Contesting the Renaissance

Contesting the Past

The volumes in this series select some of the most controversial episodes in history and consider their divergent, even starkly incompatible representations. The aim is not merely to demonstrate that history is "argument without end," but to show that study even of contradictory conceptions can be fruitful: that the jettisoning of one thesis or presentation leaves behind something of value.

Published

Contesting the Crusades
Norman Housley

Contesting the German Empire 1871–1918
Matthew Jefferies

Vietnam: Explaining America's Lost War
Gary R. Hess

Contesting the French Revolution
Paul Hanson

The Israel-Palestine Conflict: Contested Histories
Neil Caplan

Contesting the Renaissance
William Caferro

In preparation

Witch Hunts in the Early Modern World
Alison Rowlands

Reformations
C. Scott Dixon

The Rise of Nazism
Chris Szejnmann

Contesting the Renaissance

William Caferro

WILEY-BLACKWELL
A John Wiley & Sons, Ltd., Publication

This edition first published 2011

Blackwell Publishing was acquired by John Wiley & Sons in February 2007. Blackwell's publishing program has been merged with Wiley's global Scientific, Technical, and Medical business to form Wiley-Blackwell.

Registered Office
John Wiley & Sons Ltd, The Atrium, Southern Gate, Chichester, West Sussex, PO19 8SQ, United Kingdom

Editorial Offices
350 Main Street, Malden, MA 02148-5020, USA
9600 Garsington Road, Oxford, OX4 2DQ, UK
The Atrium, Southern Gate, Chichester, West Sussex, PO19 8SQ, UK

For details of our global editorial offices, for customer services, and for information about how to apply for permission to reuse the copyright material in this book please see our website at www.wiley.com/wiley-blackwell.

Library of Congress Cataloging-in-Publication Data

Caferro, William.
Contesting the Renaissance / William Caferro.
p. cm. – (Contesting the past)
Includes bibliographical references and index.
ISBN 978-1-4051-2369-3 (hardcover: alk. paper) – ISBN 978-1-4051-2370-9 (pbk. : alk. paper) 1. Renaissance. 2. Renaissance–Historiography. I. Title.
CB361.C24 2011
940.2'1072–dc22

2009053145

A catalogue record for this book is available from the British Library.

Set in 10/12.5pt Photina by SPi Publisher Services, Pondicherry, India
Printed and bound in Malaysia by Vivar Printing Sdn Bhd

1 2011

Contents

Acknowledgments

There is probably no penance sufficient for writing a book of this nature. It is at once presumptuous and inadequate and will arrive at the bookstore already out of date.

My commitment to the project has nevertheless been strong, and derives from both my scholarly interests and the vicissitudes of my professional career. The latter began teaching early modern Europe (then called Renaissance/Reformation Europe) and shifted to the Middle Ages. The transformation owes to the ambiguity of my research field – fourteenth-century Italian economic history – which occupies uncertain ground in the grand historical narrative. The urban landscape and advanced commercial practices of Italy fit poorly the medieval label as traditionally understood (especially by job committees at American universities), while the fourteenth century seems too early for consideration as early modern, particularly in comparison to England and France, which remained under the medieval veil of darkness. One recalls Robert Lopez's famous statement that Italy was "never medieval, but no medieval trend left it unaffected." Understanding the ambiguity stands at the core of my current scholarly agenda, and is the starting point of this book.

This volume is in no way intended as a comprehensive study of Renaissance historiography, if indeed that is possible. It aims only at relaying representative themes and approaches. The chapters begin with old iconic works, which serve as entrée into broader historiographical discussions. The authors may, as colleagues point out, have been superseded by recent scholarship, but I believe that including them is at the very least useful in situating and understanding present arguments. The intention is also partly archaeological: to make available to students these works, which have become increasingly difficult to access and indeed have at times been caricatured in the current literature. Each chapter takes as its subtitle a question derived from the older literature.

Nevertheless, I am aware that examination of even the limited topics covered in this book raises more questions than it answers. The demarcation lines between one field and another are not clear cut, and the very act of arranging them into chapters runs contrary to recent Renaissance scholarship that has advocated breaking down disciplinary barriers, an approach I very much agree with. The discourses themselves are often ill-fitting and not easily reconciled. Scholarly approaches differ according to generation and nationality. Basic assumptions abandoned in one discipline sometimes remain accepted in others. The status quo is often confused and it is difficult to state precisely where the scholarship is at any point.

I did not try to disguise such issues. Rather, I have sought to present as much as possible the complexity of the debates, following the eddies and spirals within them, without (hopefully) losing clarity and the main lines. The broad aim has been to be as inclusive as possible, to avoid personal judgment and the type of selective citation that has plagued my own field of economic history. I have included the work of non-historians (anthropologists, economists, literary critics, social theorists, psychologists), who have been critical in shaping the field. I have also included the work of popular writers, who, despite the slights aimed at them by professionals, have been similarly influential.

Many colleagues and friends have inspired and guided this project over the years. I want in particular to acknowledge the critical assistance of Bill Connell, whose knowledge of the subject is unparalleled and without whom there would be no book. I would also like to thank Judith C. Brown, Samuel K. Cohn, Steven A. Epstein, Christine Meek, Anthony Molho, Edward Muir, John Najemy, and Sharon Strocchia for their enormous help, both explicit and implicit. I thank my colleagues in the History Department at Vanderbilt University, especially Helmut Walser Smith, who helped me improve chapter 1. I wish to express my gratitude also to the Institute of Advanced Studies where I spent a semester finishing the manuscript and benefited from the mentorship of Caroline Walker Bynum, Nicola di Cosmo, Luigi Capogrossi-Colognesi, Giles Constable, Irving and Marilyn Lavin, and Giacomo Todeschini. I am greatly indebted to Susan M. Stuard of Haverford College, whom I admire more than I can express here. I thank also my childhood friend Marshall Gordon, who tried to unpack my academic prose, and my undergraduate student Hannah Hayes, who tried to do the same. I wish to acknowledge three special places – J.J.'s Market in Nashville, TN, the Daily Grind (now defunct) in Champaign-Urbana IL, and Hungarian Pastry Shoppe in NYC – where I did much of the editing and revising of this book.

Finally, I want to thank the editors of the series, Tessa Harvey and Gillian Kane, for their patience with me, having gone so far beyond my appointed deadlines.

I dedicate the book to my wife and closest friend Megan Weiler. I dedicate it also to my graduate mentors, John Boswell, Harry Miskimin, and Jaroslav Pelikan. My professional career has taken me far from where I began in my studies with them. But it was under their guidance that I came to love history and this book, whatever its weaknesses, is manifestation of that emotion and my great debt to them.

William Caferro

1
The Renaissance Question

Few historical periods have elicited more discussion than the Renaissance. It defies easy categorization, confounds basic definition, and has thus remained a topic of vigorous debate. Scholars have contested virtually every aspect of it, from its causes and general characteristics, to its temporal and regional boundaries, to whether indeed the label is at all valid. The discourse has occasioned a vast literature that has only grown larger in subsequent years, with new approaches and techniques borrowed from anthropology, psychology, gender studies, and literary criticism.

The identification of the era as a distinct one dates back to the period itself, to the writings of contemporaries who were aware of their importance and priority. The key figure was Francis Petrarch (d. 1374), who consciously separated himself from the "barbarism" that preceded him, on the basis of his love and understanding of the classics. In *Letters on Familiar Matters*, Petrarch characterized the period from the adoption of Christianity by the Roman emperors in the fourth century up to his own age as one of "tenebrae" or "darkness." In doing this Petrarch subverted the traditional notion among medieval Christian writers who associated the "dark age" with the period prior to the advent of Christianity. Petrarch made his determination on linguistic and cultural grounds, in terms of the good Latin and high culture of what he called "antique" Rome as opposed to the bad Latin and decline in learning in the later period.[1] Subsequent humanists, both in Italy and elsewhere in Europe, reinforced the distinction. Flavio Biondo (d. 1463) in his *History of Italy from the Decline of the Roman Empire (Historiarum ab inclinatione Romanorum imperii decades*, 1439–53) drew a clear chronological boundary between his own age and the thousand years that preceded it. He located Rome's decline as beginning with the sack of city by Goths in 410 (which he erroneously dated as

412) and lasting until 1412, a period corresponding roughly to the modern concept of the Middle Ages. Matteo Palmieri (d. 1474) drew a still sharper contrast, depicting the era after the fall of Rome as culturally barren, about which he thought it was "best to be silent altogether." Conversely, his own age was one of "majestic rhythm." He praised his fellow Florentines Giotto (d. 1337) and Leonardo Bruni (d. 1444) as having restored arts and letters. A generation later, the great Dutch humanist Erasmus (d. 1536) remarked that everywhere "splendid talents are stirring."[2]

Protestant writers of the Reformation further sharpened the distinction between the new and old age by associating the earlier period with the evils of the papacy and the church. They accused popes and scholastic theologians of subverting the true faith and encouraging the formation of a society based on superstition and ignorance. In this schema the Renaissance became a precursor to Reformation, which manifested itself by means of divine providence. Protestant scholars sought out tangible signs of God's will. The English theologian John Foxe saw one such in the advent of the printing press in the fifteenth century. Theodore Beza, Calvin's successor at Geneva, stressed the fall of Constantinople to the Turks in 1453 and the arrival of Greek scholars in Italy. The interpretations of both men have cast long shadows on the subsequent secular literature.

The formulation of the modern concept of the Renaissance owes much to Rationalist and Romantic intellectual movements of the eighteenth and nineteenth centuries, a period during which historical studies became more systematized. Enlightenment writers stressed the notion of history as one of progress, of the evolution and development of society. The great French philosophe Voltaire (d. 1778) equated the Renaissance with the awakening of human reason and "Italian genius." In his *Essay on the Manners and the Spirit of Nations* (1756), Voltaire drew parallels between the ancient Greeks and fifteenth- and sixteenth-century Italians, pairing such figures as Guicciardini and Thucydides, Ariosto, and Homer, often to the advantage of the Italians. He portrayed Cosimo de' Medici and his son Lorenzo as precursors to the enlightened despots of the eighteenth century, and Florence, their home, as an updated Athens. The Italian achievement was, however, coupled with a darker side of moral confusion and violence. "Intelligence, superstition, atheism, masquerades, poetry, treason, devotion, poison, assassinations, a few great men, an infinite number of clever and yet unfortunate scoundrels: that is what Italy was."[3]

The Romantic historian Jules Michelet (d. 1874) gave wide currency to the term "Renaissance," the title he used for the seventh volume of his *History of France* (1855).[4] Michelet perceived of the Renaissance on a grander scale than Voltaire, as a European-wide phenomenon involving all aspects of life, characterized by the "discovery of the world and the discovery of man," a phrase that has gained a special place in the historiography of the period. Michelet singled out as prime features of the Renaissance the revival of antiquity, scientific discoveries and geographical exploration. The emphasis on the latter led him to perceive such men as Columbus and Copernicus as Renaissance figures.

Unlike Voltaire, however, Michelet did not focus on fifteenth-century Italy, but stressed instead the role of sixteenth-century France. The bridge between the two places was the French invasion of the peninsula in 1494, which brought Italian influences to France. The French Renaissance reached its apogee in the court of Francis I.

Michelet's lasting achievement was to make the Renaissance into a concrete historical period. The notion of "rebirth" inherent in the term Renaissance was for Michelet above all a rebirth of the human spirit, a "heroic outburst of an immense will." In this sense, even Martin Luther was a Renaissance figure insofar as the spirit of the age led him to the break with the Church.

It was, however, Michelet's Swiss counterpart Jacob Burckhardt (d. 1897) who most set the modern terms of discussion. Burckhardt wove the various strands of Enlightenment and Romantic thought, as well as that of German philosophical-historical writers, into a powerful synthesis in his great book entitled *The Civilization of the Renaissance in Italy*. In the Enlightenment tradition, he identified the Renaissance as a period of progress and the emergence of reason.[5] Like Voltaire, he located the Renaissance in Italy and called the Italians "the first born among the sons of Europe." He stressed the role of "individualism," which he equated with the appearance of the modern man and modern world.

The Civilization of the Renaissance in Italy is so famous that its contents have often been assumed rather than carefully assayed. Scholarly refutations of the book have sometimes proceeded along lines that Burckhardt himself would not have recognized. For this reason it is worthwhile to look closely at its organization and argument.

What most interested Burckhardt was gaining access to the character of the age, pinpointing the "spirit" of the Renaissance. Burckhardt's emphasis on individualism, and the key role played by great men bears the stamp of Hegel's "*geistige Individualität*," while his interest in uncovering the roots of modernity shares characteristics of the approach of his contemporary Karl Marx (d. 1883), who like Burckhardt was a student at the university of Berlin.[6] Burckhardt nevertheless emphasized cultural rather than economic forces. Burckhardt self-effacingly called his work "*ein Versuch*" or "an attempt," intended as an interpretation, short of employing all available evidence. He promised to follow with a separate treatment of art, which he felt warranted its own attention. But he never completed that work.

The Civilization of the Renaissance in Italy is divided into six parts. The first two are the most widely read by modern students in the English speaking world. In them, Burckhardt traced the political circumstances in Italy. His main thesis is expressed in the famous subtitle of the first section, "The State as a Work of Art," by which Burckhardt meant that the state was a "calculated conscious creation." He depicted the Italian political environment as one of violence and uncertainty, which produced the individualism and egocentrism characteristic of the Renaissance. These traits were readily apparent in the great mercenary captains, the so-called *condottieri* of the fifteenth century, men of illegitimate birth, who by dint of their skill and cunning rose to leadership of armies and took over the states they served.

Burckhardt's treatment of individualism is the central theme of the book, and constitutes his most original contribution. The concept is fully developed in the second part, "The Development of the Individual." Here Burckhardt gives his oft-quoted description of the Middle Ages as "laying dreaming and half awake beneath a common veil." The veil was composed of "faith, illusion and childish prepossession" and man perceived of himself only in terms of a general category, such as race, family, or corporation. It was in Italy that the veil melted away, replaced by the self-conscious individual, who recognized himself as such. The terms "individual" and "individualism" are, for Burckhardt, elastic ones, applied in various ways. At base they constitute dedication to self-interest and freedom from authority, both moral and political.

Burckhardt devoted the third part of his book to the revival of antiquity and the link between the Renaissance and the renewed interest in classical literature. He viewed the "spirit" of the Renaissance as prior to the intellectual renewal, embedded in the "genius of the Italian people" and not specifically reflected in the work of the humanists. The humanists were Renaissance men insofar as they reflected the traits of individualism and modernity.

In the last three parts, Burckhardt fleshed out the ways that individualism affected the age. The section entitled "The Discovery of the World and of Man" makes clear his debt to Michelet. It examines oversees exploration, scientific discovery, the natural world and literature. The section on "Society and Festivals" places the individual in his social setting. "Morality and Religion" presents a dark picture of "grave moral crisis" in Italy, which grew from the influence of pagan antiquity, difficulties within the church, and, above all, unbridled egoism.

Burckhardt's great legacy was to present the Renaissance as an all-encompassing event, touching on varied aspects of life and society. His book took time to reach its audience, a development that Burckhardt himself lamented.[7] It did not correspond to the dominant trends in contemporary German academia, which favored specialization and the learned monograph.[8]

But Burckhardt's ideas gained wide currency soon enough.[9] The elegance of his writing had obvious appeal, as did the force of his argumentation. Moreover, there already existed considerable interest in the Renaissance throughout Europe. A year before the appearance of *The Civilization of the Renaissance in Italy*, the German scholar Georg Voigt had published a multi-volume work on the humanist revival of antiquity (*Rediscovery of Classical Antiquity*, 1859), which, like Burckhardt, posited a decisive break between the Renaissance and the period that preceded it. Voigt also found a place for individuality, which was reflected in the work of humanist writers. Similarly, in Italy, the historian Pasquale Villari wrote of a distinctive Renaissance "spirit." In biographical works such as *The Life and Times of Girolamo Savonarola* (1859–61) and *The Life and Times of Niccolò Machiavelli* (1877–82), Villari noted the individualistic nature of the period and the workings of Italian genius. Writing at a time of heightened nationalism owing to Italian reunification, Villari also condemned the moral and political corruption of the Renaissance, which he believed contributed to the peninsula's domination by foreign powers.

Burckhardt's work also found a receptive audience in the English-speaking world, where there was already substantial interest in the Renaissance, both in academic and non-academic circles.[10] Much of the latter consisted of accounts by travelers, poets, and artists, often highly emotional in nature, who paid homage to the aesthetic beauties of the period.[11] At the turn of the eighteenth century, the wealthy Liverpool attorney William Roscoe published two biographies of the Medici family, on Lorenzo the Magnificent (1796) and Pope Leo X (1804). The books were printed in numerous editions and did much to popularize the great Renaissance family.

In America popular writers drew comparisons between the world of fifteenth-century Florence and their own. They saw in the earlier period the seeds of American society, specifically "modernity" for which America was now the paradigm. In England, where the study of the Renaissance was more professionalized, the art critic John Ruskin had already, by the time of the publication of Burckhardt's *Civilization*, written extensively on Renaissance art, which he did not admire. The literary critic Walter Pater (d. 1894) was then beginning his career and would, like Burckhardt, stress the importance of the Renaissance as a reflection of the general spirit of the age, and of fifteenth-century Italian society as its apotheosis.[12] But the Renaissance in England remained its own entity. The critic Matthew Arnold coined the term "Renascence" (in *Culture and Anarchy*, 1869), giving a distinctly English slant to the concept coming into vogue.[13]

The broad acceptance of the Burckhardtian Renaissance in the English-speaking world owed most to the work of John Addington Symonds. The son of a medical doctor, Symonds was what might be called today a freelance scholar. He was notoriously neurotic, and spent much time in a Swiss health resort recovering from physical illness. He shared with Burckhardt an unabashed love for Italian culture and referred to the Renaissance as the "most marvelous period the world has ever known." His magnum opus was a seven-volume work entitled *The Renaissance in Italy* (1875–86) that he initiated unaware of Burckhardt's earlier work. This became known to Symonds as he was completing his book and he gratefully acknowledged his debt.

Symonds's *Renaissance in Italy* is arranged in a manner similar to Burckhardt, although its central thesis is not so tightly organized. Symonds's style is more rhetorical, a characteristic some attribute to the fact that he wrote at his health resort, which did not have a library.[14] Like Burckhardt, Symonds equated the Renaissance with the emergence of modernity, whose salient characteristics were the birth of "liberty" and "political freedom," the power of "self-determination," recognition of the beauty of the outer world and of the body through art, the liberation of "reason" in science and "conscience" in religion and the restoration of the "culture to intelligence."[15] Symonds's views have had a wide-ranging, if sometimes unacknowledged, influence on Anglo-American scholars, who have often conflated his ideas with those of Burckhardt.

Burckhardt's tradition was passed down elsewhere, in various guises in historical works with varying agendas. Scholars extended his ideas, most notably in the areas of intellectual, social and economic history, where Burckhardt's observations were more intuitive than comprehensive. Wilhelm Dilthey (d. 1911), a philosopher in the first instance, established a methodology for the study of intellectual life. He developed the notion of *Geisteswissenschaften*, sometimes translated as "intellectual (or human) sciences," which treated ideas as dynamic and developing in their historical context. They were the product of the whole person, including his irrational side. There was therefore a close connection between the individual and the culture of an age, a notion with obvious parallels in Burckhardt, and which encouraged subsequent scholars to look for specific Renaissance intellectual trends. Dilthey's influence is reflected in the work of Ernst Cassirer, who focused on fifteenth and sixteenth century Italy and saw in Renaissance intellectual life the seeds of modern science.[16] Alfred von Martin and E. P. Cheyney closely examined economic and social trends. Von Martin affirmed Burckhardt's individualistic tendencies with regard to Renaissance merchants or "bourgeois urban entrepreneurs" as he called them, who embodied the spirit of modern capitalism. Cheyney stressed the role of trade in the Renaissance and saw increased accumulation of wealth as the development that marked the passage from the medieval to modern world.[17]

Burckhardt's influence also carried over to the fields of art history and literature, which had long been viewed as important aspects of the Renaissance, but which had been treated separately by scholars, detached from broader historical processes. The effect of *The Civilization of the Renaissance in Italy* was to bring the strands together, to encourage scholars to link their studies under the common rubric of cultural history, determined by the "spirit" of the age. In his three-volume *The History of Art during the Renaissance* (1889–95), Eugene Müntz, a follower of Burckhardt, described artistic achievements in terms of spirit of the Italian people. He emphasized the role of individuality and of man's discovery of the world and himself.

It is important to emphasize, however, that even as Burckhardt became widely accepted, the Renaissance remained a highly contested and controversial construct. There existed concurrent interpretations, notably those that placed greater emphasis on the revival of antiquity. John Ruskin saw interest in the classical past as the essential feature of the Renaissance, which led to a substitution of pagan values for Christian values, a development he condemned.[18] Even followers of Burckhardt did not always agree on details. The extension and amplification of the Swiss scholar's ideas necessarily involved revision of them. Already in 1908, Karl Brandi spoke of a growing diversity of opinion and a "Renaissance problem."[19]

An obvious problem with Burckhardt's Renaissance was that it was limited to Italy. Where did this leave the Renaissance in other parts of Europe? There was no synthesis comparable to that of Burckhardt for Northern Europe. The discourse centered on the Reformation, for which the Renaissance was at best a precursor. The "traditional" interpretation (if it may be so judged) of the northern Renaissance emphasized three basic aspects: (1) its genesis in Italy and transmission, in altered form, northward; (2) the importance of humanism and interest in antiquity; and (3) its fundamentally modern quality. The influence of Burckhardt is apparent with regard to points one and three. But scholars tended to focus more on detailed features of the movement rather than search for a guiding spirit.

The extension of a Renaissance to France was perhaps most natural. It followed directly from Michelet, who located it in the sixteenth century, beginning with the French invasion of Italy in 1494. In the late nineteenth and early twentieth centuries scholars emphasized a French "discovery of Italy," of its culture and intellectual trends that in turn stimulated "native" genius. This genius, according to G. Lanson, manifested itself primarily in literature and art.[20] The former included the work of humanists, for which the court of King Francis I served as a locus of activities.

The application of the term Renaissance to England was more limited. Scholars associated it largely with literary developments, particularly the work of William Shakespeare (1564–1616). In *History of English Literature* (1863–4), Hippolyte Taine established a precedent by affixing the label (which he divided into the "pagan" and "Christian" Renaissance) to the period starting with Edmund Spenser (1552–1599) and ending with John Milton (1608–1674). The chronology remains popular in English literature departments at American universities. The critic C. S. Lewis denied, however, the existence of a literary Renaissance in the sixteenth century, stressing the prolongation of medieval trends in England. Historians have meanwhile linked the Renaissance to the Tudor/Stuart monarchies. But they too have emphasized continuity with the Middle Ages as well as English exceptionalism, treating the monarchies for their own sake rather than in terms of broad European-wide movements. The influential historian G. R. Elton accepted the utility of the term Renaissance for literature, but rejected its relevance as applied to society and politics.[21] He preferred the term "early modern" for the latter.

The notion of a German Renaissance was slow in forming. Despite the central role played by German speaking scholars in the development of the concept, there was little impulse to apply the term to a region so closely associated with the Reformation. Paul Joachimsen, writing at the beginning of the nineteenth century, claimed that the Renaissance in German lands was "mere mummery," imitative of Italy.[22] He nevertheless did much of the practical work of establishing a connection to Italy in his study of the early German humanists Rudolf Agricola (1443–1485) and Johann Reuchlin (1455–1522), whom he saw as inspired by their Italian forebears. Later scholarship would place less emphasis on the derivative aspects of German humanism and more on novelty, particularly with respect to religion. This has allowed for tighter connections between the Renaissance and the Reformation (see chapter 4).

The Revolt of the Medievalists

The most strident challenges to Burckhardt's claims, however, came from "below," from medievalists. They disputed Burckhardt's negative depiction of the Middle Ages as a period "hidden under a veil," characterized by superstition and corporate religious affiliation. They argued instead that Renaissance qualities such as rationality and individuality existed earlier. Where Burckhardt posited a fundamental break in history, medievalists saw continuities. Dissent gained momentum in the first decades of the twentieth century and was dubbed by the historian Wallace K. Ferguson "the revolt of the medievalists," a name that has stuck.[23]

The revision was led by two notable scholars, the Dutch historian Johann Huizinga and his American counterpart Charles Homer Haskins. Huizinga's critique was largely implicit. Using evocative language and imagery, he demonstrated in his book *Autumn of the Middle Ages* (1919) how some of the features of Burckhardt's Renaissance in Italy were also operative in the Burgundian Netherlands in the fourteenth and fifteenth centuries. Huizinga found similar artistic virtuosity and a desire for fame and honor. But these were bound up not with modern sensibilities but with the quintessential medieval ethic of chivalry and response to the devastating effects of the Black Death in 1348. For Huizinga the period was, in Burgundy and France, the "autumn of the Middle Ages."[24]

Charles Homer Haskins dealt with Burckhardt more explicitly, tracing several of the Swiss historian's assertions back to the twelfth century. Haskins gave his book the provocative title *The Renaissance of the Twelfth Century* (1927). He argued that the twelfth century, "the very century of Saint Bernard and his mule," was "fresh, vigorous" and innovative. He cited as evidence the advent of new artistic styles, (Romanesque and Gothic), the emergence of vernacular literature, revival of interest in the classics, recovery of Greek science and the beginning of universities and new legal systems. He made clear that the twelfth-century Renaissance was an international movement and thus broad in scope.

Huizinga's and Haskins's works have achieved a fame and influence comparable to that of Burckhardt. Their overall aims were, however, measured. Neither writer denied the existence of the Renaissance, but wished only to minimize its inflated importance. Huizinga accepted Burckhardt's claims for Italy.[25] Haskins made clear in his introduction that he intended only to show that the "Renaissance was not so unique or so decisive as has been supposed" and that conversely the Middle Ages was "less dark and static."[26] Likewise, it is important not to overstress the originality of the two historians. Their interest in the earlier period had roots in the work of prior scholars. For all his interest in the Renaissance, Jules Michelet, for example, gave at least as much attention to the Middle Ages and emphasized the achievements of several figures from the period, including the mystic Joachim da Fiore. The nineteenth-century scholar Paul Sabatier wrote at length about the life and deeds of Francis of Assisi (d. 1226), the founder of the Franciscan movement, stressing Francis's humanity and individuality, his awareness of nature and beauty, his discovery, if you will, "of the world and man."[27] Sabatier's Francis was not a Renaissance man per se, but he was an innovator, a rebel against rigid church authority and in that sense a "modern man," a depiction with obvious Burckhardtian overtones. Sabatier's interpretation found its way into later works, particularly those of art historians, and remains current.

Other medievalists, however, undertook more virulent critiques of Burckhardt. Étienne Gilson saw no value at all in the Renaissance label, claiming that the period created nothing new and was actually less vibrant than the Middle Ages. For him the Renaissance was "not the Middle Ages plus man," but "the Middle Ages minus God" and "in losing God the

Renaissance was losing man himself." Lynn Thorndike expressed similar contempt. He asserted, contra Ernst Cassirer, that the "so-called Renaissance" (as he called it) saw no advances in the sciences, but was in fact strikingly inferior to the Middle Ages in that regard.[28]

It was, however, Burckhardt's claims to individuality and modernity that evoked the most sustained criticism from medievalists. Following in Haskins's tradition, R. W. Southern in several important and widely read books characterized the twelfth century as one in which there were the stirrings of rational thought and the rehabilitation of nature. He emphasized the careers of great "individuals" such as Peter Blois, Guibert of Nogent, and John of Salisbury and used the term "medieval humanism" to describe their work, which has gained wide currency. Similarly, Joseph Reese Strayer, who studied with Haskins, posited the origins of the modern state in the Middle Ages, outlining the growth of royal bureaucracies and the development of "modern" law and legal systems already in the twelfth century.[29]

Some scholars pushed the revival back still further, finding "Renaissances" in the monastic culture of Northumbria in the seventh century, the court of Charlemagne in the eighth and ninth centuries, and the circle of the German Ottonian Emperors in the tenth and eleventh centuries.[30] The proliferation of Renaissances occasioned Erwin Panofsky's well-known attempt to distinguish among them. He described the medieval versions as "Renascences," which were limited in scope and effect and thus mere forebears to the Burckhardtian Italian Renaissance, which was truly broad-based and transformative.[31]

Medievalist claims to modernity have nevertheless persisted. Colin Morris gave a particularly strong statement on behalf of the twelfth-century roots of individualism in his often reprinted (by the Medieval Academy of America) *The Discovery of the Individual, 1050–1200* (1985). Drawing primarily on literary sources, Morris argued that the advent of individualism in the twelfth century was a transformative event, a wholly "unique western phenomenon" such that it represented "an eccentricity among cultures."[32] The thesis deprived Burckhardt's Renaissance of any priority, and indeed effectively eliminated it altogether.

Morris's hyperbole exposes the risks involved in the search for modernity. Morris argues against a phantom, laying out the "conventional" Burckhardtian account of individualism that Burckhardt would not in fact have recognized. Indeed, it was not taken from Burckhardt, but from Bishop Stephen Neill, an obscure nineteenth-century textbook writer. The effort to defeat this straw man leads Morris to overstate his claims for modernity – to exceed the excesses of Burckhardt, who wrote at a time when systematic study of the Middle Ages had not yet begun.

More recent scholarship has questioned notions of medieval modernity. Influenced by poststructural and postmodern historiographical trends, historians have shown greater reluctance to read the present into the past. In an important review article, Paul Freedman and Gabrielle Spiegel traced the recent tendency among medievalists (since the late 1970s) to avoid teleological searches for modernity in favor of attempts to understand the period on its own terms. Rather than finding analogues with the present day, scholars have placed emphasis on "alterity," often extremes in behavior such as aberrant sexual practices, demonic rites and, more generally, medieval fascination with things that were grotesque and strange. As we shall see, similar trends have also influenced scholarship on the Renaissance.

The "revolt of the medievalists" nevertheless had a profound and lasting effect on the discourse regarding the Renaissance. At base, it made scholars more aware of the realities of the earlier period and more inclined to view events that occurred during the Renaissance in terms of it. Today, there is hardly a textbook on the Renaissance in the English language that does not begin with disclaimers about the importance of the Middle Ages or with chapters devoted to the "medieval heritage."[33] Standard Renaissance figures like Petrarch are treated in terms of their medieval context; signal Renaissance works like Castiglione's *Courtier* or Machiavelli's *Prince* are studied in terms of medieval literature, the former with respect to the literature on courtly love, the latter in terms of medieval "mirror" books of advice to rulers.[34]

The accommodation of revision did not entail any less commitment to the Renaissance as its own unique age. William Bouwsma spoke of historians "sorting data into two heaps, one marked "continuities," the other "innovations."[35] If the Middle Ages had its own unique characteristics, so too did the Renaissance, sufficient to distinguish it from its predecessor. The Renaissance was a period of "accelerated" transition, in which earlier trends moved more quickly and more decisively toward modernity.

The challenge of medievalists also encouraged Renaissance scholars to look more closely at the issue of periodization. Burckhardt did not arrange his work in chronological order, preferring a thematic approach. Temporally he drew his examples from the period from Emperor Frederick II in the mid-thirteenth century to the sack of Rome in 1527. The chronology overlapped the claims of medievalists. Huizinga's Middle Ages occurred in the fourteenth and fifteenth centuries.

Where was the dividing line, was it the same in each country? Where did one place ambiguous figures such as Dante, who, according to the famous mixed metaphor, stood with one foot in the Middle Ages and "saluted the rising star of the Renaissance" with the other?[36]

The problem of periodization has proved singularly vexing. The "professionalization" of historical studies in modern times has only exacerbated the issue, as university course catalogs and academic affiliations have necessitated the drawing of distinct temporal lines of division among historical fields and encouraged scholars to fit their subjects into neat self-contained packages. John Hale has suggested that the packages may correspond to a basic human impulse to align the historical past with the contours of our own lives, which are necessarily bounded. In any case, periodization remains a pervasive if often unacknowledged problem. We shall deal with the issue more extensively below.[37]

"Golden Age" and "Problem Child"

The study of the Renaissance in the English-speaking world received a sharp stimulus during the 1930s and 1940s. The rise of fascism in Europe created an exodus of scholars, many of whom were Jewish, fleeing religious persecution. The émigrés included Hans Baron, Erwin Panofsky, Paul Oskar Kristeller, Ernst Kantorowicz, and Felix Gilbert, who went to America; Nicolai Rubinstein and Ernst Gombrich, who went to England.[38] The Italian Roberto Lopez, deprived of his academic post in Genoa, found an intellectual home at Yale University. Although the men did not all agree with Burckhardt, they were strongly influenced by him. German scholars brought with them the rich historical tradition of their country, including the approaches of Hegel (1831), Ranke (1886), and Dilthey (1911), as well as those of Karl Lamprecht (1915), Friedrich Meinecke (1954), and others. Following in the path of their intellectual predecessors, they treated the Renaissance in broad terms, using it as a means to search for greater understanding of the historical processes – the approach that inspired Burckhardt.

The émigrés showed particular interest in politics and political forms. Hans Baron and Felix Gilbert drew inspiration from Meinecke, who saw in the Renaissance the beginnings of republicanism and modern democratic ideology. Their work corresponded well with prevailing attitudes in Britain and America, engaged in war with Hitler and the axis powers, during which the ideals of liberal democracy were at stake.[39] Hans Baron argued that republicanism emerged in Florence in the early fifteenth century as a direct consequence of war with the Milanese tyrant Giangaleazzo Visconti, whom he compared to Hitler (and Napoleon).[40] Meanwhile, Paul Oskar Kristeller focused on intellectual trends, most notably humanism. His presence at Columbia University inspired numerous doctorates in the field. Robert Lopez at Yale encouraged wide interest in economic history. Lopez (d. 1987) reversed the long-accepted notion, implicit in Burckhardt, that there was a connection between economic prosperity and the cultural achievements of the Renaissance. He argued instead that the flourishing of the arts derived from economic "hard times" resulting from the Black Death in 1348. The Lopez thesis, as it came to be called, touched off a heated debate and moved the study of the economy, from the margins to the center of the scholarly discourse (see chapter 5).

The stimulus provided by the émigrés brought the study of the Renaissance to what was called "a golden age." The Renaissance emerged not only as an important moment in European civilization, but as the *key* moment. The opening of European archives after the World War II further stimulated research and facilitated a range of empirical studies, which filled in details of larger theoretical issues.[41] In 1958, Federico Chabod published a "preliminary" bibliography of the literature that ran for 48 pages.[42]

The profusion of studies and approaches, however, further complicated the picture. Wallace K. Ferguson, dubbed by Lopez as the "umpire" of postwar Renaissance historiography, devoted his career to producing what he called a "comprehensive synthesis." He called the Renaissance the "most intractable problem child of historiography." But his tone was nevertheless optimistic, reflecting the great interest in the subject and its assured status in the historical canon. He advocated a systematic analysis, which was meaningful only if applied to all of Europe.[43] Ferguson saw dispute as arising from narrow scholarly concentration on a single aspect or region.[44] He argued that while the rate of change varied from one place to another, the accrual of slow increments ultimately produced major transformations. Ferguson's work formed the basis of many subsequent monographs as well as numerous textbooks. His contribution has, however, often gone unacknowledged and for that reason is stated here at some length.

According to Ferguson, a fundamental precondition for study of the Renaissance was acceptance of the notion of periodization, which he affirmed by restating the philosopher R. G. Collingwood's dictum that it represented "the mark of advanced and mature historical thought."[45] Ferguson set the precise if admittedly arbitrary years for the period as lasting from 1300 to 1600. Following the Germanic historical tradition, Ferguson saw the Renaissance as constituting a basic shift in *Weltanschauung* (world view). The shift began in the fourteenth century and was characterized by a transformation of the economy from an agrarian to a commercial one; of politics from feudal arrangements to centralized government, of religion from the unity of Catholic worship to Protestantism, and, finally, of the emergence of secular learning and natural science. Ferguson retained Burckhardt's claims to modernity and saw Italy as the focal point of change, from whence the Renaissance radiated out to the rest of Europe and included advances in music, theater, art, and science.

Ferguson's schema remains evident in North American textbooks, which are often arranged in a similar manner, both structurally and thematically. This is especially apparent in those written in the 1960s and 1970s, which are still used in American classrooms.[46] The importance of the textbooks should not be understated, as they are the means by which students gain their first impression of the Renaissance, impressions that are often enduring, even among those who go on to become scholars.

Cultural and Literary Turns

The broad scholarly synthesis advocated by Ferguson did not, however, occur. The postwar impulse toward consensus gave way to skepticism. The shift coincided with changing political and social attitudes. The mid/late sixties and early seventies were a time of questioning the "establishment," of increased concern with social causes and injustice, with civil rights and political protest. This reflected itself in the academy, where scholars moved away from traditional topics such as the study of elites in favor of subjects that were not part of the standard canon.

Accordingly, the "revolt" this time came primarily from scholars interested in social issues. The French Annales School provided an important impetus. It stressed treating history in its totality, as an integrated whole that functioned on multiple levels.[47] It de-emphasized the deeds of great men, and focused more on structures and the broad spectrum of human existence. The school grew from the journal, *Annales d'histoire économique et sociale*, founded by Marc Bloch and Lucien Febvre back in 1929. It gained institutional status after World War II under the guidance of Fernand Braudel, who brought it temporally to the Renaissance. His pioneering *Philip II and the Mediterranean* (published in French in 1949 and translated into English in 1974) dealt with the sixteenth century, with the Mediterranean as a whole, emphasizing physical and man-made structures rather than elite culture. Braudel stressed the *longue durée*, the long view of historical time, corresponding to geographical and demographic rhythms.

The approach privileged social and economic developments over politics. Annaliste scholars such as Ernest Labrousse and Emmanuel Le Roy Ladurie went further in the direction of social history. They examined more closely the masses and advocated the study of them through quantification of "serial" data such as grain prices, which revealed the monotony of their existence.[48]

Historians also borrowed techniques from the fields of sociology and anthropology, especially from the work of Clifford Geertz. In *The Interpretation of Cultures* (1973), Geertz argued for the primacy of culture in understanding human society. Man is what he does and thus can be properly apprehended only by close examination of his cultural context. This involves interpreting signs and rituals, which allow access to meaning within the culture itself. Geertz used the term "thick description" to describe this detailed analysis of human behavior in its cultural context.[49]

Geertz's work, along with that of Victor Turner and Mary Douglas, provided historians with the tools to apprehend everyday life and behavior.[50] This has proven especially useful at gaining access to Renaissance religious practices, a hitherto much-neglected area of study. Geertz differed fundamentally with Enlightenment writers, who treated human nature as constant and readily identifiable in history. If human nature did not exist apart from its culture, it was now more difficult to read oneself back into history.[51]

Inspired by Geertz, the literary critic Stephen Greenblatt took direct aim at Burckhardt's concept of individuality. In his studies of sixteenth-century English literature, Greenblatt argued that there was no objective self. The individual was a "cultural artifact," formed by political, cultural, and social forces.[52] The self was thus constructed or "fashioned" in interaction with outside forces. This "new historicist" school, as Greenblatt and his followers have been called, drew also upon the "poststructural" approach of the French philosopher Michel Foucault (d. 1984), who denied the existence of an objective self as well as the coherency of historical categories.

A further methodological challenge to Burckhardt came from social historians interested in women and sexuality. In an essay written in 1977, Joan Kelly posed the provocative question: "Did women have a Renaissance?" She took as her starting point Burckhardt's famous but unqualified statement that "women stood on a footing of perfect equality with men." Kelly's answer was negative. She argued that the same economic and political opportunities that improved the lives of men had an adverse effect on women, that women's status actually fell with respect to their medieval counterparts.[53]

Kelly's essay served as a starting point for the study of Renaissance women. She focused on noble and upper-class women. Subsequent scholars examined the lower classes and more marginal figures. Joan Scott pioneered a new approach, which explored gender, how society constructed the notions of what it was to be male or female. In her essay "Gender, a Useful Category of Historical Analysis," Scott advocated an integrated program of study whereby gender became a category like race and class. Like other social historians, she relied on techniques of anthropology, literary studies, and sociology.[54]

The new categories produced new studies. Scholars sought out empirical evidence in European archives. They examined a range of non-elite, nontraditional topics, such as working-class people, magicians, prostitutes, the homeless, and indigent.[55] The state archive in Florence was a particularly popular destination for study. Its rich collection of documentary material includes the famous tax assessment, the *catasto* (1427), from which it was possible to reconstruct much of the social world of that important city. David Herlihy and Christiane Klapisch-Zuber gave a detailed analysis of the document in their book, *Les Toscans et leurs familles* (1978) (translated into

English in 1985 as *Tuscans and their Families*). The work bears the obvious influence of the Annales School and its interest in quantifying data (Klapisch-Zuber is in fact a student of Braudel). But the authors relied also on a new tool of historical study, the computer, to process the data.[56]

The intense interest in social history, with recovering the lives of the so-called "lost people," gave rise in the 1970s and 1980s to the study of micro-history. Microhistory began in the Italian academy and was linked, like the Annales School, to a journal (*Quaderni storici*).[57] The aim of its proponents was to produce ethnographic histories of everyday life by studying the individual in his or her social setting. Rather than examine large amounts of quantifiable data, scholars looked at a few sources or even a single text, a legal case or trial record. The technique has been viewed as the antithesis of Annales, and indeed was posed as such by its main adherent, Carlo Ginzburg, who expressed frustration at the annaliste accumulation of data and his desire to create an indigenous Italian social history in its place. In truth, however, microhistory developed more as an extension of Annales, the culmination of trend within it toward more regional and local studies. Emmanuel Le Roy Ladurie, advocate of analysis of long term serial data, himself wrote a microhistory, about the southern French town of *Montaillou*, from inquisition records, which allowed him to "see the world in a grain of sand."[58]

Microhistorical studies remain popular in England, Italy, and America. They include, Ginzburg's own *The Cheese and the Worms*, (published originally as *Il formaggio e vermi, il cosmo di un mugnaio del 500*, 1976, and translated into English in 1980), which told the story of a sixteenth-century Italian miller whose heretical views on the nature of the cosmos landed him before the inquisition; Natalie Zemon Davis's *The Return of Martin Guerre* (1983), about an imposter who returned from war in France; Judith Brown's *Immodest Acts* (1986), about a lesbian nun in an Italian convent; Edward Muir's *Mad Blood Stirring* (1997), about feuding in the Friuli region of Italy, and, most recently, William J. Connell and Giles Constable's, *Sacrilege and Redemption in Renaissance Florence* (2005), about a Florentine nobleman who hurled dung at a fresco of the Virgin Mary after a bad run of gambling at a local tavern.[59]

At the same time that historians illuminated uncharted social worlds, they also called into question the cultural and intellectual primacy traditionally accorded Italy. Rather than stress a straight-line transmission of the Renaissance from Italy to other parts of Europe, scholars changed the polarities. They looked at the flow of ideas and innovation in both directions. They demonstrated, for example, how new techniques of oil painting devised in fifteenth-century Netherlands were transferred to Italy and how the works of humanist writers were altered as they were translated into other languages and disseminated throughout Europe (see chapter 4). In this, historians have drawn on "reception theory," a school of literary criticism associated with the University of Constance in Germany (1970s). Reception theorists advocated shifting the emphasis from the producer of the text and the text itself to the receiver and the receiver's relationship to the text.[60] The historian Peter Burke has been among the most forceful in applying this to the Renaissance. Rather than distinguish between Italy and the rest of Europe, Burke has stressed the dynamic interaction among cultures.[61]

Such approaches left little space for the Renaissance as traditionally understood. Viewed from the perspective of the masses, history was, in Emmanuel Le Roy Ladurie's words, "motionless." Little or nothing changed for those living in the countryside from the eleventh century until the Industrial Revolution. Standard periodizations therefore had no meaning. This was likewise the point of Joan Kelly's argument, which cast doubt on whether the same periodization could be applied to both men and women. The challenge brought into question the "Whig" progressive view inherited from the Enlightenment that treated history as a meaningful unfolding of events, arranged into neat, self-contained eras.

Historians readjusted their horizons. Where Wallace Ferguson had called for broad synthesis in the 1950s, scholars now advocated "selectivity" and more restricted terms.[62] Even enthusiastic proponents of the Renaissance such as Denys Hay called for limited interpretations. In the second edition of *The Italian Renaissance in its Historical Background* (1976) he stated that the Renaissance, and the past more generally, seldom dealt in "transformation scenes."[63] Robert Lopez in 1970 took to task historians who overstated the Renaissance by means of shifting geographical focus. He criticized Erwin Panofsky for exaggerating the originality of Italian artists by means of comparison with their medieval German forebears. A more apt approach was to compare artistic styles within a single place. In Florence, Lopez noted, the progression from medieval to Renaissance was far more gradual, evidenced by the early Romanesque facade of San Miniato, the Gothic belfry of Santa Maria del Fiore and the Renaissance front of Santa Maria Novella.[64]

The art historian Ernst Gombrich advocated disposing of the Renaissance period marker altogether and replacing it with the term "movement" (1974). Gombrich described the Renaissance movement as "something proclaimed" by its participants and proponents, which by its very nature attracted "fanatics and hangers on," but also had its share of opponents and "neutral outsiders." This helped account for self-awareness of the first Renaissance figures, the widespread fervor they and their followers caused, as well as the contradictory trends.[65]

Gombrich's interpretation has influenced scholars on both sides of the Atlantic. It is evident in the work of Peter Burke, who has by degrees come to refine it further, defining the Renaissance most recently as "an organizing concept which has its uses."[66]

Some go still further, advocating the elimination altogether of the term Renaissance, replacing it with "early modern." They argue that the latter label, already in use in the nineteenth century, is more egalitarian, more suited to inclusion of the "vast sea" of human activity. The term Renaissance is inherently elitist and value-laden, associated with western chauvinism and claims of superiority.[67] Conversely, "early modern," is more congruent with the backgrounds of many modern scholars themselves, who, unlike previous generations, less often come from the upper-class elite.[68]

Early modern has gained popularity, particularly among literary critics and historians of Northern Europe. But the label is not without its own problems. If, as advocates proclaim, it offers an escape from Burckhardt's emphasis on elite culture, it does not avoid the great Swiss historian's teleological stress on modernity. In this sense, it is no less value laden than the term Renaissance, and is no real alternative to the traditional narrative schema of history. Indeed, it accentuates the notion of modernity, encouraging scholars to elongate the period, to push it forward temporally, closer to the present day. As the "revolt of the medievalists" brought attention to the beginnings of the era, the shift to the early modern heading has often led to focus on finding the end point. The endpoint is in turn located in the eighteenth and nineteenth centuries, and has led scholars to view the period more closely in terms of our own world.

The term "early modern" has in any case not always been applied uniformly. Historians often juxtapose it with Renaissance, using the two words as synonyms, without openly acknowledging the fact. They apply Renaissance more narrowly to Italian developments, and early modern to non-Italian developments. Intellectual and artistic trends such as humanism are placed under the rubric of Renaissance, while politics, especially the formation of nation states, is placed under the heading early modern. The shifts add to the confusion.

Pessimism, Accommodation, and the Public Domain

The revisions appeared to threaten the existence of the Renaissance as a viable historical field. In 1978, William Bouwsma, then president of the American Historical Association, judged the Renaissance to be on the "point of collapse." He noted a shift from "skepticism" of the central claims of Renaissance scholarship to "agnosticism and even indifference" and claimed that the subject had become "little more than an administrative convenience."[69] In addition to the new socially based research, Bouwsma pointed to a general philosophical turn in the academy toward poststructural and postmodern approaches that denied historical continuity and the intelligibility of such things as modernity. He cited in particular the influence of Michel Foucault and his denial of basic historical categories and patterns.[70] The Renaissance became the keynote of an outdated, chauvinistic mode of history, the grand narrative with a "single plot," whose purpose was to demonstrate the superiority of western culture.

But the Renaissance has proved remarkably resilient. For one thing, not all scholars have accepted the revisionist scholarship. They continue to use the traditional well-worn rubrics. Indeed, the historiography of the Renaissance is, like the period itself, filled with divergent patterns. Opposing trends exist side by side seemingly unaffected by each other. Some historians attack the Annales concept of history, accusing it of substituting an apocalyptic myth of modernization for the ideal of continuous development. Others denounce the postmodern inclination to see the Renaissance as "half-alien," arguing that the chief value of historical study is its ability to tell us something about ourselves.[71] Lisa Jardine's highly acclaimed *Worldly Goods: A New History of the Renaissance* follows unapologetically in the tradition of Burckhardt, positing modernity in the Renaissance. "The world we inhabit today [...] is a world which was made in the Renaissance."[72] Conversely, Robin Kirkpatrick's recent textbook on Renaissance Europe begins with a series of qualifications carefully outlining the limits of the Renaissance, which was neither strikingly original nor modern. Kirkpatrick drew heavily on literary and philosophical trends such as reception theory and the work of Foucault.[73]

An important factor in the persistence of the Renaissance is its currency with the non-academic public. Burckhardt's enduring appeal owes in part to the fact that he viewed Renaissance Italy in the manner of an excited tourist. It is this same impulse that has induced people from around the world to travel to Florence, Venice and others places where the effects of the Renaissance, notably the work of artists and architects, are most apparent. The images keep alive the period, stimulate the imagination, as they did earlier for John Addington Symonds. William Roscoe, Robert Browning, and others. Popular culture has afforded the Renaissance a "stable niche," which has included reproductions of famous artwork on refrigerator magnets and calendars and the application of the term for hotel chains and urban renewal projects.[74] The Renaissance in short transcends the scholarly world and thus resists scholarly attempts to do away with it. It resides in the public domain, where it remains an attractive synonym for progress. A recently discovered protein was given the name "renaissance," on the grounds that it had "multifarious functions" – a sort of a biological "*uomo universale*" in the Burckhardtian sense.[75]

The public Renaissance is booming. And despite the preferences of some professional scholars, public perceptions and popular opinion do affect the academy. Wealthy dilettantes, with often narrow interest in elite culture, have endowed fellowships and grants, which facilitate access to archives and libraries that have made possible the very studies that have challenged the Renaissance label. Mainstream presses continue to solicit and publish books on the Renaissance for a popular market. Similarly, university presses, despite their attention to more specialized topics and greater insulation from commercial pressures, have sometimes encouraged the use of the term Renaissance for the sake of sales. The "lay" interest has in short helped keep relevant the subject and the label.

Even those scholars who have studied ostensibly non-Renaissance topics have often worked comfortably under the label. Margaret King used the term for her book on women (*Women of the Renaissance*, 1991) and in her recent textbook described the Renaissance as of "such tremendous importance that students [...] should devote an entire semester to its study."[76] Numerous others recent books have used the label despite dealing with non-traditional topics. These include J. R. Mulryne, *Court Festivals of the European Renaissance* (2000); Julian Yates, *Error, Misuse, Failure: Object Lessons from the English Renaissance* (2000); Lu Ann Homza, *Religious Authority in the Spanish Renaissance* (2000); Ian Maclean, *Logic, Signs and Nature: Learned Medicine in the Renaissance* (2001); Joanne Ferraro, *Marriage Wars in Late Renaissance Venice* (2001); Andrew Landis and William Eiland, *Visions of Holiness: Art of Devotion in Renaissance Italy* (2001).[77]

It should not be assumed, however, that the authors were directly responsible for their titles. As professional historians know all too well, the determination is often made by the press, and has more than once been the subject of considerable tension between author and editor.

Nevertheless, what have sometimes been called "anti-Renaissance" trends by their opponents have in fact often stimulated research, opening up new vistas rather than closing them. The new historicist interpretation of individuality has, for example, encouraged study of the self in its broader historical context. It has provided a means for understanding the often ambiguous and crafted behavior of Renaissance figures and has helped reanimate discussions of style of living, civility, and politeness. Even Foucault, who posed a seemingly insurmountable challenge to the traditional historical method, has found a place in Renaissance historiography. Scholars have taken up subjects that he studied, including insanity, criminality, and sexuality. They employ Foucault's notions of power, its exercise through language and symbol and importance in human relations.[78]

It is thus possible to accept elements of postmodernism and remain an enthusiastic proponent of the Renaissance.[79] Freed from the strictures of demonstrating progress and modernity, scholars have juxtaposed traditionally antithetical categories such as the secular and religious worlds, wealth and poverty, rationality and irrationality. They have placed philosophy and magic more surely in the context of Renaissance intellectual trends, the former including continued interest in Aristotle.[80] In shifting away from emphasis on elites, scholars have employed more egalitarian language and categories. In her recent history of the Renaissance, Alison Brown replaced the old rubric "rebirth of interest in classics" with a new category, "passions and enthusiasms" that connected Renaissance love of classical learning with book collecting and interest in non-canonical works and non-intellectual frontiers. Scholars have "de-centered" the Renaissance in order to better relativize European Christian culture in terms of Islam, Byzantium, and Judaism.[81] They have situated Europe in a "global" context, in terms of the New World and the East, reaching as far as China and the Indian subcontinent.[82] They have stressed the cultural and economic interactions, cross-influences on Renaissance art, architecture, fashions. and consumption.[83]

It would be incorrect, however, to assume that the new scholarship has wholly superseded Burckhardt or that the work of the Swiss historian has been, as one recent author put it, "hopelessly shattered." Scholars continue to use Burckhardt as the authority against which to position and thus validate their work. In that sense Burckhardt shall perhaps always remain relevant, and "Burckhardt bashing" will continue to be an "Oedipal ritual" among contemporary scholars.[84] Many of the original debates arising from his work remain operative, transformed into new guises. The current emphasis on culture is in keeping with Burckhardt's most fundamental aim, to treat culture as that which "moves the world" and is conditioned by historical circumstance.[85] Sometimes lost in the stereotype that has become Burckhardt is that he incorporated into his analysis aspects of everyday life, including games, humor, and dance. His interest in festivals does not set him so far apart from those now studying ritual. Burckhardt's focus on violence and eye for lurid detail have remained popular among social historians, whose work is now more grounded in a social, anthropological, and linguistic context and applied to a broader sector of society, including middle and lower classes.[86] Meanwhile, Burckhardt's notion of the discovery of the world and man is reflected in the recent work of historians of science, who stress the Renaissance "fascination with nature" with "wondrous" phenomena. John J. Martin has argued broadly in favor of retaining Burckhardt's claim for the modernity of the Renaissance on the grounds that it suited well the world that Burckhardt inhabited. It seems inappropriate today only because our world is a postmodern one.[87]

This convergence of the old and new is perhaps most evident in John Hale's recent history of the Renaissance. The title of the book, *The Civilization of Europe in the Renaissance*, is conscious homage to Burckhardt. Like the Swiss historian, Hale defines the period as one in which there emerged a "new and pervasive attitude" and "dramatic changes in fortune." But Hale organizes his discussions and chapters into categories more in line with the current discourse. He speaks of Renaissance "passions" and "receptions," and treats western developments in terms of other cultures.[88]

A New Beginning and "Enviable Position"

The result is that at present the Renaissance remains a dynamic topic. The pessimism of the late 1970s has been replaced by greater optimism. Edward Muir in his essay "Italian Renaissance in America" (1995) claimed that Renaissance historians were in "an enviable position."[89] Peter Burke, after excusing himself for yet another book on the Renaissance (1998), asserted that there "were never so many people writing on different aspects" of the subject.[90] Randolph Starn, in the Josephine Waters Bennett lecture presented to the Renaissance Society of America in 2006, spoke of "widening the margins" of research and "accommodating turns in the workaday agendas" of scholars.[91]

But if the Renaissance is flourishing, it is doing so without a new synthesis to take Burckhardt's place. The trend among scholars has been to tread lightly, to avoid, as one historian wrote, "universality like the plague." This may indeed reflect the historical profession as a whole. It is nevertheless more difficult to speak of consensus or general agreement. There have been few attempts to provide an overview or even a review of historiographical developments.

Consequently, old problems of definition and periodization persist, and indeed have only grown worse. Some retain Wallace K. Ferguson's dating of the period, from 1300 to 1600.[92] Others do not. Margaret King's recent book traces the Renaissance from 1350 to 1700; Stella Fletcher uses the years 1390 to 1530; while John Martin prefers 1350 to 1650.[93] A look at recent American textbooks for Western Civilization courses, the most typical manner in which students are first introduced to the Renaissance, reveals considerable divergence, particularly with respect to the endpoint (see table 1.1).

The differences are greater upon closer inspection. The Sherman and Salisbury textbook, for example, places the Renaissance between the years 1300 and 1640. But the timeline provided begins in 1320, when Dante wrote the *Divine Comedy*, and ends in 1648, with the conclusion of the Thirty Years War.[94] The Hause and Maltby book uses two periodizations: one from 1350 to 1500 corresponding to political developments, and another from 1340 to 1520 corresponding to intellectual developments. The Kagan, Turner, and Ozment book uses the term Renaissance only for Italy.

Table 1.1 *The Renaissance in recent American Western Civilization textbooks*

Authors	*Title*	*Publication date*	*Renaissance years*
Kagan, Turner, Ozment	*Western Heritage*	2004	1375–1527
Levack, Muir, et al.	*The West*	2004	1350–1550
Chambers, Hanawalt, et al.	*Western Experience*	2005	1300–1500
Coffin, Stacey, et al.	*Western Civilizations*	2005	1350–1550
Hause, Maltby	*Western Civilization*	2005	1340–1520
Greer, Lewis	*Western World*	2005	1300–1600
Sherman, Salisbury	*The West in the World*	2006	1300–1640
Spielvogel	*Western Civilization*	2006	1350–1550
McKay, Hill, Buckler et al.	*A History of Western Society*	2008	1350–1550
Hunt, Martin, Rosenwein et al.	*The Making of the West*	2005	1400–1500
Kishlansky, Geary et al.	*Civilization in the West*	2008	1350–1550

Sources: Kagan (Englewood Cliffs, NJ: Prentice Hall, 2004); Levack (New York: Pearson/ Longman, 2004); Chambers (New York: McGraw Hill, 2005); Coffin (New York: W. W. Norton, 2005); Hause (Belmont, CA:Wadsworth, 2005); Greer (Belmont, CA: Wadsworth, 2005); Sherman (New York: McGraw Hill, 2006); Spielvogel (Belmont, CA: Thomson, 2006); McKay (Boston: Houghton Mifflin, 2008); Hunt (Boston: Bedford/St Martin, 2005); Kishlansky (New York: Pearson Longman, 2008).

Periodization has differed also according to the background of the author. American scholars have shown a tendency to start the Renaissance in the fourteenth century and end it in the sixteenth. Europeans frequently focus on later years, eliding the Renaissance with the so-called "long" sixteenth century, a term popularized by Braudel, going from roughly 1450 to 1620. In the English academy the year 1500 has long been considered a crossover point from the medieval world. French scholars have been inclined to follow general dates set out by Michelet, starting the Renaissance with the French invasion of Italy at the end of the fifteenth century.[95] Bernard Cottret's recent study of the Renaissance begins in 1492 and ends in 1598 (the Edict of Nantes), with emphasis on the activities at the court of Francis I.[96]

There is in short no real consensus. The distinction between the Renaissance and Reformation movements remains problematic, and for all the literature devoted to the subject, the point of separation with the Middle

Ages has hardly been established. Daniel Waley and Peter Denley's *Late Medieval Europe* deals with the period from 1250 to 1520, leaving little room for a Renaissance, at least by American standards.[97] The Italianist Anthony Molho called his study of marriage in fifteenth- and sixteenth-century Florence, *Marriage Alliance in Late Medieval Florence*. But his colleague David Herlihy titled his book on the economy of thirteenth-century Pisa, *Pisa in the Early Renaissance*.

There is lack of consistency even in the work of the same scholars, who have shown a tendency to rethink the issue throughout their careers. In his first history of Renaissance Europe, published in 1971, J. R. Hale dealt with the years 1480–1520.[98] At the end of his career, in *The Civilization of Europe in the Renaissance*, Hale shifted the temporal limits of the period from 1450 to 1620, in essence the "long" sixteenth century. Even the umpire of Renaissance historiography, Wallace Ferguson, changed his mind. He advocated the years 1300–1600 in his "Suggestions for a Synthesis" (1951). But in his textbook, published a decade later (1962), he used the years 1300–1520. The terminal date corresponds to the deaths of Leonardo da Vinci (1519) and Raphael (1520) and the condemnation of Martin Luther (1521).

Some scholars divide the Renaissance into stages or generations. They use the rubrics "early, high, and late," the same employed by medievalists for their period. The stages represent degrees of penetration and diffusion of the movement. Petrarch, an early figure, is emblematic of a "limited," early Renaissance that involved few participants. Leonardo da Vinci (d. 1520) is representative of the "high" Renaissance, now a pervasive phenomenon, most evident in terms of artistic developments.

The motive forces and defining characteristics are, however, variable. Historians arrange their period markers according to differing criteria. Bouwsma linked his concept of Renaissance to psychological states. The early Renaissance represented a period of "hope"; the late Renaissance an era of "anxiety."[99] Robert Lopez, in a spectacularly misguided metaphor, compared the three ages of the Renaissance to the life cycle of a "beautiful woman." The early Renaissance corresponded to her youth, when she was filled with "confident expectation."[100] The "high" Renaissance was a time of maturity, during which she fluctuated between "self assurance and disenchantment." The "late" Renaissance represented old age and "despondency."[101]

The temporal range has depended heavily on subfield. Intellectual historians often privilege events of the fourteenth century, art historians those of the fifteenth century. The current emphasis on "global" Renaissance willy nilly places stress on the sixteenth century, the era of the Atlantic voyages. Continuity is confused by subcategories that arbitrarily separate persons and events. In America, Christopher Columbus (1451–1506) is introduced to students as a product of the Age of Reconnaissance, Niccolò Machiavelli (1469–1527) as a product of the Italian Renaissance, and Martin Luther (1483–1546) as the starting point of the Reformation. It is thus unknown to most students that the men were contemporaries.

The problems of definition and periodization are not likely to be solved, nor are the varied approaches and methodologies apt to be reconciled. For all its jagged edges, the true value of the Renaissance problem has been its ability to continue to provoke debate. As Paula Findlen has stated, the importance of the period lay in what it tells us about making and remaking the past, as a "testing ground for new approaches to history."[102] The debate has raised issues that have gone on to have scholarly lives of their own that have developed and evolved in interesting ways, in some cases into sub-disciplines. In this sense the current discourse has, in a basic way, returned to days of the émigré scholars of the postwar years of the twentieth century. It is the purpose of this volume to trace and evaluate these debates.

Notes

1 For Petrarch's priority see T. E. Mommsen, "Petrarch's Conception of the Dark Ages," *Speculum* 17 (1942): 226–42.

2 E. Harris Harbison, *The Christian Scholar in the Age of the Reformation* (New York, 1956), p. 87.

3 Voltaire, *Essai sur les moeurs et l'esprit des nations, oeuvres completes*, vol. 7 (Paris, 1883–5), p. 167.

4 The French writer Seroux d'Agincourt is credited with being the first to use the term in the late eighteenth century. J. B. Bullen, *The Myth of the Renaissance in Nineteenth Century Writing* (Oxford, 1994), p. 9.

5 Felix Gilbert, *History: Politics or Culture? Reflections on Ranke and Burckhardt* (Princeton, 1990); Lionel Gossman, *Basel in the Age of Burckhardt: A Study of Unseasonable Ideas* (Chicago, 2000).

6 Georg G. Iggers, *The German Conception of History: The National Tradition of Historical Thought from Herder to the Present* (Middletown, CT, 1983).

7 Burckhardt lamented that he had not yet sold 200 copies 18 months after the book appeared. See Denys Hay, ed., *The Renaissance Debate* (New York, 1965), p. 4 and Peter Gay's introduction to the S. G. C. Middlemore edition of Burckhardt's *The Civilization of the Renaissance in Italy* (New York, 1982), pp. xviii–xix.

8 Specialization was encouraged by the growth at this time of scholarly journals throughout Europe and in America. Wallace K. Ferguson, *The Renaissance in Historical Thought: Five Centuries of Interpretation* (Cambridge, MA, 1948), p. 197.

9 Burckhardt was translated into Italian in 1876, English in 1878, and French in 1885.

10 J. R. Hale, *England and the Italian Renaissance: The Growth of Interest in its History and Art* (London, 1954), pp. 84–107; Anthony Molho, "The Italian Renaissance,

Made in the USA," in *Imagined Histories, American Historians Interpret the Past* (Princeton, 1997), pp. 264–7; Theodore E. Stebbins Jr, *The Lure of Italy: American Artists and the Italian Experience, 1760–1914* (Boston and New York, 1992).

11 Bullen, *Myth of the Renaissance*; Marcello Fantoni, "Renaissance Republics and Principalities on Anglo-American Historiography," in *Gli anglo-americani a Firenze. Idea e construzione del Rinascimento*, ed. by M. Fantoni (Rome, 2002), p. 37.

12 Walter Pater, "The Renaissance: Studies in Art and Poetry" in *Selected Writings of Walter Pater*, ed. by Harold Bloom (New York, 1974), pp. 20–1.

13 Hale, *England and the Italian Renaissance*, p. 7. See also the essays in John E. Law and Lene Østermark-Johansen, eds., *Victorian and Edwardian Responses to the Italian Renaissance* (Aldershot, 2005).

14 Hale, *England and the Italian Renaissance*, pp. 169–96; Ferguson, *Renaissance in Historical Thought*, p. 204.

15 John Addington Symonds, *Renaissance in Italy*, vol. 1, p. 22; Ferguson, *Renaissance in Historical Thought*, p. 200.

16 Ernst Cassirer, *Individuum und Kosmos in der Philosophie der Renaissance* (Leipzig, 1927). This was translated into English as *The Individual and the Cosmos*.

17 E. P. Cheyney, *The Dawn of a New Era, 1250–1453* (New York, 1936), p. 2; Alfred von Martin, *The Sociology of the Renaissance* (New York, 1932).

18 Bullen, *Myth of the Renaissance*, pp. 9, 90.

19 Karl Brandi, *Das Werden des Renaissance* (Göttingen, 1908).

20 G. Lanson, *Histoire de la littérature française* (Paris, 1894).

21 G. R. Elton, *Return to Essentials: Some Reflections on the Present State of Historical Study* (Cambridge, 1991), p. 431; Michael Hattaway, *A Companion to English Renaissance Literature and Culture* (Malden, MA, 2000); C. S. Lewis, *English Literature in the Sixteenth Century Excluding Drama* (Oxford, 1954), p. 2; Ferguson, *Renaissance in Historical Thought*, pp. 354–7.

22 Paul Joachimsen, *Geschichtsauffassung und Geschichtschreibung in Deutschland unter dem Einfluss des Humanismus* (Leipzig and Berlin, 1910), p. 16. See also Ferguson, *Renaissance in Historical Thought*, pp. 255–6.

23 Ferguson, *Renaissance in Historical Thought*, pp. 330–85.

24 Johan Huizinga, *The Autumn of the Middle Ages*, trans. by Rodney J. Payton and Ulrich Mammitzsch (Chicago, 1996, originally published in 1919); Charles Homer Haskins, *The Renaissance of the Twelfth Century* (Cambridge, MA, 1927).

25 Johan Huizinga, "The Problem of the Renaissance" (1920), reprinted in *Men and Ideas* (New York, 1960).

26 Haskins, *Renaissance of the Twelfth Century*, p. 5.

27 Paul Sabatier, *Life of Saint Francis of Assisi*, trans. by Louise Seymour Houghton (New York, 1908, originally published in French in 1894).

28 Étienne Gilson, "Humanisme médiéval et renaissance," in *Les idées et les lettres* (Paris, 1932), p. 192; Lynn Thorndike, *A History of Magic and Experimental Science*, vol. 5 (New York, 1923–58).

29 R. W. Southern, *The Making of the Middle Ages* (New Haven, 1953) and *Medieval Humanism* (New York, 1970); Joseph R. Strayer, *On the Medieval Origins of the Modern State* (Princeton, 1970).
30 See, among others, Robert Bartlett, *The Making of Europe* (Princeton, 1993).
31 Erwin Panofsky, "Renaissance and Renascenses," *Kenyon Review* 6 (1944), pp. 201–6.
32 Colin Morris, *The Discovery of the Individual, 1050–1200* (Toronto, 1972), p. 2.
33 Peter Burke, *The Renaissance*, 2nd edn. (London, 1997), p. 4.
34 Peter Burke, *The Fortunes of the Courtier* (University Park, PA, 1995); Felix Gilbert, *Machiavelli and Guicciardini* (Princeton, 1965).
35 William J. Bouwsma, "The Renaissance and the Drama of Western History," in *A Usable Past: Essays in European Cultural History* (Berkeley and Los Angeles, 1990), p. 350.
36 Haskins, *Renaissance of the Twelfth Century*, p. 9.
37 J. R. Hale, "The Renaissance Label," in *Background to the English Renaissance*, ed. by J. B. Trapp (1974), pp. 30–42.
38 Molho, "Italian Renaissance," pp. 270–1.
39 Fantoni, "Renaissance Republics," pp. 35–53.
40 Hans Baron, *The Crisis of the Early Renaissance: Civic Humanism and Republican Liberty in an Age of Classicism and Tyranny* (Princeton, 1955), p. 40.
41 Edward Muir, "The Italian Renaissance in America," *American Historical Review* 100 (Oct. 1995): 1107–8.
42 Federico Chabod, *Machiavelli and the Renaissance* (London, 1958), pp. 201–49.
43 Wallace K. Ferguson, "The Interpretation of the Renaissance: Suggestions for a Synthesis," *Journal of the History of Ideas* 12 (1951): 483–95.
44 Wallace K. Ferguson, *Europe in Transition, 1300–1520* (Boston, 1962), p. vii.
45 R. G. Collingwood, *The Idea of History* (Oxford, 1946), p. 53.
46 Robert Ergang, *The Renaissance* (Princeton, 1967); Lewis W. Spitz, *The Renaissance and Reformation Movements* (St Louis, MO, 1987); De Lamar Jensen, *Renaissance Europe*, (Lexington, MA, 1981).
47 Peter Burke, *The French Historical Tradition: The Annales School 1929–1989* (London, 1990); Lynn Hunt, ed., *The New Cultural History* (Berkeley and Los Angeles, 1989).
48 Emmanuel Le Roy Ladurie, "Motionless History," *Social Science History* 1, 2 (Winter 1977): 115–36.
49 Clifford Geertz, "Thick Description: Toward an Interpretive Theory of Culture," in *The Interpretation of Cultures* (New York, 1973), pp. 3–30.
50 Victor Turner, *The Ritual Process: Structure and Anti-Structure* (Chicago, 1969); Mary Douglas, *Purity and Danger: An Analysis of the Concepts of Pollution and Taboo* (London, 1966).
51 Clifford Geertz, "The Impact of the Concept of Culture on the Concept of Man," in *Interpretation of Cultures*, pp. 34–7.
52 Stephen Greenblatt, *Renaissance Self-Fashioning: From More to Shakespeare* (Chicago, 1980).

53 Joan Kelly, "Did Women Have a Renaissance?" in *Becoming Visible: Women in European History*, ed. by Renate Bridenthal and Claudia Koonz (Boston, 1977), pp. 137–64.
54 Joan Scott, "Gender: A Useful Category of Historical Analysis," *American Historical Review* 91 (1986): 1053–75.
55 Muir, "Italian Renaissance in America," pp. 1107–8.
56 David Herlihy and Christiane Klapisch-Zuber, *Tuscans and their Families* (New Haven, 1985, originally published as *Les Toscans et leurs familles*, 1978).
57 English language translations of selections from the journal are in Edward Muir and Guido Ruggiero, eds., *Microhistory and the Lost People of Europe* (Baltimore, 1991).
58 Emmanuel Le Roy Ladurie, *Montaillou: The Promised Land of Error* (New York, 1978).
59 The genre has, however, had its scholarly critics. See Dominick LaCapra, "The Cheese and the Worms: The Cosmos of a Twentieth Century Historian," in *History and Criticism* (Ithaca, 1985), pp. 45–70.
60 The group includes Hans Rovert, J. H. Jauss, Manfred Fuhrmann, and Wolgang Iser. See J. H. Jauss, *Towards an Aesthetic of Reception* (Manchester, 1982).
61 Burke, *Renaissance*, p. 29.
62 Bouwsma, "Renaissance and the Drama of Western History," p. 357.
63 Denys Hay, *The Italian Renaissance in its Historical Background* (Cambridge, 1976), p. 2.
64 Robert S. Lopez, *The Three Ages of the Italian Renaissance* (Charlottesville, VA, 1970), p. 5.
65 E. H. Gombrich, "The Renaissance – Period or Movement," in *Background to the English Renaissance*, ed. by A. G. Dickens, J. B. Trapp, et al. (London, 1974), p. 25.
66 Burke, *Renaissance*, p. 6, and *The European Renaissance: Centres and Peripheries* (Oxford, 1998), p. 1.
67 Burke, *Renaissance*, p. 5.
68 Leah S. Marcus, "Renaissance and Early Modern Studies," in *Redrawing the Boundaries: The Transformation of English and American Literary Studies*, ed. by Stephen Greenblatt and Giles Gunn (New York, 1992), pp. 41–63.
69 Bouwsma, "Renaissance and the Drama of Western History," p. 350.
70 Michel Foucault, *The Order of Things* (New York, 1970).
71 Bouwsma, "Renaissance and the Drama of Western History," p. 356 and "Eclipse of the Renaissance," *American Historical Review* 103, 1 (Feb. 1998): 115.
72 Lisa Jardine, *Worldly Goods: A New History of the Renaissance* (London, 1996), p. 436.
73 Robin Kirkpatrick, *The European Renaissance* (London, 2002), pp. 1–5.
74 Paula Findlen and Kenneth Gouwens, "The Persistence of the Renaissance," *American Historical Review* 103, 1 (1998): 52; Paul Grendler, *The European Renaissance in American Life* (Westport, CT, 2006); Allen J. Grieco, Michael Rocke, and Fiorella Gioffredi Superbi, eds., *The Italian Renaissance in the Twentieth Century* (Florence, 2002); Randolph Starn, "A Postmodern Renaissance?" *Renaissance Quarterly* 60 (2007): 2.

75 L. N. Antar and G. J. Bassell, "Sunrise at the Synapse: The FMRP mRNP Shaping the Synaptic Interface," *Neuron* 37 (2003): 555–8.

76 Margaret L. King, *Women of the Renaissance* (Chicago, 1991) and *The Renaissance in Europe* (London, 2003), p. xiii. Contrast this, however, with Merry E. Wiesner, who shifted labels: *Working Women in Renaissance Germany* (New Brunswick, 1986); *Gender, Church and State in Early Modern Germany* (New York, 1998); and as Merry E. Wiesner-Hanks, *Women and Gender in Early Modern Europe* (Cambridge, 1993).

77 Some earlier examples include Edward Muir, *Civic Ritual in Renaissance Venice* (Princeton, 1981); Richard Trexler, *Public Life in Renaissance Florence* (Ithaca, 1980); Guido Ruggiero, *Binding Passions: Tales of Magic, Marriage and Power at the End of the Renaissance* (Oxford, 1993).

78 Guido Ruggiero, "Excusable Murder: Insanity and Reason in Early Renaissance Venice," *Journal of Social History* 16, 1 (Autumn 1982): 109–19 and *The Boundaries of Eros: Sex Crime and Sexuality in Renaissance Venice* (Oxford, 1985); Michael Rocke, *Forbidden Friendships: Homosexuality and Male Culture in Renaissance Florence* (New York, 1996); James M. Saslow, *Ganymede in the Renaissance: Homosexuality in Art and Society* (New Haven, 1986); Carol Thomas Neely, "Recent Work in Renaissance Studies: Psychology. Did Madness Have a Renaissance?" *Renaissance Quarterly* 44, 4 (Winter 1991): 776–9.

79 Starn, "Postmodern Renaissance?" pp. 1–24.

80 James Hankins, *Plato in the Italian Renaissance*, 2 vols. (Leiden, 1990); Brian P. Copenhaver, "Did Science Have a Renaissance?" *Isis* 83, 3 (Sept. 1992): 387–407; Charles B. Schmitt, "Reappraisals in Renaissance Science," *History of Science* 16 (1978): 200–14; B. P. Copenhaver and C. Schmitt, *Renaissance Philosophy* (Oxford, 1992).

81 Burke, *European Renaissance*, p. 4; Alison Brown, *The Renaissance* (London, 1999), p. 97; Guido Ruggiero, ed., *A Companion to the Worlds of the Renaissance* (Oxford, 2002), pp. 4–5.

82 Starn, "Postmodern Renaissance?" pp. 10–11; Peter Burke, "Renaissance Europe and the World," in *Palgrave Advances in Renaissance Historiography*, ed. by Jonathan Woolfson (New York, 2005), pp. 52–70; John J. Martin, ed., *The Renaissance World* (New York, 2007).

83 Robert Schwoebel, *The Shadow of the Crescent: The Renaissance Image of the Turk 1453–1517* (Nieuwkoop, 1969); Gerald MacLean, ed., *Re-Orienting the Renaissance: Cultural Exchanges with the East* (Basingstoke, 2005); Margaret Meserve, *Empires of Islam in Renaissance Historical Thought* (Cambridge, MA, 2008). A review of the recent literature on Islam and the Renaissance is in Francesca Trivellato, "Renaissance Italy and the Muslim Mediterranean in Recent Historical Work," forthcoming in *Journal of Modern History*.

84 Starn, "Postmodern Renaissance?" p. 5.

85 Bouwsma, "Renaissance and the Drama of Western History," p. 359.

86 John K. Brackett, *Criminal Justice and Crime in Late Renaissance Florence, 1537–1609* (Cambridge, 1992); Trevor Dean and K. J. P. Lowe, eds., *Crime, Society and the Law in Renaissance Italy*, (Cambridge, 1994); Thomas V. Cohen and Elizabeth

S. Cohen, *Words and Deeds in Renaissance Rome: Trials before Magistrates* (Toronto, 1993); Thomas V. Cohen, *Love and Death in Renaissance Italy* (Chicago, 2004).

87 William Eamon, *Science and the Secrets of Nature: Books and Secrets in Medieval and Early Modern Culture* (Princeton, 1994); Paula Findlen, *Possessing Nature: Museums, Collecting and Scientific Culture in Early Modern Italy* (Berkeley and Los Angeles, 1994); Loraine Daston and Katherine Park, *Wonders and the Order of Nature, 1150–1750* (New York, 1998); John J. Martin, *The Myth of Renaissance Individualism* (New York, 2004).

88 John R. Hale, *The Civilization of Europe in the Renaissance* (New York, 1993), pp. xxiv, 189–350.

89 Muir, "Italian Renaissance in America," p. 1118.

90 Burke, *European Renaissance*, p. 1.

91 Starn, "Postmodern Renaissance?" p. 17.

92 Ferguson, "Interpretation of the Renaissance," pp. 483–95.

93 King, *Renaissance in Europe*; Stella Fletcher, *The Longman Companion to Renaissance Europe* (New York, 2000); John J. Martin, *The Renaissance: Italy and Abroad* (New York, 2003).

94 Dennis Sherman and Joyce E. Salisbury, *The West in the World* (New York, 2006), pp. 364–5.

95 Hugues Daussy, *La renaissance vers 1470–1560* (Paris, 2003).

96 Bernard Cottret, *La renaissance, 1492–1598* (Paris, 2000).

97 Daniel Waley and Peter Denly, *Later Medieval Europe*, 3rd edn. (London, 2001); George Holmes, *The Later Middle Ages, 1272–1485* (New York, 1962).

98 J. R. Hale, *Renaissance Europe 1480–1520* (Oxford, 1971).

99 William Bouwsma, *The Waning of the Renaissance, 1550–1640* (New Haven, 2001), p. 112.

100 Lopez, *Three Ages of the Italian Renaissance*, pp. 7–8.

101 Theodore K. Rabb, *The Last Days of the Renaissance and the March to Modernity* (New York, 2006), pp. xix–xxi, 120–60.

102 Paula Findlen, "Possessing the Past: The Material World of the Italian Renaissance," *American Historical Review* 103 (Feb. 1998): 83–114 (quotes are p. 113).

2

Individualism: Who Was the Renaissance Man?

I know how fraught with uncertainty this hope of fame may be, and I realize how little we may see its consequences. Therefore I have lived my life as best I might; and in some hope of the future, I have scorned the present [. . .] For this course seems but honorable, and even if any hope I have of fame should fail me, my ambition is worthy of praise, inasmuch as longing for renown is natural.

Girolamo Cardano[1]

For both amateur and professional historians, a traditional starting point for discussion of the Renaissance has been individualism. They associate the period with the achievements of talented, "self-aware" men. Giorgio Vasari (d. 1574) focused his famous account of the "revival" (*rinascita*) of Italian art on the series of great artists, culminating in the "genius" of Michelangelo. Jules Michelet defined the era as one of "the discovery of the world and man," which in turn led to man's "rediscovery of his own self." In *The Civilization of the Renaissance in Italy*, Jacob Burckhardt placed "individualism" at the heart of his analysis and made it the essential quality of the Renaissance man, distinguishing him from his medieval counterpart, who lay "half-awake beneath a common veil," woven of "faith, illusion and childish prepossession."[2] Burckhardt's individualism was uniquely Italian, developed in the context of local politics, which by their calculated and treacherous nature produced self-serving men, who succeeded according to their skill and ability. Birth and inherited status meant little; illegitimacy often fared best.

Burckhardt's construct has been the most influential and enduring aspect of his thesis. The Renaissance persona or "spiritual individual" (*geistiges*

Individuum) was a highly developed form, a modern man, whose attributes grew from his "boundless ambition" and "thirst after greatness." He was an autonomous actor, aware of his own uniqueness as well as that of others. Medieval man, by contrast, was conscious of himself only as "a member of a race, people, party, family or corporation, through some general category."

These personal qualities formed the basis of the larger achievements of the Renaissance. They found expression in the lives of a wide range of individuals, including the philosophers Nicholas of Cusa and Giovanni Pico della Mirandola, the explorers Christopher Columbus and Hernan Cortes, the condottieri Francesco Sforza and Federico da Montefeltro as well as merchants and politicians such as the Medici.

The list is not inclusive. The term individualism has been applied in numerous and often inconsistent ways. It was coined in early nineteenth-century France, by political conservatives, who used it as a pejorative for eccentricity and isolation that threatened the established political order. German Romantics revised this view, adding positive qualities such as originality and genius. Burckhardt's drew on both traditions, seeing in individualism genius and originality combined with isolation that produced anxiety.[3]

The construct was carried into the twentieth century and underlies much of our current understanding. Nevertheless, the elastic nature of the term has engendered a great deal of debate among modern scholars. This has taken place not only among historians, but across disciplines, among literary critics, sociologists, anthropologists, psychologists, and psychiatrists. The scholarship has sought both to modify Burckhardt and to go beyond him altogether. Medievalists, here as elsewhere, called into question chronology, tracing the roots of individualism to earlier periods. Renaissance social, intellectual, and cultural historians have extended their studies across class and gender lines, demonstrating the sustained importance of "corporate" associations – of family, guilds and the church – categories that were not exclusive.[4] Postmodern and new historicist literary critics meanwhile have questioned the very existence of the autonomous individual, viewing the self as a "fiction" fashioned by its context.[5] Historical/psychoanalytic work has stressed relational aspects of identity: how the self was shaped in opposition to an "other," notably by "encounters" with natives of the New World and with Islam.[6] Recent approaches have also emphasized the development of specifically Renaissance modes of behavior including politeness, sincerity, and crafted ambiguity. John Martin has argued that the era witnessed the emergence for the first time of "an inner self" and the awareness, if at times hazy, of the boundaries between it and the outer world.[7]

As with all aspects of Renaissance historiography, various trends exist at once and are not easily reconcilable. The current discourse has, however, proceeded with a greater sense of the limits of the priority of the West. Where individualism was once perceived as a great dividing line between European civilization and the rest of the world, it is now seen as having contemporary parallels in Asia, particularly in contemporary China and Japan.[8]

The Development of the Individual and the Discovery of the World and Man

What is at once evident about Michelet and Burckhardt's individualism is its gendered and elitist nature. The great self-aware individuals were all men. Michelet's representatives of the "heroic age" of self-discovery were Columbus, Copernicus, and Galileo. John Addington Symonds gave his discussion of the individual the subtitle "Men of the Renaissance" and stated plainly that the great achievements of Italy were the work of "men of power."[9] Burckhardt took as his *uomo universale,* "all-sided man," the Florentine humanist and architect Leon Battista Alberti, who coupled illegitimacy of birth (his mother was a slave) with imposing intellectual and physical skills, the latter including the ability jump over another man's head in a single bound.[10] The sixteenth-century French essayist Michel Montaigne (1533–1592), whose introspective search for self-knowledge ("Que sçais-je?") defined his life, denied this activity to commoners and women. The "true advantage" of the latter was their beauty, which made them attractive to men.[11]

Given the emphasis it is not surprising that the study of the Renaissance has been characterized, perhaps more so than any other historical period, by biographies of great men. The trend was apparent already in the eighteenth century in the works of William Roscoe and Pasquale Villari, and continued into the modern era with "profiles" of Renaissance figures and various collected lives (see table 2.1).[12] The tradition of male genius was emphasized in textbooks; Robert Ergang, writing in 1955, equated the Renaissance to the activities of "many men of great genius."[13] Few would now go so far, but the great Renaissance men live on in the now familiar subsection and embedded box in textbooks, which in recent years have included the occasional woman who exhibited similar traits as men (see chapter 3). There remains a tendency, more pervasive than professional scholars would like to admit, to periodize the Renaissance in terms of the lives of prominent male figures.

A common starting point in both popular and scholarly work is Francis Petrarch. Petrarch's career embodied many of the basic characteristics that scholars have associated with Renaissance individualism. He sought, through study of classics, earthly fame and glory and was keenly aware of

Table 2.1 *Sample of profiles of Renaissance "individuals" in textbooks and collected lives*

Individual	*Source*
Petrarch	Rabb, Plumb, Schwoebel, Spitz, Jenson, Zophy
Machiavelli	Plumb, Spitz, Breisach, Zophy, Gundersheimer
Columbus	Jensen, Spitz, Checksfield, Zophy
Montaigne	Rabb, Schwoebel, Checksfield
Michelangelo	Plumb, Spitz
Da Vinci	Plumb, Ergang, Jensen, Spitz, Lucas, Gundersheimer
Cellini	Ergang, Spitz

Sources: M. M. Checksfield, *Portraits of Renaissance Life and Thought* (New York, 1965), pp. 73–97, 145–63; L. Spitz, *Renaissance Europe* (St Louis, MO, 1971), pp. 14, 187, 219, 223, 242, 263; H. S. Lucas, *The Renaissance and Reformation* (New York, 1934); R. Ergang, *The Renaissance* (New York, 1967), pp. 168, 192; J. H. Plumb, *Renaissance Profiles* (New York, 1961); R. Schwoebel, *Renaissance Men and Ideas* (New York, 1981); T. K. Rabb, *Renaissance Lives* (New York, 1993); E. Breisach, *Renaissance Europe, 1300–1517* (New York, 1973), pp. 135–7; D. L. Jensen, *Renaissance Europe* (Lexington, MA, 1981), pp. 292, 165; J. W. Zophy, *A Short History of Renaissance and Reformation Europe* (Englewood Cliffs, NJ, 1996), pp. 66–8, 128–9, 135–7; W. L. Gundersheimer, ed., *The Italian Renaissance* (Englewood Cliffs, NJ, 1965), pp. 123–36, 163–81.

his own uniqueness. "Everything Petrarch read or learned," wrote Georg Voigt in the nineteenth century, "[...] he related to his own person."[14] Petrarch's genius was, however, conflicted and anxious, a fact he himself made plain in *My Secret* (1347–53), which outlined the struggle between his desire for earthly fame and for salvation of his soul. Petrarch explained his plight to his interlocutor, the church father Augustine of Hippo, who suggested he abandon his ambition and contemplate death. "The glory of men and the immortality of your name mean much more to you than they should."[15] In "On the Ascent of Mount Ventoux," Petrarch expressed both appreciation for the natural beauty of the Alpine landscape around him and concern about his salvation, for which his ascent up the mountain served as a metaphor.

Petrarch provided a model for the next generation of humanists, who expressed their self-reflective genius through their writing, in imitation of the ancients. The humanist brand of individualism was often vain and arrogant. Petrarch and his followers occasionally employed their rhetorical skills to ridicule both their inferiors and each other. Burckhardt viewed this satiric wit as an essential component of individualism, achieving its fullest expression in the sixteenth century in the work of Pietro Aretino (1491–1556).[16] Petrarch displayed admirable skill in the genre, deriding, in a well-known letter, a local doctor with whom he had personal disagreement. He described him as little more than a mechanic. "Cure your patients if you can," Petrarch wrote, "if not, kill them and demand payment when they are dead."[17]

Petrarch's fifteenth-century counterpart Poggio Bracciolini (d. 1459) described his fellow humanist Francesco Filelfo as a "reeking goat" and "horned monster" and Lorenzo Valla as the creation of the devil, who left him on earth so that he could do greater harm to humanity. Valla in turn ridiculed Bracciolini's linguistic skills, suggesting that he learned Latin from his stable boy.[18] Valla's most forceful revenge, however, was his greater posthumous fame.

Perhaps the most striking instances of genius cum vanity were in the art world. The art historian Rudolf Wittkower described painters as an "idiosyncratic caste with immensely strong leading individuals."[19] He based this assessment largely on Giorgio Vasari, whose famous *Lives of the Artists* provides many examples. When asked by papal officials to supply evidence of his skill for a commission in Rome, the artist Giotto di Bondone arrogantly drew a simple circle ("tondo"), saying that "it is more than sufficient" (and indeed it was). Donatello smashed his own work (a life sized bronze head) rather than receive less than he thought it was worth. The young Michelangelo evoked such jealousy in his fellow art student, Torrigiani, that the latter struck him in the face with a trowel, disfiguring him for life. Michelangelo's own ego revealed itself at the presentation of his *David* in the city of Florence. When the *gonfaloniere* Piero Soderini criticized the nose of the statue for being "too large," Michelangelo ascended the scaffold with a heap of dust in his hand. He feigned chiseling, and tossed the dust below. Michelangelo, Vasari tells us, "then laughed to himself, feeling compassion for those who, in order to appear that they understand, do not realize what they are saying." Soderini was nevertheless pleased and claimed that the stone had "come alive."[20]

Vasari's biographical sketches stress the conflicts and struggles of the artists, with themselves and with their patrons.[21] Michelangelo himself wrote of internal misery that accompanied his creativity. The characteristics linked artist to writer. The latter were likewise eccentrics and anxious people, whose creative impulses produced in them a sense of isolation and fear. Petrarch complained of melancholy and despair. At the age of thirty-eight, Michel Montaigne removed himself from public life, to his country estates to examine his thoughts by means of a new literary genre, the essay. Montaigne wrote of the necessity of reserving a "back room" ("arriere boutique") in which to search within himself and establish his "real liberty."[22]

One discerns in these traits modern notions of genius and creativity. It is this familiarity that has made the traditionalist depiction of individualism so compelling, particularly in non-academic circles. An idealized portrait of the Renaissance man is that given by Baldassare Castiglione in his *Courtier* (1528). The book is set at the court of the Duke of Urbino, with characters drawn from real life. Castiglione, a nobleman, soldier and ambassador from Mantua, took much of his long career to write it. The work proved enormously influential, published in numerous editions and languages. In part 1, the interlocutors discuss the characteristics of the ideal courtier. They stress qualities such as courage, education, good grooming, athletic and martial skill and above all "grazia" or grace, which encompassed the others. Grace was bestowed upon man by nature, but could, to a degree, be learned by imitation. For Castiglione, grace was a style and elegance, free of all affect. To further elucidate this point, Castiglione coined a new term "*sprezzatura*," without exact English equivalent, but intended to convey a sense of studied "nonchalance."[23]

The precise meaning of *sprezzatura* has elicited considerable discussion, about which we will speak more fully later. Peter Burke called *The Courtier* "a guide to self representation," an instruction manual that depicted man not so much as he was, but as he should be, in the context of the elite at court.[24] Castiglione's use of *grazia* mirrored that of Vasari, who applied the term to artists, whose work possessed a natural endowment and elegance.[25] The meaning parallels Burckhardt's notion of "*uomo universale*," whose persona and speech appeared "faultless." Interestingly, however, Burckhardt did not include Castiglione in his discussion of the "development of the Individual," but in a section on society, festivals, and social etiquette.[26]

The Courtier was one of numerous Renaissance "conduct" books, a genre that was popular in the sixteenth century. The books outlined the proper modes of behavior, both at court and in the urban setting. Giovanni della Casa's *Galateo*, published in 1558, focused on manners and table etiquette, as did Thomas Elyot's *The Boke named the Governour* (1531) and Roger Ascham's *The Scholemaster* (1571). The conduct books often offered advice to women, particularly with regard to chastity. Some, such as Juan Luis Vives's *The Education of a Christian Woman* (1523), emphasized gender distinctions, advising men on the ways to behave in the public sphere, while admonishing women to remain at home in the domestic sphere (see chapter 3).[27]

The proliferation of conduct books affirms the strong interest that Renaissance society had in the self. This is further verified by the popularity of biography and autobiography as literary genres. Petrarch wrote a collection of lives of ancient men, *De viris illustribus (On famous men)*, based on Cicero. His friend Giovanni Boccaccio wrote the lives of both famous men and women, including contemporaries. The Florentine bookseller Vespasiano da Bisticci (1421–1498) arranged his *Vite di uomini illustri* by profession, giving biographies of notable contemporaries such as Lorenzo and Cosimo de' Medici and Federico da Montefeltro.[28] The Roman bishop and humanist Paolo Giovio (d. 1552) offered sketches of ancients, contemporaries, Italians, non-Italians and even non-Europeans in his *Elogia*.

Humanists wrote biographies of each other, helping to insure their lasting fame. Boccaccio wrote about Petrarch, as did the German humanist

Rudolf Agricola. The Englishman Thomas More wrote about Giovanni Pico della Mirandola. William Roper wrote a biography of Thomas More (1556), who was his father-in-law.

Autobiography was also a widespread Renaissance literary form.[29] Among the most well known is that of goldsmith/soldier/lover/brawler Benvenuto Cellini (d. 1571), begun in 1558 and completed in 1566. After more than 400 years the work retains its ability to shock, possessing the color and suspense of a modern crime thriller. The Romantic poet Goethe (d. 1832), who translated it into German in 1803, described it as reflecting both the positive and negative aspects of individualism, of self-liberation and creativity on the one hand, and conflict and isolation from the world on the other.[30] Burckhardt described Cellini as a "whole man," who could "do all and dares do all, and who carries his measure in himself."[31]

Cellini makes clear from the outset of his work the importance of self-commemoration and exaltation. "All men of whatsoever quality they be, who have done anything of excellence [...] should describe their life with their own hand."[32] Cellini then unabashedly boasted of his artistic skill, his important connections and his sexual exploits, with both women and men. He complained bitterly of rivals, fellow artists and goldsmiths, who denied him his repute. He told of feuds and fights, including several homicides he committed as the result of minor slights.

A similarly rounded though less violent self-portrait was that given by the Milanese physician and mathematician Girolamo Cardano (1576). Born a year after Cellini, Cardano offered a startlingly complete description of himself, including his preference for fish over meat, his occasional insomnia, the wart over his left eye, and the number of teeth (15) that remained in his mouth by age seventy-four. Cardano expressed a strong desire for glory and fame, aware that the path would lead to "torment" and "exhaustion" and ultimately a short life.[33] Cardano secured his earthly fame primarily through his medical and mathematical writings, which he carefully lists in chapter 45 of his autobiography. Like Cellini, Cardano's fame produced conflict with the world, especially battles with intellectual rivals, that engendered in him a sense of anxiety and isolation, about which he speaks at length.

The works of Cellini and Cardano, published, translated, and widely circulated in the nineteenth century, exerted strong influence on the traditional construct of Renaissance individualism. Autobiography was, however, by no means an exclusively Italian genre. The Pomeranian notary Bartolomew Sastrow (1520–1603) wrote a personal memoir, as did the English composer Thomas Whythorne (1528–1595). In France, the soldier Blaise de Montluc (1500–1574) recounted his thoughts and experiences in his *Commentaries*; and in the Netherlands, the Flemish philologist and humanist Justus Lipsius (1547–1606) recorded his reflections on the world around him. There also emerged at this time artisan autobiographies, written by non-elites, including tanners and craftsmen, who, as James Amelang has shown, often expressed similar senses of alienation and solitude.[34]

A distinctive species of autobiographical work was the *ricordanze (libri di famiglia)*, which developed among the merchant class in the city of Florence. More than a hundred of them have survived; many have yet to be examined. They were a mélange of diary and business account, with legal authority such that they could be presented in court as evidence in disputes. They do not exist for other Italian cities and it is not entirely clear why this is so.[35] Nevertheless, they were often revealing of their authors. The *ricordanze* of Buonaccorso Pitti (d. 1410) reads like a picaresque novel, relating the details of Pitti's career as a merchant, ambassador, soldier and, most conspicuously, a gambler, a habit he shared with Girolamo Cardano.[36]

The visual analog of biography and autobiography was portrait and self-portrait. The art historian John Pope-Hennessy considered the two genres synonymous with the "Renaissance cult of personality."[37] Pisanello (1395–1455) in Italy and Jean Fouquet (1420–1481) in France rendered the likenesses of local aristocrats and merchants at courts. Pisanello also initiated the practice of making commemorative coins of rulers, in imitation of the Romans.

Jean Fouquet was likely responsible for first independent self-portrait, a small oval picture in gold on black enamel in 1450. The Dutch artist Maarten van Heemskerck (1498–1574) rendered likenesses of himself, as did the German painter Albrecht Dürer (1471–1528), among the most accomplished at the genre.[38] The independent self-portrait became increasingly common in the sixteenth century. Giorgio Vasari, an artist as well as writer, did a portrait of himself (1567) that hangs in the Uffizi, the building he designed. Parmigianino (1503–1540) gave conspicuous demonstration of his skill, presenting himself as he appeared in a convex mirror (1523–4), with physical distortions.

Literary and visual genres were often linked together. Renaissance biographies had portraits affixed to their subjects, following a model established in antiquity by the ancient Roman writer Varro. The second edition of Vasari's *Lives* (1568) contained 144 pictures of the artists described therein. Editions of the work of Dante (1521), Erasmus (1533), and Shakespeare (1623) all had portraits of their authors attached as frontispieces.[39]

The visual representations reinforced notions of individualism. Piero della Francesca's famous portrait of Federico da Montefeltro in profile (1465–6), with his wife, emphasized Federico's high status and dignity. Piero's subsequent representation of Federico in an altarpiece clad in armor praying stressed his devotion. The portrait of Baldassare Castiglione (1514–15) by Raphael projected images of unaffected self-confidence consonant with the main themes of *The Courtier*.[40]

Overseas Explorations

A conspicuous instance of individualism was overseas explorations. Michelet's discovery of man was linked to the discovery of the New World. Burckhardt saw the explorers and the discovery of America as emblematic of the Renaissance "self-conscious spirit of inquiry" that was a key component of individualism. The explorers' search for fame, their self-aggrandizing individualistic impulses, produced what De Lamar Jensen has called "the most profoundly altering activity of the Renaissance."[41]

The emphasis on the importance of the explorers and discovery of the New World found a congenial audience in American classrooms. It connected America directly to the European Renaissance. Christopher Columbus is the essential figure, an individual who challenged the medieval worldview and whose journey for Spain in 1492 constituted, in the words of a popular historian, the "rise of the modern age."[42] This notion has recently been repeated by the renowned scholar Jacques Le Goff, who pointed to Columbus and the subsequent Treaty of Tordesillas (1494) as the beginning point of modernity.[43]

Individualism and concern for personal reputation were particularly apparent in the careers of the conquistadores. According to J. H. Parry, the men possessed Machiavellian *virtù* that allowed them to improvise in a new setting.[44] Hernan Cortes (1485–1547) and Francisco Pizarro (1475–1541) subdued powerful civilizations by means of cunning and daring. Cortes arrived in Mexico in 1519 with only 66 men and 16 horses, led his army through the jungles of Vera Cruz to the highlands of the Mexican plateau, to island city of Tenochtitlán, where he defeated the powerful Aztecs. Eleven years later, Pizzaro led a band of 100 infantry and 60 cavalry to the high Andes and defeated the Incas. Cortes grandly described his deeds in his diary, in which he compared himself to Julius Caesar and Alexander the Great. His companion Bernal Diaz gave careful detail of local flora and fauna and wild animals, demonstrating a Renaissance appreciation of nature.[45]

A similar sense of priority and achievement is evident in the career of Amerigo Vespucci (d. 1512). He relayed his exploits in two famous letters, *Mundus Novus* (1504) and *Quatuor Navigationes* (1505), in which he claimed, like Cellini and Cardano, to tell of his experience so 'that my record may live for future generations."[46] The letters gained wide currency and popularity, and by 1520 were available in 60 editions. The German mapmaker Martin Waldseemuller (d. 1521) included a copy of them in his *Cosmographie introductio* (Introduction to Cosmography, 1507), along with a portrait of Amerigo and named the New World after him (America).[47]

Whether the individualism exhibited by the explorers was the same as that of their humanist counterparts is, however, an open question.[48]

The anguished vanity of a Petrarch and the acquisitive *virtù* of Cortes do not at once appear to be the same thing. Humanists were often silent about the deeds of the explorers, while the explorers, conversely, seemed little aware of the work of humanists. Amerigo Vespucci presents perhaps the most apparent straight-line connection. He was a "son of the Florentine Renaissance," working before his voyages for the Medici bank.[49] The popularity of his letters owed in part to his classical learning and literary style, which had humanist rhetorical flourishes. Like the humanists, Vespucci situated present events in terms of the ancients. He described that "savages" of America, for example, as "more inclined to be Epicurean than stoic."

J. H. Parry saw the explorations as reflective of a general "Renaissance spirit" that pervaded Spain and the court of Queen Isabella in the fifteenth and sixteenth centuries. He noted the popularity of Renaissance Italian literary and intellectual trends and the translation of Ariosto's *Orlando Furioso* into Spanish. Samuel Edgerton focused more narrowly on Florence, arguing that there was a direct causal link between the Renaissance and the Atlantic voyages through the work of Paolo Toscanelli (d. 1482), a Florentine astronomer, mathematician and friend of Filippo Brunelleschi.[50] Interested in finding a sea route to the Indies, Toscanelli studied the *Geographia* of the second-century Greek astronomer Ptolemy. The *Geographia* was transported to Florence by the Byzantine scholar Manuel Chrysoloras in 1396. Its arrival was, for Edgerton, an epoch-making event, whose significance was enhanced by the fact that it coincided precisely with the beginning of civic humanism and Masaccio's use of new techniques of perspective. Toscanelli wrote to the king of Portugal advocating the sea route, and ultimately helped inspire Christopher Columbus's study of Ptolemy, which served as inspiration for his voyage and thus the discovery of the New World.[51]

The Medieval Individual

Nevertheless, for many scholars the overseas explorations point precisely away from the Renaissance. They see the voyages as a distinctly medieval endeavor, inspired by notions of Christian crusading.[52] The technological innovations that allowed the explorers to sail greater distances were not strictly speaking Renaissance ones, but the result of evolution of techniques from the Middle Ages, during which some of the greatest advances were made.

Portugal, the small state that initiated the Atlantic adventure, had little ostensible connection to the Renaissance. Its great prince, Henry the Navigator, was, despite his sobriquet, not himself an explorer, nor much of a seaman. He encouraged exploration to fulfill the predictions of astrologers who had pronounced for him "great and noble conquests" and to establish commercial ties with Genoa and Venice, which had preceded Portugal in involvement in coastal African trade.[53]

William H. Prescott in his classic study of the conquest of Mexico portrayed Cortes not as the embodiment of the spirit of the Renaissance, but as a representative of an "age of religious fervor.[54] Columbus's journey for Spain in 1492 coincided with the last phases of the Spanish *reconquista*, the centuries long Christian crusade against the Muslims. The year brought the seizure of the last Moorish kingdom at Granada, and repression and exile of Jews and Muslims. Columbus was himself an intensely religious man, who expressed a desire to convert the natives and brought with him to the New World the works of Saint Francis of Assisi.

The explorers and their employers were also influenced by medieval travel accounts and the legends contained in them. They believed, for example, in the existence in the fabulously rich Christian king, Prester John, who lived in the east among the pagans, near the lands of the Amazon women, described at length in the popular travel diary of the Englishman John Mandeville (*Travels and Travels*, 1366). The Portuguese explorer Vasco da Gama brought letters of introduction to Prester John with him on his journey around the tip of Africa.

For the medievalist Robert Bartlett, even the Renaissance sense of "discovery" displayed by the explorers had roots in the Middle Ages. Bartlett argued that a similar zeal had been expressed during the European expansion in the twelfth and thirteenth centuries, when the eastern frontier was conquered and the local pagans there were Christianized. Bartlett called this widening of Europe's internal boundaries the "Europeanization" of Europe.[55]

Medievalists focused still more attention on the earlier roots of individualism. They point out that despite the claims of Renaissance historians, literary genres such as biography and autography were not new; nor was the information relayed in them necessarily original or true. Renaissance authors blatantly copied material from earlier works. Paolo Giovio derived his "facts" from myth and legend and did not try to disguise it. Moreover, as Alison Knowles Frazier has pointed out, medieval genres such as saint lives remained popular with humanist writers.[56]

Medieval autobiographies were, like their Renaissance counterparts, decidedly self-aware. Authors spoke of their desire for fame and glory as well as their worries and anxieties.[57] In his memoir, *De vita sua sive monodiarum suarum libri tres*, Guibert of Nogent (d. 1125) makes statements about his love of classics, his desire for recognition, his discomfort with physical love, and his irrational fears of sexual mutilation. The last led the historian John Benton to label Guibert a "disturbed man."[58] Peter of Blois (d. 1203), author of a series of autobiographical letters, declared, in a manner reminiscent of Petrarch, the need to pass beyond "the darkness of ignorance" of the day to "the enlightenment of science" through study of the ancients. "Let the dogs bark, let the pigs grunt! I will nonetheless be a disciple of the ancients."[59]

The existence of such notable figures encouraged Charles Homer Haskins to seek his Renaissance in the twelfth century. Richard Southern associated the men with the emergence of "medieval humanism," a term we will discuss in further detail later (see chapter 4). Perhaps no character more exemplified the traits of medieval egoistic individuality than Peter Abelard (d. 1142). His *History of My Calamities*, in the form of a letter to a friend, gave an unflinching account of Abelard's professional career, as a brilliant student and then teacher in cathedral schools in France, who treated the lecture hall and the academic world as a species of intellectual battlefield. He told of his "unfortunate" affair with his student, Heloise that resulted in a cruel revenge and his personal and professional downfall. Abelard relays his story with a deep sense of tragedy and self-obsession, a theme evident also in his famous correspondence with Heloise.

Abelard lacked the requisite athletic skills of Burckhardt's "*uomo universale*." But his persona and sense of himself nevertheless gave him the Burckhardtian aspect of a "modern" man. Indeed, Le Goff described Abelard as a "modern intellectual."[60] Abelard's status in this regard is heightened by the contrast between his career and that of his contemporary and antagonist, Bernard of Clairvaux, the Carthusian monk, who opposed the rationality and logic advocated by Abelard and who spearheaded Church efforts to condemn him.

Medievalists have adduced additional examples of "unique" personas. They point to Gerbert of Aurillac (d. 1003), who studied astronomy and mathematics among the Muslims, and Roger Bacon (d. 1292), who undertook experimental scientific studies, using lenses for magnification, correcting errors in the calendar, and speculating on various mechanical devices, including ones that could fly (see chapter 7). The historian Walter Ullmann has examined the effect of medieval individualistic behavior on political institutions; Peter Dronke has looked at individualism in its literary, religious, and psychological settings.[61]

The studies have provided support for medievalist claims against the priority of Renaissance individualism. But like their Renaissance counterparts, scholars of the Middle Ages have employed the term individualism loosely, and not always in consistent ways. Indeed, some have made claims that go far beyond those made by Burckhardt. Colin Morris in his influential and oft-reprinted study of medieval individualism, saw it as a unique phenomenon that constituted a fundamental point of separation between the history of the West and that of other cultures. The claim is used by Morris to establish the Middle Ages as the key turning point in history (see chapter 1).[62]

Recent scholarship has presented a more contextualized view of medieval individualism that deemphasizes notions of modernity and originality. Caroline Walker Bynum has argued that the medieval "self" was not secular. It involved a search for an "inner self" that often took place inside a monastery and was indistinguishable from the search for God. Introspection did not in any case preclude involvement in the collectivity. The self adapted to its environment, and was formulated according to extant models of behavior.[63]

Collectivity and Family

In a similar manner, Renaissance scholars have questioned individualism's secular nature and distance from collective forms. Charles Trinkhaus argued that the individualistic impulses of Renaissance man were intrinsically linked to his search for God (see chapter 7).[64] Meanwhile, individuality did not conflict with membership in groups. Renaissance man belonged to corporations such as guilds, confraternities, and the church. He was a citizen of the state and a member of a family, categories that were not exclusive.[65]

Scholars have stressed the singular importance of family. Natalie Zemon Davis argued that in sixteenth-century France family and lineage provided the context for the creation of the individual. "Everywhere the family was conceived of as a unit from which one took identity and passed it on to the next generation." Individuals understood their successes and failures in terms of the family.[66] They sought fame not only for its own sake, but to bring honor to the clan. Even reactions against the family, in particular against the strictures of patriarchy, were forms of self-definition. "Embeddedness," as Davis wrote, "did not preclude self-discovery, but rather prompted it."[67]

This was especially the case in Italy, the home of Burckhardt's self-made man. Studies have shown how individualistic forms of self-expression were embedded in the family context, as well as in other group associations.[68] For all the details the authors of Florentine *ricordanze* gave about themselves, they usually began by invoking family lineages and stating their hope that by attaining greater status they would further glorify it. Benvenuto Cellini coupled his overt yearnings for fame with statements of his intention to establish "an honorable foundation" for his forbears.[69] In rejecting the notion of individuality in fifteenth- and sixteenth-century Florentine society, the historian Anthony Molho concluded that "family tradition, family expectations, family patrimonies provided a moral compass which guided individual actions."[70]

The precise role played by family has been the subject of its own debate. According to one interpretation, the family provided the context for economic individualism in the city of Florence. Political, legal, and economic changes in the fourteenth and fifteenth centuries reduced the power and solidarity of Florentine patrician clans and freed their members to behave more individualistically. The extended clans or *consorterie* of the earlier period, who pooled their fiscal resources and lived under one roof, lost cohesion by the fifteenth century. This discouraged collective behavior and encouraged independent individual investment. Since patrician families were leaders of the Florentine business world, the economy became a more "individual enterprise."[71] The building of Renaissance palaces that occurred at this time were the "aesthetic articulation" of the physical separation from the individual household from its corporate forebear.[72]

The interpretation, reminiscent of Alfred von Martin (see chapter 5), gave institutional context to Burckhardtian individualism. It presupposed the evolution during the Renaissance of nuclear "modern" families, living together in single units in a single space. William Kent has challenged this notion, arguing that the structure of patrician families in Florence remained complex and varied and often large and cohesive. Even where there were smaller units, members of the extended clan often lived nearby, in the same parish and district connected by paternal ties. There thus remained an "active sense" of lineage within the broader economic community.[73] David Herlihy and Christiane Klapisch-Zuber's analysis of the Florentine *catasto* of 1427 showed divergent patterns of family organization, according to class. Patrician families exhibited strong patrilinear solidarity and adherence to networks of relatives and friends. Poorer families, however, demonstrated strikingly less solidarity.[74]

The evidence for other places supports the more diverse picture. Jacques Heers and Diane Owen Hughes have shown the persistence of large clans and the tightening of lineage bonds among the elite in Genoa.[75] Studies of family structure north of the Alps reveal variation with respect to place and circumstance. Extended families living under one roof, sharing economic resources, were a rare phenomenon, and, to the extent that they existed, were located mostly in rural spaces.[76] Peter Laslett counted few nuclear units in England, France, Germany, and the Low Countries.[77] The social anthropologist Jack Goody warned against adopting "the myth of the extended family," an assumption, common to nineteenth-century scholarship, that small families necessarily evolved from larger ones.[78]

The corporate nature of Renaissance individualism has been affirmed in numerous studies. Florence, for all its famous individuals, was nevertheless a prototype of collectivity. There was evidence of "corporatism" in the social, economic, and political organization of the city.[79] Christiane Klapisch-Zuber emphasized the role of kinship networks of "parenti, vicini and amici" in providing the milieu for advancement. The location of one's home became a place to make connections and to find business associates.

Confraternities functioned similarly, bringing together people often from diverse backgrounds.[80]

Networks were of central importance in the art world. Rather than agonized isolation, artists often worked closely with family, kin, and neighbors. They were members of guilds and workshops and maintained dialogues with their patrons, who were often institutions – confraternities, hospitals or supervisory boards of churches. Work on the Florentine cathedral was, since 1331, controlled by the wool merchants' guild, which hired artists and supervised their projects. They negotiated subjects and themes. When the friars of the church of San Francesco at Borgo San Sepolcro hired the artist Sassetta to paint the triptych on the high altar (*The Legend of the Wolf*, 1437–40), they outlined the physical dimensions of the project, the materials he should use, as well as iconography and themes.[81] William Kent described the typical private Florentine art patron, whom he called "Giovanni X," as a merchant, who focused on his neighborhood and family. He often endowed a chapel in honor of his family at a local church. The chapel, like the contemporary *ricordanze*, projected images of family solidarity. They included the heraldic family insignia of the agnatic line.

In addition, Renaissance artists often worked together. The Venetian painter Gentile Bellini undertook joint commissions with his brother Giovanni. Donatello and Michelozzo pooled their money for several projects in the years from 1425–34. Individualistic genres such as portraiture were often generic or idealized in nature.[82] They emphasized the social roles and status of their subjects, showing them with family insignia or with symbols of their professions. According to Patricia Simons, portraits of absent or dead husbands could assert very real control over wives and children, who would have meals in the presence of the images and converse with them.[83]

Renaissance biographies served a similar function. They often presented lives not as they were actually lived, but in an idealized manner intended to emphasize specific traits or moral virtues. Humanists wrote hagiographies and saint lives according to the medieval tradition.[84] Giorgio Vasari's *Lives of the Artists* has been described by Paul Barolsky as a "masterpiece of Renaissance fiction," comparable to the *novellieri* of Boccaccio. Vasari's agenda included a desire to promote the social standing of artists against the contemporary tendency to see them as mere practitioners of the mechanical arts and thus socially inferior. This was likewise part of Benvenuto Cellini's motive in his autobiography.[85]

Notions of collectivity are also apparent in the overseas explorations. Denys Hay argued that the discovery of the New World and the threat of Islam encouraged Europeans to reevaluate the space they lived in, to form a more collective sense of identity, perceiving themselves for the first time as "Europeans." He traced the beginnings of a European consciousness to the fourteenth century, but saw it accelerating in the years from 1450 to 1520, with the discovery of the New World and with preoccupation of the threat of the Turks, who captured Constantinople in 1453.[86] It was ironically a pope, Pius II, the leader of Christendom (the traditional form of pan-European identification), who helped coin the term "European," in letters to an ambassador in Venice just after fall of Constantinople in 1453. The Bohemian king George Podiebrad (d. 1471) called for a union of European states to confront the Turkish challenge in a treatise entitled *One Europe*. Podiebrad envisioned a common treasury and assembly, not unlike today's European Union. The term European gained wide currency in the sixteenth century. Pierfrancesco Giambullari used it for the title of his book, *Storia dell'Europa* (1566).[87]

Europe's awareness of itself as a collective entity was also evident in the cartography of the period. The symbolic map of the Middle Ages, with Jerusalem at its center, gave way to more precise, mathematical projections in which Europe figured prominently. The German mapmaker Martin Waldseemuller produced the first map of Europe without an idealized Jerusalem at its center. His Dutch counterpart, Gerardus Mercator made a monumental five-foot map of Europe (1544), with careful representation of forests, mountains and cities. Abraham Ortelius presented Europe as enthroned over the whole world in his world atlas, *Theatrum orbis terrarum* (A Theater of the Terrestrial World, 1572). This helped establish, as Jerry Brotton has argued, Europe's importance in the emerging Atlantic world while marginalizing the Muslim east.[88] The printing press gave wide currency to the maps. Ortelius's *Theatrum orbis terrarum*, the costliest printed work in the sixteenth century, appeared in 40 editions. The presses also encouraged the commercialization of mapmaking, which allowed the market, rather than courts and political patronage, to determine the nature of representation of the world.

The Black Death and the Cult of Remembrance

In contextualizing individualism, scholars have looked more closely at exogenous forces. They have given a great deal of attention to the Black Death (1348) and subsequent plagues and famines of the fourteenth and fifteenth centuries that greatly reduced Europe's population. Plague and demographic contraction represent a clear point of separation with the Middle Ages, during which there had been no major epidemics since the sixth century.[89]

Scholars have stressed the effect of the plague on Renaissance *mentalité* – how pervasive death and fear of mortality conditioned attitudes toward oneself and the world. In his famous contemporary description of the plague in the *Decameron*, Giovanni Boccaccio spoke of opposing reactions. Some turned away from the world to religious asceticism; others lived for the day, with a heightened sense of freedom. The art historian Millard Meiss highlighted the former, noting a shift in Siena and Florence from "individual consciousness" in the work of pre-plague artists such as Giotto and Duccio, toward themes of asceticism and guilt characteristic of the work of the thirteenth century.[90] The argument is, however, difficult to sustain beyond Tuscany, and more recent scholarship has warned against positing too direct links between visual change and historical events.[91]

Historians have meanwhile emphasized a greater self-awareness produced by the plague. Jacques Chiffoleau has argued that the fear of death increased the impulse to self-commemoration. Using evidence from 3,500 last testaments (1340 to 1460), Chiffoleau traced a shift toward more flamboyant funerals among the wealthy in the French city of Avignon. He described the funerals as "theaters of death," which involved a careful "calculus of salvation" that was essentially "modern" in nature.[92] Sharon Strocchia has likewise noted the emergence of flamboyant funeral styles in post-plague Florence, characterized by "conspicuous consumption."[93] Samuel K. Cohn has examined evidence of self-commemoration below the level of the elite in Tuscany and Umbria and argued that there existed a "cult of remembrance," a desire for earthly fame, among the lower classes, particularly after the second outbreak of the plague in 1363. Cohn demonstrated that peasants and ordinary citizens (including women) eschewed the traditional practice of dispersing their legacies at death and instead stockpiled their assets, commissioning chapels in their honor and perpetual masses to preserve their earthly memory.[94]

Cohn's foray into the "psychological subsoil" of the Renaissance represents a substantial revision of Burckhardt's elitist view of individualism.[95] As with the upper classes, self-commemoration among ordinary citizens was corporate in nature. They stressed the importance of lineage. Their funerary chapels contained family crests, intended to honor the clan. Commemoration of the individual, here as elsewhere, was thus bound up with honoring of ancestors.

The Performative, Postmodern, and Relational Self

The revisionist research has made clear that the Renaissance individual belonged to several categories at once and that these were complicated and required subtlety to negotiate. To this end, individuals consciously crafted images of themselves, projected by means of public performance. Castiglione stressed this point in *The Courtier*. The man at court sought to "make a good impression."[96] The term *sprezzatura* was suggestive of this. It signified "an art that hid art." The word, according to Eduardo Saccone and Daniel Javitch, contained also a measure of disdain for social inferiors, who could not interpret the social code.[97]

Scholars have closely examined the performative aspect of the self in the urban setting. Ronald Weissman described the Renaissance Florentine persona as a consciously "ambiguous" one, necessarily so in order to negotiate the web of often conflicting relations, including family, friends, and neighbors. Individualism in Florence thus owed its very existence to its corporate setting. The Florentine individual concerned himself with "impression management," which required dissimulation, cryptic speech, and sometimes outright lying.[98] The Florentine humanist Leon Battista Alberti described the world (in his *Book of the Family*) as "so full of human variety, differences of opinion, changes of heart, perversity of custom, ambiguity and obscurity" that one had to be "far-seeing in the face of frauds, traps and betrayals."[99] The Florentine diarist Giovanni Morelli instructed men to "keep discussions open with everyone, and if you need to use different and unworthy words with different men in order to argue your own part, do it [...]"[100]

The self consciously crafted persona was not uniquely Italian. A conspicuous example was the great Dutch humanist, Desiderius Erasmus. According to the historian Lisa Jardine's depiction of him, Erasmus manipulated contemporary visual and print media to fashion himself as a secular monk, who succeeded by dint of his intrinsic gifts without art. He created a "multidimensional cultural persona" around the image of the great church father Jerome, whose guise he often assumed in print and portraits, most of which he commissioned himself. The image was, according to Jardine, at variance with the realities of his life, during which in fact he achieved limited academic recognition and clerical preferment.[101]

The example of Erasmus nevertheless emphasizes the enduring quality of Renaissance facades, which in the Dutchman's case remain a basic part of modern day perceptions of him. But not all scholars have accepted the notion of an autonomous self, no matter how ambiguously crafted. New historicist literary critics have depicted the Renaissance self as a wholly passive entity acted upon by external forces. They see it as a cultural artifact that reflects larger social, political, economic, and religious forces. Stephen Greenblatt has been most prominent in arguing this point, coining the still popular term "self-fashioning." "The simplest observation," he wrote, "is that in the sixteenth century there appears to be an increased self-consciousness about self-fashioning of human identity as a manipulable artful process."[102] Greenblatt demonstrated this in analyses of several prominent sixteenth-century English figures, including Thomas More, Edmund Spenser, and William Tyndale.

Greenblatt drew upon the work of the sociologist Clifford Geertz and philosopher Michel Foucault. The former stressed the cultural context of human behavior, the latter denied of the existence of an objective self.[103]

The postmodern approach has exerted strong influence on the academy over the past 25 years. Historians, despite sometimes reflexive hostility, have nevertheless often used it as a tool to gain greater understanding of the Renaissance individual and his relationship with society. Mario Biagioli drew on new historicism to gain insight into Galileo's career. Rather than treat his "genius" in the traditional manner, as manifest and untethered, Biagoli argued that Galileo is best understood in terms of the Medici court, where he gained favor and patronage.[104] Similarly, art historians have treated portraiture more closely in its cultural and social context. They have demonstrated the subjective nature of genre, which involved conscious fashioning on the part of painter and patron. Princes who commissioned portraits used them to give expression to their political and social aspirations. Artists painted themselves not as they necessarily were, but as they wished to be seen, with an eye toward establishing more firmly their social roles and status.[105] Paul Barolsky has demonstrated how Michelangelo used the deformity of his nose, broken by Torrigiani's trowel, to craft his image in self-portraits as a latter-day Socrates, ugly on the outside but virtuous on the inside.[106]

New historicist methods have also informed the study of the overseas explorations and the discovery of the Americas. Scholars now de-emphasize notions of "conquest" and hegemonic individualism in favor of "encounters" and the ways in which each side influenced the other.[107] Tzvetan Todorov argued that New World natives, whose existence was hitherto unknown, presented an "other" against which Europeans came to measure and define themselves and gain a sense of their own cultural identity.[108] Todorov's interpretation reflects the influence of reception theory, which stresses the role of the receiver in cultural and intellectual exchanges. It also reflects notions of relational identity in the psychoanalytical studies of Jacques Lacan, which have gained wide currency with respect to overseas explorations in the work of the cultural anthropologist Michel de Certeau.[109]

The impressions of Europeans of the inhabitants of the New World were recorded in travel accounts, which became a popular literary genre in the sixteenth century. The genre included first-hand descriptions of the explorers as well as professional histories, some by men who had never actually traveled to the New World. The works described the local people, their customs, as well as their environment. Many descriptions were negative, emphasizing acts of cannibalism and aberrant sexual practices. They were sometimes accompanied by visual images, drawn from classical sources and medieval legend.[110]

Nevertheless, whatever the original intention, the works ultimately produced a greater understanding among Europeans of the natives, of themselves and of humanity more generally. Anthony Pagden has argued that this was the natural outcome of the interchange regardless of the objective of the traveler.[111] The Spanish court historian of the Indies Gonzalo Fernandez de Oviedo (1478–1557) derided the customs of the natives of the Antilles, but nevertheless provided a great deal of basic information about their mores, manners and even eating habits, which included perhaps the first ever description of the pineapple. The Dutch missionary Jean de Léry, skeptical of the capacity for the Christianity of the Tupinamba people of Brazil, provided detailed information on their dress, appearance and customs.[112] The Spanish Franciscan Bernardino de Sahagún (d. 1590) wrote his account of Aztec customs in Nahuatl, the native language, which he had learned during his many years as a missionary and teacher of the children of dignitaries.[113]

The increased knowledge of the natives engendered debate about them. The most famous occurred between Bartolomé de Las Casas (d. 1566) and Juan Ginés de Sepúlveda, in Spain at Valladolid in 1550. The disagreement centered on issues of humanity, based on Aristotle's doctrine of natural slavery: whether the natives were by nature inferior and if so whether conversion to Christianity was of any use.[114] Las Casas, a planter and slave owner who had lived in Hispaniola (modern day Haiti), argued that the Spanish treatment of the natives was cruel and in his treatise *Very Brief Account of the Destruction of the Indies*, maintained that the slaves were owed equal dignity as fellow human beings. Ginés de Sepúlveda, a humanist scholar, refuted these views, contending that the natives were slaves by nature, and thus inherently inferior. This was proved by their practice of human sacrifice and cannibalism.

What emerged in the debate at Valladolid was a relativist notion of culture and of the human condition. Scholars have suggested that the debate was a critical moment in which Europeans came to perceive themselves as civilized.[115] Others stress a new inclination among contemporaries to condemn their own civilization in terms of the new. The Milanese author Girolamo Benzoni (1519–1570), who had passed 14 years in the New World, denounced Spanish behavior toward natives in his *History of the New World* (1565).[116] Garcilaso de la Vega (1539–1616), the son of an Incan princess and Spanish conquistador, wrote a history of Peru and Incas (*The Royal Commentaries of the Incas*, 1609) that lauded the virtues of the Incas: their achievements in philosophy, poetry, belief in one God and the founding of towns in accordance with natural law.[117]

Recent scholarship has also focused on assessing the degree to which the new understandings of humanity and self-identity applied to Europe's

Islamic neighbor to the East, the Ottoman Empire. According to Tzvetan Todorov, the encounter with New World "natives" was unique because Europe had no idea they existed. Nevertheless, there is a great deal of evidence of contemporary European preoccupation with Islam, and of cultural, intellectual, and economic exchange between the sides.

Historians, implicitly influenced by the modernist work of Edward Said, have stressed how Europeans viewed Islamic civilization as a species of "other," against which to measure their own society. Humanist writers in particular showed significant interest in Islam, particularly after the fall of Constantinople (1453) and heightened fears of the advance of Ottoman armies. James Hankins has demonstrated how humanists wrote as much about the Turks as notions of "human dignity." They advocated crusades against the enemy, whom they depicted less as religious infidels and more in political and cultural terms as a threat to the survival of good letters. Humanists applied the Latin term "immanis," meaning inhuman or savage, to Muslims, the lexical opposite of "humanitas."[118]

There was nevertheless peaceful and productive exchange between the two worlds. Several recent studies highlight the influence of Islam on Western architectural styles (Venice) and the interchange of goods such as tapestries and medals.[119] The portolan maps used in the first phases of European exploration were produced in Islam. Vasco da Gama took along with him to the New World an Arab navigator/astronomer. One of the most popular travel writers of the sixteenth century was the Muslim, Al-Hassan Al-Wazzan, captured in war in 1518, baptized by the pope (Leo X, a Medici), and known as Leo Africanus. Africanus' *History and Geography of Africa* (1550) gained wide circulation throughout Europe and was translated into French, Spanish, and English. It provided a firsthand description of Morocco, replacing romantic notions with more specific information. In Natalie Zemon Davis's estimation, Africanus represented a transitional figure between the Christian and Muslim worlds, who, though outwardly a Christian, remained inwardly and proudly Muslim. He saw Islam as a means by which the diverse peoples of Africa were unified.[120]

Although outwardly isolationist, the Ottomans likewise showed interest in the West. The Ottoman sea captain, Piri Reiss (as he was known in the West) included Columbus's voyages in his map of the world (1517). Reiss also produced a manual, "Maritime matters" (1526), that described the Portuguese exploration of the African coast and voyages to the Indies.[121]

Whether or not the Renaissance constituted a turning point in relations with the Muslims remains to be determined. Interactions between the East and West reached deep into the Middle Ages and have received much attention from scholars with respect to the Crusades (1095–1291) and the so-called *pax Mongolica* (1250–1350), during which the pagan Mongols allowed western merchants (notably Marco Polo) access to Central Asia and the Middle East.[122] As Margaret Meserve has recently shown, Renaissance humanists based much of their writing on Islam not on contemporary sources, but on medieval chronicles.[123]

Civility and the Divided Self

Like so much of the Renaissance historiography, no single approach to individualism has prevailed. The topic is too broad and complex for that. The Burckhardtian construct has largely been abandoned, compared by a recent scholar to an "old flying machine" in a museum.[124] Postmodern approaches remain popular, but they have been subjected to searching critique. John Martin pointed out that although new historicists reject Burckhardt's autonomous and modern self, they offer no escape from his association of the past with the present. The Renaissance self, whether a fiction or not, remains in their schema a distant image of the modern day. Thus one heroic narrative has replaced another, with the Renaissance again in the role of an important historical turning point.[125]

There continues to be strong scholarly interest in *mentalité*. Recent studies have examined Renaissance behavioral characteristics, looking more closely at the many conduct books produced in the sixteenth century. In his recent masterful history of the Renaissance, John Hale described civility as a defining feature of the period.[126] In doing so, he followed the tradition of Denys Hay (who saw civility – politeness and manners – as an indisputable trait of the Renaissance), who was in turn influenced by the German sociologist Norbert Elias. Elias traced the beginning of modern notions of civility (*civilité*) to sixteenth-century France. He attributed the development to the consolidation of the nation state and advent of absolute monarchy (see chapter 6), which eliminated the independent power of the feudal aristocracy and effectively reduced them to courtiers. Renaissance civility was distinct from prior medieval notions of courtesy and involved table manners, etiquette, and a heightened sense of embarrassment and shame. It reached a peak at Louis XIV's court in the seventeenth century, from where it diffused throughout Europe.[127]

Elias followed closely Burckhardt's emphasis on elite culture and politics. His northern geographical focus, however, led him to emphasize political stability rather than chaos. Robert Muchembled traced the roots of civility to Italy during the time of the French invasion (late fifteenth/early sixteenth century), whence it was transferred north. Marvin Becker moved the advent back further, to fourteenth-century Italy, stressing the role of the political culture there.[128]

If, however, civility was the representative behavioral feature of Renaissance, what may be said of the evidence of dissimulation, calculated ambiguity and cruel treatment of natives by the explorers? Such contradictions have been addressed by the historian John Martin, who has offered the most comprehensive current treatment of the subject.[129] Like Elias, Martin stressed the importance of the sixteenth century. But rather than civility, Martin saw the emergence in the period of notions of "prudence" and "sincerity." Prudence lost its medieval association with virtue and became in the Renaissance a strategy of self-projection that involved disguising one's true intentions. Sincerity became a new moral category that stressed harmony between one's inner feelings and outer actions.[130] Martin saw the Renaissance self as negotiating the two. What was novel, however, was the understanding that the "interior self" lay at the core of one's being. The Renaissance therefore witnessed the advent of a new relationship between the inner self and the outer world, the beginning of the awareness that there was in fact a distinction between the two. Renaissance identity was less about a particular stance vis-à-vis the outer world, but about how a certain stance might affect one's relation to that world and other human beings.[131]

Martin's thesis allows room for a Burckhardtian "discovery of the individual." It also allows a role for external forces in shaping the self. More broadly, it provides a useful category to group diverse Renaissance individuals from Petrarch to Montaigne, and sets the terms for future discussion.

Notes

1 Girolamo Cardano, *The Book of My Life*, trans. by Jean Stoner, intro. by Anthony Grafton (New York, 2002), p. 34.

2 Burckhardt treats the issue most conspicuously in part 3, titled "The Development of the Individual," pp. 93–117 and in part 4, "Discovery of the World and Man," pp. 197–246.

3 On the vagaries of use of the term "individualism" in the nineteenth century, see Konrad W. Swart, "Individualism in the Mid-Nineteenth Century (1826–1860)," *Journal of the History of Ideas* 23, 1 (Jan.–Mar. 1962): 77–90; Steven Lukes, *Individualism* (Oxford, 1973), pp. 17–23; J. B. Bullen, *The Myths of the Renaissance in Nineteenth-Century Writing* (Oxford, 1994), pp. 12–16; John J. Martin, *Myths of Renaissance Individualism* (New York, 2004), pp. 8–9.

4 Samuel K. Cohn, "Burckhardt Revisited from Social History," in *Language and Images of Renaissance Italy*, ed. by Alison Brown (Oxford, 1995).

5 Stephen Greenblatt, *Renaissance Self-Fashioning: From More to Shakespeare* (Chicago, 1980).

6 Edward Said, *Orientalism* (New York, 1978); Jacques Lacan, *The Language of the Self: The Function of Language in Psychoanalysis*, trans. by Anthony Wilden

(Baltimore, 1997); Michel de Certeau, *The Writing of History*, trans. by Tom Conley (New York, 1988); Tzvetan Todorov, *The Conquest of America and the Question of the Other*, trans. by Richard Howard (Oklahoma, 1999).

7 John J. Martin, "Inventing Sincerity, Refashioning Prudence: The Discovery of the Individual in Renaissance Europe," *American Historical Review* 102, 5 (Dec. 1997): 1309–42.

8 Carmi Schooler, "The Individual in Japanese History: Parallels To and Divergences From the European Experience," *Sociological Forum* 5, 4 (Dec. 1990): 569–94; Peter Burke, "Representation of the Self from Petrarch to Descartes," in *Rewriting the Self: Histories from the Renaissance to the Present*, ed. by Roy Porter (London, 1997), pp. 27–8.

9 John Addington Symonds, *The Renaissance in Italy*, vol. 1 (New York, 1935), pp. 331–52, quote p. 332.

10 Jacob Burckhardt, *The Civilization of the Renaissance in Italy*, trans. by S. G. C. Middlemore (New York, 1982, originally published in 1860), pp. 98–100. See also Wallace K Ferguson, *The Renaissance in Historical Thought: Five Centuries of Interpretation* (Cambridge, MA, 1948), pp. 189–19.

11 Roger Smith, "Self Reflection and Self," in Porter, *Rewriting the Self*, p. 52.

12 William Roscoe, *Life of Lorenzo de' Medici, called the Magnificent* (London, 1796); Pasquale Villari, *The Life and Times of Girolamo Savonarola*, trans. by Linda Villari (New York, 1888, originally published as *La storia di Girolamo Savonarola e de'suoi tempi*, Florence, 1859–61).
(Florence, 1859–61) and *Niccolò Machiavelli e i suoi tempi* (Florence, 1877).

13 Robert Ergang, *The Renaissance* (New York, 1967), p. 2.

14 Georg Voigt, *Die Wiederbelebung des classischen Alterthums oder das erste Jahrhundert des Humanismus*, 2 vols. (Berlin 1859). I've used the Italian translation, *Il Risorgimento dell'antichità classica ovvero il primo secolo dell umanesimo*, vol. 1 (Florence 1888), pp. 80–1 (quote on p. 81).

15 Francis Petrarch, *The Secret*, ed. and intro. by Carol E. Quillen (New York, 2003), pp. 90–2, 134.

16 Burckhardt, *Civilization*, pp. 107–17.

17 Francis Petrarch, *Invectives*, ed. and trans. by David Marsh (Cambridge, MA, 2003), pp. 7, 12.

18 Poggio Bracciolini, *Facetiae* (London, 1928), pp. 105–6.

19 Rudolf Wittkower, "Individualism in Art and Artists: A Renaissance Problem," *Journal of the History of Ideas* 22, 3 (Jul.–Sep. 1961), p. 298.

20 Giorgio Vasari, *The Lives of the Artists*, trans. by Julia Conway Bondanella and Peter Bondanella (Oxford, 1991), pp. 22, 153–4, 421, 428.

21 Paul Barolsky, *Michelangelo's Nose: A Myth and its Maker* (University Park, PA, 1990) and *Why Mona Lisa Smiles and Other Tales by Vasari* (University Park, PA, 1991). See also Patricia Lee Rubin, *Images and Identity in Fifteenth-Century Florence* (New Haven, 2002).

22 Michel Montaigne, "On Solitude," *The Complete Essays*, ed. by M. A. Screetch (New York, 1993), p. 270.

23 For the discussion on *sprezzatura* see, among others, Wayne Rebhorn, *Courtly Performances: Masking and Festivity in Castiglione's Book of the Courtier* (Detroit,

1978) and Harry Berger, Jr, *The Absence of Grace: Sprezzatura and Suspicion in Two Renaissance Courtesy Books* (Stanford, 2000).

24 Peter Burke, *The European Renaissance: Centres and Peripheries* (Oxford, 1998), p. 219.

25 Vasari, *Lives*, pt. 2, pp. 55–7.

26 Burckhardt, *Civilization*, pp. 269–71.

27 Rudolf Bell, *How to Do It: Guide to Good Living for Renaissance Italians* (Chicago, 1999).

28 Margery A. Ganz, "A Florentine Friendship: Donato Acciaiuoli and Vespasiano da Bisticci," *Renaissance Quarterly* 43, 2 (Summer 1990): 372–83.

29 Burke, "Representation of the Self," p. 21.

30 Hans Baron, "Burckhardt's Civilization of the Renaissance a Century after its Publication," *Renaissance News* 13, 3 (Autumn 1960): 211.

31 Burckhardt, *Civilization*, p. 233.

32 *The Life of Benvenuto Cellini, written by himself*, intro. by John Pope-Hennessy and trans. by John Addington Symonds (London, 1960), p. 1. On Cellini's debt to Vasari, see Victoria C. Gardner, "*Homines non nascuntur, sed figuntur*: Benvenuto Cellini's Vita and Self-Presentation of the Renaissance Artist," *Sixteenth Century Journal* 28, 2 (Summer 1997): 447–65.

33 Cardano, *Book of My Life*, chs. 6, 9.

34 James S. Amelung, *The Flight of Icarus: Artisan Autobiography in Early Modern Europe* (Stanford, 1998).

35 William Connell, "*Libri di famiglia* and the Family History of Florentine Patricians," *Italian Culture* 8 (1990): 279–92; James Grubb, "Memory and Identity: Why Venetians Didn't Keep Ricordanze," *Renaissance Studies* 8 (1994): 375–87.

36 Buonaccorso Pitti, *Two Memoirs of Renaissance Florence: The Diaries of Buonaccorso Pitti and Gregorio Dati*, ed. by Gene Brucker (Prospect Heights, IL, 1991).

37 John Pope-Hennessy, *The Portrait in the Renaissance* (Princeton, 1966).

38 Joseph L. Koerner, *The Moment of Self-Potraiture in German Renaissance Art* (Chicago, 1993).

39 Burke, *European Renaissance*, pp. 222–3.

40 John T. Paoletti and Gary M. Radke, *Art, Power and Patronage in Renaissance Italy*, 3rd edn. (Upper Saddle River, NJ, 2005), pp. 414–16.

41 De Lamar Jensen, *Renaissance Europe: Age of Recovery and Reconciliation* (Lexington, MA, 1981), p. 279 and *The Expansion of Europe* (Boston, 1967); J. H. Parry, *The Age of Reconnaissance* (New York, 1963); Carlo M. Cipolla, *Guns, Sails and Empires, 1400–1700* (New York, 1965).

42 In his popular paperback, Barnett Litvinoff equated the year 1492 with the "rise of the modern age," with Columbus as its herald. Barnett Litvinoff, *1492: The Decline of Medievalism and the Rise of the Modern Age* (New York, 1991).

43 Jacques Le Goff, *The Birth of Europe*, trans. by Janet Lloyd (Oxford, 2005), pp. 192–4.

44 J. H. Elliott saw Cortes as a Renaissance figure. J. H. Elliott, "The Mental World of Hernan Cortes," *TRHS*, 5th series, 17 (1967): 41–58.

45 Hernan Cortes, *Letters from Mexico*, ed. and trans. by Anthony Pagden (New Haven, 1986); Bernal Diaz, *The Conquest of New Spain*, trans. by J. M. Cohen (New York, 1970).

46 Felipe Fernández-Armesto, *Amerigo: The Man Who Gave His Name to America* (New York, 2007). English language translations of Amerigo's letters are in *Amerigo Vespucci*, ed. by Luciano Formisan and trans. by David Jacobson (New York, 1992).

47 J. R. Hale, *Renaissance Exploration* (New York, 1968) and J. R. S. Philips, *The Medieval Expansion of Europe* (Oxford, 1988).

48 J. H. Elliott, *The Old World and the New, 1492–1650* (Cambridge, 1970), pp. 151–6.

49 German Arciniegas, *Amerigo and the New World* (New York, 1955), pp. 302–14.

50 Samuel Y. Edgerton, *The Renaissance Rediscovery of Linear Perspective* (New York, 1975), pp. 120–2.

51 Edgerton, *Renaissance Rediscovery*, p. 115.

52 Le Goff, *Birth of Europe*, p. 193; Todorov, *Conquest of America*, p. 12.

53 Parry, *Age of Reconnaissance*, p. 36; Jerry Brotton, *Trading Territories: Mapping the Early Modern World* (New York, 1998), pp. 60–6.

54 William H. Prescott, *History of the Conquest of Mexico* (New York, 1843), p. 112. Full text available online at the Scholar's Lab, University of Virginia Library, at http://etext.virginia.edu/toc/modeng/public/PreConq.html, accessed Feb. 2010.

55 Robert Bartlett, *The Making of Europe: Conquest, Colonization and Cultural Change, 950–1350* (Princeton, 1993).

56 Alison Knowles Frazier, *Possible Lives: Authors and Saints in Renaissance Italy* (New York, 2004).

57 Aaron Gurevitch, *The Origins of European Individualism*, trans. by Katherine Judelson (Oxford, 1995), pp. 110–55.

58 John E. Benton, "The Personality of Guibert Nogent," *Psychoanalytic Review* 57 (1970–1): 563–86 and *Self and Society in Medieval France: The Memoirs of Abbot Guibert of Nogent* (New York, 1970); Jay Rubenstein, *Guibert of Nogent: Portrait of a Medieval Mind* (London, 2002); Paul J. Archambault, *A Monk's Confession: The Memoirs of Guibert of Nogent* (University Park, PA, 1995).

59 Jacques Le Goff, *Les Intellectuels au Moyen Age* (Paris, 1957), p. 14; Richard Southern, *The Making of the Middle Ages* (New Haven, 1953) p. 210.

60 Le Goff, *Birth of Europe*, p. 58.

61 Walter Ullmann, *The Individual and Society in the Middle Ages* (Baltimore, 1966); Peter Dronke, *Poetic Individuality in the Middle Ages* (Oxford, 1970); Robert W. Hanning, *The Individual in Twelfth-Century Romance* (New Haven, 1977); Richard W. Southern, *Medieval Humanism and Other Studies* (New York, 1984).

62 Colin Morris, *The Discovery of the Individual, 1050–1200* (Toronto, 1972).

63 Caroline Walker Bynum, "Did the Twelfth Century Rediscover the Individual?" *Journal of Ecclesiastical History* 31 (1980): 1–17 and *Jesus as Mother: Studies in the Spirituality of the High Middle Ages* (Berkeley, 1982). See also Jean-Claude Schmitt, "La découverte de l'individu: Une fiction historiographique," in *La fabrique, la*

figure et la feinte. Fictions et statut des fictions en psychologie, ed. by P. Mengal and F. Parot (Paris, 1989), pp. 213–36.

64 Charles Trinkhaus, *In Our Image and Likeness: Humanity and Divinity in Italian Humanist Thought*, 2 vols. (Chicago, 1970).

65 Cohn, "Burckhardt Revisited," p. 219 and *The Cult of Remembrance and the Black Death: Six Renaissance Cities in Italy* (Baltimore, 1992).

66 Natalie Zemon Davis, "Boundaries and the Sense of Self in Sixteenth-Century France," in *Reconstructing Individualism: Autonomy, Individuality and the Self in Western Thought*, ed. by Thomas C. Heller, Morton Sosna, and David E. Wellbery (Stanford, 1986), p. 53.

67 Davis, "Boundaries," p. 63.

68 Willam Kent, "Individuals and Families as Patrons of Culture in Quattrocento Florence," in Brown, *Languages and Images*.

69 *Cellini*, pp. 1–3.

70 Anthony Molho, *Marriage Alliance in Late Medieval Florence* (Cambridge, MA, 1994), p. 348.

71 Richard A. Goldthwaite, *Private Wealth in Renaissance Florence: A Study of Four Families* (Princeton, 1968), p. 255.

72 Goldthwaite, *Private Wealth*, p. 258.

73 Francis William Kent, *Household and Lineage in Renaissance Florence* (Princeton, 1977).

74 David Herlihy and Christiane Klapisch-Zuber, *Tuscans and their Families* (New Haven, 1985, originally published as *Les Toscans et leurs familles*, 1978), pp. 363–4.

75 Jacques Heers, *Le clan familial au Moyen Age: Etude sur les structures politiques et sociales des milieux urbains* (Paris, 1974) and *Genes au XVe siecle* (1961); Diane Owen Hughes, "Urban Growth and Family Structure in Medieval Genoa," *Past and Present* 66 (Feb. 1975): 3–28.

76 Barbara Diefendorf, "Family Culture, Renaissance Culture," *Renaissance Quarterly* 40 (1987): 664, 666. For England see David Cressy, "Kinship and Kin Interaction in Early Modern England," *Past and Present* 113 (Nov. 1986): 38–69.

77 Peter Laslett, *Family Life*, (Cambridge, 1977), pp. 12–39.

78 Jack Goody, "The Evolution of the Family," in *Household and Family in Past Time*, ed. by P. Laslett and R. Wall (Cambridge, 1972).

79 John M. Najemy, *Corporatism and Consensus in Florentine Electoral Politics, 1280–1400* (Chapel Hill, 1982).

80 John Henderson, *Piety and Charity in Late Medieval Florence* (Oxford, 1994); Christopher Black, *Italian Confraternities in the Sixteenth Century* (Cambridge, 1989); James Banker, *Death in a Community: Memorialization and Confraternities in an Italian Commune in the Late Middle Ages* (Georgia, 1988); Nicholas Terpstra, *Lay Confraternities and Civic Religion in Renaissance Bologna* (Cambridge, 1995).

81 James R. Banker, "The Program for the Sassetta Altarpiece in the Church of San Francesco in Borgo San Sepolcro," in *I Tatti Studies: Essays in the Renaissance* 4 (1991): 11–58.

82 Evelyn Welch, *Art and Society in Italy, 1350–1500* (New York, 1997), pp. 83–6, 96–7; Lorne Campbell, *Renaissance Portraits: European Portrait-Painting in the 14th, 15th and 16th Centuries* (New Haven, 1990), pp. 25–6, 41–60.
83 Patricia Simons, "Portraiture, Portrayal and Idealization: Ambiguous Individualism in Representations of Renaissance Women," in Brown, *Language and Images*, p. 274.
84 Frazier, *Possible Lives*.
85 Barolsky, *Why Mona Lisa Smiles*, p. 5; Gardner, "Homines non nascuntur, sed figuntur," pp. 447–65; Burke, "Representation of the Self," pp. 27–8.
86 John R. Hale, *The Civilization of Europe in the Renaissance* (New York, 1993).
87 Denys Hay, *Europe: The Emergence of an Idea* (New York, 1966, pp. 73, 99; Burke, *European Renaissance*, p. 216.
88 Brotton, *Trading Territories*, pp. 168–9.
89 David Herlihy, *The Black Death and the Transformation of the West* (Cambridge, MA, 1997); Samuel K. Cohn, *The Black Death Transformed: Disease and Culture in Early Renaissance Europe* (London, 2002).
90 Millard Meiss, *Painting in Florence and Siena after the Black Death* (Princeton, 1951), pp. 4, 12, 59–74, 165; Miklos Boskovits, *Pittura fiorentina alla vigilia del Rinascimento, 1370–1400* (Florence, 1975).
91 Welch, *Art and Society*, p. 27; Paoletti and Radke, *Art, Power and Patronage*, pp. 157–9.
92 Jacques Chiffoleau, *La Comptabilité de l'au-delà: les hommes, la mort et la religion dans la région d'Avignon* (Rome, 1980).
93 Sharon Strocchia, *Death and Ritual in Renaissance Florence* (Baltimore, 1992); Paul Binski, *Medieval Death: Ritual and Representation* (London, 1996).
94 Cohn, "Burckhardt Revisited," p. 219; *Death and Property in Siena, 1205–1800* (Baltimore, 1989), pp. 281–8, and *Cult of Remembrance*.
95 Cohn, "Burckhardt Revisited," p. 288.
96 Baldassare Castiglione, *The Book of the Courtier* (New York, 2002) p. 24.
97 Eduardo Saccone, "The Portrait of the Courtier in Castiglione," *Italica* 64 (1987): 1–10; Daniel Javitch, "Il Cortegiano and the Constraints of Despotism," in Robert W. Hanning and David Rosand, eds., *Castiglione: The Ideal and Real in Renaissance Culture* (New Haven, 1983), pp. 34–5.
98 Ronald F. E. Weissman, "The Importance of Being Ambiguous: Social Relations, Individualism and Identity in Renaissance Florence," in *Urban Life in the Renaissance*, ed. by Susan Zimmerman and Ronald F. E. Weissman (London, 1989), p. 272.
99 Leon Battista Alberti, *I libri della famiglia*, trans. R. N. Watkins (Columbia, SC, 1969), p. 266.
100 Giovanni di Pagolo Morelli, *Ricordi* (Florence, 1969), pp. 282–3.
101 Lisa Jardine, *Erasmus, Man of Letters: The Construction of Charisma in Print* (Princeton, 1993), p. 5.
102 Greenblatt, *Renaissance Self-Fashioning*, p. 2.
103 Clifford Geertz, *The Interpretation of Cultures* (New York, 1973), p. 49; Michel Foucault, *The Order of Things: An Archaeology of the Human Sciences* (New York,

1970), pp. 386–87 and *Power/Knowledge: Selected Interviews and Other Writings, 1972–1979*, ed. and trans. by Colin Gordon (New York, 1980).

104 Mario Biagioli, *Galileo, Courtier: The Practice of Science in the Culture of Absolutism* (Chicago, 1993).

105 Joanna Woods-Marsden, "'Ritratto al Naturale': Questions of Realism and Idealism in Early Renaissance Portraits," *Art Journal* 46, 3 (Autumn 1987): 213–14 and *Renaissance Self-Portraiture* (New Haven, 1998), pp. 1, 5; E. H. Gombrich, "The Mask and the Face: The Perception of Physiognomic Likeness in Life and Art," in *The Image and the Eye* (Oxford, 1982); Simons, "Portraiture, Portrayal and Idealization," pp. 263–311; Rubin, *Images and Identity*.

106 Barolsky, *Michelangelo's Nose*, pp. 7–12.

107 Alison Brown, *Renaissance* (London, 1999), p. 98.

108 Todorov, *Conquest of America*, p. 12.

109 Lacan, *Language of the Self*; Ida Altman and Reginald D. Butler, "The Contact of Cultures: Perspectives on the Quincentenary," *American Historical Review* 99, 2 (Apr. 1994), pp. 478–503; de Certeau, *Writing of History*; Stephen Greenblatt, *Marvelous Possessions: The Wonder of the New World* (Chicago, 1991) and *New World Encounters* (Berkeley, 1993); Anthony Grafton, *New Worlds, Ancient Texts: The Power of Tradition and the Shock of Discovery* (Cambridge, MA, 1995).

110 Santiago Sebastián, *O Brave New People: The European Invention of the American Indian* (Albuquerque, 1996).

111 Anthony Pagden, *European Encounters in the New World* (New Haven, 1993), pp. 17–87.

112 Anthony Pagden, *The Fall of Natural Man: The American Indian and the Origins of Comparative Ethnology* (New York, 1982), p. 109.

113 Munro S. Edmundson, ed., *Sixteenth-Century Mexico: The Work of Sahagún* (Albuquerque, 1974).

114 Bartolomé de Las Casas, *In Defense: The Defense of the Most Reverend Lord, Don Fray Bartolomé de Las Casas, of the Order of Preachers, Late Bishop of Chiapa, against the Persecutors and Slanderers of the Peoples of the New World Discovered across the Seas*, ed. and trans. by Stafford Poole (Illinois, 1974) and *The Devastation of the Indies: A Brief Account*, trans. by Herma Briffault (Baltimore, 1992); Juan Ginés de Sepúlveda, *Tratado sobre las justas causas de la guerra contra los Indios*, trans. by Marcelino Menendez y Pelayo and Manuel Garcia-Pelayo (Mexico, 1941).

115 D. A. Brading, *The First America: The Spanish Monarchy, Creole Patriots, and the Liberal State 1492–1867* (New York, 1991), pp. 80–8; David M. Traboulay, *Columbus and Las Casas: The Conquest and Christianization of America, 1492–1566* (Maryland, 1994), p. 167.

116 Burke, *European Renaissance*, p. 212.

117 Brading, *First America*, pp. 225–72 and "The Incas and the Renaissance: The Royal Commentaries of Inca Garcilaso de la Vega," *Journal of Latin American Studies* 18, 1 (May 1986), pp. 14–15.

118 Said, *Orientalism*; James Hankins, "Renaissance Crusaders: Humanist Crusade Literature in the Age of Mehmed II," *Dumbarton Oaks Papers* 49 (1995): 111–207. See also Robert Schwoebel, *The Shadow of the Crescent: The Renaissance Image of the Turk 1453–1517* (Nieuwkoop, 1969); Gerald MacLean, ed., *Re-Orienting the Renaissance: Cultural Exchanges with the East* (Basingstoke, 2005) and "When West Looks East: Some Recent Studies in Early Modern Muslim Cultures," *Journal for Early Modern Cultural Studies* 7, 1 (Spring/Summer 2007): 96–112; Nancy Bisaha, *Creating East and West: Renaissance Humanists and the Ottoman Turks* (Philadelphia, 2004); L. P. Harvey, *Muslims in Spain, 1500 to 1614* (Chicago, 2005).

119 Deborah Howard, *Venice and the East: The Impact of the Islamic World on Venetian Architecture 1100–1500* (New Haven, 2000); Lisa Jardine and Jerry Brotton, *Global Interests: Renaissance Art between East and West* (Ithaca, 2000).

120 Natalie Zemon Davis, *Trickster Travels: A Sixteenth-Century Muslim between Worlds* (New York, 2006).

121 Brotton, *Trading Territories*, pp. 117, 168–9.

122 Janet Abu Lughod, *The Medieval World System* (Oxford, 1989).

123 Margaret Meserve, *Empires of Islam in Renaissance Historical Thought* (Cambridge, MA, 2008), pp. 15, 117.

124 William J. Connell, ed., *Society and Self in Renaissance Florence* (Berkeley, 2002), p. 6.

125 Martin, "Inventing Sincerity," pp. 1311, 1339; see also Lee Patterson, "On the Margin: Postmodernism, Ironic History and Medieval Studies," *Speculum* 65 (1990): 87–108.

126 Hale, *Civilization of Europe*, pp. xix, 355–417.

127 Norbert Elias, *The Civilizing Process: Sociogenetic and Psychogenetic Investigations*, trans. by Edmund Jephcott, rev. edn. ed. by Eric Dunning, Johan Goudsblom, and Stephen Mennell (Oxford, 1994).

128 Robert Muchembled, "Manners, Courts and Civility," in *A Companion to the Worlds of the Renaissance*, ed. by Guido Ruggiero (Oxford, 2002), pp. 156–172; Marvin Becker, *Civility and Society in Western Europe, 1300–1600* (Bloomington, 1988).

129 Martin, "Inventing Sincerity," and *Renaissance Individualism*, pp. 4–20.

130 On sincerity see also Lionel Trilling, *Sincerity and Authenticity* (Cambridge, 1972), pp. 1–14; Peter Burke, *The Historical Anthropology of the Early Modern Italy: Essays on Perception and Communication* (Cambridge, 1987), pp. 233–5.

131 Martin, *Renaissance Individualism*, pp. 13–14.

3

Gender: Who Was the Renaissance Woman?

Judging from the treatises of all philosophers and poets and from all orators – it would take too long to mention their names – it seems that they speak from one and the same mouth [. . .] that the behavior of women is inclined to and full of every vice [. . .] As I was thinking this, a great unhappiness and sadness welled up in my heart, for I detested myself and the whole feminine sex, as though we were monstrosities in nature.

Christine de Pizan[1]

In a famous essay published in 1977, Joan Kelly asked whether the term Renaissance could also be applied to women.[2] She took as her starting point Burckhardt's well-known but unqualified statement that "women stood on a footing of perfect equality with men." Kelly's answer was negative. She argued that the same economic and political opportunities that improved the lives of men had an adverse effect on women.

Kelly's essay gave impetus not only to the study of Renaissance women, but called into question the basic schema of periodization: whether the same could be employed for both sexes. The past three decades have witnessed enormous growth in research on Renaissance women. This has coincided more generally with the development of women's history and gender studies as popular academic disciplines.[3] Kelly took a literary approach, examining medieval courtly literature in terms of Renaissance conduct books. Historians have since employed a wide range of methodologies, borrowing from the fields of anthropology, sociology, psychology, and others. They have searched archives and uncovered wholly new information, illuminating the legal, familial, religious, and economic context in which women operated. Following the lead of Joan Scott, scholars have focused on gender: how society constructed the notions of what it was to be male or female, how women exercised agency and power in the face of secular and religious restrictions. Gender is treated as a category similar to race and class, according to which we may understand the complex connections among the various forms of human interaction.[4] The study of women inherently involves also the study of men.

The research on the Renaissance has shown that the realities of women's lives differed from those of men and from each other. Women's experiences depended on a wide range of factors, including social and economic circumstance, physical location (urban or rural), as well as marital status, age, health, and family dynamics.[5] While most scholars would still agree with Kelly's pessimistic conclusions, they would also argue that the period witnessed important developments. Chief among these was an increased awareness and discussion of gender issues and the emergence of strong dissenting views, an "other" voice, against the inherited misogynistic tradition.

The Inherited Tradition

As with the study of men, a popular early approach to Renaissance women's history was the biography of the prominent individual. The tradition predates Burckhardt and has involved presenting what Natalie Davis has called "women worthies" to place beside notable men.[6] A favorite subject has been Isabella d'Este, the duchess of Mantua. This "first lady of the Renaissance" possessed all the basic attributes associated with the Burckhardtian Renaissance persona. She was well educated and accomplished (learned in both Latin and Greek, skilled at the flute) and an enthusiastic patron of the arts, whose circle included the painters Raphael, Titian, and Leonardo da Vinci. When Isabella's husband Lodovico Gonzaga was captured in war, she ruled Mantua in his stead and even led armies into battle.[7]

The list of worthies includes others, typically prominent political and religious figures from aristocratic backgrounds: Caterina Sforza of Forlì; Catherine de' Medici, queen regent of France; Queen Elizabeth I of England; and Teresa of Avila (1515–1582), the visionary Spanish saint.[8] Their biographies have added to our overall knowledge, but they also present a skewed picture of women's experience. By segregating them from men, scholars have de-historicized and separated them from the broader historical processes.[9] The studies do little to distinguish Renaissance women from their medieval forebears. Indeed, Isabella d'Este's career bears semblance to that of the twelfth-century queen Eleanor of Aquitaine (d. 1204), who presided over a vibrant intellectual court, and Isabel of Conches (d. 1130?), a generation earlier, who led armies.

The reality was that Renaissance women of all classes faced profound limitations. They encountered legal restraints and were hindered by accepted attitudes and inherited tradition. Men played the role of provider, working in the public sphere; women were reduced, in Barbara Hanawalt's words, to "homebodies," confined to domestic and familial matters. Men gained a sense of identity from their professional affiliations and public office. Women's identity owed to their sexuality. Masculine honor varied according to class – aristocratic notions bound to loyalty and bravery; middle and working class notions tied to honesty, integrity and good craftsmanship. Feminine honor was constant, linked to sexuality and the necessity, for all classes of women, to maintain their chastity. In this way, male identity and honor were active and positive entities, while female identity and honor were passive and negative entities. Women possessed unique power through sexual indiscretion and improper behavior, to destroy the status and distinction of their whole families. This justified women's removal from the public sphere and denial of education and employment, the most basic means of advancement.

The gender roles were grounded in scripture and the writings of theologians. Eve, the temptress, was responsible for the fall of mankind. Mary, the sinless virgin, the mother of Jesus, brought redemption. The images dominated Christian perceptions of women. The church fathers Jerome and Augustine held virginity above marriage as the ideal state. "Death came through Eve: life has come through Mary," Jerome wrote in his letter to Eustochium. "For this reason the gift of virginity has poured most abundantly upon women, seeing that it was from a woman that it began."[10] The early writers expressed an unmistakable misogyny. Among the claims made by Jerome against marriage was that "matrons want many things, costly dresses, gold jewels [...] she complains that one lady is dressed better than she." He concluded that "to support a poor wife is hard, to put up with a rich one is torture."[11]

Jerome and the church fathers drew upon misogynistic notions expressed by classical writers. In the first book of *Politics* (the section "On the Household"), Aristotle asserted that man was by nature superior to women, who were "incomplete" men and thus a species of "deformity."[12] He ranked women just above slaves in the natural hierarchy of things, to be ruled by their husbands albeit, Aristotle allowed, by means of consent in the manner of a constitutional monarchy. Plato argued in the *Timaeus* that all beings began as males and were regenerated into women if they lived "cowardly or immoral" lives.[13] The Greek physician Galen (AD 129–200) gave detailed biological justifications for women's inferiority, emphasized "vital heat," a force in bodies that men possessed in greater quantity than women. This pushed male genitalia to the outside, the perfect form, but left women's genitals on the inside, thus imperfect. Men were therefore warm and dry beings; women, conversely, were cold and wet. As heat was inclined to move upward toward the heavens, men became endowed with "higher" qualities such as intelligence and rational thought (as well as baldness, the "burning up" of hair). Women possessed lesser qualities, associated with the earth and the body, such as carnality, inconstancy, and deception.[14]

These views passed into the Middle Ages. Plato's *Timaeus* was one of the few classical Greek texts available in Latin translation for much of the period and thus remained highly influential. The full corpus of Aristotle's work was reintroduced to the West in the twelfth and thirteenth centuries. Scholastic theologians "harmonized" Aristotle's views with Christian theology.[15] Thomas Aquinas (d. 1274) argued for the inferiority of women both on Christian grounds, as the result of Eve's temptation by the devil, and on Aristotelian terms, as the result of her inherent biological inferiority.[16] The ideas were reinforced by popular trends, including the veneration of Mary, which stressed Mary's human role as grieving mother and as *mediatrix*, intercessor between ordinary citizen and God. This further strengthened the Mary/Eve–good woman/bad woman dichotomy.

During the Renaissance, the classical and Christian notions of women were asserted most conspicuously in the works of humanists. Leon Battista Alberti, drawing on Plato and Aristotle, argued in *Book of the Family* (1432–4) that it was the husband's duty to restrict the activities of his wife to the house and the domestic sphere. Alberti closely modeled his book on *Oeconomicus*, an openly misogynistic work by a lesser known Greek philosopher Xenophon. Alberti's Venetian contemporary, Francesco Barbaro (1390–1454) expressed similar sentiments in *On Wifely Duties* (1416), written in the form of a letter to Lorenzo de' Medici on the occasion of his marriage. Barbaro drew on Xenophon as well as Augustine, Aristotle, and Plutarch and argued for the necessity of the subordination of women on the grounds that it maintained patriarchy, which was critical to political authority – an assertion that, as we shall see, proved particularly influential.[17]

The popularity of Xenophon reflects the importance of gender roles.[18] Xenophon's negative views on women appeared in numerous works, including the Swiss humanist Heinrich Bullinger's *Der Christlich Eestand* (Christian State of Matrimony, 1540), which went through nine editions, and the Englishmen John Dod and Robert Cleaver's *A Godlie Forme of Householde Government* (1610), a popular seventeenth century treatise on marriage and family life. Aristotelian and Galenic notions of women were repeated in the popular pediatric manual, *The Rose Garden*, by the German physician Eucharius, who traced gender differences to the "hot and dry seed" in men and "coldness and moisture" in women. An English writer, Edmund Tilney, in the late sixteenth century wrote that the best way for a woman to preserve her reputation was to never leave the house.[19]

Law and Family

Gender distinctions were enforced by law. European legal codes limited women's autonomy by restricting their right to hold property and represent themselves in court. Early medieval Germanic law codes had justified women's secondary status on the grounds that they were unable to perform the feudal obligation of military service. But such restrictions were often allowed to lapse, with the result that women possessed some *de facto* autonomy. This changed with the introduction of Roman law (along with the Aristotelian corpus), first in Southern Europe in the twelfth and thirteenth centuries and in the north in the sixteenth century. The triumph of Roman law owed much to the work of the humanists, who included law in their classical studies (see chapter 4).

Scholars have viewed Roman law as having a largely negative impact on woman. Feudal-based restrictions in medieval codes were replaced by gender-based restrictions. Roman law outlined specifically female attributes such as "fragility, imbecility, irresponsibility and ignorance" that justified denying them independent legal status. It grouped women with peasants and "the simple-minded" as lacking responsibility for their own actions and thus credibility in legal testimony.[20]

Roman law stressed the importance of patriarchy. Husband and fathers had absolute powers (*patria potestas*) within the family, which in turn was a necessary component of kingly authority. The sovereign's power over the state was an extension of the father's authority over the family. The emerging absolute monarchies of the sixteenth century thus found Roman law conducive to their aims. The French political theorist Jean Bodin in his *Six Books of the Commonwealth* (1576) spoke of the family as the "source and origin of all republics." The father stood as sovereign of the family as the king to his subjects.[21] French law did not allow married women separate identities from their husbands, or the right to own property (see chapter 6).

Joan Kelly saw the rising absolute state as the principal cause of the subjection of aristocratic women. Others scholars have taken a broader perspective, noting differences according to class. Restrictions applied most directly to upper class women, who possessed economic means and social standing, but less so to lower and middle class women. Prescriptive law did not always represent actual practice. Jurists were selective in what they took from Roman law, and codes varied from place to place. The city of Florence had particularly harsh laws, representing a "veritable prison" for women, who needed men to represent them in legal matters.[22] The laws in neighboring Pisa were, however, more lenient. The small town of Poppi, near Arezzo, followed the Pisan model; the city of Lucca, near Pisa, followed the Florentine example.[23]

The legal scholar Thomas Kuehn has argued that there was no single concept of woman in Roman law, that the law was more an "abstraction." He noted that even in Florence women gained *de facto* rights to own and dispose of property and to serve as guardians to children. This was the result not only of loopholes in Roman law, but also of the influence of concurrent legal systems that remained in force, including canon and civil law. In France, the same principles of political patriarchy that legally privileged males permitted women willy nilly to assume the role of head of the household when men died, to prevent the dissolution of the family and political anarchy. The evidence has led some to question whether the legal subservience of women in Europe was entirely gender based. Thomas Kuehn has minimized the gendered aspects of Roman law, preferring the term "legal personhood." Barbara Diefendorf has emphasized how the tight connection between the nature of the family and the welfare of the state in France made law there above all a political issue.[24]

The degree of agency and autonomy possessed by women has been further tested in archival studies. Using Florentine diaries, *ricordanze* (business memoirs) and the *catasto* records of 1427, the French scholar Christiane Klapisch-Zuber has argued that marriage and the dowry system of the city disenfranchised women by denying them their inheritances and favoring male lineages. Florentine marriage "strategy" aimed at creating strong patrilinear networks, which, in that highly commercialized city, involved business alliances. Florentine "family values" therefore depended on masculine objectives, which reduced women, in Klapisch-Zuber's evocative term, to "passing guests" in their own houses: their identities determined by their relations to men, first their fathers, who arranged their marriages, and then their husbands, who received them. Lacking self-determination, wives became Griseldas, patiently, as in Boccaccio's famous tale, enduring humiliation and subjugation. When women of marriageable age lost their husbands, they were placed in the difficult position of having to choose between remarriage, which would involve leaving their dead husband's household and their children, or staying single, which would defy family marriage strategies that centered on creating new networks. In the first instance she became a "cruel mother," both affectively and economically, since abandonment of her children meant also not providing for them financially. The very choice raised resentment toward women on all sides, and reinforced stereotypical notions that associated femininity with inconstancy and disorderliness.[25]

Klapisch-Zuber's thesis has loomed large in the historiography, particularly among Italianists. It stresses the importance of a woman's dowry (a sum paid by the bride's family to the groom) in reducing her to a commodity. The dowry system dated to Roman times and was revived in Europe with the advent of Roman law. The Germanic tradition of *morgengabe*, whereby the husband provided money to the bride, was retained in the form of a trousseau, a small gift by the husband on the wedding day, often a hope chest (*cassone*) in Italy, which contained gendered images of the proper domestic role of women. But the dowry system constituted big business, and in Italy it was a critical means by which political and business networks were made. As Anthony Molho and Julius Kirshner have shown, the size of dowries in Florence grew to large proportions in the fifteenth century. In 1425 the city set up a dowry fund (*monte delle dote*), which functioned both as means of investment for families to accrue money at interest and as an instrument of public finance, used by the state to raise money for wars and other exigencies.

The growing size of dowries has led scholars to examine the degree to which the dotal system may have also placed constraints on men, who had to raise the money. In his studies of Venice, Stanley Chojnacki argued, contra Klapisch-Zuber, that large dowries of aristocratic women gave them significant latitude. The sums represented a large portion of the wealth of aristocratic families, which in turn encouraged the Venetian state, concerned with maintaining the status and prestige of its leading families, to protect dotal rights. Women thus entered marriages in powerful positions, which became even more so during widowhood when their dowries reverted to them or their chosen heirs. Economic power tightened affective bonds, as women's wealth induced men to court them "more assiduously."[26] The "power of love," as Chojnacki called it, was apparent in the language of male testaments, which by the fifteenth century employed such terms as "dilecta" (beloved) "uxor" (wife) and "molier charissima" (my dearest wife).[27] Husbands named wives as executors of their wills and sought vocational choices for their daughters.

The Florentine and Venetian examples present sharp contrasts, and have provided the basic reference points for further scholarly discussion. The evidence elsewhere suggests substantial local variation.[28] Studies of Genoa, for example, show that the dotal system did little for elite women, who faced severe limitations, particularly from the fifteenth century and beyond.[29] Scholars of England have argued both sides.[30] They have noted how English law explicitly protected male rights, by means of primogeniture. Lawrence Stone, in a well-known and much-debated thesis, maintained that the rise of Puritanism and increased English patriarchy minimized women rights, which, contra Chojnacki, lacked affective ties until the eighteenth century. But Alan MacFarlane, in an equally controversial thesis, argued that strong affective ties existed in England back into the Middle Ages. Anthony Fletcher has maintained that prescriptive legal restrictions on English women were at variance with their *de facto* right, particularly their very visible presence in public in audiences at theaters in London in Elizabethan times.[31]

The contradictions remain significant.[32] Martha Howell has demonstrated that women's legal rights decreased in urban centers of the Low Countries from 1300 to 1550, but not as a result of increased patriarchy or absolutist trends, but in the context of less centralized governments and economic prosperity.[33] The advent of Protestantism throughout Europe meanwhile brought marriage more under the control of monarchs and secular powers, who further restricted women's freedoms. Catholicism responded to Protestant actions by enforcing greater uniformity of canon law, which often worked against women.

Geography and social class were important factors. Restrictions on upper-class women in Italy and southern Europe appear to have been greater than the restrictions on their counterparts in northern Europe. Studies of the latter suggest that men and women waited until their late twenties to get married, when men had acquired economic independence. This allowed the couples more autonomy from their parents and families. In southern and eastern European women married at younger ages, typically in their teens, to older men, in their late twenties and early thirties. The couples often stayed with their parents and families, enhancing inequalities and the subservience of women.

Throughout Europe there is evidence that women of the middle and poorer classes had greater self-determination. Their dowries were smaller, and thus they were not as bound by state law. Economic necessity and the rhythm of rural life thus placed couples on a more equal footing.

Economy and Work

The legal and social status of women was closely connected to their economic roles. Defining the precise nature of those roles has, however, been a particularly vexing problem. Women's economic activities are difficult to isolate. Their work often fell under the heading of domestic "chores," while men's work, which took place outside the household, was considered "production" (see chapter 5). Restriction to the domestic sphere precluded travel from one region to another and thus involvement in long distance trade.[34] Women were denied participation in craft guilds.

Women's economic contribution was nevertheless vital to society. In the countryside and agricultural setting, women shared responsibilities with men. They took care of poultry and small animals, raised fruit and vegetable gardens and span cloth. They worked in the fields during harvests and even transported goods to local rural markets. In western Norway where the primary male occupation was fishing, women appear to have done most of the farming. The extant letters of Anne Baillet, the wife of a prominent Parisian judge, show that she effectively managed the family estates when her husband was away, giving detailed instructions to overseers on how to inspect mills, review accounts, and draw up inventories of goods at a manor house.[35]

Studies of urban women indicate that they took part in various occupations. Florentine women worked as bakers, vintners, carpenters and occasionally as butchers and goldsmiths.[36] German women worked in mines, though restricted to less dangerous jobs above ground. Throughout Europe, women worked as servants – often poor girls, as young as seven or eight years old, in the households of the rich. They worked year-round, assisting in running the household. The Florentine *catasto* of 1427 lists servant (*fante*) as the most common female occupation in the city. In France and Germany, servants found employment through female agents with social standing. The state regulated their activities and received compensation from both the servant and her employer.

Elite households employed female slaves and wet nurses to help care for newly born infants. The latter were generally older women, married and with children of their own, who worked for short periods, and earned the highest wages among domestic servants.[37] The former were often young girls, non-Christians, from Mongol Eastern Europe (in Italy) or northern Africa (in Spain and Portugal), who worked until manumitted by their owners.[38] Female slaves were an important part of the social fabric of Renaissance Italian society. Affairs with masters produced illegitimate children.[39]

The terms of employment for wet nurses and slaves were set by men.[40] Opportunities for working outside the home were generally better for married women than unmarried ones, since society feared less their potential for "misbehavior."[41] But women's employment nevertheless depended also on her life cycle and was therefore inherently variable. The same woman could begin her career as a household servant and then, when married, be hired as a wet nurse, and still later, when older and her children grown, work in a beer brewing establishment or for a textile firm.

Brewing and cloth making were frequent occupations for women, and have consequently been much studied by scholars. The former (which included production of hard cider) took place primarily in northern Europe. Beer was made at home or in establishments close to it, and thus maintained women in their domestic spaces. Wages were in any case low, insufficient to allow women to live on their own. English "ale wives" came both from the upper and lower strata of society, exclusive of the poor.[42] They worked often in difficult circumstances to supplement family income.

Spinning may have been the most widespread occupation, involving women from all over Europe, who worked "domestically" for their families and "professionally" for mercantile firms. Surplus was sometimes marketed locally. Commercial wool cloth and silk firms employed women to spin threads, a task that required more patience than skill, and could be done at home. The fifteenth-century Florentine merchant, Tommaso Spinelli, had thirty female silk spinners on his payroll, the largest part of his work force, but the lowest paid. The highest salary went to skilled weavers, who were all men.[43]

Women also participated in the labor force as healers and midwives, occupations that often involved formal apprenticeships and were, as in Nuremberg and Naples, supervised by town officials. Expertise was gained primarily through experience. Women healers often specialized in the care of women, for issues concerning reproduction, sexuality, and contraception. They were occasionally called upon to concoct love potions. Midwifes, a subset of the healer category, assisted women at birth and with prenatal care.[44]

Prostitution was the lowest category of employment. It was pervasive throughout Europe, treated by authorities as an inevitable vice that protected honorable women from the lust of young men, or, as in Florence, that minimized the likelihood of homosexual behavior among men, which was a still more serious crime.[45] In any case, prostitution developed into what Leah Otis has described as an "institution with its own regulation and rules."[46] Cities had public brothels, which like other businesses, were taxed by governments. Prostitutes wore distinctive clothes – often caps with bells on their heads and high heels on their feet – that set them apart from honest women. Using tax registers, David Herlihy argued that prostitution was the largest female profession in the city of Bologna in 1395.[47] Social stigma existed then as today. But recent studies of Rome and Florence indicate that prostitutes sometimes mingled with "honest" folk and that social restrictions and stigma increased dramatically throughout Europe during the Protestant Reformation, when prostitution gained a more negative moral connotation.[48]

The level of participation of women in the overall European work force is difficult to assess. Men were reluctant to allow women access to their crafts and the sense of personal identity that went along with it. In the countryside, women could assist their husbands in the fields, but were often denied use of the plow, which was a metaphor of male virility.[49] Urban craft guilds actively excluded women from participation. They structured themselves around the male lifecycle – apprenticeship began at puberty, mastership coincided with mature adulthood. They left no room for female activities such as pregnancy or childrearing. To limit the possibility of passive participation, guilds specifically prohibited members from teaching their crafts to their daughters and wives. Medical guilds, hostile to healers and midwives, often accused them of sorcery and witchcraft, charges that, as we shall soon see, followed all too easily from their involvement in health-related issues. Women were not allowed to attend university and thus did not have access to the most distinguished part of the medical establishment.[50]

Guilds took a leading role in restricting women's participation in the labor force during the plague and demographic crises in the fourteenth and fifteenth century. The crises appear prima facie to have created opportunities for women, given the overall shortage of labor. But in studies of the city of Nuremburg, Merry Wiesner has shown that guilds became more restrictive in the face of the challenge, more zealous in protecting male priority in the workplace. The demographic crisis elicited a heightened sense of "guild honor," reflected in an intensification of male rituals and "male bonding."[51] The exclusion was reinforced by the Reformation and Catholic reform, which produced legislation aimed at placing women more surely under the authority of men.

Similarly, David Herlihy demonstrated how Florentine urban guilds, rather than hire women, recruited male peasants from the countryside, from as far away as the Low Countries and Germany, to replenish the plague-depleted work force. He noted too the role of technology and specialization in reducing further the economic participation of women, which largely disappeared in the fourteenth and fifteenth centuries. Women shifted into domestic production and the domestic sphere [52] P. J. P. Goldberg's studies of the English town of York confirmed the pattern. But Goldberg placed the turning point in the fifteenth century, arguing that female participation in the workforce increased in the immediate aftermath of the plague in 1348, but then declined when the full weight of the "economic crisis" occurred.[53]

The consideration of the effects of plague is part a still broader discourse on the impact of macro-economic forces on the status of women.[54] Scholars have in particular debated the effects of capitalism on women. The discussion derives from Marx's notion that capitalism necessarily enhanced patriarchy, which drove women decisively out of the workplace into the domestic sphere.[55] This was given historical locus in the Renaissance by Alice Clark, who argued that the advent of capitalism in England in the late sixteenth century to the late eighteenth century forced women out of the workplace. Their skills were unsuited to large-scale capitalistic enterprises that were then developing.[56] Clark's thesis exerted a strong influence on Joan Kelly, who likewise blamed the emerging capitalist economy for forcing women into the domestic sphere. Martha Howell's empirical studies of the urban economies of Leiden, Cologne, Liege, Douai, and Frankfurt am Main appear to have confirmed the pattern.[57]

The negative view of capitalism has been accompanied by a positive view of the Middle Ages. Scholars have viewed it as an economic high point for women.[58] The positive depiction of the Middle Ages goes back to the nineteenth century in the work of Karl Bucher, and was popularized in the twentieth century by Joan Kelly, Eileen Power, and David Herlihy.[59] Herlihy depicted the eleventh century as a species of paradise for women workers, with female landholding at its apex and wide-spread participation in the textile industry, including female workshops, *gynaecea*, dating back to antiquity, in which women worked all aspects of production, including carding, spinning, dying weaving, and embroidering. The period also saw the establishment of guilds of women retailers in Paris and Rouen, and a guild of female silk makers in Cologne.

But scholars hotly debate the notion, implicit and explicit, that medieval women experienced a "golden age." Judith Bennett has argued for continuity from 1300 to1700. Female occupations may have changed, but the basic circumstances of employment remained the same. Women worked low-skilled, low-status, and low-paying jobs. Women brewers continued to earn meager wages, despite changes in the structure of the business. There was, in short, no transformation; the framework of economic subordination remained the same. The idyllic *gynaecea* had been staffed by slaves, who often worked also as prostitutes.[60]

But here as elsewhere, scholars point to exceptions to the rule.[61] Even as social and economic forces moved to limit women's opportunities, there were numerous success stories. The French widow Charlotte Guillard inherited her husband's printing business and ran it successfully for 20 years, directing a labor force of 25–30 workers. Glickl bas Judah Leib (known by her Christianized name Glückel of Hameln), a Jew from Hamburg, took a debt-ridden business left by her husband and amassed a substantial fortune with it.[62] She recounted her extraordinary career in her memoirs. She described attending fairs, traveling to markets, and drawing on a network of friends within the Jewish community with whom she stayed when on journeys. She remarried at age 54, and entrusted her fortune to her new husband, who promptly squandered it.

There is likewise evidence of female ownership of taverns and inns. The famous English mystic, Margery Kempe, owned a brewing establishment, though she did not do especially well managing it. Women sold goods at city marketplaces; in sixteenth-century Poland perhaps three-quarters of the retailers at the public market were female. German women sold pretzels and sauerkraut, and after the discovery of the New World, marketed new commodities such as sugar, chocolate, tea, and calico. Even where guild restrictions were strong, we find *de facto* participation of women, who helped their brothers and fathers in workshops. In the city of Leiden, male drapers gave over their businesses to their wives when called to public office.[63] Women found employment in posts such as grain inspector, cloth measurer, and even tax collector.

The realities led Judith Brown to argue that there was in fact an economic Renaissance for women. She demonstrated in particular how working conditions improved in seventeenth-century Tuscany. Opportunities expanded for women, particularly in the burgeoning silk industry in Florence. Women were involved in all phases of the manufacturing process.[64]

Convents and "Living Saints"

The institutional church presents perhaps the most obvious example of societal constraints placed on women. It denied them direct participation as clergy or in the office of bishop. Ritual and liturgy stressed female subservience and obedience. Eve and Mary remained powerful images that reinforced female stereotypes.

The restrictions were not uniquely Christian, but existed also in Judaism and Islam.[65] Christianity, however, possessed a means of physically sequestering women in convents, which had been established alongside male monastic houses at the beginning of the Middle Ages. As with men, the cloister was for women a means of worship and expression of piety. But convents served also the broader secular function of reducing the number of single females in society and ensuring chastity. Fathers, particularly from the aristocratic class, sent daughters there rather than dower them, providing an "honorable" solution for families with numerous girls in an era of rising costs of dowries.[66]

The situation made for unwilling nuns. The Venetian sister, Arcangela Tarabotti (d. 1652) gave eloquent voice to the issue in *Simplicity Betrayed (La simplicita ingannata)*, condemning fathers (her own especially) for betraying the innocence of their young daughters in order to protect their wealth. She compared them to "the worst tyrants in the world" and their daughters to "little song birds," ensnared in nets, forever deprived of their liberty. Tarabotti argued that coercion made for bad nuns, who were unlikely to attain perfection "since God has shown himself to hate any act which is not born of voluntary disposition."[67]

As Tarabotti's writings suggest, however, the convent had the advantage of providing women with access to education that they may not otherwise have had. It also allowed an escape from the traditional cycle of marriage and child bearing and could confer substantial significant secular power on its members. Convents, like monasteries, often owned substantial amounts of land, connecting them to secular political, economic, and social networks. Abbesses dealt with local authorities, and even became focal points of resistance to that authority. As abbess of her Venetian convent, Tarabotti stood up against both ecclesiastical and secular authorities, who sought to change the rules regarding the order. The German abbess Caritas Pirckheimer defended her monastery against Protestant reformers.[68]

The nature of convent life has been subject of much recent study.[69] Nuns performed plays, musical works and wrote histories of their orders and houses.[70] In Germany, they produced "sister" books, documenting daily life and religious experiences. Tarabotti and Pirckheimer both wrote memoirs; the latter's *Denkwurdigkeiten* (1524–8) described in great detail her thoughts and intellectual interests. Nuns were involved in financial transactions that required facility with sophisticated accounting practices. Their houses served as patrons to artists. In Florence, nunneries actively participated in the political, social, and economic affairs of the city – the last including production of textiles.[71]

Women expressed piety also through lay associations, which did not involve being cloistered or accepting a formal rule. Among the most popular of these were the Beguines, which grew to large numbers in German-speaking lands and the Low Countries. As much as 7.5 percent of the overall population of fourteenth-century Cologne was involved. Women took a mutual pledge of piety, chastity and poverty. They lived and worked together, but remained in the world. The institutional church was, however, uncomfortable with autonomy of the Beguines, and with female lay associations more generally.[72]

Holiness was itself, however, a means of empowerment. Gabriella Zarri has demonstrated how "living saints" (*sante vive*), women renowned for their piety, used their special status to exercise authority and influence secular rulers and public officials.[73] Catherine of Siena (d. 1380), a Dominican tertiary and ascetic who had mystic visions and worked among the poor and infirm, was nevertheless a potent political force.[74] Although barely literate, she communicated her ideas through letters, often strongly worded, to her scribe, sent to influential people, including the pope, whom Catherine referred as "babbo," colloquial Tuscan for "daddy." The Spanish nun Teresa of Avila, a visionary mystic and member of the strict Carmelite order, traveled throughout Spain, establishing reformed Carmelite houses and gaining audience and influence at the court of Queen Isabella.[75]

In this manner, religion was an important means of female self-expression.[76] The *sante vive* were powerful figures in the Renaissance world, whose careers compare favorably to those of male counterparts such as Savonarola and Bernardino of Siena who, despite their renunciation of worldly affairs, took leading secular roles (see chapter 7). But the path for holy women was a narrow one. They faced close scrutiny and more skepticism than did men. Their behavior was often reflexively viewed as aberrant and extreme rather than pious and devout. Female ascetics were, for example, more often inclined than men to fast and deny themselves food, exposing themselves to charges of mental disorders. Catherine of Siena nourished herself at times by eating the pustules of those sick people she cared for. Teresa of Avila subjected herself to prolonged fasting and mortification of the flesh. Ascetic men were, on the other hand, more likely to renounce their wealth or careers, decisions that, although dramatic, appeared more measured and moderate, and more in line with societal norms. As Caroline Walker Bynum has shown, the differences derived largely from the fact that food was the one commodity that women, as domestic creatures, controlled, and thus could in fact renounce.[77]

The Renaissance portrait of female piety does not go especially far in distinguishing them from their medieval forebears. Fears of female sexuality, of autonomous or extreme behavior in both the institutional and non-institutional setting, were not new.[78] There had been powerful abbesses and *sante vive* in the Middle Ages, who gained great distinction and influence. Caritas Pirckheimer's career is, for example, seen as in the tradition of the eleventh century German abbesses Hrostvitha of Gandersheim, to whom Caritas was in fact compared to in her own day. Hrostvitha was a prolific author of plays and histories and counseled kings and important government officials. Mystics like Catherine of Siena and Teresa of Avila had medieval analogs in the figures of Christina Ebner or Hildegard of Bingen, the former author of a memoir and favorite of the Holy Roman Emperor Charles IV, the latter the author of 20 works, including treatises on medicine.[79]

The most obvious distinction between the two periods was the great changes brought about by the Reformation and Catholic response to it.[80] The advent of Protestantism brought the dissolution of convents and monasteries. Martin Luther, John Calvin, and Martin Bucer elevated the status of marriage, viewing it as an honorable state. But while opening new opportunities, scholars have argued that reform also created new restrictions. Protestantism allowed women more active participation in congregations, and, as with men, more direct access to the word of God. Wives of Protestant ministers took leading roles in congregations and communities; Anabaptists allowed women access to the priesthood.[81] Catholic reformers established new female religious orders, including the Ursulines in Brescia founded by Angela Merici (1535), which consisted of non-cloistered laywomen, who served the poor and sick and earned their living by making clothes and teaching. Mary Ward established in England a network of schools directed by laywomen called the Institute of the Blessed Virgin, fashioned on the Jesuit order. By 1631 there were 300 schools, whose curriculum included instruction in Latin and Greek.

But advances were met by retrenchment on the part of authorities. Reformers were no more comfortable than their medieval Catholic predecessors with female sexuality or the presence of women in the public domain.

The elevation of the status of marriage in Protestantism was accompanied by greater emphasis on child rearing and the family, and on patriarchy, which ultimately produced, according to one scholar, a "social demotion" for women.[82] Meanwhile, the Protestant elimination of convents removed an alternate lifestyle, which, as noted, had its virtues, particularly in terms of education and freedom from marriage.

Reformed Catholicism was similarly restrictive. As church officials moved from "countering" the Reformation to reforming practices within, the role of women suffered. The church withdrew its support of the Ursulines and Mary Ward's Institute. The Ursulines were ordered to accept vows and placed under the authority of local bishops; Mary Ward's schools were suppressed, and when she publicly objected, she was imprisoned as a heretic and schismatic. The church also moved forcefully to eradicate other lay groups such as the beguines.

Catholicism also promoted patriarchy. The cult of Joseph, of minor significance in the Middle Ages, gained prominence in the sixteenth century. Church officials now projected Joseph as a strong patriarchal figure. Where the "medieval" Mary had been depicted as an adult woman, caring for her infant child, the sixteenth-century Mary was rendered as an adolescent, protected by an older but still vigorous Joseph. To create room for the cult of Joseph, the church deemphasized the cult of Mary's mother, Anne, which had been popular in the late Middle Ages.[83]

Witchcraft and Sorcery

The most disturbing development in Europe was the great witch craze that reached a peak in the sixteenth and seventeenth centuries.[84] Religious and secular authorities portrayed witchcraft as an international conspiracy that threatened the basic fabric of society. Scholars have adduced numerous causes for this, including demographic changes, wars, inflation, bad harvests, and most obviously the highly charged religious atmosphere of the time. Women nevertheless bore a disproportionate share of the blame. From 1480 to 1700 more women were executed in Europe for witchcraft than for any other crime. According to Margaret King, the number of women burned at the stake exceeded the number elevated to sainthood by a hundred to one.[85]

The frequent prosecution of women for sorcery was one of the most profound gender differences of the period.[86] Suspicion fell easily upon women, who were involved in aspects of life in which magic could be seen as an operative force. They cared for animals, which might mysteriously die; they prepared food, which could spoil: they nursed children and the infirm, who might suddenly die.[87] Midwives and healers were especially prone to the charges if their cures did not work. The typical accused woman was usually old, unmarried, poorly educated, and quarrelsome, thus easily associated with superstition and malice.[88]

Scholars have adduced a variety of reasons for the victimization of women.[89] Margaret King saw the witch hunts as a species of "war" waged by learned and powerful men against women.[90] Mary Daly argued that the hunts were a means by which male authorities tried to suppress independent women.[91] Robert Muchembled saw the prosecution of women as part of a larger social struggle in which the elite sought to control popular culture and force its values on the rural world. Women were targeted because they transmitted values in their roles as teachers of their children.[92] Lyndal Roper, applying psychoanalytic theory, interpreted the prosecution of women as reflective of "pre-Oedipal fantasies" of malevolent maternity and ambivalent feeling of women toward each other. Roper demonstrated how in seventeenth-century Augsburg the accusers were often recent mothers and the accused often post-menopausal women, who served as live-in help for infants. The older women upset established domestic hierarchies. Their access to babies just after birth gave them *de facto* power that led to conflict, suspicion, and envy with the younger mothers.[93]

Scholars have offered additional reasons, including increased female life expectancy with respect to men, which left more unmarried and unattached women, the group that was most suspect. Christina Larner has emphasized the broad role of political consolidation and rise of more centralizing monarchs for whom suppression of witches served as a means of extending control. It need be stressed, however, that the belief in witches and their demonic power was widespread in Europe, among intellectuals as well as common folk. The French legal scholar, Jean Bodin argued (*Démonomanie des sorciers*, 1580) that laws should be suspended for the prosecution of witches, since sorcery was a crime against God. Even progressive individuals like Erasmus and Montaigne, although they expressed skepticism about witchcraft, still accepted its reality.[94]

There was nevertheless a lack of uniformity of practice across Europe. The witch hunts varied from region to region and according to the attitudes of local officials. In some places, men were more often targeted than women.[95] Overall, prosecutions were most frequent in Northern Europe, in parts of Germany and France, and less frequent in Southern Europe. Nevertheless, both Catholics and Protestant authorities burned witches.[96]

The role of misogyny was, however, unmistakable. The famous guide to prosecution of witches, the *Malleus maleficarum* (1486) was openly anti-woman. It provided an etymology for the term "femina," which derived from "fe" (faith) and "minus" (less), that is, faithless. The authors of the book, the Dominican inquisitors Heinrich Kramer and Jacob Sprenger, employed a range of classical and Christian arguments, depicting women as carnal, credulous, and imperfect, and inferior to men. Women's slippery tongues and insatiable lust allowed the devil to seduce them, as he had Eve. The *Malleus maleficarum* ran through 14 editions from 1487 to 1520.

Querelle des Femmes

The persecutions and institutional restrictions notwithstanding, it was in the sixteenth century that some of the strongest voices asserting the rights of women emerged. Indeed, there developed at that time a broad based and vigorous debate over the qualities of women, their dignity, mental abilities, place in society, and the value of educating them. This has come to be known by modern scholars as the "*querelle des femmes*" or "woman's question." It was primarily a literary phenomenon that engaged both female and male writers, the latter including humanists such as Desiderius Erasmus and Juan Luis Vives. Thousands of tracts were produced, in a variety of languages, including Latin, French, German, Italian, Spanish, and English, representing all three faiths, Catholic, Protestant, and Jewish. The printing press allowed the tracts to be widely disseminated.[97]

For many scholars the *querelle* is the aspect of women's experience that fits most comfortably under the label "Renaissance." Gerda Lerner in her long view of women's history asserted that it constituted the first serious discussion of gender as a social construct in western history.[98] At the core of the discussion was what it meant to be female and male, what were the characteristics, the proper modes of behavior for each.

The key figure was Christine de Pizan (1401–1471). For Elissa Weaver, Christine alone justified saying yes to Joan Kelly's challenge, that there was a Renaissance for women.[99] Christine was Venetian by birth, but lived most of her life in France, where her father was physician and astrologer to King Charles V. She pursued a literary career, which took on professional dimensions when her father, who had overseen her education, and her husband, who had supported her, died. Christine then supported herself, her children, and her mother by writing. Christine self-effacingly referred to her literary voice as little more than that of "a tiny cricket that flaps its wings frantically." But her male contemporaries took her far more seriously, comparing her to "a crow that sang more loudly when its song was praised and food dropped in its beak."[100]

Christine refuted the misogynist slights in *The Romance of the Rose* (1225), a popular medieval French work on courtly love, and in Matheolus' *Lamentations*, a more obscure Latin work on women and marriage. She wrote of the latter that "just the sight of this book made me wonder how it happened that so many different men [...] are so inclined to express [...] so many wicked insults about women and their behavior."[101] The former, left uncompleted by William of Lorris, took on a strong anti-women bias in the hands of Jean de Meung, whose lengthy additions cataloged the vices of women, including fickleness, deceit, and lack of faith.

Christine gave her most comprehensive defense of women in *The Book of the City of Women (Le Livre de la Citè des dames*, 1405), a dialogue between the author and three allegorical female figures representing Reason, Rectitude, and Justice. The women command Christine to build a city to protect females – past, present, and future – on the model of the Amazon queens and warriors of antiquity, who had conquered the Persian king Cyrus and established a matriarchal society.

Christine argued against the long tradition of defamation, beginning with the ancient philosophers. She accused them of acting from resentment and jealousy, projecting onto women their own sins and insecurities. Christine conceded that the female body might be weaker than the male body, but she denied Aristotelian and Galenic notions of female imperfection or that gender roles were biologically determined. The burdens of child rearing rendered women subject to men. Women possessed the same virtues and same intelligence, but had fewer opportunities to express their talent. If women were similarly taught "they would learn as thoroughly and understand the subtleties of all the arts and sciences as well as sons." Christine revised the standard interpretation of Mary and Eve, affording the former a greater role than the latter. "If anyone would say that man was banished by Lady Eve, I tell you that he gained more through Mary than he lost through Eve, when humanity was conjoined to the Godhead."[102]

Christine modeled the *City of Women* on Giovanni Boccaccio's *Concerning Famous Women (De mulieribus claris*, 1380). Boccaccio offered a list of praiseworthy women dating from classical times. But, unlike Boccaccio, who praised women who "overcame" their physical and mental weakness and acted like men, Christine lauded women on their own terms and treated gender as socially constructed. Her work therefore deserves to be seen as revolutionary in its context.[103]

Others writers followed Christine's example. Isotta Nogarola (1418–1466), the daughter of a Veronese noble, wrote a series of letters and a treatise addressing issues of gender identity. In *Dialogue on the Equal or Unequal Sin of Adam* (1451) Nogarola defended Eve against the charge of having caused the fall of mankind.[104] Unlike Christine, however, Nogarola based her defense on Eve's inferiority to Adam, that as the lesser party she could not have been responsible for man's fall. Stronger statements appear in the work of Moderate Fonte and Lucrezia Marinella, two Venetian noblewomen. In *The Worth of Women (il merito delle donne*, 1600) Fonte refuted both biblical and Aristotelian claims against women. Her main character, Corinna, expressed the intention to "remain free of men," so as not to have to subordinate herself in any way to them. In *The Nobility and Excellence of Women and the Defects and Vices of Men* (*Le nobilta et eccellenze delle donne et i diffetti, e mancamenti de gli uomini*, 1600), Lucrezia Marinella argued that Eve was superior to Adam, and that women were in general superior to men. "If women [. . .] wake themselves from the long sleep that oppresses them, how meek and humble will those proud and ungrateful men become."

Margaret King has described Moderate Fonte and Lucrezia Marinella as "proto-feminists." Marinella responded in part to the misogyny of male writers, in particular to Giovanni Passi's *The Defects of Women* (*I donneschi diffetti*, 1599), which listed the inherent defects of women and advocated restricting them to domestic roles.

But men also supported women, and argued on their behalf. Both Erasmus (*The Institution of Christian Marriage*, 1526) and Vives (*The Education of a Christian Woman*, 1523) allowed women if not political and domestic equality to men a measure of spiritual equality and advocated education for the daughters of aristocrats.[105] The contemporary German humanist, Heinrich Cornelius Agrippa von Nettesheim, argued more strongly on behalf of women's capacity for reason and even superiority to men in some respects.[106] In *On the Nobility and Excellence of Women* (*De nobilitate et praecellentia sexus foeminei... declamatio*, 1529) Agrippa followed Marinella in arguing that Eve was superior to Adam She was made from Adam's rib, thus out of bone rather than clay, a superior material. Eve's milk sustained life, and through menstruation rid the body of poisons, while Adam, not Eve, brought sin into the world. Women deserved political rights, including the privilege to hold public office, a view that was also held by Agrippa's English counterpart Thomas Elyot (*The Defense of Good Women*, 1540).

The interest of male writers in the subject has been taken as evidence by scholars of women's growing status in society. But scholars also wonder whether the participation of men in the *querelle* indicates it was more a literary game, aimed at displaying rhetorical skills, satire and wit, a popular sport among male humanists. Erasmus and Vives' support for women was in fact tepid; they viewed female virtues as gender specific. Some male writers took absurd positions or wrote on both sides. The anonymous author of *Disputatio Nova* (1595) pondered whether women should be considered human beings, while Edward Gosynhill slighted women in one poem, *The Schoolhouse of Women*, and then praising them in another, *The Praise of Women*, published a year later.

The motives of men are made more suspect by the fact that many wrote for female patrons. This was the case with most of the positive portrayals listed above. Agrippa dedicated his work to Margaret of Burgundy; Thomas

Elyot to Anne of Cleves (Henry VIII's fourth wife); Erasmus and Vives wrote for Catherine of Aragon (Henry VIII's first wife). Even Boccaccio's *Concerning Famous Women* in the fourteenth century, the first of the genre, was dedicated to a woman, Andrea Acciauoli.

The most notorious example of the rhetorical aspect of the *querelle* is the third book of Castiglione's *The Courtier*. Both sides, pro and con, are presented there in the form of a debate between two leading male protagonists, Gasparo Pallavicino and Giuliano de' Medici. Gasparo voices the traditional misogyny, drawing upon the Aristotelian argument that women were defective and incomplete males and thus inferior. Giuliano de' Medici argues, on the other hand, that the two sexes possessed equal mental and spiritual faculties. "There have always been women who have done all that men have done." This, Giuliano, notes was true physically and intellectually, with respect even to war and philosophy.

Castiglione's own views have been the source of considerable discussion. Joan Kelly argued that Castiglione held negative and patronizing attitudes toward women. The active participants in the debate were all men, women served as passive witnesses. Valeria Finucci has extended this further, asserting that women functioned throughout *The Courtier* as adornments at the court and politely excused themselves from conversations when the subject turned to weighty matters.[107]

But if male writers exploited the *querelle* genre, the issues raised in the debate were real enough. The sincerity of the assertions of Tarabotti, Fonte, and Marinella are undeniable, as are those expressed by the pseudonymous Jane Anger, who in *Protection of Women* (1589) railed against the falsehoods of men and maintained that they could not survive without women. The ideas were influential and carried over to the next generation, stated more forcefully by writers such as Marie le Jars de Gournay (1565–1645), Anna Maria van Schurman (1607–1678) and others. In *L'Egalite des homes et des femmes (The Equality of Men and Women*, 1622) Gournay argued that men and women were by nature equal and that Christ came into the world as a man only because the misogynistic Jewish tradition would not have allowed him to achieve anything as a female.[108]

The reality of the issues raised by the *querelle* is confirmed in visual images. Painted chests and cabinets given as part of wedding trousseaus contained scenes, biblical and classical, depicting proper female roles.[109] The rape of the Sabines reminded women of their role in bearing children for the good of the state; the sufferings of Griselda encouraged women to bear patiently with the trials and humiliations put upon them by their husbands. Echoes of the *querelle* were also evident in popular songs and prints. The latter were hung in taverns and people's homes and often juxtaposed female virtues with vices.

Education and Humanism

A key issue for participants in the *querelle des femmes* was education. Christine de Pizan argued that only through equal access to learning did women stand a chance of raising themselves to the level of men. University and advanced training were closed to women, and would not be opened until the modern era. What learning was available was rudimentary, consisting of an hour or so of study, with emphasis on reading from manuals of prayers or lives of virtuous women – material seen as sufficient for managing domestic affairs. Teaching took place in the home or in local often unlicensed elementary schools. Reading and writing were taught separately, with decidedly less emphasis on the latter. Writing required a stylus, which was expensive and represented a financial commitment that parents were reluctant to make for daughters.[110] The result was what scholars have called a "semi" or "split literacy" among women, which restricted their intellectual horizons. Studies suggest that literacy was lowest in rural areas of Southern and Eastern Europe and higher in urban areas in northwest Europe.[111]

The humanist course of study, with its emphasis on rhetoric and eloquence in preparation for service in the public sphere, was inherently unsuited to women (see chapter 4). The famous humanist teacher Pier Paolo Vergerio argued that "liberal studies," were intended exclusively for the sons of aristocrats, to give them "judgment" to further their careers for the state.[112] Even Erasmus and Vives, who advocated for educational training for women, excluded its use for public service. The education of females was a means of promoting the Christian ideal of chastity. "Let few see her and none at all hear her," Vives wrote.[113]

But women nevertheless attained rank as humanists and had distinguished careers, gaining notice in the public sphere.[114] Most were, like Christine de Pizan, from well-to-do families, with solicitous fathers, who oversaw their education. Women below the elite were more easily excluded, as also were men. Class was therefore an important factor and even female advocates of education like Anna Maria van Schurman believed the privilege proper to women of means, who possessed the requisite time and freedom from domesticity. Schurman's French contemporary, Louise Labé (1520–1566) expressed the same opinion, although she was among the few women writers of the period who was not of the elite, but the daughter of a French rope maker.[115]

Restrictions notwithstanding, it is possible to speak of a female humanist tradition in Europe. The roster includes Italians such as Isotta Nogarola, Laura Cereta, and Cassandra Fedele, and northerners like Caritas Pirckheimer from southern Germany, Margaret Roper of England, Anna

Maria van Schurman of Holland, Marguerite d'Angoulême (1492–1549), Louise Labé, and Marie Jars de Gournay of France.

Like their male counterparts, the women mastered classical languages and literature.[116] Laura Cereta openly expressed a longing for fame and immortality.[117] Isotta Nogarola wrote orations against the Turks and a life of Saint Jerome, drawn from Cicero, Plutarch, biblical and patristic sources.[118] Schurman mastered Hebrew, Chaldean, Arabic, and Syriac, wrote an Ethiopian grammar book and laid out an extensive education program for women in *Whether a Christian Woman should be Educated* (1638).[119]

Schurman believed that the basic goal of education was to make women better Christians. But, unlike Erasmus, she argued that learned women also helped the public good and thus the state, by producing wise and devout subjects.[120] Louise Labé argued that women should be educated for their own sake and urged that they publicly display their knowledge. "If any of us excel let her do so proudly, and not resist the glory she will win." The ideas inspired women reformers of the next generation, including Mary Astell (1666–1731), who established academies for the education of women.

The list of accomplished women includes Marguerite d'Angoulême (1492–1549), sister of the King Francis I, whose *Heptameron*, fashioned on Boccaccio's *Decameron*, contains stories of assertive women and critical statements about marriage and is still widely read in modern classrooms. It includes musicians and artists. Francesca Caccini (1587?), daughter of a prominent Neapolitan noble, was a composer-singer at the Medici court in Florence. Properzia de' Rossi (1490–1530) gained famc as a sculptor, carving first peach stones and eventually mastering the techniques of marble. Sofonisba Anguissola (1532–1625) studied informally with Michelangelo and became court painter for Philip II of Spain.[121] Anguissola inspired others including Irene di Spilimbergo (1541–59), Lavinia Fontana (1552–1614), and Artemisia Gentileschi (1593–1632). There were likewise notable women artists in the Netherlands in the seventeenth-century including Judith Leyster, whose paintings were until recently taken as those of her friend Frans Hals.[122]

Unnatural Beings and Book-Lined Cells

Consideration of the visual arts again demonstrates the limited opportunities available to women. Properzia de Rossi received public commissions, but she was an exception. More generally, women were denied this as well as permission to pursue traditional artistic themes such the male nude. They therefore focused on domestic and devotional themes. Sofonisba Anguissola painted what was immediately accessible to her, including herself, her family, and members (mostly female) of the Spanish court. Her famous Chess Game (1555) depicts her with her three sisters Lucia, Minerva, and Europa (1555).

Much of the creative output of women occurred in the domestic setting, including in arts that did not possess the status of painting and sculpture. Women were, for example, pioneers in embroidery. Stylistic developments in the sixteenth century parallel some of those of painting, with increasing recourse to naturalistic forms and greater attention to perspective. In the public realm, female artists were innovative within their limited spheres. Artemisia Gentileschi portrayed the figure of Judith, an important political symbol in her native Florence, in a decidedly feminist manner, cutting off the head of Holofernes (1612–13) in a savage way, evoking female power.

Women's skill elicited praise from male contemporaries, but often in backhanded ways. Men treated accomplished women as ornaments to family honor or as a means to further their own reputation and careers. Cassandra Fedele's father Angelo, for example, hoped to use his daughter's talents to advance his position at the Venetian court. Female skill was viewed as gender specific. Women's natural gifts included attention to detail and the ability to imitate rather than to think originally. The combination of genius and melancholy that was (see chapter 2) a basic characteristic of Renaissance individuality was distinctly masculine. Women writers and artists whose work brought anxiety and melancholy were seen as flawed or troubled people. Male contemporaries viewed their achievements in the public realm as "wondrous" and thus unnatural. Giorgio Vasari devoted a biography to Properzia de Rossi. But he judged her "miraculous" artistic skill inferior to that of her male counterparts on the grounds that she was unable to "escape her female nature."[123]

Success for women in the public sphere lay in their ability to "overcome" their sex. The transformation involved acquiring male virtues. Boccaccio made this point in his catalog of famous women, as did Christine de Pizan's patron Jean Gerson, who lauded her as a "manly female." Women themselves sometimes stood in their way of their counterparts. Laura Cereta complained of "babbling and chattering" women who strongly opposed her intellectual ambitions.

Such attitudes limited the artistic and intellectual production of women, which was small in comparison to that of men. Despite her erudition and eloquence, Margaret Roper published only one work (posthumously), a translation into English of *The Devout Treatise on the Pater Noster* (1542) by Erasmus, a family friend. The treatise dealt with piety and family loyalty, subjects proper to women. Meanwhile, marriage often meant the end of serious work. Cassandra Fedele's literary career began at age twenty-two, but ended 12 years later, when she married. She returned to her studies when widowed, at age ninety-one.

Public life was unnatural for even the most accomplished women. Intellectual and cultural boundaries were often policed by attacks on their sexual behavior. Male humanists compared their female counterparts to Amazons, the legendary warriors, who were antagonistic to men. Marie Jars de Gournay was accused of having an affair with Montaigne, whose work she helped edit.[124] Louis Labè was charged by John Calvin (who condemned her views on education) with providing sexual services for local nobles and clergy.[125]

As Margaret King has argued, the charges created doubts in women, isolating them intellectually, and forcing them to retreat from the public sphere to their homes, to what she has called "book lined cells," which were in effect self-constructed prisons.[126] Isotta Nogarola pursued a career as a humanist, avoiding both marriage and the cloister, living with her mother. By eighteen, she had secured a reputation among her male counterparts, who were complimentary. But her public life as a humanist lasted briefly, ended at twenty-three, when she was falsely accused of sleeping with her brother. Her humanist tutor Guarino Guarini renounced her and she abandoned her career for the convent.

Patronage and Power

As the preceding discussion makes clear, there was little room in public life for women. Nevertheless, they were never wholly absent from it. The most "visible" locus of their activities was at courts, as ladies in waiting, as countesses and duchesses, and, in a few cases, as rulers of states.

Consideration of the court returns our discussion to where it began, with Joan Kelly. Women at court served as patrons, helping to facilitate the intellectual and artistic activities synonymous with the Renaissance. Marguerite of Navarre stood at the center of a circle of humanists at the court of her brother, Francis I. Anne of Brittany (1477–1514), queen to both Charles VIII and Louis XII collected tapestries and commissioned a French translation of Boccaccio's *Concerning Famous Women*. Marie de' Medici (1573–1642), queen of Henry IV, served as patron to Peter Paul Rubens and personally oversaw the rebuilding of the Luxembourg palace and expansion of the Chateau of Monteaux-en-Brie.[127] Countess Isabella d'Este (1474–1539) of Mantua brought Ariosto, Titian, Raphael, Andrea Mantegna, and Leonardo da Vinci to her court.[128] The English queen Catherine of Aragon, the first wife of Henry VIII, was patron to Erasmus and Juan Luis Vives.

As with men (see chapter 2), patronage was for women a means of projecting power and constructing identity. Recent scholarship has emphasized diverse activities.[129] Isabella d'Este, for example, patronized traditionally "feminine" domestic projects such as religious painting and decorative arts.

But she also sponsored "masculine" ones including public statuary. Isabella's zeal as collector of art (sculpture in particular) involved her in direct public competition with male collectors, a competition she waged enthusiastically, with male members of her own family.[130] Studies of women patrons below the level of the elite suggest that their tendencies, like those of men, shifted according to a range of factors, including marital status and geographical location. Cynthia Lawrence has shown how female patronage often changed after the death of a husband.[131] Margarita Pellegrini of Verona had followed the accepted convention of displaying her husband's coat of arms in the family chapel (1529–57). Once he died, however, she shifted to her own distinctly "feminine" themes, dedicating the family chapel to Saint Anne, the patron of childbirth and mothers.

Patronage was likewise an important theme in the Middle Ages, and indeed Joan Kelly highlighted the activities of prominent court patrons such as Matilda of Tuscany (d. 1115) and Eleanor of Aquitaine (d. 1204).[132] But the Renaissance period was distinct from the medieval period in that there existed full-fledged women rulers, such as Elizabeth I Tudor, Isabella of Castile, and Christina of Sweden for which there was no medieval parallel. The ascendancy of the Renaissance monarchs owed to historical accident, the absence of male heirs.[133] Their exercise of political power was deeply paradoxical in a society that, as we have seen, championed political patriarchy, absolute state authority and the overwhelmingly denied women the right of citizenship. Renaissance political power was inherently masculine in nature. John Knox, writing in reaction to the rule of Mary Stuart in Scotland, called female monarchs "repugnant to nature" and contrary to scripture. The French political theorist Jean Bodin in his *Six Books of the Commonwealth* argued that the state, like a household, relied on the authority of a single man.

The circumstance required skillful negotiation and projection of power. Elizabeth Tudor is credited with displaying unparalleled skill at this, carefully molding popular opinion by playing on the image of her virginity, unwedded to a mortal man, betrothed instead to the English state.[134] She employed images of the Virgin Mary in her speeches and was often visually represented by artists as Astraea, the daughter of Zeus, or as Diana, the virgin huntress. Elizabeth also used androgynous images to display distinct authority.[135]John Aylmer, a contemporary supporter of Elizabeth, described the queen (*Harborowe for Faithfull and Trewe Subjects*, 1559) as possessing two bodies – her natural female body, which left her subject to male authority in the home, and her political body, which allowed her to rule. In this manner, Aylmer effectively distinguished sex from gender.

Other female rulers gave similar attention to images.[136] Queen Christina of Sweden (1626–1689) presented herself in paintings as the Roman goddess Minerva Pacifica, a symbol of both wisdom and virginity but ready for war to preserve her freedom. Catherine de' Medici used the emblem of Artemisia of Caria, the armed but chaste queen of Halicarnassus, who ingested her dead husband's ashes to express her fidelity and absorption of his power. The queen regent of the Netherlands, Margaret of Austria (1480–1530) took the traditional pose of male rulers in a devotional diptych, praying directly to the Christ-child rather than, in the traditional feminine manner, praying to the Madonna.[137]

The examples demonstrate the constructed nature of Renaissance gender and how women used images to exercise power and agency in public spaces. The images were, as Natalie Davis has shown, transferable. Men drew on feminine images, most typically the stereotype of "disorderly female" at carnivals or during political revolts against authority. This freed them from responsibility, while at the same time creating a sexual energy and power to embolden them to speak the truth.[138]

Renaissance and Early Modern

The use of gendered images and the exercise of female agency in the political world are vibrant fields in Renaissance studies. Recent scholarship has drawn on philosopher/sociologist Jurgen Habermas's concept of the "public sphere," to understand the informal ways in which women influenced the public political discourse, in convents, lay communities, salons, and theaters. Seventeenth century Parisian salons, for example, brought together upper class men and women in which they read works, discussed ideas and put on dramatic productions.[139]

With regard to the original question raised by Kelly, whether women had a Renaissance, the balance of scholarly opinion remains largely negative. Indeed, scholars appear less inclined to use the term Renaissance in their studies, preferring the "less lyrical" label "early modern," which they see as more inclusive of Northern European trends as well as a wider range of women's activities, including those below the level of the elite.[140] The term also facilitates discussion of religious developments without recourse to the equally value laden term, Reformation, which begs its own explanation with regard to women. The term Renaissance has retained its appeal primarily among students of Italy and France, particularly those interested in the *querelle* tradition and deeds of elite, accomplished women.[141] But even with regard to Italy and France, the Renaissance label has lost ground, running afoul of disciplinary boundaries and subfields. The artists Sofonisba Anguissola and Artemisia Gentileschi, for example, often characterized as "Renaissance" women, painted in styles that belong more properly to the mannerist and baroque traditions respectively.

Nevertheless, the Renaissance and early modern labels have not been treated as exclusive. The reality, here as elsewhere, is that historians of gender have used the two together in works. Catherine R. Stimpson has argued that this is desirable, that "early modern" functions as a "supplementary name" that broadens the meaning of Renaissance. But, again as elsewhere, the "early modern" label tends to stretch the temporal period of investigation forward to the eighteenth century and the modern world, encouraging teleology, with scholars judging Renaissance events in terms of the current developments.[142] In this respect, the historiography on Renaissance gender may be compared with that on the Renaissance economy (see chapter 5). Nevertheless the tendency has helped sharpen distinctions with the Middle Ages.[143]

Such issues remain, however, much debated. Judith Bennett has argued against the notion of change in women's circumstances in the period from 1300 to 1700.[144] Susan Stuard has pointed out, to the contrary, that long-term continuity has its own problems, erasing the basic transition points in women's history.[145] The historiography is singularly rich and has, perhaps more so than in any other subfield, incorporated a wide-range of methodologies, both theoretical and empirical, facilitating a genuinely interdisciplinary dialogue across fields.

Notes

1 Christine de Pizan, *The Book of the City of Ladies*, trans. by Earl Jeffrey Richards (New York, 1982), pp. 4–5.
2 Joan Kelly, "Did Women Have a Renaissance?" in *Becoming Visible: Women in European History*, ed. by Renate Bridenthal and Claudia Koonz (Boston, 1977), pp. 137–64; Judith Bennett, "Medieval Women, Modern Women: Across the Great Divide," in *Feminists Revision of History*, ed. by Ann Shapiro (New Brunswick, 1994).
3 Linda K. Kerber, "Gender," in *Imagined Histories*, ed. by Gordon Wood and Anthony Molho, eds. (Princeton, 1998), p. 41.
4 Joan Scott, "Gender: A Useful Category of Historical Analysis," *American Historical Review* 91 (1986): 1053–75; Gisela Bock, "Women's History and Gender History: Aspects of an International Debate," *Gender and History* 1 (Spring 1989): 7–30 and *Women in European History* (Oxford, 2002).
5 Margaret King, *Women of the Renaissance* (Chicago, 1991); Merry E. Wiesner, *Women and Gender in Early Modern Europe*, 2nd edn. (Cambridge, 2000); Monica Chojnacka and Merry E. Wiesner, eds., *Ages of Woman, Ages of Man: Sources on European Social History, 1350–1750* (London, 2002).
6 Natalie Zemon Davis, "Women's History in Transition: The European Case," *Feminist Studies* 3 (1975–6): 83–103.
7 Popular biographies of Isabella d'Este include Julia Cartwright Ady's *Isabella d'Este: Lioness of Mantua, 1474–1539*, 2 vols. (New York, 1903); Edith P. Meyer,

First Lady of the Renaissance: A Biography of Isabella d'Este (Boston, 1970); and Daniela Pizzagalli, *La signora del Rinascimento: Vita e splendori di Isabella d'Este alla corte di Mantova* (Rome, 2001).

8 For Catherine de' Medici, see Pierre de Bourdeille Brantôme, *Illustrious Dames of the Court of the Valois Kings*, trans. by Katharine Prescott Wormeley Lamb (London, 1912); N. M. Sutherland, *Catherine de' Medici and the Ancien Régime* (London, 1921); and R. S. Knecht, *Catherine de' Medici* (New York, 1998). For Elizabeth, see M. Creighton, *Queen Elizabeth* (New York, 1899); T. Y. Crowell and Katharine Susan Anthony, *Queen Elizabeth* (New York, 1929); J. E. Neale, *Queen Elizabeth* (New York, 1934).

9 N. Z. Davis, "Women's History in Transition," p. 83; Judith Brown and Robert C. Davis, eds., *Gender and Society in Renaissance Italy* (New York, 1998), p. 3; Gerda Lerner, *The Creation of Feminist Consciousness: From the Middle Ages to Eighteen-Seventy* (Oxford, 1993).

10 A. Wright, ed., *Select Letters of St Jerome* (Cambridge, MA, 1963), p. 114.

11 Jerome, *Letters in the Select Works Nicene and Post Nicene Writers*, trans. by H. Fremantle, vol. 6 (Edinburgh 1892), pp. 102–3.

12 Aristotle, *Politics*, trans. by A. L. Peck (Cambridge, MA, 1943), p. 460.

13 Plato, *Timaeus and Critias*, trans. by Desmond Lee (New York, 1977), p. 122.

14 Thomas Laqueur, *Making Sex: Body and Gender from the Greeks to Freud* (Cambridge MA, 1990); Monica H. Green, *Making Women's Medicine Masculine: The Rise of Male Authority in Pre-Modern Gynaecology* (Oxford, 2008).

15 Ian Maclean, *The Renaissance Notion of Woman* (Cambridge, 1988), pp. 6–7.

16 Wiesner, *Women and Gender*, p. 18; Maclean, *Renaissance Notion of Woman*, pp. 7–8, 12.

17 Margaret L. King, *Venetian Humanism in an Age of Patrician Dominance* (Princeton, 1986), pp. 92–8.

18 Lorna Hutson, "The Housewife and the Humanist," in *Feminism and Renaissance Studies*, ed. by Lorna Hutson (New York, 1999), pp. 82–105 and *The Usurer's Daughter: Male Friendship and Fictions of Women in Sixteenth Century England* (London, 1994).

19 Jean Howard, "Cross-Dressing, the Theater and Gender Struggle in Early Modern Europe," *Shakespeare Quarterly* 39 (1988): 418–40.

20 Wiesner, *Women and Gender*, p. 32.

21 Barbara Diefendorf, "Gender and Family," in *Renaissance and Reformation France, 1500–1648*, ed. by Mack Holt (Oxford, 2004), p. 99.

22 Julius Kirshner, "Materials for a Gilded Age: Non-Dotal Assets in Florence (1300–1500)," in *The Family in Italy from Antiquity to the Present*, ed. by Richard Salle and David Kertzer (New Haven, 1991). See also Romeo de Maio, *Donna e Rinascimento* (Milan, 1987), pp. 86, 99.

23 Giovanna Benadusi, *A Provincial Elite in Early Modern Tuscany* (Baltimore, 1996); Christine Meek, "Women between Law and Social Reality in Early Renaissance Lucca," in *Women in Italian Renaissance Culture and Society*, ed. by Letizia Panizza (Oxford, 2000), pp. 182–93.

24 Thomas Kuehn, *Law, Family, and Women: Toward a Legal Anthropology of Renaissance Italy* (Chicago, 1994) and *Heirs, Kin and Creditors in Renaissance*

Florence (Cambridge, 2008); Julius Kirshner, "Wives' Claims against Insolvent Husbands," in *Women of the Medieval World: Essays in Honor of John H. Mundy*, ed. by Julius Kirchner and Suzanne F. Wemple (Oxford, 1985), pp. 256–302.

25 Christiane Klapisch-Zuber, "The 'Cruel Mother': Maternity, Widowhood and Dowry in Florence in the Fourteenth and Fifteenth Centuries," in *Women, Family, and Ritual in Renaissance Italy* (Chicago, 1985).

26 Stanley Chojnacki, "The Power of Love: Wives and Husbands in Late Medieval Venice," in *Women and Power in the Middle Ages*, ed. by Mary Erler and Maryanne Kowaleski (Athens, Georgia, 1988), pp. 127–9, 132, "Patrician Women in Early Renaissance Venice," *Studies in the Renaissance* 21 (1974): 176–203, and "Kinship Ties and Young Patricians in Fifteenth Century Venice," *Renaissance Quarterly* 38 (1985): 240–70. The essays are collected in Stanley Chojnacki, *Women and Men in Renaissance Venice* (Baltimore, 2000).

27 Chojnacki, "Power of Love," p. 132.

28 Joanne M. Ferraro, "Family and Clan," in *A Companion to the Worlds of the Renaissance*, ed. by Guido Ruggiero (Malden, MA, 2002), p. 176 and *Marriage Wars in Late Renaissance Venice* (Oxford, 2001).

29 Diane Owen Hughes, "Urban Growth and Family Structure in Medieval Genoa," *Past and Present* 66 (1975): 3–28 and "From Brideprice to Dowry in Mediterranean Europe," *Journal of Family History* 3 (1978): 262–96. See also Anthony Molho, *Marriage Alliance in Late Medieval Florence* (Cambridge, MA, 1994); Trevor Dean and K. J. P. Lowe, eds., *Marriage in Italy, 1300–1550* (Cambridge, 1998).

30 Lawrence Stone, *Family, Sex and Marriage in England, 1500–1800* (New York, 1977); Alan MacFarlane, *Marriage and Love in England, Modes of Reproduction, 1300–1840* (London, 1986); John Gillis, *For Better or Worse: British Marriages 1600 to Present* (Oxford, 1985); Miriam Slater, *Family Life in the Seventeenth Century: The Verneys of Claydon House* (London, 1984).

31 Anthony Fletcher, *Gender, Sex, and Subordination in England 1500–1800* (New Haven, 1995).

32 Even in Florence, women had legal recourse with respect to their dowries and the right to reclaim it should their husbands become insolvent. Thomas Kuehn, "Person and Gender in the Laws," in *Gender and Society in Renaissance Italy*, ed. by Judith A. Brown and Robert C. Davis (New York, 1998), p. 89; Kirshner, "Wives' Claims," pp. 257, 287, 301.

33 Martha C. Howell, *The Marriage Exchange: Property, Social Place, and Gender in the Cities of the Low Countries* (Chicago, 1998).

34 Martha C. Howell, *Women, Production and Patriarchy in Late Medieval Europe* (Chicago, 1986); Barbara A. Hanawalt, ed., *Women and Work in Preindustrial Europe* (Bloomington, 1986), p. viii; Louise A. Tilly and Joan W. Scott, eds., *Women, Work, and Family* (New York, 1978); Daryl M. Hafter, ed., *European Women and Preindustrial Craft* (Bloomington, 1995); Olwen Hufton, *The Prospect Before Her: A History of Women in Western Europe, 1500–1800* (London, 1995).

35 Diefendorf, "Gender and Family," p. 106.

36 Samuel K. Cohn, *Women in the Street: Essays on Sex and Power in Renaissance Italy* (Baltimore, 1996). For Florentine women, see also Isabelle Chabot, "La reconnaissance du travail des femmes dans la Florence du bas Moyen Age: Contexte idéologique et réalité," in *La donna nell'economia, sec. XIII–XVIII*, ed. by Simonetta Cavaciocchi (Prato, 1990), pp. 563–76; Roberto Greci, "Donne e corporazioni: La fluidità di un rapport," in *Il lavoro delle donne*, ed. by Angela Groppi (Rome, 1996), pp. 71–91.

37 Leah L. Otis, "The Municipal Wet Nurses of Fifteenth-Century Montpellier," in Hanawalt, *Women and Work*, pp. 83–113; Christiane Klapisch-Zuber, "Blood Parents and Milk Parents: Wet Nurses in Florence, 1300–1530," in *Women, Family and Ritual*, pp. 132–64.

38 Charles Verlinden, *L'Esclavage dans l'Europe médiévale*, 2 vols. (Paris, 1955); Iris Origo, "The Domestic Enemy: The Eastern Slaves in Tuscany in the Fourteenth and Fifteenth Centuries," *Speculum* 30 (1955): 321–99; Susan Mosher Stuard, "To Town to Serve: Urban Domestic Slavery in Medieval Ragusa," in Hanawalt, *Women and Work*, pp. 39–55 and "Ancillary Evidence for the Decline of Slavery," *Past and Present* 149 (1995): 3–28.

39 Philip Gavitt, *Charity and Children in Renaissance Florence: The Ospedale degli Innocenti, 1410–1536* (Ann Arbor, 1991); Thomas Kuehn, *Illegitimacy in Renaissance Florence* (Ann Arbor, 2002).

40 Judith Bennett, "History that Still Stands: Women's Work in the European Past," *Feminist Studies* 14, 2 (Summer 1988), p. 275.

41 Hanawalt, *Women and Work*, pp. x–xi.

42 Judith Bennett, "The Village Ale-Wife: Women and Brewing in Fourteenth-Century England," in Barbara Hanawalt, *Ale, Beer and Brewsters in England: Women's Work in a Changing World* (Oxford, 1996), pp. 24–5.

43 William Caferro, "The Silk Business of Tommaso Spinelli, Fifteenth-Century Florentine Merchant and Papal Banker," *Renaissance Studies* 10 (Dec. 1996): 417–39.

44 Katherine Park, *Doctors and Medicine in Early Renaissance Florence* (Princeton, 1985) and *Secrets of Women: Gender, Generation, and the Origins of Human Dissection* (New York, 2006); Sandra Cavallo and David Gentilcore, eds., "Spaces, Objects and Identities in Early Modern Italian Medicine," a special edition of *Renaissance Studies* 21 (2007). On the progressive exclusion of women from the health care profession, see Green, *Making Women's Medicine Masculine*.

45 Michael Rocke, *Forbidden Friendships: Homosexuality and Male Culture in Renaissance Florence* (Oxford, 1993).

46 Leah L. Otis, *Prostitution in Medieval Society: The History of an Urban Institution in Languedoc* (Chicago, 1985), p. 139.

47 David Herlihy, *Opera Muliebria: Women and Work in Medieval Europe* (Philadelphia, 1990), p. 158.

48 Elizabeth S. Cohen, "Seen and Known: Prostitutes and the Cityscape of Late Sixteenth Century Rome," *Renaissance Studies* 12 (1998): 392–409; John K. Brackett, "The Florentine *onestà* and the Control of Prostitution, 1403–1680,"

Sixteenth Century Journal 24 (1993): 273–300; Ruth Karras, "Prostitution and the Question of Sexual Identity in Europe," *Journal of Women's History* 11 (1999): 159–77.

49 Eileen Power, *Medieval Women*, ed. by M. M. Poston (Cambridge, 1975), p. 60; Hanawalt, *Women and Work*, p. xiii.

50 Nancy Siraisi, *Medieval and Early Renaissance Medicine* (Chicago, 1990), pp. 27, 35, 44, 46.

51 Merry E. Wiesner, "Guilds, Male Bonding and Women's Work in Early Modern Germany, *Gender and History* 1 (1989): 125–37.

52 Herlihy, *Opera Muliebria*, p. 155.

53 P. J. P. Goldberg, *Women, Work, and Life Cycle in a Medieval Economy* (Oxford, 1992).

54 Karl Marx, *Capital: A Critique of Political Economy*, vol. 1, trans. by Ben Fowkes (New York, 1977).

55 This is in Frederich Engels, *The Origin of the Family, Private Property, and the State* (New York, 1972, originally published 1884).

56 Alice Clark, *Working Life of Women in the Seventeenth Century* (London, 1992, originally published 1919).

57 Howell, *Women, Production, and Patriarchy*.

58 Karl Bucher, *Die Fraunfrage im Mittelalter* (Berlin, 1882); Bennett, "Medieval Women, Modern Women," p. 151.

59 See Judith Bennett's comments in her review article, "History that Still Stands," pp. 269–83.

60 Bennett, "Medieval Women, Modern Women," pp. 154, 158, 168.

61 Judith Brown and Jordan Goodman, "Women and Industry in Florence," *Journal of Economic History* 40, 1 (1980): 73–80.

62 Glickl bas Judah Leib, *The Memoirs of Glückel of Hameln*, trans. by Marvin Lowenthal (New York, 1977); Natalie Zemon Davis, *Women on the Margins: Three Seventeenth-Century Lives* (Cambridge, MA, 1995).

63 Martha Howell and Robert Duplessis, "Reconsidering the Early Modern Urban Economy: The Cases of Leiden and Lille," *Past and Present* 94 (1982): 49–84.

64 Judith Brown, "A Woman's Place Was in the Home: Woman's Work in Renaissance Tuscany," in *Rewriting the Renaissance: The Discourses of Sexual Difference in Early Modern Europe*, ed. by Margaret W. Ferguson, Maureen Quilligan, and Nancy J. Vickers (Chicago, 1986) p. 222.

65 Wiesner, *Women and Gender*, pp. 213–63 and *Gender, Church, and State in Early Modern Germany* (New York, 1998), pp. 31–78.

66 M. King, *Women of the Renaissance*, p. 86; Kate J. P. Lowe, *Nuns' Chronicles and Convent Culture in Renaissance and Counter-Reformation Italy* (New York, 2003).

67 M. King, *Women of the Renaissance*, p. 89.

68 Craig Monson, *Disembodied Voices: Music and Culture in an Early Modern Italian Convent* (Berkeley, 1995).

69 An excellent and comprehensive guide to the current literature on convents is in Sharon T. Strocchia, "Convent Culture," in Oxford Bibliographies Online.

70 Elissa B. Weaver, *Convent Theater in Early Modern Italy: Spiritual Fun and Learning for Women* (Cambridge, 2001).
71 Silvia Evangelisti, *Nuns: A History of Convent Life, 1450–1700* (Oxford, 2007); Lowe, *Nuns' Chronicles*, p. 2; Sharon T. Strocchia, "Naming a Nun: Spiritual Exemplars and Corporate Identity in Florentine Convents, 1450–1530," in *Society and Individual in Renaissance Florence*, ed. by William Connell (Berkeley and Los Angeles, 2003), pp. 215–40 and *Nuns and Nunneries in Renaissance Florence* (Baltimore, 2009), pp. 72–151.
72 Konrad Eisenbichler, "Italian Scholarship on Pre-Modern Confraternities in Italy," *Renaissance Quarterly* 50, 2 (Summer 1997): 567–80; Walter Simons, *Cities of Ladies: Beguine Communities in the Medieval Low Countries, 1200–1565* (Philadelphia, 2001); Sharon T. Strocchia, "Sisters in Spirit: The Nuns of Sant' Ambrogio and Their Consorority in Early Sixteenth-Century Florence," *Sixteenth Century Journal* 33 (2002): 745–77.
73 Gabriella Zarri, *Le sante vive: Profezie di corte e devozione femminile tra '400 e '500* (Turin, 1990) and *Recinti: Donne, clausura e matrimonio nella prima età moderna* (Bologna, 2000); Lerner, *Creation of Feminist Consciousness*.
74 Margaret L. King and Albert Rabil, Jr, *Teaching Other Voices: Women and Religion in Early Modern Europe* (Chicago, 2007). For Catherine, see F. Thomas Luongo, *The Saintly Politics of Catherine of Siena* (Ithaca, 2006).
75 Gillian T. W. Ahlgren, *Teresa of Avila and the Politics of Sanctity* (Ithaca, 1996); Jodi Bilinkoff, *The Avila of Saint Teresa: Religious Reform in a Sixteenth-Century City* (Ithaca, 1989); Alison Weber, "Spiritual Administration: Gender and Discernment in the Carmelite Reform," *Sixteenth Century Journal* 31, 1 (Spring 2000): 123–46.
76 King and Rabil, *Teaching Other Voices*, p. 7; Barbara Diefendorf, *From Penitence to Charity: Pious Women and the Catholic Reformation in Paris* (Oxford, 2004).
77 Caroline Walker Bynum, *Holy Feast and Holy Fast: The Religious Significance of Food to Medieval Women* (Berkeley and Los Angeles, 1987).
78 Dyan Elliott, *Spiritual Marriage: Sexual Abstinence in Medieval Wedlock* (Princeton, 1993).
79 Lerner, *Creation of Feminist Consciousness*, p. 93; Bonnie S. Anderson and Judith P. Zinsser, *A History of Their Own*, vol. 1 (New York, 2000).
80 Natalie Zemon Davis, "City Women and Religious Change," in *Society and Culture in Early Modern France* (Stanford, 1965), pp. 108, 118, 119.
81 N. Z. Davis, "City Women," p. 111.
82 M. King, *Women of the Renaissance*, p. 137.
83 Carolyn C. Wilson, *St. Joseph in Italian Renaissance Society and Art: New Directions and Interpretations* (Philadelphia, 2001).
84 Alan Charles Kors and Edward Peters, eds., *Witchcraft in Europe, 400–1700* (Philadelphia, 2001), p. 2; Wiesner, *Women and Gender*, p. 222.
85 M. King, *Women of the Renaissance*, p. 146.
86 Brian P. Levack, *The Witch Hunt in Early Modern Europe* (New York, 1987); Moshe Sluhovsky, *Believe Not Every Spirit: Possession, Mysticism, and Discernment in Early Modern Catholicism* (Chicago, 2007). For the medieval connection

between women and the inquisition, see Dyan Elliott, "Seeing Double: John Gerson, the Discernment of Spirits, and Joan of Arc," *American Historical Review* 107 (Feb. 2002): 26.

87 Wiesner, *Women and Gender*, p. 270; M. King, *Women of the Renaissance*, p. 145.

88 Eric Midelfort, *Witch Hunting in Southwestern Germany, 1562–1684* (Stanford, 1972).

89 Elspeth Whitney, "The Witch 'She'/The Historian 'He': Gender and the Historiography of the Witch Hunts," *Journal of Women's History* 7 (1995): 77–101; Christina Larner, *Enemies of God: The Witch Hunt in Scotland* (London, 1981).

90 M. King, *Women of the Renaissance*, p. 144.

91 Mary Daly, *Gyn/Ecology* (London, 1979); Marianne Hester, *Lewd Women and Wicked Witches: A Study of the Dynamics of Male Domination* (London, 1992); Deborah Willis, *Malevolent Nature: Witch Hunting and Maternal Power in Early Modern England* (Ithaca, 1995).

92 Robert Muchembled, *Popular Culture and Elite Culture in France 1450–1750* (Baton Rouge, 1985).

93 Lyndal Roper, *Oedipus and the Devil: Witchcraft, Sexuality in Early Modern Europe* (London, 1994), pp. 199–225.

94 M. King, *Women of the Renaissance*, p. 148.

95 Susanna Burghartz, "The Equation of Women and Witches: A Case Study of Witchcraft Trials in Lucerne and Lusanne in the Fifteenth and Sixteenth Centuries," in *The German Underworld; Deviants and Outcasts in German History*, Richard J. Evans (New York, 1998).

96 William E. Monter, *Witchcraft in France and Switzerland: The Borderlands during the Reformation* (Ithaca, 1976), p. 17.

97 King and Rabil, *Teaching Other Voices*, p. xvii; Gisela Bock, *Women in European History*, pp. 2–4; Albert Rabil, "Querelle des femmes," in *Encyclopedia of the Renaissance*, ed. by Paul Grendler, vol. 6 (New York, 1999), pp. 195–6.

98 Lerner, *Creation of Feminist Consciousness*, p. 146; Joan Kelly. "Early Feminist Theory and the Querelle des Femmes," in *Women, History and Theory: The Essays of Joan Kelly* (Chicago, 1984), pp. 65–109.

99 Elissa B. Weaver, "Gender," in Ruggiero, *Worlds of the Renaissance*, p. 204.

100 Bock, *Women in European History*, pp. 2–12.

101 King and Rabil, *Teaching Other Voices*, p. xvi; M. King, *Women of the Renaissance*, p. 220.

102 De Pizan, *City of Ladies*, p. 24.

103 See Giovanni Boccaccio, *Famous Women*, trans. and ed. by Virginia Brown (Cambridge, MA, 2001). See also Stephen Kolsky, *The Ghost of Boccaccio: Writings on Famous Women in Renaissance Italy* (Turnhout, 2005).

104 Isotta Nogarola, *Complete Writings*, ed. and trans. by Margaret L. King and Diana Robin (Chicago, 2004), pp. 138–58.

105 Bock, *Women in European History*, p. 4.

106 Weaver, "Gender," pp. 198–9; Bock, *Women in European History*, p. 3; Heinrich Agrippa, *Declamation on the Nobility and Preeminence of Women*, trans. by Albert Rabil Jr (Chicago, 1996).

107 Valeria Finucci, *The Lady Vanishes: Subjectivity and Representation in Castiglione* (Stanford, 1992). The discussion has included consideration of the historical context of participants, see William Connell, "Gasparo and the Ladies," *Quaderni d'Italianista* 23 (2002) and John Najemy, "Gianozzo and the Elders," in Connell, *Society and Individual.*

108 Bock, *Women in European History*, p. 13.

109 Jacqueline Musacchio, in Lowe and Dean, eds., *Marriage in Italy, 1300–1650* (Cambridge, 1998); Rona Goffen, *Titian's Women* (New Haven, 1997); Paola Tinagli, *Women in the Italian Renaissance* (ch. 1) (Manchester, 1997); Cristelle Baskins, *Cassone Painting, Humanism and Gender in Early Modern Italy* (Cambridge, 1998).

110 Wiesner, *Women and Gender*, pp. 143–52; M. King, *Women of the Renaissance*, pp. 164–88: Rosemary O'Day, *Education and Society, 1500–1800: The Social Foundation of Education in Early Modern Britain* (New York, 1982); Paul Grendler, "Education in the Renaissance and Reformation," *Renaissance Quarterly* 43 (1990): 774–824; Suzanne Hull, *Chaste, Silent and Obedient: English Books for Women, 1475–1640* (San Marino, CA, 1982).

111 David Cressy, *Education in Tudor and Stuart England* (London, 1975); Judith Bryce, "'Les livres des Florentines': Reconsidering Women's Literacy in Quattrocento Florence," in *At the Margins: Minority Groups in Pre-Modern Italy*, ed. by Stephen J. Milner (Minneapolis, 2005), pp. 131–61; and Sharon T. Strocchia, "Learning the Virtues: Convent Schools and Female Culture in Renaissance Florence," in *Women's Education in Early Modern Europe: A History, 1500–1800*, ed. by Barbara J. Whitehead (New York, 1999), pp. 3–46.

112 Pier Paolo Vergerio, "Defining Liberal Learning, 1403," in *Vittorino da Feltro and Other Humanist Educators*, ed. by W. H. Woodward (Cambridge, 1897), pp. 102–9.

113 Juan Luis Vives, *The Education of a Christian Woman*, ed. and trans. by Charles Fantazzi (Chicago, 2000); Wiesner, *Gender and History*, p. 153.

114 Patricia H. Labalme, ed., *Beyond Their Sex: Learned Women of the European Past* (New York, 1984).

115 M. King, *Women of the Renaissance*, p. 201.

116 Albert Rabil Jr, *Laura Cereta: Quattrocento Humanist* (Binghamton, NY, 1981); *Laura Cereta: Collected Letters of a Renaissance Feminist*, transcribed, trans., and ed. by Diana Robin (Chicago, 1997).

117 *Cassandra Fedele: Letters and Orations*, ed. and trans. by Diana Robin (Chicago, 2000).

118 Margaret King has called Isotta Nogarola the first major woman humanist in Italy. Nogarola, *Complete Writings*, p. 9.

119 Anna Maria van Schurman, *Whether a Christian Woman Should Be Educated and Other Writings from Her Intellectual Circle*, ed. by Joyce L. Irwin (Chicago, 1998); Wiesner, *Women and Gender*, pp. 160–3.

120 Constance Jordan, "Feminism and the Humanists," in *Rewriting the Renaissance: The Discourse of Sexual Difference in Early Modern Europe*, ed. by Margaret Ferguson et al. (Chicago, 1986), pp. 242–58.

121 Mary D. Garrard, *Artemisia Gentileschi: The Image of the Female Hero in Italian Baroque Art* (Princeton, 1989).
122 Frima Fox Hofrichter, *Judith Leyster: A Woman Painter in Holland's Golden Age* (Coornpijk, 1989).
123 M. King, *Women of the Renaissance*, pp. 199, 205; Frederika H. Jacobs. "The Construction of a Life: Madonna Properzia de' Rossi 'Scultrice Bolognese,'" *Word and Image* 9, 2 (Apr.–June 1993): 122–3; Anne Jacobson Schutte, "Irene di Spilimbergo: The Image of a Creative Woman in Late Renaissance Italy," *Renaissance Quarterly* 44, 1 (Spring 1991): 42–61.
124 Lerner, *Creation of Feminist Consciousness*, p. 197.
125 Wiesner, *Gender and History*, p. 156.
126 Margaret L. King, "Book-Lined Cells: Women and Humanism in the Early Italian Renaissance," in Labalme, *Beyond their Sex*.
127 Deborah Marrow, *The Art Patronage of Maria de' Medici* (Ann Arbor, 1982); M. King, *Women of the Renaissance*, pp. 160–1.
128 Werner L. Gundersheimer, "Women, Learning and Power: Eleanora of Aragon and the Court of Ferrara," in Labalme, *Beyond their Sex*, pp. 43–65; Rose Marie San Juan, "The Court Lady's Dilemma: Isabella D'Este and Art Collecting in the Renaissance," *Oxford Art Journal* 14 (1991): 67–78; Joyce de Vries, "Caterina Sforza's Portrait Medals: Power, Gender and Representation in the Italian Renaissance Court," *Women's Art Journal* 24 (2003): 23–8.
129 Wiesner, *Women and Gender*, p. 170.
130 Clifford Brown, "A Ferrarese Lady and a Mantuan Marchesa: The Art and Antiquities Collection of Isabella d'Este Conzaga (1474–1539)," in *Women and Art in Early Modern Europe*, ed. by Cynthia Lawrence (University Park, PA, 1997), pp. 53–71; for a negative view of Isabella's patronage, see David Chambers, *Patrons and Artists in the Italian Renaissance* (New York, 1971).
131 Allison Mary Levy, ed., *Widowhood and Visual Culture in Early Modern Europe* (Hampshire, UK, 2003).
132 Patricia Skinner, *Women in Medieval Italian Society* (London, 2001).
133 Constance Jordan, ed., *Renaissance Feminism: Literary Texts and Political Models* (Ithaca, 1990); Annette Dixon, ed., *Women Who Ruled: Queens, Goddesses, Amazons in Renaissance and Baroque Art* (Ann Arbor, 2002).
134 Carole Levin, "Power, Politics and Sexuality: Images of Elizabeth I," in Jean Brink, ed., *The Politics of Gender in Early Modern Europe* (Kirksville, MO, 1989); Leah Marcus, "Shakespeare's Comic Heroines: Elizabeth I and the Political Uses of Androgyny," in *Women in the Middle Ages and Renaissance: Literary and Historical Perspectives*, ed. by Mary Beth Rose (Syracuse, 1986), pp. 135–54; J. N. King, "Queen Elizabeth I: Representations of the Virgin Queen," *Renaissance Quarterly* 43 (Spring 1990): 30–74; Mary Beth Rose, "The Gendering of Authority in the Public Speeches of Elizabeth I," *PMLA* 115, 5 (Oct. 2000): 1077–82; Louis A. Montrose, "Idols of the Queen: Policy, Gender, and the Picturing of Elizabeth I," *Representations* 68 (Autumn 1999): 108–61.
135 Frances A. Yates, "Queen Elizabeth as Astraea," *Journal of Warburg and Courtauld Institutes* 10 (1947): 27–82.

136 Maureen Quilligan, *The Allegory of Female Authority: Christine de Pizan's Cité des Dames* (Ithaca, 1991).

137 Alexandra Carpino, "Margaret of Austria's Funerary Complex at Brou," in Lawrence, Women and Art, pp. 37–52; Andrea G. Pearson, "Margaret of Austria's Devotional Portrait Diptychs," *Women's Art Journal* 22 (2001): 19–25; Dagmat Eichberger, "Margaret of Austria's Portrait Collection: Female Patronage in Light of Dynastic Ambitions and Artistic Quality," *Renaissance Studies* 10, 2 (1996): 259–79.

138 Natalie Zemon Davis, "Women on Top," in *Society and Culture in Early Modern France* (Princeton, 1975), pp. 124–51.

139 Jürgen Habermas, *The Structural Transformation of the Public Sphere: An Inquiry into a Category of Bourgeois Society* (Cambridge, 1989); Wiesner, *Gender and History*, pp. 166–7.

140 Catherine Stimpson, *Rewriting the Renaissance* (Chicago, 1986), p. vii.

141 Meg Lota Brown and Kari Boyd McBride, *Women's Roles in the Renaissance* (Westport, CT, 2005).

142 Hufton, *Prospect Before Her*.

143 Weaver, "Gender," pp. 188–9.

144 Bennett, "Medieval Women, Modern Women," in *Culture and History, 1350–1600*, ed. by David Aers (London 1992), pp. 147–75: Gisela Bock, "Challenging Dichotomies: Perspectives on Women's History," in *Writing Women's History: International Perspectives*, ed. by Karen Offen, Ruth Roach Pierson, and Jane Rendall (Bloomington, 1990), pp. 1–24.

145 Susan Mosher Stuard, "Fashion's Captives: Women in French Historiography," in *Women in Medieval History and Historiography*, ed. by Susan M. Stuard (Philadelphia, 1987), pp. 59–80.

4

Humanism: Renovation or Innovation? Transmission or Reception?

Read over the poems, consider the letters, and think about the books which Petrarch [. . .] brought forth when he was alive [. . .] contemplate his eloquence, for by its means he clearly demonstrated the preeminence it has among all other humanistic studies. I have reserved praise for it until the end, since, in my judgment, it seems the greatest thing there is. For what can be better than to be the master of the emotions, to bend your auditor to where you might want and to bring him back from that place, filled with gratitude and love.

Coluccio Salutati[1]

Humanism has long stood at the core of the Renaissance debate. Scholars have viewed it not only as an intellectual prime mover, but as a unifying feature by which the Renaissance was transmitted, received and transformed into a pan-European phenomenon. According to Roberto Weiss's well-known definition, humanism "conditioned every aspect of what we now call the Renaissance."[2] It formed a bridge linking political, intellectual, literary and artistic developments. Consequently, no facet of the Renaissance has been more thoroughly studied, both in its Italian and European context.[3]

But if humanism was a critical component of the Renaissance, its precise nature has been the source of much disagreement. Scholars debate its characteristics, its relationship to its intellectual forebears, its value as an educational program as well as the ways it was altered and shaped over time and change of geographical locus. The task of separating fact from fiction is made more difficult by the claims of the humanists themselves, who portrayed their work as innovative and as constituting a break from a sterile "medieval" past. Their study of classics was nevertheless inherently backward looking and imitative, raising the question of just how original the movement actually was. The issue is a concern for modern university teachers who need to explain to their students the broad appeal, enormous enthusiasm, and widespread influence of humanism.[4]

Discussions have often begun with an evaluation of the word itself. Humanism, like "individualism," is a vague term, whose very haziness, as one prominent scholar noted, has given it a "universal and irresistible" appeal.[5] The word was not coined in the Renaissance, but in the nineteenth century by the German secondary school teacher F. J. Niethammer, who used it as a synonym for Greek and Latin classical studies then coming into vogue in schools. The literary critic Mathew Arnold popularized the term in English, whence it was appropriated by Anglophone scholars and applied to the revival of interest in classics during the Renaissance period.[6] Early writers such as Karl Hagen (d. 1870), Georg Voigt (d. 1891), Paul Joachimsen (d. 1930), Remigio Sabbadini (d. 1934), and Giovanni Gentile (d. 1944) treated humanism as a comprehensive intellectual Renaissance movement that conditioned all aspects of learning.[7] They associated it (especially Gentile) with a new view of mankind, captured in the famous assertion by Giovanni Pico della Mirandola (1463–1494) of the worth and "dignity of man." A next generation of scholars, including Hans Baron, Eugenio Garin, and Roberto Weiss, nuanced and gave firmer root to the broad interpretation. Garin described humanism as a transformative intellectual movement akin to German idealism of the nineteenth century.[8] The analysis matched well Jules Michelet's association of the Renaissance with the "discovery of mankind," and Burckhardt's stress on egoistic individualism and modernity, though neither writer was interested in humanism per se. In an influential early textbook, Sem Dresden described humanism as "the movement that brought modern Europe into being."[9]

The equation of humanism with modernity has had many implications, including a tendency to see in it as an antithesis of Christianity and the starting point of modern science (see chapter 7). The present discussion will focus on the originality of the movement, its relationship with the past, its transformation as it moved throughout Europe. The recent historiography has tended to accept the complexities and contradictions rather than attempt to resolve them. It treats the Renaissance "revival of classics" in terms of prior medieval revivals and views renovation and innovation as not mutually exclusive. Scholars accept, if not the originality of Renaissance humanists, the singularity of their contributions to various fields, especially education.

Humanism and Scholasticism

In his account of the Renaissance revival of interest in classical antiquity, Georg Voigt, the first serious student of humanism, contrasted the movement to its intellectual predecessor, scholasticism, which, since the thirteenth century, dominated university curricula and was "emblematic" of medieval thought. Scholasticism involved study of the classics, but with a Christian agenda, intended to better understand the faith in terms of the work of the Greek philosopher Aristotle. Humanism, by contrast, was representative of Renaissance thought. According to Berthold Ullmann it "canceled" scholasticism, substituting, in Voigt's formulation, the "dry and pedantic cathedral of ideas" of scholasticism" with "more concrete researches."[10] The father of the new approach, Francis Petrarch, condemned scholasticism in his writings and subsequent humanists followed his lead. Antagonisms reached an apex in Northern European universities in the sixteenth century, where humanist professors denounced their scholastic colleagues as "barbarian thickheads" and scholastic professors condemned humanists as "speechifiers" and "Greeklings"[11]

The extent of the distinction between scholasticism and humanism was an early point of contention among scholars. For Eugenio Garin, the difference was essential to establishing humanism's superiority over its predecessor and its dignity as a full-fledged intellectual movement. If humanism was not its own philosophical system then the Renaissance was inferior to the Middle Ages. Garin's contemporary, Paul Oscar Kristeller, limited the distance between the two movements and the scope of humanism more generally. In a series of influential essays over a distinguished career, Kristeller argued that humanism was not inherently antagonistic to scholasticism.[12] Scholastics concerned themselves with philosophy, and the search for truth, while humanists focused on grammar and rhetoric. The humanist interest in grammar and rhetoric grew from the medieval tradition of *dictatores*, professional rhetoricians, who practiced the art of composing documents, particularly public letters and speeches. The humanist agenda was thus educational, aimed at achieving eloquence by study of the classics. To this end humanists studied different texts than scholastics, showing especial preference for work of the Roman orator and politician Cicero. Humanists also studied Greek texts, but unlike scholastics, they worked from the originals, rather than use Latin versions.[13]

Important to Kristeller's revision was a reexamination of the term humanism. Although the word did not exist in Renaissance times, its cognate "humanist" (*umanista*) did. *Umanista* was used at Italian universities in the fifteenth century as student slang for a teacher of grammar and rhetoric. It derived from the term "*studia humanitatis*," used in classical times to denote a literary education. Cicero referred to "*studia humanitatis*" in *Pro Archaia* as a course of liberal arts that emphasized eloquence for the purpose of participation in government service. In Italian universities, *studia humanitatis* included grammar, rhetoric, poetry, history, and moral philosophy.[14] It did not, however, encompass the whole of the medieval tradition of the liberal arts, which consisted also of arithmetic and geometry and astronomy and music (the so-called *quadrivium*).

For Kristeller then, style and eloquence gave humanism its distinctive quality. Humanists were teachers of *studia humanitatis* and thus did not represent a philosophical school. Their work was separate from other currents of Renaissance thought such as Platonism and Aristotelianism, which were philosophical and also flourished in the period. "I should like to understand Renaissance humanism at least in its origins as a broad cultural and literary movement," Kristeller wrote, "which in its substance was not philosophical, but had important philosophical implications and consequences." The thesis, although distinct from that of Georg Voigt, nevertheless provided support for the earlier scholar's observation that despite the high sounding claims of humanists, their actual work did not always appear particularly creative or original.[15] Humanists were not *bad* philosophers; they were not philosophers at all.

Kristeller's interpretation has remained a point of departure for study. It appears in undergraduate textbooks and general works, which usually treat Renaissance humanism and philosophy as separate entities. It has provided impetus for scholarly studies that examine more closely humanism's continuities with the Middle Ages. Historians have searched for the roots of humanism in the medieval study of grammar and in educational treatises and practices. They have scrutinized teaching methods and grammar books as well as the careers of important figures who predated Petrarch. Ronald Witt traced successive stages of the development of humanism back to the eleventh and twelfth centuries. He noted the important influence of the French revival of grammar and poetry in the twelfth century, which constituted "a veritable cultural invasion from the north" that inspired a first generation of Italian humanism, most evident in the city of Padua in the work of Lovato dei Lovati (1240–1309) and Albertino Mussato (1261–1329), a notary and judge respectively, who wrote poetry on the model of Seneca. The men, traditionally viewed as "pre-" or "proto-" humanist figures, were, according to Witt, full-fledged humanists.[16] Petrarch represented a next generation of humanism in which Cicero became the model for oration and private letter writing and civic and religious issues grew more important. Robert Black has taken a similarly long view, stressing the influence of twelfth-century France on Italian developments. But he saw humanism as a reaction against French cultural hegemony, which had led to a decline in interest in classical studies in thirteenth-century Italy. Italian humanism grew from the legal profession, which restored Latin grammar.[17]

The revision has allowed humanism to retain its importance as a distinctive Renaissance development, while narrowing the gap with the Middle Ages. But the reassessment must be understood as distinct from a "revolt of medievalists," which occurred earlier and on its own terms. There is in fact considerable divergence between the work of medievalists and Renaissance scholars with regard to humanism. The two employ the same term, but they do not in fact interpret it in the same manner; nor do they draw on the same scholarly tradition. Charles Homer Haskins, writing before Kristeller, applied humanism in a very broad sense to the Middle Ages, making it a synonym for "the revival of the study of Latin classics" and thus a fundamental part of his "twelfth century Renaissance." He applied the term to a wide array of men, including John the Scot in the ninth century, John of Salisbury in the twelfth as well as contemporary glossators of texts.[18] Étienne Gilson equated humanism with the study of Latin and Greek classics and an appreciation for the dignity of man and love of nature. He saw this as reflected most directly in monastic culture, which joined the dignity of man and nature with love of God.[19] Walter Ullmann and Richard Southern argued in similar fashion that man found in God's humanity an appreciation of his own (see chapter 2).[20] Ullmann looked closely at political and legal factors, arguing that medieval humanism's roots lay in the "secularization" society, which began with the Investiture Controversy in the eleventh century. Richard Southern looked more closely at notions of friendship between man and God engendered both in the monastery and in cathedral schools and universities in the twelfth century.[21] Southern used the term "medieval humanism" in the title of his study and later coined the term "scholastic humanism" to describe intellectual trends during the period from 1100 to 1300. He compared John of Salisbury (d. 1180) directly to Petrarch noting their common devotion to Cicero and to rhetoric and eloquence.[22]

Southern's interpretation has been highly influential among medievalists, and the phrase "medieval humanism" remains current. But Southern's work did not gain similar traction among Renaissance scholars. This is largely because Southern did not position his thesis in terms of the Renaissance scholarly tradition. His definitions of humanism do not take into account Kristeller's work. Thus the two seminal works in the fields have little common ground and the discourses have proceeded separately, a fact so glaring that scholars rarely address the issue explicitly.

Philology, History, and the Search for Manuscripts

What seems generally agreed upon by Renaissance scholars is that humanism, whatever its starting point, involved the study of rhetoric and grammar and in so doing led to advances in other fields, such as philology, textual criticism, and historical writing.[23] Medieval writers, even the best of them, treated language in a haphazard way. Richard Southern allowed John of Salisbury "the outline" of Petrarch and Erasmus, but he admitted that

Salisbury ultimately treated classical sources with "sovereign indifference" to the actual aims of the authors.[24] Renaissance humanists introduced the notion of the study of language in context and of historical continuity. Their emphasis on rhetoric willy nilly forced them to examine carefully texts, to critique and understand language in its context. For William Bouwsma, this made the study of rhetoric itself intellectually transformative, bringing with it an appreciation of humanity, and a new concept of man, which provided coherency for the whole humanist movement.[25] Petrarch studied Ciceronian rhetoric and eloquence in the hope of attaining wisdom. His keen knowledge of the Latin language allowed him to reconstruct Livy's *History of Rome*, which had been dispersed since antiquity. Lorenzo Valla (d. 1457), the greatest Latinist of the next generation, used his critical linguistic skills to make further emendations to Petrarch's Livy, with the result that the *History of Rome* was largely restored to its original state.

Lorenzo Valla has, with Petrarch, been viewed as a key figure in humanism. His unparalleled understanding of Latin in historical context helped initiate the field of philology. His *Elegances of the Latin Language* (1440) was a popular guide to classical Latin usage and style, and *Emendationes Livianae*, a critique of Livy, demonstrated that the Roman historian sometimes got his facts wrong. In *Declamation on the Forged Donation of Constantine* (1440), Valla employed his skills at Latin to cast doubt on the "Donation of Constantine," by which popes claimed the right to their territorial state and political authority. Valla concluded that the document contained corrupted Latin usages (including the post-classical term *banna* for flag rather than the classical Roman word *vexillum*) that were not from the era of the Emperor Constantine in the fourth century, the supposed date of its composition, but from the seventh century.

The Florentine Angelo Poliziano (1454–1494) gave similar emphasis to philology in his works with Greek texts. In *Miscellanies* (1489) a collection of critical essays, Poliziano employed close textual examination, treating the oldest manuscript as the most reliable and checking Latin translations against Greek ones. His editions of the works of Greek classical authors were done with such care and erudition that many are still used by scholars today.

As Poliziano's example shows, the study of Greek was by the fifteenth century a fundamental part of the humanist program. Petrarch had tried to learn the language in the fourteenth century, but could not find a suitable teacher. But access and facility grew steadily, stimulated by the creation of a chair in Greek studies at the University of Florence in 1397, the arrival of Greek scholars at Western church councils (notably the Council of Ferrara-Florence, 1438–9) and ultimately the fall of Constantinople in 1453. Humanists eventually undertook the study of Hebrew and other ancient languages, which allowed them direct access to the bible and patristic texts as well as Jewish writings of the Kabbalah.

The study of language and of classical texts would not have been possible, however, without the availability of the ancient manuscripts themselves. Much humanist activity was devoted to recovering the "lost" texts. Humanists searched monasteries and libraries throughout Europe, in what became a form of intellectual sport. Petrarch found works by Livy, Cicero, and Tacitus, and at the time of his death had a personal library consisting of two hundred manuscripts. The Florentine humanist Poggio Bracciolini found important manuscripts in southern German monasteries at Reichenau and St Gall; his counterpart Niccolò Niccoli sent representatives as far as Denmark to acquire ancient works and was willing to "sell his farms" and personal properties to pay for them.[26] When the Byzantine scholar Manuel Chrysoloras took up his professorship in Greek studies in Florence, he brought with him numerous Greek texts, including editions of Plutarch's *Lives* and Plato's *Dialogues* (see chapter 2).

The rediscovery of the work of classical historians such as Livy, Tacitus, and Sallust encouraged humanists, as Felix Gilbert has argued, to study historical writing as an independent literary genre.[27] Medieval histories divided time in terms of Christianity. Humanists divided time according to the classical manner, by year and, like classical authors, took as subject matter wars with the inclusion of dialogue and omens.[28] Humanists conceived of history in moral terms, as a guide providing practical lessons for contemporary life. The humanist Pier Paolo Vergerio argued that history bestowed on people "the light of experience and cumulative wisdom."[29] Leonardo Bruni wrote that history made men "both wiser and more moderate."[30]

Like the classical authors, humanist historians often wrote about their native states, regions, and cities. Bruni wrote a history of his native Florence, as did Poggio Bracciolini and Niccolò Machiavelli. The Venetian humanist Bernardo Giustiniani (1408–1489) wrote about Venice; Jacob Wimpheling of Alsace, his home, and the Frenchman Robert Gaguin wrote a history of France.

Humanist history nevertheless betrayed the ambiguities of the humanist agenda. In applying classical forms to contemporary events, writers often constrained the new circumstances to fit old ones, placing new institutions and even new people in old classical categories (see chapter 2). What was unique about humanist history was its awareness that the present was distinct from the past.[31]

An Educational Revolution?

Humanists actively promoted themselves and their new ideas. Petrarch called for educational reform and the abandonment of "outdated" pedagogical ways, but gave few concrete proposals. He nevertheless inspired others, including Giovanni Conversini of Ravenna (1343–1408), who hired himself out as tutor to the households of the ruling families in Padua and Ferrara and Pier Paolo Vergerio of Padua, who wrote *On Noble Customs and Liberal Studies* (1403), the first treatise that explicitly laid out the humanist educational program. Vergerio placed emphasis on the importance of grammar, rhetoric, and eloquence as a means of forming good moral character for the purposes of public service. He dedicated the work to the son of the ruler of Padua and intended humanist studies for the (male) children of the elite (see chapter 3).[32]

The first decades of the fifteenth century saw the establishment of several humanist secondary schools in Italy. Gasparino Barzizza (1360–1430) of Bergamo opened an academy for the private instruction of boys at his house, and served also as tutor at the Visconti court at Pavia. Barzizza's student, Vittorino da Feltre, founded schools in Venice in 1421 and in Mantua in 1423 for court officials and the children of the ruler. Guarino Guarini (1374–1460) established a school in Ferrara, and authored a well-known humanist grammar book, *Regulae grammaticales* (1418), to replace the standard medieval work by the fifth–century grammarian Donatus. Guarino, who had studied in Constantinople, gave prominent place in his curriculum to Greek.

The schools helped establish humanistic studies among the ruling Italian elite and helped make courts early centers of humanist activity. Vittorino's academy counted among its alumni Lorenzo Valla and Federico II, duke of Urbino, the latter an important patron of humanists. States actively sought humanist educators, a trend attributed to "competitiveness" within the ruling classes. The "loose" structure of Italian education, which was not dominated by the church as in Northern Europe but controlled instead by secular powers and local governments, allowed states to respond quickly to incipient trends, permitting humanism to flourish. Humanist education often required little more than a single teacher or tutor.

The activities of the schools and teachers have led some scholars to speak of "an educational revolution" in Italy. They argue that academies represented a distinctly new Renaissance era in pedagogy. In addition to inculcating social and personal values on classical models, the schools taught in innovative ways. They eschewed the medieval tradition of rote memorization, requiring students instead to understand what they read. Students composed original pieces in Latin, a practice advocated by Guarino in his grammar book. According to Paul Grendler, this humanist curriculum fitted into the larger Italian educational system, which included also vernacular schools, which taught the abacus and rudimentary skills for the children of the merchant class. The educational revolution allowed the Renaissance to become "a cohesive cultural and historical epoch of great achievement."[33]

Other scholars have, however, called into question the revolutionary nature of the humanist educational program. Anthony Grafton and Lisa Jardine have argued that the reality of the humanists' achievements fell short of their claims.[34] They depict humanist teaching methods as both derivative and tedious, with much *de facto* emphasis on medieval style memorization and attention to the petty grammatical rules of Latin. Using Guarini's grammar book and student notes, Grafton and Jardine claim that humanist instruction had "more to do with its appropriateness as a commodity than with its intrinsic intellectual merits." Guarini's grammar book, though shorter than its medieval counterparts, used the same scholastic terminology as well as similar mnemonic devices. Students gained skills that allowed only the appearance of erudition. Rather than wisdom and independent thought, the course of studies was intended to promote "obedience and docility," qualities that Renaissance rulers found desirable in hiring them for public service.

Paul Grendler has maintained that, on the contrary, humanist education constituted a distinct break from the past.[35] While conceding that the course of studies required much drill and exercise, he doubted that what seems drudgery to modern critics was actually drudgery to the students. He compared the study of Latin in the schools with the study of music and athletic training nowadays, requiring practice that could easily appear tedious to the outsider. He argued that the values inherent in the subjects taught in the humanist schools inevitably had an impact on students. Collectively they instilled personal and social values distinct from the medieval past and in this regard were innovative.

Both sides of the debate evaluate humanist education in terms of the present day. Robert Black has advocated a more contextual approach, examining closely the teaching manuals that were used at the time, both in famous and lesser-known educational centers. From this vantage, humanist education appears less innovative with respect to its antecedents, but nevertheless distinct on its own terms.[36] Humanists accepted much of the medieval educational program, particularly its philological emphasis. But Italian humanists "revived" classical grammar, after the widespread adoption of anticlassical texts in the thirteenth century. Thus humanist educators may be credited, by the second half and end of the fifteenth century, with overseeing the widespread restoration of Cicero and Virgil.

Transmission and Reception

The Italian schools nevertheless provided an important means of transmitting humanism and making it a more wide spread movement. The teachers were mobile men, taking employ where they found opportunity. "Teachers should keep their ears open to new invitations [...]" wrote Giovanni Conversini, "for when they stay too long in one place their authority declines and they are considered worthless."[37] Students were also mobile. Italian schools attracted young scholars from throughout Europe, including the Hungarian Janus Pannonius (1424–1472), the German Peter Luder (1415–1472), and the Englishman John Tiptoft, earl of Worcester (1427–1470), all of whom studied with Guarino. The papacy played a key role.[38] The massive papal bureaucracy required literate men to run it and became a source of jobs for humanists. Clerics traveled throughout Europe, to church councils, spreading new ideas. Petrarch was supported for much of his career by clerical benefice and gained his initial love of classics at the papal court in Avignon.

The movement of humanist ideas was further aided by the invention of the printing press in the middle of the fifteenth century. It brought classical and humanist texts directly to readers – to physicians, theologians, jurists, and other educated people, who formed the intellectual audience for the new ideas. The presses allowed the classical revival to transcend the Mediterranean, and thus, unlike prior intellectual revivals, become a truly European phenomenon. The presses popularized Columbus's discovery of America and gave wide circulation to Vespucci's learned letters describing the New World.[39] They allowed Desiderius Erasmus, the "prince" of the humanists, to become an international figure, whose reputation and livelihood is owed largely to the popularity of his books (see chapter 2). They made the controversy arising from Johannes Reuchlin's study of Jewish cabalistic texts in southern Germany an international debate that involved humanists from throughout Europe.

Elizabeth Eisenstein considered the printing press the most significant innovation of the Renaissance. She argued that the sheer volume of production changed the "literary diet" of sixteenth-century Europe and itself encouraged intellectual ferment.[40] Martin Davies has pointed to a preexisting book culture and active trade in manuscripts prior to the advent of press.[41] He argued that printing did not cause an immediate change in the quality of editions, which were often rendered according to the manuscript version. The market for classics remained small. Lists of published books show that religious tracts, bibles, confessional manuals, and romances (i.e., non-humanist works) remained popular. Even in Florence, a center of humanist activity, few editions of Cicero or Livy were produced before 1500.[42]

The precise nature of the transmission of humanism throughout Europe has elicited a great deal of discussion. Scholars once treated it as straight-line movement of ideas, from Italy to the rest of Europe. They now place greater emphasis on the role of the receiver, how ideas were interpreted and shaped by those who acquired them (see chapter 1).[43] Peter Burke, drawing on the work of the reception theory of literary scholars, has used the metaphor of a grid or filter, arguing that what was selected by the receiver was congruent with the culture that received it. Reception thus represented its own manner of production.[44]

The process is perhaps most apparent with the vicissitudes of Baldassare Castiglione's *Courtier*, one of the most popular humanist texts of the day. It was translated into numerous languages, during which it underwent significant alterations (see chapter 2). The English translation, by Thomas Hoby in 1561, rendered the famous word "sprezzatura," the key characteristic of the Renaissance man, as "disgracing," a pejorative quite different from the generally accepted "nonchalance." The Polish translator of *The Courtier*, Lukasz Górnicki (1566) transferred the setting of the book from court at Urbino to Krakow. He replaced the discussion of the merits of the Italian language with one on the merits of the Slavic language. Górnicki left out all references to sculpture and painting, since they were unknown locally, as well as the famous debate on virtues of women. He replaced Gasparro Pallavicino's anti-women sentiments with anti-Italian ones.[45]

Florentine and Italian Humanism

Sensitivity to reception notwithstanding, it remains common practice, particularly in textbooks, to follow the lead of Voigt and Weiss and start discussions of humanism with Italy, moving by degrees to the rest of Europe.[46] The schema usually involves an initial excursus on "pre-humanism" in Padua and Naples, the latter centered on the court of Robert I of Anjou (1309–1343), who encouraged Greek learning and crowned Petrarch poet laureate of Italy.[47] The discussion proceeds then to Florence, the rest of Italy, and finally to Northern Europe. The focus is on the careers of representative figures, men who achieved fame and gave shape to the humanist movement. Their careers demonstrate the narrow "elite" base of humanism.

The influential twentieth-century scholar Berthold Ullmann attributed the priority of Italy to "a germ" or "excess of secretion" that distinguished the Italian people from those elsewhere.[48] More recent scholarship has emphasized Italy's "unique" urban character and wealth that produced a broadly literate public that facilitated the development of humanism.[49] The exceptional nature of the urban context is, however, debatable, since humanism was also popular at Italian courts as well in southern German cities (Nuremberg and Augsburg), whose economic and social makeup resembled that of their Italian counterparts. Nevertheless the argument has helped establish Florence as the initial locus of humanism, from where it "radiated" out elsewhere. Florence's commercial character and government of rich merchants required the services of a large cadre of notaries skilled in rhetoric. Lacking its own university until 1349, there was in Florence no entrenched scholastic tradition as in the north to oppose humanism. Once established, the university aided humanism with the establishment of a chair in Greek. Florentine officials attempted to hire Petrarch for the new university, but were unsuccessful.

The humanist tradition in Florence was a singularly rich one and has been the subject of a great number of studies.[50] Petrarch, though educated in Avignon, inspired developments in the city through friends and disciples, including Giovanni Boccaccio, with whom he maintained close contact. Petrarch also influenced two other leading local figures, Luigi Marsigli (1342–1394), an Augustinian monk, whose monastery was a meeting place for humanists, and Coluccio Salutati (1331–1406), a notary and chancellor of the republic (1375–1406). Salutati wrote biographies of Petrarch and Boccaccio, and accumulated a library of over 800 classical manuscripts.[51]

Scholars treat Florentine humanism in generational terms.[52] The first generation, inspired by Petrarch, placed emphasis on Cicero and saw through the establishment of Greek as a field of study. Manuel Chrysoloras (1353–1406) attracted a strong following after arriving as professor of Greek in Florence in 1397. His fellow Byzantine George Gemistos Pletho conducted a "continuing seminar" in Hellenic studies at the Council of Florence in 1439 that was widely attended by young humanists.[53]

A second generation followed that was more politically oriented. They used classical learning and rhetoric to praise Florence as a new Athens and bastion of "liberty" in the context of war with Milan and the "tyranny" of its ruler Giangaleazzo Visconti. Hans Baron coined the term "civic humanism" and argued that the year 1402, when Florence was at the point of defeat by Milan, constituted a dividing line, when humanism assumed the aspect of modern republicanism, particularly in the writings of Leonardo Bruni (1370–1444), Coluccio Salutati's successor as chancellor of the city (see chapter 6).

Bruni and the civic humanist tradition were followed by a shift in the middle of the fifteenth century to more spiritual and speculative concerns. Plato, known to the Middle Ages only through a single (atypical) dialogue, the *Timaeus*, became a popular subject of study. Leonardo Bruni translated several Platonic dialogues from Greek. Marsilio Ficino (1433–1499) recovered the main body of Plato's work and in 1484 published translations of all of Plato's dialogues, along with Neoplatonic commentaries. An informal "academy" developed around Ficino, consisting of scholars and influential politicians, supported Cosimo de' Medici, who provided Ficino with a villa at Careggi as a meeting place.

It remains an operative question whether Ficino and his followers properly fit under the rubric of humanism. Kristeller explicitly excluded Ficino from his famous definition and placed him under the heading of Renaissance philosophy. Ficino did not share the humanist interest in rhetoric and style, but saw in Plato and Neoplatonic texts a means to better understand the Christian faith. His translations included the mystical, magical work of Hermes Trismegistus, in whom he saw further links to Christianity (see chapter 7).

But distinctions are not so easily made. In studying Plato, Ficino expressed hostility toward Aristotle and the scholastic tradition, thus sharing a basic prejudice with the humanists. As James Hankins has emphasized, Ficino also shared the humanist penchant for self-promotion and for using the texts he studied for his own purposes.[54] Most important, Ficino and his academy exerted a strong influence on northern humanistic developments. Several key figures, among them the German humanist Johannes Reuchlin and the French humanist Jacques Lefèvre d'Étaples (1455–1536) studied with Ficino. Therefore although Ficino was not strictly speaking a humanist, he is often included – with qualification and disclaimers – in discussions of humanism, often grouped with his famous pupil Giovanni Pico della Mirandola.

The connection between Florentine humanism and the rest of Italy has been the subject of considerable debate. Peter Burke warned against taking a "Florentino-centric" view of events, overemphasizing the role of the city in the transmission of humanism. The warning is a fair one, but difficult in fact to heed. Burke himself began his discussion of the subject in a recent textbook with Florence.[55] The connection between the city and other parts of Italy was strong. Both Pier Paolo Vergerio and Guarino Guarini studied with Chrysoloras in Florence. Leonardo Bruni, for all his political propagandizing on behalf of Florence, worked also at the papal court in Rome. Poggio Bracciolini, Bruni's successor as chancellor, worked both in Rome and Naples. Antonio Loschi (1368–1441), author of polemics against Florence in the service of Milan, was a student of Chrysoloras and Coluccio Salutati. Finally, Petrarch, who inspired developments in Florence, passed the whole of his itinerant career outside of that city. His longest continuous residence was eight years at the court of the Visconti, who ultimately gained possession of his vast library when they captured Padua in 1388.

The common ground allowed for common characteristics. Throughout Italy, as in Florence, humanists studied the Greek language and used their rhetorical skills for political end. The Milanese humanist Pier Candido Decembrio (1392–1477) wrote propagandistic tracts on behalf of Milan, as did Francesco Filelfo (1398–1481) who penned a panegyric on the model of the *Iliad* for Francesco Sforza (*Sforziade*) when he became duke in 1450.

Lorenzo Valla's famous attack on the donation of Constantine was written while he was in the employ of King Alfonso the Magnanimous (1442–58) of Naples, who was then at odds with the pope. As Jerry Bentley has demonstrated, Alfonso employed humanists to project the desirability of monarchical rule and images of himself as a latter day Caesar. In Venice, a species of civic humanism arose in the work of Paolo Sarpi, who supported Venetian republican ideals. At the papal curia, humanists wrote in support of the ambitions of popes and the church.

Recent scholarship has, nevertheless, focused on outlining the distinct features of humanism throughout Italy. Milanese humanism is seen, for example, as placing emphasis on editing classical texts, and closely linked to local universities. Lorenzo Valla taught at the University of Pavia, where he gave lectures that formed the foundation of his *Elegances of the Latin Language*. Mario Santoro has spoken of the "Neapolitanization" of humanism in terms of the cultural and historical experiences of Naples, which was, unlike elsewhere in Italy, a monarchy.[56] Scholars of Rome and the papacy have stressed the importance of the papal bureaucracy. Pope Nicholas V (1447–1455), himself a humanist educated in Florence, collected classical works that formed the core of the Vatican library and founded an academy for the translation of Greek texts. The patronage of popes, however, was uneven. Some were indifferent and hostile to humanism. It was the papal bureaucracy, the so-called *curia romana*, the largest and most complex in Europe, that sustained humanism even when popes did not. Humanists found employment as apostolic secretaries, producing official bulls and letters that required rhetorical skill. According to John D'Amico, the bureaucracy engendered its own form of humanism, which he called "curial" humanism, reflected most prominently in the work of Paolo Cortesi (1465–1510) and Giulio Pomponio Leto (1427–1494). It was disseminated by means of informal literary academies, in which participants read their work to each other and received instruction in Latin composition. The distinct Roman features of humanism included emphasis on Latin and imitation of Cicero, but ultimately less interest in the Greek.[57]

Finally, Venice, long seen as a "failure" on account of the relatively restricted popularity of humanism (to a small leisured elite), is now seen as an important point of dissemination of humanist texts, owing to printing press of Aldus Manutius (1449–1515). Aldus, a humanist trained in Rome, established his famous shop in 1493. He introduced important technical innovations to the printing of books that constituted its own contribution to humanism. He produced quality portable editions of Latin and Greek texts, with clear typeface, free of scribal errors.[58] The republican dimension of Venetian humanism has been reexamined and is treated more as its own entity, distinct from Florence in its conservative aspect and interest in celebrating Venetian patrician rule and defending expansive policies within Italy.[59]

Humanism in Northern Europe

It is with respect to Northern Europe that the discussion about the transmission of humanism has been most problematic.[60] Here scholars draw heavily on notions of reception and examine indigenous forces that influenced and shaped the movement. For Voigt and Weiss, the diffusion of humanism was a simple matter of the traffic in men and ideas to and from Italy through the familiar routes: commerce, church councils, and papal service. Italian scholars journeyed north; northern scholars and students went south to Italy. As in Italy, a first generation mastered Latin, the next acquired Greek, which became an essential component of northern humanism. According to a famous story, the French humanist Guillaume Budé (1468–1540) was so enamored of Greek that he passed several hours on his wedding day studying a Greek grammar book.

In general, however, northern humanism had its own distinct features. These include a greater "national" dimension, emphasis on Christian reform and a larger role played by universities. The last owed largely to the fact that there did not exist in many places in the north the same articulated system of secondary schools as in Italy. Boys there went to university at thirteen or fourteen years of age, and gained their first real exposure to learning in that context. Italian students received basic secondary education first and then went to advanced study in law and medicine. Centralizing monarchs encouraged humanist curricula in northern universities as a means of extending their authority by training officials for the royal bureaucracies (see chapter 6). University centers were often also publishing centers. The Dutch city of Louvain, site of a humanistic college, the *Collegium Trilingue* (the Trilingual College) dedicated to the study of Latin, Greek, and Hebrew, was also the home of an active printing press that published translations of Aristotle and Plato as well as the work of contemporary humanist writers and books on Hebrew and Oriental languages. Humanists collaborated with printers. Josse Bade's printing shop in Paris was a meeting place for authors, teachers, and students. Erasmus lived for a time with the famous printer in Basel, Martin Froben.[61]

Recent studies place the decisive period for northern humanism in the later fifteenth and sixteenth centuries, thus separating it temporarily from events in Italy, for which the fourteenth century remains important. This did not preclude direct Italian influences. As Peter Burke has demonstrated, the largest migrations of Italian humanists to the north occurred in the second half of the fifteenth century.[62] But the Italian connection was not straight-line and the diffusion, if we may call it that, was slow, allowing native characteristics to grow. As in Italy, there existed "pre" or "proto" movements that did not constitute full-fledged humanism. Scholarly debates have revolved around establishing the point at which critical mass was achieved.

In the early twentieth century, historians of German and Dutch humanism placed strong emphasis on indigenous, non-Italian roots.[63] They favored local characteristics such as that German tradition of mysticism and the "basic inwardness" of the German people.[64] They stressed above all the activities of the Brethren of the Common Life, a lay religious community, founded in the fourteenth century by the Dutch preacher Gerard Groote (1340–1384). The Brethren were popular in Northern Europe and in the Low Countries. They devoted themselves to simple piety, the "Devotio Moderna," based on imitation of Christ and became forceful advocates of education. Their "schools" rejected scholasticism in favor of humanist study, particularly at Deventer, where the humanist headmaster Alexander Hegius (1433–1498) taught Greek and inspired future humanists including Erasmus.[65]

The indigenous theory has, however, elicited considerable hostility. Lewis Spitz accused its proponents of skating "on ice thinner than that of the Dutch canals" and pointed out that the Brethren did not operate full-scale schools, nor were they properly speaking a teaching order. Brethren academies, including at Deventer, were controlled by local governments and the church. Thus the real inspiration for humanist study came from civic leaders. Alexander Hegius was himself not a member of the Brethren.

German humanism is now seen as inspired by a combination of forces, external and internal. The major early German humanists studied on the peninsula, as did their patrons, who included government officials, jurists, and prelates. But Germany possessed some of the same social, economic, and political preconditions as Italy. Nuremberg and Augsburg were urban centers, with educated merchant elites. Rulers patronized humanists at court. Maximilian I (1493–1519) established a chair for Latin poetry and rhetoric at the University of Vienna. As in Italy, monasteries provided a locus of humanist activity. The Cistercian abbey at Adwert outside of Groningen was a meeting place for young scholars, as was the Benedictine cloister of Sponheim in southwest Germany, whose learned abbot Johannes Trithemius (1462–1505) collected a library of over 2,000 books.[66]

German humanism has been treated in generational terms, stressing its progressive independence from Italy. Scholars speak of initial wave of "wandering poets" or "migratory birds," who traveled to Italy and focused primarily on acquiring classical skills. Peter Luder (1415–1472) studied with Guarino, stayed in Italy for 20 years and returned to advocate the "new" intellectual ways in lectures at the University of Heidelberg. Rudolf Agricola (1444–1485), the so-called father of German humanism, studied law at Pavia and acquired outstanding skill in Latin and Greek, which he sought to transplant to the north "as yet unmarked by any trace of culture." Erasmus, an admirer of Agricola, credited him with bringing for the first time beyond the Alps the "gleam of better literature."

A second generation of humanists, more secure in their abilities, moved in original directions.[67] Conrad Celtis (1459–1508), the "arch-humanist," returned home after two years in Italy (where he met Marsilio Ficino among others) with a distaste for Italian intellectual haughtiness and a desire to seize cultural leadership from them. To this end, he founded a network of indigenous northern "sodalities" to promote indigenous humanistic study. The sodalities extended as far as Hungary and Poland and did much to promote humanism in Central Europe. In his written work, Celtis advocated cultural nationalism, which would become an important theme among German humanists. He published distinctly "German" works, including an edition of the Roman historian Tacitus' history of Germanic tribes, *Germania*, and the plays of the eleventh-century German abbess, Roswitha of Gandersheim. He recruited scholars to write a *Germany Illustrated* on the model of Biondo's *Italy Illustrated*. Celtis's contemporary humanist, Jakob Wimpheling (1450–1528) of Alsace boasted of never having visited Italy or indeed the neighboring province of Swabia.[68] Wimpfeling received his education at the University of Heidelberg, and wrote *Germania* (1501), a history of Alsace, in which he proudly argued, against contemporary French claims, that the region had been inhabited by Germans since the time of the Roman emperor Augustus.

Similar trends existed in the Low Countries, where humanism gained wide popularity in the sixteenth and seventeenth centuries. Universities and the printing press played important roles. By 1500 presses had been established at Utrecht, Delft, Gouda, Deventer, Zwolle, Nijmegen, Antwerp, and Leiden. According to one estimate, nearly half the books printed in the Netherlands in the sixteenth century were classics, including the works of Cicero, Greek authors, and contemporary humanists.[69] Leiden, site of a university and a press (1575), was home to two of the most influential humanists of the period, Justus Lipsius (1547–1606), and Joseph Scaliger (1540–1609).

Dutch humanism likewise had its own features. It possessed less of a national dimension than its German counterparts and involved greater participation of secondary schools for Latin and Greek, which became popular with a rising urban merchant class in cities.[70] Dutch developments were less connected to Italy and more directly affected by trends in Germany, Spain and France, and England. The German Rudolf Agricola influenced Alexander Hegius, who in turn influenced the Dutch humanist, Erasmus. Erasmus learned his Greek at Paris from the French humanist Robert Gaguin, and maintained close contact throughout his career with humanists at the Tudor court in England, including William Grocyn, John Colet and, most famously, Thomas More. It was after his visit to England in 1499 that Erasmus began his most productive period, and in Paris that Erasmus met his future disciple, the Spaniard Juan Luis Vives (d. 1540) who bypassed Italy and settled in the Netherlands in 1512, becoming what one scholar has called the "son" of Dutch humanism.[71]

Erasmus's career makes clear the international character of Dutch humanism. Born in Rotterdam, Erasmus nevertheless belonged to all of Europe, a point he himself made clear in his oft quoted response to Zwingli's offer of citizenship at Zurich, that he considered himself "a citizen of the world." But Erasmus's career also emphasizes many of the basic features of northern humanism in the late fifteenth and sixteenth centuries, including mastery of the Greek language, exploitation of the printing press, and the use of linguistic and classical skills to study the bible and patristic texts in their original languages. Erasmus's calculated use of the press allowed him an intellectual career wholly outside of the university, as an international figure, who lived, if barely, by the profits of his writings (see chapter 2). His interest in theological texts helped initiate "Christian humanism," classical study intended to better understand the faith. It shared the same basic orientation as Ficino's study of Plato, which likewise aimed at getting closer to God. In *Enchiridion on Christian Knight* (1503) Erasmus developed the notion of "*philosophia Christi*," a simple, heartfelt piety based on scripture, which he extended and amplified throughout his career. But simple piety and the close study of scripture led to critique of religious practices, often in the form of satire, an aspect of Erasmus's career for which he is perhaps best known. In this sense his career has been perceived as in the gateway of the Reformation, helping to pave the way for Martin Luther, who though not a humanist, was nevertheless influenced by the movement. Erasmus remained in the fold and openly distanced himself from Luther. But the point of separation between humanism and the Reformation is an important issue, which we will discuss further (see chapter 7).

"Christian humanism" was also an important part of the French humanist tradition. Erasmus's contemporary Jacques Lefèvre d'Étaples (1455–1536) studied the bible and patristic texts in their original languages, making translations of the Psalms and writing commentaries on the Gospel of John and the epistles of Paul. D'Étaples ran afoul of church authorities and found sanctuary at the court of King Francis I and his sister Marguerite d'Angouleme in Paris, a center of humanistic study.

The broader lines of the development of French humanism have, however, been the subject of particularly intense debate. A basic problem for scholars is that French intellectual culture (lyric poetry, romance) flourished in the Middle Ages and was indeed synonymous with the period. Therefore if humanism involved a rejection of the Middle Ages, then it involved also a rejection of France's cultural and intellectual tradition, the point argued by Ronald Witt and Robert Black with respect to Italian humanism. What space was then left for French humanism?

Henri Hauser provided an early solution, emphasizing the Italian origins of humanism, brought back by French soldiers from Italy after the French invasion of the peninsula in 1494. The movement gained strength on French soil and acquired its own characteristics, becoming tied up with religious reform. The view remains influential, though, as for elsewhere in Northern Europe, it has been modified to place greater stress on indigenous features.[72]

Recent scholarship has focused on the years from 1480 to 1540 as centrally important to French humanism. The period includes the careers of key individuals, the establishment of humanist university curricula and printing presses and the royal patronage of King Francis I. One of the earliest humanists, Guillaume Fichet (1433–1490) founded France's first press, in the basement of the Sorbonne, and, though trained in scholasticism at the University of Paris, published the works of Cicero and Lorenzo Valla's *Elegances*. Erasmus's mentor Robert Gaguin (1423–1501) maintained about him a circle of humanists that included members of faculty of the university as well as royal and local government officials. Guillaume Budé (1468–1540), King Francis I's personal secretary, was perhaps the most renowned humanist of the period, distinguishing himself as a writer of history and legal studies. With Francis's support, Budé founded the Royal College (later known as the College of France) for humanist studies.[73]

The timeline nevertheless leaves problematic the role of Francis Petrarch, who grew up in Avignon and gained his first love of classics there (1326–1353). The general trend has been to deemphasize Petrarch and the earlier period, fitting it under the now familiar heading of "prehistory," swept away by the ravages of the Hundred Years War and Church Schism. The historian Franco Simone is among the few to argue for continuity, noting that French humanism retained Petrarch's sense of historical relativism and classification of the current age as a new and distinct one. This is evident in the work of Budé, who like Petrarch, consciously separated his own era from its medieval predecessor (in *De philologia*).[74]

Disagreement persists, however, about the role of Italy. French scholars tend to minimize the connection, while the English-language counterparts are inclined to place greater emphasis on it. The American historian Eugene Rice argued that French humanism was "transplanted" from Italy, but that the French altered it to suit their own needs.[75] The French historian Jean-Claude Margolin, on the other hand, saw French humanism as possessing its own "peculiar" traits and argued for continuity with France's rich medieval past, in hostile opposition to Italian developments. Marc Fumaroli has spoken of the emergence of a distinctly French "aulic" humanism," a political-centered humanism that developed at the court of Francis I. French aulic humanists consciously eschewed the Italian tradition of oratory based on Cicero in favor of Seneca and Tacitus and their focus on prudence and stoic fortitude.[76]

The study of English humanism has followed some of the same general lines as elsewhere. Scholars have emphasized developments in the late fifteenth and early sixteenth centuries. Thomas More (1478–1535) is the dominant figure. Indeed after his death humanism is seen as largely disappearing in England.

But as with discussion of Germany, indeed more so, scholars have grappled with proto movements and the influence of Italy. There was strong traffic in students, scholars, merchants, and churchmen between the peninsula and the island. The Florentine humanist Poggio Bracciolini took up residence in England from 1418–1422. Prominent Englishmen, including dukes and clerics, studied in Italy. Nevertheless, the state of intellectual affairs in England was not particularly advanced in the earlier period. Bracciolini complained in letters to friends back home of intellectual isolation and the lack of classical texts in local libraries and monasteries.[77]

The study of English humanism has focused on the activities of the court of Henry VIII Tudor. Henry maintained about him a circle of humanists that included Thomas Linacre (1460–1524), the royal physician and tutor to his children; William Grocyn (d. 1519), the first to teach Greek regularly at Oxford; John Colet (1466–1519), the dean of Saint Paul's cathedral in London; and Thomas More, the most accomplished of the group, who would die a martyr's death after opposing Henry's decision to divorce. All the men were accomplished at the Greek language. Linacre and Grocyn had studied in Florence.[78]

Thomas More has received the overwhelming bulk of scholarly attention. This is as much for his stance regarding Henry VIII's divorce as for his humanist work.[79] More's career emphasizes the indigenous aspect of English humanism. He did not study in Italy, but gained his appreciation of classics and knowledge of the Greek language from Linacre and Grocyn at the Tudor court. The precise nature of More's humanism and the influences upon him has, however, been the subject of its own debate.[80] More's friendship with Erasmus encouraged scholars to treat his humanism in terms of that of his Dutch counterpart.[81] But recent studies have deemphasized the connection between the men. They point to More's debt to the Platonic studies of Ficino and Pico della Mirandola, who had influenced Linacre, Grocyn, and Colet. More's most famous work, *Utopia* (1515–1516), drew on Plato.

English humanism ultimately gained institutional status in universities. Italian humanists lectured at Cambridge and Oxford in the mid-fifteenth century and Grocyn had offered lectures in Greek. But there was significant resistance, and scholasticism remained a focal point of university studies.

This softened, however, in the sixteenth century, as Tudor rulers encouraged humanist curricula at universities as a means to train public servants for the royal bureaucracy. In this way, English humanism became aligned with state building (see chapter 6).

Royal courts and universities also served as focal points of humanist activity in Spain and Central Europe. The Spanish monarchs Ferdinand and Isabella promoted humanist learning as a tool of centralization intended to create educated public officials loyal directly to the monarchy. In 1508, a trilingual college was founded at Alcalà for the study of the bible in its original languages. The Hungarian ruler Matthias Corvinus patronized humanists at court, as did the Polish King Casimir. Both sought to use the rhetorical skills of humanists to affirm their royal power. A university was established at Cracow, as an offshoot of an earlier sodality set up there by Conrad Celtis. It offered humanist courses and Janus Pannonius (1424–1472), the renowned Hungarian humanist, taught there.[82]

The countries have, however, received far less attention from scholars, who tend to view humanist trends there as derivative or "off center" of the mainstream.[83] Central European humanism, for instance, focused on the careers of a small group of men, with strong ties to Italy. The Polish humanist Callimachus (1438–1496), tutor to King Casimir's children, was a Florentine expatriate, banished from the city for criminal behavior. The "father" of Hungarian humanism, Janos Vitez (1408–1472), studied in Italy and maintained close contact there throughout his career.

Spanish humanism was likewise closely connected to Italy. But the movement appears "off-center" in that the first generation of humanists in the fifteenth century wrote in the vernacular and used translations of classical and humanist text. The marquis of Santillana (1398–1458) expressed humanist love for classics and rhetoric, but did not in fact know Latin. This has raised the question whether he qualifies as a humanist. The historian Ottavio di Camillo has argued that Santillana and the early Spanish vernacular tradition was indeed humanist, reflective of a distinctive way that humanism was appropriated in Spain. It paved the way for a subsequent generation of humanists, trained in Italy and Spain, who excelled in Latin. The chief figure is Antonio de Nebrija (1444–1522), whose skills in Latin and Greek were comparable to those of his great Florentine counterpart and friend Angelo Poliziano.[84]

Imitation as Innovation

Consideration of humanism in its diverse settings makes more difficult any attempt to posit a single workable definition for it. If, as Eugene Rice has suggested, Jacques Lefèvre d'Étaples was a representative humanist figure in

France, he does fit easily within the definition of humanism as a rhetorical and philological enterprise. Lefèvre's interests included religious speculation and philosophy. The same is true of the Dutch humanist Justus Lipsius, who undertook a philological reconstruction of the work of Seneca, which engendered in him interest of the poet's stoic philosophy.

The contradictions are not at once at odds with Kristeller's famous definition of humanism, which is not so narrow as some critics maintain. Kristeller allowed humanism an indirect and powerful influence on philosophy.[85] But discomfort remains over where precisely to draw the line. Textbooks and general studies, whatever explicit definition they give of humanism (and it is usually Kristeller's) often include philosophers in the discussion. They do so by distinguishing between those who were humanists proper and those who were inspired by humanism. In his survey of Italian developments, George Holmes included Marsilio Ficino and Giovanni Pico della Mirandola as part of a "second phase" of humanism.[86] But Holmes took care to call the men, and those in their circle, "humanist inspired" rather than humanists. Charles Nauert's recent textbook explicitly denies Ficino the title of humanist, but includes him in the discussion of Florentine humanism, by means of subheading, that at once sets him apart, but allows reference to his ideas and influence. In her textbook, *The Renaissance in Europe*, Margaret King treats humanism in a chapter entitled "Human Dignity and Humanist Studies: The Career of Humanism (1350–1530)," a heading that maintains a basic distinction between Ficino and Pico (grouped under "Human Dignity") and the humanists, but facilitates discussion of the two trends together.[87]

The approach reflects a basic methodological problem. It is difficult to offer a broad history of humanism that is inclusive of Northern European developments without reference to Ficino and Pico, who had such a profound influence beyond the Alps. As we have seen, many of the major northern figures studied with them and took up their interest in Plato and Neoplatonic thought. Moreover their notion of "human dignity" provides a unifying feature of the Renaissance intellectual ethic that seems well applied to both the pursuit of eloquence as well as to philosophical speculations. It was, as De Lamar Jensen states in his textbook, the "philosophical phase" represented by Ficino and Pico that had "something to offer to northern humanists" and thus "propelled" humanism across the Alps. Eugene Rice used the term "humanist philosophy of man," which remains popular in textbooks.[88]

Nevertheless the unity implicit in the notion of human dignity is more illusory than real. The Florentine humanist Gianozzo Manetti (1396–1459) asserted the importance of the dignity of man in his eponymous, *On the Dignity and Excellence of Man*. But he positioned his argument against the slights to human dignity in medieval literature, particularly in the work of Pope Innocent III (1198–1216), whose *On the Misery of Human Life* depicted human nature as fallen and corrupt. The philosopher Pico della Mirandola's famous praise of mankind in his *Oration on the Dignity of Man* was quite different. It was much broader philosophical statement, a reinterpretation of Aristotle's notion of the order of being. Pico placed man at the top of the scale, but with the understanding that his ascent owed to his actions and that if these were lacking he could lose his place.

While such contradictions are not easy to convey in general works, there has been among scholars a trend toward a broader conception of humanism that treats it as intellectual and cultural movement that encompassed not only grammar, rhetoric, poetry, history, and moral philosophy, but also biblical studies, political thought, science, and theology, stretching into the seventeenth century and involving vernacular literature (see chapter 7). Historians emphasize how humanists and philosophers shared the same texts, and although they approached them in different ways – the philosopher searching for truth and wisdom, the humanist for eloquence – the results were not always very different.[89] Humanists facilitated philosophical study by producing critical editions of texts. The very practice of imitation was itself innovative. Kenneth Gouwens, drawing from the field of cultural psychology, argued that the study and imitation of the classics produced a "cognitive turn" among humanists, who viewed themselves in new ways, intimately connected to the subjects they studied. Meanwhile, as William Bouwsma has argued, humanist rhetorical culture led of its own accord to a new conception of men.[90] Shifts in the study of rhetoric in the middle of the fifteenth century induced humanists to eschew conjoining wisdom and eloquence, as Petrarch had, in favor of separating eloquence from wisdom, a basic feature of the work of Platonists like Ficino. The distance between humanists and philosophers was further shortened by the penchant of both to appropriate classics for the purpose of self-promotion. The philosopher Ficino may have understood Plato better than humanist Leonardo Bruni did, but neither properly understood Plato apart from their own personal/professional agendas.[91] Charles Nauert has favored more negative language, seeing humanism as a species of "intellectual solvent," that struck down traditional beliefs and thus ultimately allowed innovation.[92]

Notes

1 From "On Petrarch's Eloquence," in *Renaissance Debates on Rhetoric, ed. and trans. by* Wayne Rebhorn (Ithaca, 2000), p. 19.

2 Roberto Weiss, *The Spread of Italian Humanism* (London, 1964), p. 46.

3 Albert Rabil Jr, ed., *Renaissance Humanism: Foundations, Forms and Legacy*, 3 vols. (Philadelphia, 1988); Riccardo Fubini, *L'umanismo italiano e i suoi storici* (Milan,

2001); Donald R. Kelley, *Renaissance Humanism* (Boston, 1991); James Hankins, "Renaissance Humanism and Historiography Today," in *Renaissance Historiography*, ed. by Jonathan Woolfson (New York, 2005); Benjamin Kohl, *Renaissance Humanism, 1300–1550: A Bibliography of Materials in English* (New York, 1985); Christopher S. Celenza, *The Lost Italian Renaissance: Humanists, Historians, and Latin's Legacy* (Baltimore, 2004); Kenneth Gouwens, "Perceiving the Past: Renaissance Humanism after the Cognitive Turn," *American Historical Review* 103, 1 (Feb. 1998): 55–82; Riccardo Fubini, *Humanism and Secularization, Petrarch to Valla*, trans. by Martha King (Durham, 2002); Angelo Mazzocco, ed., *Interpretations of Renaissance Humanism* (Leiden, 2006); Mark Jurdjevic, "Hedgehogs and Foxes: The Present and Future of Italian Renaissance Intellectual History," *Past and Present* 195 (2007): 241–68.

4 Charles G. Nauert, *Humanism and the Culture of Renaissance Europe* (Cambridge, 1995 and 2nd edn., 2006).

5 Paul Oskar Kristeller, "The Philosophy of Man in the Italian Renaissance," in *Renaissance Thought and Its Sources*, ed. by Michael Mooney (New York, 1961, originally published in 1955), p. 120.

6 A history of the use of the term humanism is in Vito R. Giustiniani, "Homo, Humanus, and the Meanings of 'Humanism,'" *Journal of the History of Ideas* 46 (Apr.–Jun. 1985): 167–95.

7 Karl Hagen, *Germany's Religious and Literary Relations in the Age of the Reformation*, 2 vols. (1841–3); Georg Voigt, *Die Wiederbelebung des classischen Alterthums oder das erste Jahrhundert des Humanismus*, 2 vols. (Berlin, 1859); Paul Joachimsen, *Geschichtsauffassung und Geschichtschreibung in Deutschland unter dem Einfluss des Humanismus* (Leipzig, 1910) and "Aus der Entwicklung des italienischen Humanismus," *Historische Zeitschrift* 121 (1920): 189–233; Remigio Sabbadini, *Il metodo degli umanisti* (Florence, 1922); Giovanni Gentile, *Studi sul Rinascimento* (Florence, 1920) and "La concezione humanistica del mondo," *Nuova antologia* 277 (1931): 307–17.

8 Eugenio Garin, *Italian Humanism: Philosophy and Civic Life*, trans. by Peter Munz (New York, 1965).

9 S. Dresden, *Humanism in the Renaissance*, trans. by Margaret King (New York, 1968).

10 Garin, *Italian Humanism*, pp. 2–3.

11 Erika Rummel, *The Humanist-Scholastic Debate in the Renaissance and Reformation* (Cambridge, MA, 1995), p. 11.

12 Paul Oskar Kristeller, "Humanism and Scholasticism in the Italian Renaissance," in Mooney, *Renaissance Thought*, pp. 92–119. See also *Renaissance Thought II: Papers on Humanism and the Arts* (New York, 1965) and *Renaissance Concepts of Man and Other Essays* (New York, 1972).

13 Kristeller, "Humanism and Scholasticism," pp. 93–100.

14 Kristeller, *Renaissance Thought II*, pp. 9–10; Jean-Claude Margolin, *Humanism in Europe at the Time of the Renaissance*, trans. by John Farthing (Durham, NC, 1989), p. 3.

15 Celenza, *Lost Italian Renaissance*, pp. 10–11.

16 Ronald Witt, "Medieval 'Ars Dictaminis' and the Beginnings of Humanism: A New Construction of the Problem," *Renaissance Quarterly* 35, 1 (Spring 1982): 1–35; "Medieval Italian Culture and the Origins of Humanism as a Stylistic Ideal," in Rabil, *Renaissance Humanism*, vol. 1, pp. 29–70; *"In the Footsteps of the Ancients": The Origins of Humanism from Lovato to Bruni* (Leiden, 2000), pp. 21, 497; and "Kristeller's Humanists as Heirs of the Medieval Dictatores," in Mazzocco, *Interpretations of Renaissance Humanism*, pp. 21–35.
17 Robert Black, *Humanism and Education in Medieval and Renaissance Italy* (Cambridge, 2001); "The Origins of Humanism," in Mazzocco, *Interpretations of Renaissance Humanism*, pp. 38–71; and "The Renaissance and Humanism: Definitions and Origins," in Woolfson, *Renaissance Historiography*, pp. 103–8.
18 Charles Homer Haskins, *The Renaissance of the Twelfth Century* (Cambridge, MA, 1939), pp. 10, 17, 93–4, 101, 114–17.
19 Étienne Gilson, "Humanisme médiéval et renaissance," in *Les idées et les lettres* (Paris, 1932). This was argued also by Jean Leclercq in *The Love of Learning and the Desire for God*, trans. by Catharine Misrahi (New York, 1961).
20 Walter Ullmann, *Medieval Foundations of Renaissance Humanism* (Ithaca, 1977).
21 Richard Southern, *Medieval Humanism* (New York, 1970), pp. 29–30, 37.
22 Southern, *Medieval Humanism*, pp. 31, 105–7, 110, 113.
23 Nauert, *Humanism and Culture*, p. 37.
24 R. W. Southern, *Scholastic Humanism and the Unification of Europe*, vol. 1 (Oxford, 1995), pp. 21, 125, 129.
25 William Bouwsma, "Changing Assumptions in Later Renaissance Culture," *Viator* 7 (1976), see now *A Usable Past: Essays in European Cultural History* (Berkeley and Los Angeles: 1990), pp. 74–92.
26 Werner L. Gundersheimer, *The Italian Renaissance* (Englewood Cliffs, NJ, 1965), pp. 46–7; Peter Burke, *The Renaissance*, 2nd edn. (London, 1997), p. 27.
27 Felix Gilbert, *Machiavelli and Guiccardini: Politics and History in Sixteenth Century Florence* (New York, 1985), p. 203.
28 Gilbert, *Machiavelli and Guiccardini*, pp. 208–11.
29 Benjamin G. Kohl, "Humanism and Education," in Rabil, *Renaissance Humanism*, vol. 3, p. 12.
30 Donald R. Kelley, "Humanism and History," in Rabil, *Renaissance Humanism*, vol. 3, p. 238.
31 Burke, *Renaissance*, pp. 19–20.
32 Naeurt, *Humanism and Culture*, p. 45; Kohl, "Humanism and Education," pp. 12–13. See also W. H. Woodward, *Vittorino da Feltre and Other Humanist Educators* (Cambridge, 1897).
33 Paul F. Grendler, *Schooling in the Renaissance: Literacy and Learning, 1300–1500* (Baltimore, 1989).
34 Anthony Grafton and Lisa Jardine, *From Humanism to the Humanities* (Cambridge, MA, 1986).
35 Grendler, *Schooling in the Renaissance*, pp. 17–35.
36 Black, *Humanism and Education*, pp. 1–11, 366–8.
37 Black, *Humanism and Education*, p. 4.

38 Roberto Weiss called the papacy a "powerful propagating factor" of humanism. Weiss, *Spread of Italian Humanism*, pp. 86–97.
39 Anthony Grafton, *Commerce with the Classics: Ancient Books and Renaissance Readers* (Ann Arbor, 1997).
40 Elizabeth L. Eisenstein, *The Printing Press as an Agent of Change*, 2 vols. (Cambridge, 1979), p. 169 and *The Printing Revolution in Early Modern Europe* (Cambridge, 1983).
41 Martin Davies, "Humanism in Script and Print in the Fifteenth Century," in *The Cambridge Companion to Renaissance Humanism*, ed. by Jill Kraye (Cambridge, 1996).
42 D. E. Rhodes, *Gli annali tipografici fiorentini del XV secolo* (Florence, 1988).
43 For reception theory, see J. H. Jauss, *Towards an Aesthetic of Reception* (Manchester, 1982).
44 Burke, *The European Renaissance: Centres and Peripheries* (Oxford, 1998), p. 8.
45 Burke, "The Courtier Abroad Or the Uses of Italy," pp. 40–51 and *The Fortunes of the Courtier: The European Reception of Castiglione's Cortegiano* (University Park, PA, 1996).
46 Georg Voigt started with Florence first, then to other republics such as Siena to Venice, the courts, the papal curia, and finally beyond the Alps. Charles Nauert structured his survey in a similar way, as did Albert Rabil in the first two volumes of his *Foundations of Humanism*.
47 Nicholas Mann, "The Origins of Humanism," in Kraye, *Cambridge Companion*, pp. 14–17; see also Rabil, *Renaissance Humanism*, vol. 1, pp. 5–16, 10–14 and Roberto Weiss, *The Dawn of Humanism in Italy* (London, 1947), pp. 19–20.
48 Berthold L. Ullmann, "Some Aspects of the Origin of Humanism," *Philological Quarterly* 20 (1941): 212–23.
49 Gundersheimer, *Italian Renaissance*, p. 5.
50 Robert Black "Education and the Emergence of a Literate Society," in *Italy in the Age of the Renaissance, 1300–1550*, ed. by John Najemy (Oxford, 2004), pp. 18–36. See also Lauro Martines, *The Social World of Florentine Humanists, 1390–1460* (Princeton, 1963); George Holmes, *The Florentine Enlightenment* (London, 1969), *Florence, Rome and the Origins of the Renaissance* (London, 1986), and "Humanism in Italy," in *The Impact of Humanism on Western Europe*, ed. by Anthony Goodman and Angus MacKay (New York, 1990); Ronald G. Witt, *Hercules at the Crossroads: The Life, Work and Thought of Coluccio Salutati* (Durham, NC, 1983); Gene Brucker, *The Civic World of Early Renaissance Florence* (Princeton, 1977).
51 Deno Geanakoplos, "Italian Humanism and the Byzantine Émigré Scholars," pp. 353–4; Charles L. Stinger, "Humanism in Florence," in Rabil, *Renaissance Humanism*, vol. 1, p. 175.
52 Holmes, "Humanism in Italy," pp. 118–36.
53 Geanakoplos, "Italian Humanism," p. 357.
54 James Hankins, *Plato in the Italian Renaissance* (Leiden, 1990).
55 Burke, *Renaissance*, pp. 5, 38.
56 Mario Santoro, "Humanism in Naples," in Rabil, *Renaissance Humanism*, vol. 2, pp. 296–331.

57 John F. D'Amico, *Renaissance Humanism in Papal Rome* (Baltimore, 1983), p. xiv and "Humanism in Rome," in Rabil, *Renaissance Humanism*, vol. 1 pp. 264–95.
58 M. J. C. Lowry, *The World of Aldus Manutius: Business and Scholarship in Renaissance Venice* (Ithaca, NY, 1979).
59 Margaret L. King, "Humanism in Venice," Rabil, *Renaissance Humanism*, vol. 1, pp. 209–10 and *Venetian Humanism in an Age of Patrician Dominance* (Princeton, 1986).
60 Denys Hay, *The Italian Renaissance in its Historical Context* (Cambridge, 1977); Goodman and Mackay, *Impact of Humanism*; Roy Porter and Mikulas Teich, eds., *The Renaissance in National Context* (Cambridge, 1992).
61 Jean Claude Margolin, "Humanism in France," in Goodman and Mackay, *Impact of Humanism*, p. 164.
62 Peter Burke, "The Spread of Humanism," in Goodman and MacKay, *Impact of Humanism*, pp. 3–4.
63 Nauert, *Humanism and Culture*, pp. 105–6.
64 Lewis Spitz, "Humanism in Germany," in Goodman and Mackay, *Impact of Humanism*, p. 203; N. L. Brann, "Humanism in Germany," in Rabil, *Renaissance Humanism*, vol. 2, pp. 123–55.
65 Albert Hyma, *The Christian Renaissance: A History of the Devotio Moderna* (Grand Rapids, MI, 1924, updated, Hamden, CT, 1965).
66 James H. Overfield, *Humanism and Scholasticism in Late Medieval Germany* (Princeton, 1984).
67 Spitz, "Humanism in Germany," pp. 208–9.
68 Nauert, *Humanism and Culture*, p. 115.
69 G. D. Painter, *Catalogue of Books Printed in the XVIth Century now in the British Museum* (1962), pp. ix, 143.
70 James K. Cameron, "Humanism in the Low Countries," Goodman and Mackay, *Impact of Humanism*, pp. 137–140; Nauert, *Humanism and Culture*, p. 111.
71 Cameron, "Humanism in the Low Countries," p. 148.
72 Henri Hauser, "De l'humanisme et de la Reforme en France," *Revue historique*, 64 (1897): 258–97; Wallace K. Ferguson, *The Renaissance in Historical Thought: Five Centuries of Interpretation* (Cambridge, MA, 1948), pp. 262–3.
73 Jean-Claude Margolin, *L'humanisme en Europe au temps de la Renaissance* (Paris, 1981).
74 Franco Simone, *Il Rinascimento francese: Studi e ricerche* (Turin, 1965).
75 Eugene Rice, "Humanism in France," in Rabil, *Renaissance Humanism*, vol 1 p. 109.
76 Marc Fumaroli, *L'âge de l'éloquence* (Geneva, 1980).
77 Roberto Weiss, *Humanism in England during the Fifteenth Century* (Oxford, 1957), pp.13–21; Denys Hay, *Polydore Vergil: Renaissance Historian and Man of Letters* (Oxford, 1952).
78 Nauert, *Humanism and Culture*, pp. 114–15.
79 Richard J. Shoeck, "Humanism in England," in Rabil, *Renaissance Humanism*, vol. 2, p. 6; Douglas Bush, "Tudor Humanism and Henry VIII," *University of Toronto Quarterly* 7 (1938), pp. 162–77 and *The Renaissance and English Humanism* (Toronto, 1939).

80 Alistair Fox, *Thomas More, History and Providence* (Oxford, 1982); Richard Marius, *Thomas More: A Biography* (New York, 1984).
81 J. K. McConica, *English Humanists and Reformation Politics under Henry VIII and Edward VI* (Oxford, 1965).
82 Marianna D. Birnbaum, "Humanism in Hungary," Rabil, *Renaissance Humanism*, vol. 2, pp. 293–334; Rósza Feuer-Tóth, *Art and Humanism in Hungary in the Age of Matthias Corvinus* (Budapest, 1990); Harold B. Segel, *Renaissance Culture in Poland: The Rise of Humanism, 1470–1543* (Ithaca, 1989).
83 Birnbaum, "Humanism in Hungary," p. 300.
84 Ottavio di Camillo, "Humanism in Spain," in Rabil, *Renaissance Humanism*, vol. 2, pp. 55–7.
85 Kristeller, "Philosophy of Man," p. 126.
86 Holmes, "Humanism in Italy," pp. 118–36.
87 Margaret King, *The Renaissance in Europe* (New York, 2003), pp. 65–99.
88 De Lamar Jensen, *Renaissance Europe*, (Toronto, 1981), pp. 113–14; Eugene F. Rice, *The Foundations of Early Modern Europe, 1460–1559* (New York, 1970), p. 77. The recent history of the Renaissance and Reformation Europe by Jonathan Zophy contains the subheading "Humanists as Philosophers." Jonathan W. Zophy, *A Short History of Renaissance and Reformation Europe* (Upper Saddle River, NJ, 1996), p. 73.
89 Jill Kraye, "Philologists and Philosophers," in *Cambridge Companion*. The schema harkens in many ways back to Paul Joachimsen's statements at the beginning of the twentieth century. He saw humanism as existing in various types – aesthetic, political, and critical. Paul Joachimsen, "Aus der Entwicklung des italienischen Humanismus," *Historische Zeitschrift* 121 (1920), pp. 189–233.
90 Gouwens, "Perceiving the Past," pp. 55–82; Bouwsma, "Changing Assumptions," pp. 74–92.
91 Hankins, *Plato in the Renaissance*, vol. 1, pp. 99–100.
92 Nauert, *Humanism and Culture*, pp. 205–6.

5

Economy: Hard Times or Prosperity?

Let me say then that thirteen hundred and forty eight years had already passed after the fruitful incarnation of the Son of God when into the city of Florence, more noble than any other Italian city, there came the deadly pestilence. Without pause it spread from one place and it stretched its miserable length over the West [. . .] Therefore out of sheer necessity there arose among those who remained alive customs, which were contrary to the established practices of the time.

Giovanni Boccaccio[1]

The discovery of America, and that of the passage to the East Indies by the Cape of Good Hope, are the two greatest and most important events recorded in the history of mankind.

Adam Smith[2]

The discourse among economic historians has focused not only on the nature of the economy, but on whether the term "Renaissance," coined by intellectual and cultural historians, is at all applicable to the field of study. A chief obstacle has been the existence of an alternate category, capitalism, which coincides temporally with the Renaissance. Karl Marx (d. 1883), Burckhardt's contemporary at the University of Berlin, stressed the importance of the period from the fourteenth to the sixteenth century as one of transition from the feudal mode of production to the capitalist one.[3] Max Weber (d. 1920) located capitalism in the sixteenth century, linking it to the advent of Calvinism and the so-called "Protestant ethic." Werner Sombart (d. 1941) dated its emergence to the fifteenth century, distinguishing it from petty trade in wares by artisans and craftsmen of the Middle Ages.[4]

Studies of capitalism dominated the early scholarship on economic history. Writing on the eve of World War II, the American economic historian Frank Nussbaum asserted that "economic history does not know a Renaissance." The concept was already subsumed under the heading of "early capitalism."[5] The notion of an economic Renaissance was further undermined by the influence of the French Annales School (founded in the 1920s), which stressed the *longue durée*, a division of time that eschews historical labels in favor of larger, cyclical economic patterns.[6] Annaliste scholars used quantitative evidence (prices and wages mostly) to trace long economic term trends. François Simiand (d. 1935) spoke of "conjunctures," alternating phases of expansion and contraction (A and B phases) of the economy, which had little to do with political and social events or traditional period markers.

The term Renaissance remains problematic to economic historians, who treat developments on their own terms in specialized textbooks for courses devoted specifically to economic history. Nevertheless, important events occurred in the years from 1300 to 1600, the temporal space traditionally afforded the Renaissance, including the Black Death and the Atlantic explorations that had significant economic consequences and have occasioned a great deal of scholarly study. Italianists have taken the lead in linking the phenomena (notably the Black Death) to Renaissance cultural developments. Students of Northern Europe have generally shunned the label in favor of "early modern" and focused instead on situating events (beginning with the Atlantic explorations) in terms of modern industrialization. The macro or "big picture" approach is currently undergoing revision by scholars interested in individual agency and the financial activities of ordinary consumers.[7]

Early Tradition: Renaissance and Capitalism

Jacob Burckhardt paid little attention to economic issues in his *Civilization of the Renaissance in Italy*, but his emphasis on progress had important consequences for study of economy. It suggested a vibrant Renaissance economy, or at least one better than its medieval counterpart. Burckhardt's stress on modernity matched well the basic objectives of Karl Marx, who saw in capitalism the essence of the modern world. It is thus not surprising that the two discourses soon came together. The point of coincidence was individualism. Burckhardt's self-reliant, calculating Renaissance individual came to be seen as possessing the same qualities of the capitalist entrepreneur. That Burckhardt's individual was from Italy, the most commercially advanced region in Europe, strengthened the link.

An international group of scholars fleshed out the connection. In 1924 the Norwegian historian Halvdan Koht equated Renaissance individualism with capitalism, which he saw as most apparent in the business community of Florence.[8] The German sociologist Alfred von Martin turned Burckhardt on his head, treating individualism as an economic phenomenon that wholly transformed medieval "corporate" forms such as feudalism, urban guilds, and politics into more "rational enterprises."[9] The American historian H. M. Robertson, following closely von Martin, argued that economic individualism was synonymous with rational enterprise, which created a sense of honor and justice among Renaissance businessmen.[10]

The equation of capitalism with the Renaissance ran concurrent, however, with attempts to locate the phenomenon in the Middle Ages. In this respect, Renaissance economic history has differed from other subfields in that it did not face a re-evaluation or "revolt" from medievalists, but the two sides developed conjointly. The great Belgian scholar Henri Pirenne (1862–1935) argued that capitalism existed already "beyond a doubt" in the twelfth century. He saw the period from 1000 to 1300 as one of substantial economic growth, owing to increased population, the resurgence of long distance trade and, most importantly, the rise of cities and an urban middle class.[11] Medieval cities, especially in Northern Europe (and above all Pirenne's native Belgium) constituted wholly new entities, distinct from Roman and ancient predecessors.[12] They became centers of capitalistic behavior, and thus loci of modernity, which included the birth of modern democracy.

Pirenne's ideas gained wide currency both in scholarly works and in general textbooks, the latter including one written by Pirenne himself.[13] Edward P. Cheyney's English language textbook *Dawn of a New Era*, published in 1936, linked the rise of the West with economic modernity stemming from the medieval expansion of trade and accumulation of wealth, reaching its peak in the middle of the thirteenth century.[14] Alfons Dopsch's *Economic and Social Foundations of European Civilization*, published a year later, highlighted various forms of "capitalistic" behavior, including the activities of the German Hanse, a federation of towns and merchants that controlled the East-West trade along the Baltic.[15] Robert Lopez applied the term "the commercial revolution" to the period from 1000–1300, an appellation that remains popular. Armando Sapori advocated use of "Renaissance" to describe the economy of thirteenth-century Italy.[16]

The search for capitalistic forms and behavior inspired detailed studies of cities, merchants, and commerce. In the 1930s and 1940s there was notable interest in trade and business, the latter including the wool cloth and banking industries, two of the most important and well documented of the era. Italian scholars took the lead, drawing on the singularly rich archival sources there. Sapori wrote pioneering studies of major Florentine banking companies including the Bardi, Peruzzi, and the del Bene.[17] Frederic Lane examined Venetian trade and the ship-building industry, Sylvia Thrupp and Eileen Power investigated English trade and cloth industry and Abbott Payton Usher and Richard Ehrenberg detailed banking practices in the Mediterranean and southern Germany respectively.[18] These joined studies of state fiscal practices, of taxation and public finance and funded debts—the last an innovation begun in Italian cities in the fourteenth century and later used in the Netherlands and England and nowadays by contemporary states. Its use in the earlier period tightened the association between Renaissance and economic modernity.[19]

The empirical studies represented a shift away from earlier sociological and theoretical approaches, which had aimed at locating the "spirit" of capitalism rather than specifics. The change was stimulated by greater access to European archives, particularly after World War II. The study of business history in the English-speaking academy was encouraged by N. S. B. Gras, who urged scholars to eschew examining the economy from the "outside," in terms of laws, legislation and to look instead from the "inside," through close study of documentary evidence such as account books, diaries, notarial records, and correspondence.[20] Among the most prominent of the postwar generation of business historians were Raymond de Roover and his wife Florence Edler de Roover, who produced seminal studies of Belgian and Florentine merchant banking, the Italian silk industry, and maritime insurance practices. Raymond de Roover, trained as an accountant, explained clearly the sophisticated organization and commercial practices of the famed Medici bank, a study that is still the standard in the field.[21]

Business history remains a popular field among economic historians. They have extended their reach into numerous additional industries including cotton, and beer making, to name a few. They have uncovered wholly "new" sources, including private archives such as those of the Spinelli family, Florentine papal bankers at the time of the Medici, whose operations offer comparative perspective on their more famous contemporaries.[22] The studies possess a strong regional aspect, often dealing with businesses in prominent commercial cities.[23] Interest in state finance and taxation has waned, in favor of more politically based studies that deal with the fisc in terms of state formation and Weberian notions of modern bureaucratic forms (see chapter 6).

Students of Italian business have tended to stress its modernity. They have seen echoes of the present day in the use of the *commenda*, a fiscal instrument that allowed merchants to share risk.[24] In Genoa, ordinary people invested in *commenda* giving it the aspect of a modern stock market. Raymond de Roover compared the structure of the Medici bank to a modern holding company. Bills of exchange, a credit instrument employed by the Medici and other contemporary banks to evade church restriction on usury, were used to speculate in the international money market and remit funds without recourse to specie. Venetian "giro" banks, as Reinhold Mueller has shown, relied like their modern counterparts on fractional reserve and thus created "bank money," expanding monetary supply. The Fugger housed their workers in company-built residences, *fuggerie*, which have been compared to a modern factory town.[25] Most modern and capitalistic seeming of all was the use of double entry book keeping, an accounting technique that allowed systematic calculation of profits, with each transaction recorded twice, as both a debit and a credit, and a balance struck.[26] Max Weber, Werner Sombart, and Joseph Schumpeter saw double entry as emblematic of a "rational" approach to business and thus a driving force behind capitalism. This interpretation found its way into early textbooks, which posited double entry as the basic innovation that marked the advent of Renaissance capitalism.

Double entry has spawned its own lengthy debate among scholars. They question its dating and whether the rational calculation it entailed could have also been done by means of a "medieval" single entry method. All agree, however, that its origins were Italian and that the technique disseminated widely from there to the rest of Europe. Its diffusion was aided by manuals like that of Luca Pacioli, a mathematician, monk, and friend of Leonardo da Vinci, whose *Summa de arithmetica* (1494) offered a clear and complete description of Venetian "bilateral" style, with debits facing credits. Modern day accountants claim Pacioli as the founder for their profession.[27]

The emphasis on business and commerce has often involved close attention to the lives of merchants, who are described as individualistic and capitalistic by nature. Jakob Strieder's study of the Fugger bank focused on Jacob "the rich" Fugger (1459–1525), whom he called a "rational individualist" and "capitalist." Raymond de Roover labeled the Medici bankers "capitalist," the same term applied by Robert Lopez to the Genoese captain/pirate/entrepreneur Benedetto Zaccaria (d. 1307), who created a monopoly in the trade of alum, a fixative for dyes essential to the wool cloth industry.[28] The French merchant Jacques Coer (d. 1456) has likewise been fitted under the rubric of "individualist/capitalist," owing not only to his far-reaching commercial activities, but also his personal life, which involved accusations of poisoning the king's mistress.[29]

Although all the men have been viewed as capitalists, they have not all been seen as Renaissance figures. As elsewhere, temporal and geographic considerations condition the use of the term. According to De Roover, the Medici were Renaissance figures, whose capitalistic urges paid for the Renaissance art and building projects that beautified their native (Renaissance) city Florence. But Benedetto Zaccaria, whose life played itself out in the thirteenth century, was, in his biographer's estimation, a medieval figure, as was Jacques Coer, who though capitalist and cunning, lived in fifteenth-century France, the city of Lyon, where the Renaissance had not yet occurred. The French scholar Yves Renouard believed that the term Renaissance should be restricted to Italian merchants on the grounds that in addition to their business activities they were the principal consumers of Renaissance culture, notably the work of humanists (see chapter 4).[30]

The urban and merchant model did not, however, take into account developments in the countryside, where most people lived, even in Italy. Henri Pirenne drew a sharp distinction between the urban and rural spheres; the latter remained "feudal," with the rising capitalist city eventually overwhelming it. The English historian M. M. Postan described cities as "nonfeudal islands in the feudal seas."[31] In general scholars used two labels: "medieval" to describe activities (i.e., feudalism) in the countryside and "Renaissance" for the activities in the city. Consideration of the two sectors together was primarily the work of Marxist scholars who pondered the extent to which cities grew and sustained themselves by exploiting their rural lands. The Italian Gaetano Salvemini argued that Florence's economic greatness came directly at the expense of its countryside, which it oppressed with taxes. Studies of other Italian cities have, however, suggested greater variation. Florence's less potent neighbor Siena, for example, did not behave harshly toward its hinterland, but was receptive to it, aware that its own economic well-being was intrinsically linked.[32]

The relations between the city and the countryside has, as shall be discussed further below, been an issue of significant scholarly interest, taken up by participants in the "transition" and proto-industry debates for capitalism in the sixteenth and seventeenth centuries. The ambiguous nature and "medieval" aspect of countryside in the earlier centuries has meanwhile encouraged scholars to distinguish, as did Marx, between "merchant capitalism" and "industrial capitalism." The former related to cities and trade, the latter to factories, "free" labor, and full-scale capitalism of the nineteenth century, which encompassed all of society. Thus while positing the Medici as the Catholic antithesis to Max Weber's Calvinist spirit of capitalism, Raymond de Roover nevertheless described them as merchant capitalists.[33]

The Crises of the Fourteenth and Fifteenth Centuries: Hard Times, Prosperity, and Investment in Culture

The fourteenth century represents a point of passage in the discussion of the Renaissance economy, and of the European economy more generally. After centuries of demographic growth and economic expansion (1000–1300),

Europe experienced a series of crises – famine, plague, and war – that lasted for more than 100 years. Population decreased by one-third or one-half, according to various estimates.

Modern histories recount the crises in vivid detail. The "Great Hunger" of 1315–17 struck hard in Northern Europe, reducing population in some areas by as much as 10–25 percent.[34] It was followed by the Black Death, which swept through all of Europe (1347–50), to the Middle East and the steppes of Asia from where it had come. According to the standard account, the plague entered Europe on Genoese trading ships, by way of the Crimea, making landfall at Messina in Sicily and Genoa, spreading along trade routes.

Some economic historians explained the crises by means of Malthusian diagnosis. Drawing on the work of the eighteenth-century economist Thomas Malthus (*Essay on the Principal of Population*, 1798) they argued that Europe's population had exceeded food supply, causing famines and epidemics that acted as "checks," bringing the two back into line. M. M. Postan and Wilhelm Abel applied this directly to the last decades of the thirteenth century, when, they claimed, the boundaries of productive land had reached its limits, and, when rural estates such as at Winchester in southern England and in northern France and Germany show diminished yields of wheat, barley, and rye.[35] The Malthusian interpretation saw the process as both cyclical and inevitable, given that population increased geometrically and food supply arithmetically. It de-emphasized the Black Death as an all-encompassing event, and, in the manner of the Annales tradition to which it is closely allied, minimized the importance of historical labels such as Renaissance.

But the Black Death has remained a key event in many studies, and as we have already seen, especially among students of the Renaissance (see chapter 2). It coincided with intellectual and artistic developments associated with the period, with the careers of Petrarch and Boccaccio, the latter author of a detailed account of the plague in his *Decameron*. The demographic crisis clearly altered the economic status quo, raising obvious questions whether the phenomena were connected.

The cultural implication of the crises was the work of Robert Lopez (d. 1987). In his famous essay, "Hard Times and Investment in Culture," Lopez argued that the cycle of plague and famine produced a European-wide depression followed by stagnation. The demographic decline, in conjunction with the end of the "Mongolian peace" (1350) that had allowed western merchants to trade with the East, caused a contraction of trade and overseas markets. Lopez cited evidence of steep declines in yields of tolls and the contraction of two of the largest industries of the era: wool cloth and banking. He argued that in the face of economic "hard times," contemporaries ceased investing in their now unprofitable businesses and turned instead to the new humanistic culture that was then developing. Economic uncertainty increased the value of this culture, which Lopez understood as primarily art work and building projects. As the economic status of businessmen decreased, art patronage became a means of stabilizing their social status.[36]

The argument, first outlined in a lecture at a symposium at the Metropolitan Museum in 1952, was elaborated upon by Lopez in subsequent articles. It was incorporated into the Cambridge Economic History of Europe, in textbooks and gained wide currency among cultural and art historians.[37] Lopez saw the increase in cultural investments during the Renaissance as relative not absolute. The Middle Ages had seen investment in cathedrals, castles, and art. But an inverse proportion existed between cultural and business activity, such that the northern French towns that built the largest cathedrals in the High Middle Ages were not the most commercially advanced, and the Italian city of Genoa, an economic power in the Middle Ages, had the peninsula's smallest cathedrals. Lopez went so far as to suggest (tentatively) that investment in culture may have ended the Renaissance. The attempts by Pope Leo X, a member of the Medici family, to beautify the Vatican forced him to raise money through the sale of indulgences, which alienated Luther and thus sparked the Reformation.

It is worth relaying the details of the Lopez thesis because it is so famous and its fame has led to caricature and misrepresentation. "Investment in culture" did not mean, as one recent critic has argued, that citizens bought art "to store in bank safes" as if "present-day brokers."[38] Lopez did not view art as an investment in the modern sense. His intention was to outline in general terms a cultural turn by investors aimed at sustaining their social status. Lopez's approach was contextual, that of a medievalist who had devoted the majority of his career to illuminating the details of the commercial revolution from 1000 to 1300, but who accepted the reality of a cultural and intellectual Renaissance for the later years.[39] Lopez's pessimistic portrayal of the Renaissance economy was itself not new. Henri Pirenne had earlier described the years after 1330 as ones of a "cessation of all advance." Lopez's originality lay in connecting economy to Renaissance without recourse to the concept of capitalism and to notions in Burckhardt and von Martin of individuality and modernity. In this way, he consciously turned aside the work of the previous generation of scholars.[40]

The Lopez thesis was important also because it touched off a spirited debate that placed the economy at the center of Renaissance studies for more than two decades, a status that it has yet to regain. The discourse was distinguished not only by the vast amount of scholarship marshaled in defense of one point or the other, but by the tone of participants, who wrote what were as much manifestos as economic histories.[41] Carlo M. Cipolla denounced Lopez and his supporters as a "sect" and dismissed their assertions of declines in aggregate production as "dangerous and misleading." The European demographic crisis did not "depress" the economy, it brought about a new equilibrium in which per capita earnings were the same or higher than before.[42]

The debate focused on the effects of plague on trade and industry. Studies of customs revenues in the cities of Barcelona and Marseilles supported Lopez, showing declines in revenue beyond population loss.[43] Benjamin Kedar traced losses in trade in Venice and Genoa and changes in mentality among merchants, who became more pessimistic and averse to taking fiscal risks – emotional depression thus accompanied commercial depression.[44] Lopez's opponents meanwhile cited examples of growth industries as well as cities and regions that remained prosperous. They pointed to shifts to higher priced luxury goods to compensate for declines in the overall volume of trade. The city of Florence turned to production of high-end woolen cloths and development of a native silk industry that increased nearly fivefold from 1430 to 1445. Local silk merchants like Tommaso Spinelli recorded substantial profits as high as 30 percent on his investment. Declines in traditional wool cloth production in Florence and Flanders, the industry leaders of the Middle Ages, were offset by increases in Milan, Venice, and above all in England. England shifted from supplying raw wool to producing finished cloth. Meanwhile, cotton production increased in southern Germany offsetting declines in Italy. Lombardy cultivated woad, a blue dye used to stain fabric. "Factor substitution" reduced the recourse to expensive labor.[45] Sheep rearing required less labor and thus replaced cereal farming in some areas. The large scale conversion of arable land in England into pasture, occasioned Thomas More's famous sixteenth-century couplet:

> Sheep have eaten up our meadows and our downs
> Our corn, our wood, whole villages and towns.[46]

In Castile, the sheep grazers' union, the Mesta, active since the thirteenth century, became a powerful institution. Shepherds there shifted to raising Merino sheep, which produced high priced wool for luxury cloths.[47]

The debate was joined also by monetary theorists, who looked beyond demography and production figures to investigate the effects of money supply on economic developments. Harry Miskimin, using mint records in France and England, demonstrated shortages of specie that fettered commercial activities in the fourteenth and fifteenth centuries.[48] John Day spoke of a "Great Bullion Famine," during the era, which was most acute in the years from 1395 to 1415. John Munro argued that monetary contraction in England and Low Countries reached a critical stage from the 1370s to

1470s.[49] Peter Spufford emphasized the lack of silver, caused by diminished yields from mines in Saxony, Bohemia, and Tyrol, Europe's major sources, which had become exhausted.[50]

Not all agreed on the causes, locus, and extent of the bullion famine. Some scholars stressed imbalances in payments with the Islamic East; others emphasized hoarding and reductions in stocks owing to the velocity of circulation and the industrial use of metals by churches and in building construction and for luxury goods. Nathan Sussman has called into question whether indeed there were shortages in France, pointing to errors in calculations by earlier scholars.[51]

The discourse among monetary historians has proceeded on its own terms, beyond the Lopez thesis. This is true of the literature more generally. Scholars have treated the Black Death and demographic crisis as part of broader patterns, examining structural changes in markets and the realignment of trade networks. They focus on standard of living, and debate, not the cultural and intellectual effects of the mortality, but its social and economic meaning, whether it constituted a "golden age" for peasants and laboring classes owing to increased wages and decreased grain prices.[52] To this end, scholars have looked closely at wages and prices, the latter often relating to the building industry, for which much quantitative data has survived. Research on the peasantry and the countryside in France and Italy has centered on sharecropping, a system dating from the Middle Ages, by which owners of lands provided seed and loans to tenants in return for a share of the produce. David Herlihy argued that the extension of the system in Tuscany (*mezzadria*) during the plague era helped share risks and was favorable for peasants. P. J. Jones has asserted to the contrary that the system favored landowners. Philip Hoffman's studies of France suggest losses and benefits on both sides.[53]

Disagreement about standard of living persists. Short-term price and wage trends suggest greater variability than long term ones, with fluctuations that did not always favor laborers. The basic uncertainty of life and thin margin for existence made, as Christopher Dyer has argued, the notion of "good times" inherently problematic.[54]

It is with respect to Italy, and the city of Florence in particular, that the scholarship remains most concerned with connecting the economy to Renaissance culture.[55] No city has received more attention from economic historians or has richer archival source materials. Even Burckhardt, for all his inattention to fiscal issues, acknowledged that Florence was singularly possessed of "accurate information on financial affairs."[56] David Herlihy and Christiane Klapisch-Zuber, in *Tuscans and their Families*, employed computers to analyze the massive Florentine tax assessment of 1427, the so-called *catasto*.[57] This allowed them to illuminate in detail the social and economic fabric of Florence and its territorial state. Although Herlihy was a student of Lopez, the book does not concern itself with issues of hard times and prosperity but falls more naturally under the rubric of Annales history – with its comprehensive treatment of quantifiable data – the vantage of its co-author Klapisch-Zuber, a student of Fernand Braudel (see below).

Herlihy and Klapisch-Zuber described a Florentine society in which there was both great wealth and great poverty and uneven distributions of resources. The political historian Hans Baron, stressing the former, argued that great riches encouraged in the city, in the work of humanists, a new, positive view of wealth, which exalted its civic and moral value. This represented a distinctly Renaissance view of economy, different from the medieval view, which, influenced by Franciscan attitudes, advocated poverty as the ideal.[58]

The most rigorous recent claims to Florentine prosperity have been those of Richard Goldthwaite.[59] In several important works, Goldthwaite has stressed capital accumulation and social fluidity of Florentine wealth, which served as a precondition for luxury or "conspicuous" consumption in the fifteenth and sixteenth centuries.[60] Goldthwaite urged scholars to pay closer attention to the demand side (rather than production) and asserted that plague and crises brought new opportunities and increases in real income to artisans, particularly those involved in the building industry, of which "nothing was more conspicuous and more expensive."[61] The ranks of the consumers were constantly changing, thus sustaining demand, which involved all levels of society, including the secular and religious realm.[62]

The ideas were extended to Italy as a whole. The uniqueness of the peninsula lay in its urban concentration of wealth, which provided "permissive" economic causation for the great artistic and architectural flourishing of the period. Investment in culture was not, as in Lopez, intended to maintain or establish social place; Renaissance culture was reflective of qualitative change by which culture was created.

Goldthwaite's work is perhaps best understood as a response to Lopez, although the two scholars never directly addressed one another. They shared, however, the same basic aim, to establish a direct link between economic and cultural developments.[63] Lopez looked backward, situating his findings for the Renaissance economy in terms of the earlier medieval commercial expansion, while Goldthwaite focused on the fifteenth and sixteenth centuries, comparing Italy with contemporary Europe. Like Lopez, Goldthwaite's ideas have gained force not only among economic historians, but also cultural and art historians, who have treated consumption in a still larger sense as a metaphor for the Renaissance itself, applicable to the intellectual and material realm, the consumption of books and ideas. Lisa Jardine described the Renaissance as a celebration of the "urge to own" in which there was unprecedented demand for "worldly goods" and a "culture of consumption." This included wholly new goods brought back from the New World and East that further stimulated consumer demand.[64]

The notion of conspicuous consumption remains popular among historians. It is part of a more optimistic view of the economy that has emerged since Robert Lopez's death (1987). The view has included stress on constructive aspects of the "crises" of the fourteenth and fifteenth centuries. Scholars have employed Joseph Schumpeter's term "creative destruction" to describe the long term positive impact of demographic decline, which brought institutional changes that ultimately set Europe on the path to greater growth.[65]

The ideas are not without their critics.[66] Conspicuous consumption posits its own variety of Burckhardtian modernity. Focus on the demand side, though a useful counter to the earlier emphasis on supply and production, runs the risk of devolving into anecdotal history. Goldthwaite's optimistic conclusions about the Renaissance economy were derived primarily from study of successful business enterprises owned by the wealthy Florentine elite.

Recent scholarship has sought to broaden the range of variables and move beyond the narrow focus on plague and demography. It has looked more closely at the economic effects of warfare, which was rampant at the time and coincided directly with plague and famine, making it difficult to separate the impact of the one from the other. The most well known conflict of the period was the Hundred Years War (1337–1453) fought between England and France. The greatest incidence of war was, however, most likely in Italy, where the tradition of civic rivalry among the numerous independent states in close geographic proximity occasioned constant conflict. This was further exacerbated by the use of mercenary soldiers to fight wars. They formed "free" companies in times of peace, looting and pillaging the countryside, activities that made warfare perpetual.[67]

Wars were by far the most expensive activities undertaken by states. Indeed, the very practice of warfare was highly economic in nature. Opponents generally avoided pitched battles, which were considered too risky. They favored instead wars of attrition, wearing down each other economically, by means of blockades of trade routes and attacks on merchants. Armies wreaked havoc on rural lands, burning enemy barns, stealing livestock, destroying vines, and terrorizing peasants. Such activities forced the abandonment of villages, which had important economic consequences. The French historian Guy Bois described the coincidence of war, plague, and famine in fourteenth-century France as producing a "Hiroshima like" effect in parts of the countryside, decimating whole regions that, due to lack of money and political will, often remained so for many years. Productive laborers were frequently the first to desert, leaving behind less able men, and reducing output. Similar shifts in human capital occurred also in Italy, where skilled rural and urban workers left to escape hardships, induced often by tax breaks and concessions from rival states, who sought their services. The movement of silk weavers (1328) from war ravaged Lucca to Venice helped to establish the lucrative industry in that city. In general, rich states, able to offer the best terms, were the most successful in the competition for skilled workers.

The costs of warfare challenged even the most prosperous states to meet them. They required enormous outlays of money, which were gained from the citizenry by means of taxes and loans. Renaissance tax systems were highly complex. In Italy states employed a wide range of direct and indirect taxes as well as loans, both "forced" and "voluntary," which offered return at interest. Revenue from indirect taxes (*gabelles*) was used to repay the loans, thus the two sources were intrinsically linked, both increasing greatly during wars. Taxes took money away from the system and reduced the resources available to consumers. M. M. Postan argued that high taxes in England attendant the Hundred Years War meant lost opportunities for investments in business and other more productive enterprises. According to Anthony Molho, Florence experienced significant economic drain as a result of its wars with Milan in the early fifteenth century. Increases in indirect taxes struck most heavily on the middle and lower classes, while only a wealthy few with political ties to the ruling regime received full remuneration from loans. The evidence suggests that there was a class dimension to the economic effects of war.[68] War's impact was also felt differently in different places. In general, smaller more agrarian states struggled more than larger more commercially active ones. The former resorted to such expedients as pawning communal territory to lenders and borrowing money from foreign states and princes.[69]

Scholars need, however, to proceed with caution. The study of taxation and public finance tends to encourage pessimistic views of the economy, while the study of business practices of the elite inclines researchers to produce optimistic views. There remains much more research to be done, particularly with regard to warfare. Indeed, it is difficult provide a balance sheet.[70] The negative effects of war were accompanied also by more favorable ones. Soldiers' wages were, for instance, recycled back into the economy in the form of purchases. War stimulated industries such as the Milanese armor business and the Arsenale in Venice as well as petty businesses of more local arms makers.[71] It remains for scholars to situate war more firmly in terms of other economic phenomena, to determine whether it altered basic economic patterns or simply accentuated those already present.[72]

The Long Sixteenth Century and the Early Modern Economy

The cycle of plague, famine, and crises ended in the sixteenth century. Europe's population regained its pre-plague level by the 1570s. Cities grew larger, industrial and agricultural output expanded, a direct sea route to the Indies was established, a New World was discovered and a global economy emerged, with the Atlantic for the first time at the center of activity. Scholars group the phenomena under the heading of the "long sixteenth century," a term popularized by Fernand Braudel that corresponds roughly to the years 1450 to 1620, allowing also the inclusion of social, political, and religious events – the rise of nation-states and Protestant Reformation – which had important economic consequences.

The focus on these years entailed a shift in the scholarly discourse. Economic historians who study the phenomena stress "modernity," but less so in terms of the Renaissance. Harry Miskimin, a student of Robert Lopez, was among the few to apply the Renaissance label to the whole period from 1300–1600, describing the years 1300–1460 as the "early Renaissance" and those from 1460–1600 as the "late Renaissance." Most scholars have, however, preferred the term "early modern" and situate events beginning in 1450/1500 in terms of the nineteenth century and the start of modern industrialization and the factory system.[73] The approach is teleological (see chapter 3) and shows little concern for making explicit connections between economic and cultural developments. The primary interest is in illuminating the "big picture," the grand thesis that explains the "rise of the West." The vantage is pan-European and comparative, with focus on finding the causes of the "great divergence," as Kenneth Pomeranz has recently called it, the point at which European economies moved beyond those of China and Islam; in short how the West "won" and the world became divided into "developed" and "underdeveloped "nations.[74]

The discourse is heavily influenced by Marxian theory and the Annales School, both of which treat industrialization as the key moment in European history. More so than earlier, economists have taken a leading role in the discourse, speculating on numerous factors including technology (W. W. Rostow), trade and social relations, political institutions, and property rights (New Economic School, Douglass North).[75]

Historians have tended to treat the sixteenth century together with the seventeenth. The first was an era of expansion, although not uniform. The second was a time of contraction, what Eric Hobsbawm famously called a "general crisis." The response to the crisis formed the point of separation for the economies of European states. The Dutch and the English emerged as "winners," as "modern" economies, freed from demographic cycles and able to sustain long term per capita growth and rise in income without population increase.[76]

Overseas Explorations/Price Revolution/ Consumption and Slavery

Grand theses notwithstanding, there have also been many local and individual studies. As for the earlier period, scholars have examined specific industries and business firms, agricultural practices, as well as money supply, war and public finance.

The transatlantic voyages and passage to the Indies have received a great deal of attention. The eighteenth-century economist Adam Smith called them the "most important events recorded in the history of mankind."[77] The starting date of the long sixteenth century as 1450 coincides with the Portuguese explorations of the African coast and Atlantic Ocean, which brought control over the Atlantic islands (Madeira) and set the stage for Vasco da Gama's journey to Calicut in 1498 and the opening of a direct route to the spice islands in the Indies that challenged Venice's domination of trade of luxury goods from the East, a key feature of medieval Mediterranean trade.[78] The Atlantic voyages culminated in the discovery of the Americas and the establishment of colonies by the Spanish, French, Dutch, and English, which created an Atlantic economy.

Historians initially emphasized the immediate long-term economic stimulus for Europe, what one overly enthusiastic scholar called a 400-year boom.[79] Few now make such claims. They treat the "rise of the Atlantic economy" as a slow and partial process that did not affect Northern Europe as a whole, but, as Jonathan Israel has noted, only a "fringe."[80] The full consequences of the establishment of colonies and "favorable balance of trade" were not felt until the latter seventeenth and eighteenth centuries. Prosperous states such as the Netherlands benefited also from local trade in the Baltic as well as by means of agricultural innovation.

Portugal, the initiator of the long distance voyages, was an unlikely candidate for international leadership. Its economy was relatively undeveloped in the fifteenth century and its impetus along the African coast was conditioned to a large degree by a "medieval" Christian crusading zeal against the pressure of the expanding Almoravid empire in Morocco. The Portuguese demonstrated little business acumen. They controlled the new trade in spices by means of military coercion and their early success in marketing depended not on underselling the Venetians, but in denying them access to their traditional suppliers. When old Mediterranean networks and routes reformed, the Venetians recaptured much of their trade and by 1530s were again in a strong position.[81] When Portugal's royal and military strength declined in the second half of the sixteenth century, its trade largely disappeared.

A much-debated consequence of the European conquests was its impact on money supply. The Spanish conquistadors – Cortes in 1520 in Mexico and Pizarro in 1530 in Peru – found new sources of silver, notably at Potosì (1545) in Peru (modern-day Bolivia), which alone quadrupled the value of previous imports of precious metals. The dramatic influx of specie produced what Earl J. Hamilton called (in *American Treasure and the Price Revolution*, 1934) a "price revolution" in sixteenth-century Europe. This in effect reversed the bullion famine of the previous two centuries, described by scholars who had been inspired by Hamilton. The flood of metals in Europe caused the price of goods to increase dramatically from 1500 to 1620. Patterns varied from region to region and according to commodity. Grain prices were the most volatile, rising as much as seven times in nominal terms in some places, accompanied by increases in rents. Wages and the price of manufactured goods lagged behind, thus causing a loss of real income, which favored landholders over tenants.[82] The trends were widely noted by contemporaries, including by the French political theorist, Jean Bodin, who saw a direct connection between the treasure from America and the general rise of prices in France.

As with the discourse on the fourteenth and fifteenth centuries, scholars have engaged in intramural debates on the timing and precise effects of the increased bullion stocks. Some point to evidence that Europe experienced inflation before the arrival of New World silver, spurred by demographic recovery, increased economic activity, which in turn increased the scale and velocity of exchange, driving up prices. New technologies revived production of German mines in the last years of the fifteenth century, which reached a peak in the early 1520s, just as the overseas supplies were found. Others have deduced political factors: the debasements of coinage and greater availability of credit also increased money supply. They question the basic validity of Hamilton's thesis, noting that the 200 percent price increase he traced over the course of the sixteenth century constitutes less than one percent increase yearly, modest by modern standards.[83] The increase in bullion also had positive effects, providing greater liquidity, which brought down interest rates and favored international exchanges, allowing Western Europe to overcome its traditional trading deficit with the Baltic region and the East.[84]

Whatever the effect on monetary stocks, Atlantic trade ultimately altered traditional patterns. It led to the establishment of new trade networks and brought to Europe a new set of goods and commodities. The Spanish transported home the potato and maize, which helped increase European food supply and reduce the likelihood of famine.[85] They imported cocoa, from South America, which in pure form was thought fit "only for pigs," but with the addition of sugar and other spices, became popular in Europe at the tables of aristocrats and the well-to-do. The New World also became a source of tobacco in the sixteenth and seventeenth centuries, and by the late seventeenth and eighteenth centuries, coffee and tea (Indies). The new commodities encouraged a "consumer society," in which goods were desirable also for their novelty and prestige.[86] By the eighteenth century this included distinct shopping areas, bars and eating places and more generally the notion of leisure time and activities.[87]

A commodity that was in particularly great demand in the period was sugar. It had been cultivated in Sicily and Cyprus in the Middle Ages, and in Muslim Egypt and Syria. But supplies were limited, and honey remained the traditional sweetener. As a result of the explorations, the Portuguese set up plantations in the Azores and then in Brazil.[88] By the sixteenth century demand for sugar increased fourfold and by the middle of the seventeenth century the Portuguese were sending more than 22 tons of sugar to Europe from their colony in Brazil, giving rise to the saying "Whoever says Brazil says sugar and more sugar."[89]

The popularity and profitability of sugar stimulated the traffic in black African slaves, the most tragic aspect of the overseas voyages. Sugar cultivation was labor intensive. Cane took 12 months to ripen, and required many workers to process it through its various stages. The Portuguese imported slaves from Africa to do this work, a trade they had become involved in during the middle of the fifteenth century while exploring the African coast. The Genoese had preceded the Portuguese, transporting Africans to the Mediterranean and Asia Minor for domestic service in the Middle Ages. The Atlantic trade was on a more vast scale, and involved harsher physical labor. By 1700, more than a million and a half slaves were imported to the Americas. The numbers grew still more in the eighteenth century, for which there has survived the most detailed records. Slavery became an important part of the larger Atlantic trading networks and involved the participation of African states.[90]

"Transition to Capitalism": Cities, Nation States, and World Systems

Atlantic trade also stimulated the growth of urban centers. The city of Antwerp became a main entrepôt of trade, marketing Portuguese spices from the Indies, as well as German metals, Italian silks, and English cloth. The city's population doubled from 1450 to 1550. The high concentration of merchants facilitated exchange and credit transfers, lowered transaction costs, and made the city a financial clearinghouse for Europe. Unlike in the

Middle Ages, when fairs met seasonally, transactions at Antwerp took place throughout the entire year. The city constructed a permanent hall along the waterfront, a Bourse, to house these activities under one roof.

The growth of European cities from 1500–1800 has been viewed as critical to the overall development of the European economy and to capitalism. Scholars have drawn again on the work of Henri Pirenne. But the "early modern urban revolution" is judged differently from its medieval counterpart in that it favored Northern Europe (England, Low Countries, Germany, and France) over the Mediterranean (Italy, Iberia, southern France). The population of the north increased 18 percent (from 36 to 42.5 million) as opposed to 11 percent in the Mediterranean (from 18.3 million to 20 million).[91] Unlike in the Middle Ages, there were few new cities; rather, extant cities grew larger. According to Jan de Vries, urbanization patterns after 1600 were more structured and less autarchic than their medieval predecessors.[92] The vast majority of people still lived in the countryside, but Europe overall became more urbanized, with the highest density in the Low Countries.

Urban developments served as the focal point of the "transition" debate, which arose in the 1950s and reached a peak in the 1970s, contemporaneous with the Lopez thesis and the hard times–prosperity debate. The transition debate (which makes no reference to Lopez) was largely theoretical and interpretive, initiated by economists who based their interpretations on available evidence rather than original research. At issue was ascertaining the point at which labor became free and merchant capitalism gave way to industrial capitalism. Maurice Dobb and Paul Sweezy, Marxist economists, traced the stages of development, with emphasis on the sixteenth and seventeenth centuries. Maurice Dobb argued that urban expansion and international trade in the sixteenth century produced capitalism in cities, but was not in itself sufficient to end feudalism in the countryside, which died a separate death by means of its own internal contradictions.[93] There was therefore a gap between the end of the old mode and the birth of the new one, which Dobb saw as emerging in seventeenth-century England. Paul Sweezy argued that increased trade transformed cities and by necessity the countryside as well, making the collapse of feudalism coeval with the birth of capitalism.[94]

The two views formed the basis of subsequent debate, played out in the pages of the journal *Science and Society* and later reproduced in a book entitled *The Transition from Feudalism to Capitalism*. Robert Brenner reassessed both Dobb and Sweezy in a sweeping study that minimized the role of international commerce and stressed instead class struggles within the feudal world, between lords and peasants in the countryside, which produced different outcomes in different places.[95] Brenner accused prior scholars of drawing conclusions too narrowly from the English example, the eventual home of the Industrial Revolution. He advocated looking more broadly at Europe, where there existed diverse social relations. Unique conditions paved the way for industrialization in England, while the social and economic realities of Eastern Europe led to the subordination of peasants and the advent of a second serfdom.[96]

At issue in both the transition debate and Brenner's revision of it was the state of labor relations in the countryside. This was also of central importance in the "proto-industry" debate, which arose alongside it. Franklin Mendels argued that increased trade and demand for goods in the sixteenth and seventeenth centuries encouraged manufacturers (particularly in Northern Europe) to base their operations in the countryside and employ peasant labor, allowing them to circumvent urban guild restrictions and produce goods more cheaply for the international market. An export-oriented linen industry was, for example, established in Flanders as a compliment to agricultural production. The proto-industries allowed accumulation of capital in the countryside and inculcated skills to rural labor, helping to "free" them in the Marxian sense. This formed the precursor to the Industrial Revolution of the nineteenth century, making it the culmination of increased scope and scale of businesses that had been going on for centuries.[97]

Proto-industry has sparked its own debate, as scholars question the degree to which the sites of rural industry corresponded to the places where industrialization actually occurred. The primacy of cities in the development of capitalism nevertheless remains important. They were, according to the well-known Annales scholar Fernand Braudel "cathedrals" of ideas. In his three volume *Civilization and Capitalism*, Braudel stressed a progression of "capital" cities of increasing size and economic might, a linear unfolding of economic dominance from Florence in the thirteenth century to Amsterdam in the seventeenth, culminating with London, which stood as a prelude to industrialization. Braudel described capitalism and cities as "much the same thing."[98] But cities only went so far in transforming the world. They fed off "the old mode without altering it" and ultimately gave way to nation states, which brought the final phase of industrial capitalism. The "failed" city was thus the necessary prelude to the nation state.[99]

A close look at Braudel's analysis reveals that it is not free of ambiguity. He described capitalism in various ways, as a multi-faceted entity that existed in different guises in different places and indeed was not necessarily a system all of its own.[100] Jan de Vries de-emphasized the priority of capital cities, arguing that they should be situated instead in broader urban networks, treated in relation to each other, and with their hinterlands.[101] Thus like adherents of proto-industry, de Vries saw industrial revolution as more an evolution.

Braudel's schema nevertheless retains popularity, in textbooks and general histories. The "rise of nation states" is a key component in discussions of the early modern economy (see chapter 6). The nation state facilitated the overseas explorations and allowed the means to exploit the resources found abroad. The Portuguese voyages of Dias and Da Gama in the 1480s and 1490s and the Spanish voyages of Columbus for Spain were all state sponsored. The Dutch and the English governments created trading companies, the Dutch and English East India Companies, to manage affairs. Rulers employed "mercantilist" practices aimed at gaining a favorable balance of trade to accrue bullion, placing import tariffs on the goods of competitors, fostering native industry, and requiring trade to be done in native ships.

Scholars impute still more to the nation state. They see it as representing an advanced political form, a step forward in the evolutionary scale from the city-state (see chapter 6). It was larger in size and population, possessed greater internal cohesion, fewer local tariffs and greater coercive force. This helped create economies of scale that lowered transaction costs. Political consolidation also improved enforcement of contracts, stimulated labor mobility and technological diffusion. It produced standing armies, and with them wars of increased scale and cost that accentuated their advantage over city states and helped produce a military revolution that led to technical innovations in war that ultimately facilitated world domination, as a precondition for economic domination.

Political consolidation has also been credited with producing institutional innovation. Douglass North argued that the nation states of the sixteenth and seventeenth centuries, most notably England, redefined property rights, protecting private ownership, which included also patent laws and intellectual rights. The changes provided incentive for economic initiative, by bringing private returns into parity with social returns, the good of the individual synchronized with the good of the society and economy. This paved the way for technological advance, which in turn ultimately paved the way for the industrial revolution.[102]

The rise of the nation states also provided the context for the sociological studies of Immanuel Wallerstein, author of one of the most complex and controversial arguments relating to the development of capitalism. Like Braudel whom he admired, Wallerstein traced the ascent of capitalism over three volumes.[103] The prime mover was again the commercial expansion of the sixteenth and seventeenth centuries, which made possible large-scale accumulation of capital. This in turn helped finance agricultural production and created a worldwide "division of labor" in which the different sectors had their own economic roles. The capitalist "world system" unfolded in stages from 1450 to 1670.[104]

He called the sectors "the core, periphery, and semi-periphery." The core states – England, Holland, and France – had strong central governments and bureaucracies as well as standing armies. This allowed the "bourgeoisie" to gain control over international commerce, the profits of which allowed them to monetize rural space and thus encourage rural entrepreneurs and industrialization (England). The peripheral states – Poland and Latin America – had weak central governments and their resources, grain and bullion primarily, were expropriated by the core, which led to the subjugation of the peasantry (Poland). The semi-peripheral states – Italy, Spain, and southern Germany – were zones that had previously been in the core, but were now in decline. They had strong trading sectors, notably in banking, but no longer dominated trade and thus did not benefit from the world system to the same degree that the core states did.

Agency and Innovation

Wallerstein's work demonstrates the wide gap that separates studies of early modern economy from those of Renaissance economy. Wallerstein used the term Renaissance, but loosely, stripped of any association with culture. His broad sociological approach to capitalism recalls that of Alfred von Martin. But unlike von Martin, Wallerstein minimizes the role of individual agency, which had allowed the earlier scholar to link capitalism to the Renaissance. Wallerstein emphasis is squarely on macro-economic developments, capitalism as a "top-shelf entity," as Braudel called it.

It is the role of individual agency that many recent economic studies now seek to recover. But in so doing, scholars deal with a different set of players than earlier. The wealthy businessman and Renaissance "merchant-individual" have been replaced by artisans, laborers, and women (see chapter 2). This has allowed access to previously unexplored sectors of the economy, including the difficult-to-quantify domestic sphere. The new emphasis has, however, encouraged movement away from the grand narrative and use of the term Renaissance, for which there is little apparent application.

The changing approaches to the "Renaissance economy" may be traced in university textbooks. Lewis Spitz, in his *Renaissance and Reformation Europe*, first published in 1971, followed closely von Martin's schema, associating the Renaissance economy with capitalism and individualism. Ernst Breisach's *Renaissance Europe*, published in 1973, began discussion of the economy with statement of the Lopez thesis and the hard times-prosperity debate. Robin Kirkpatrick's *Renaissance Europe*, published almost 30 years after Breisach (2002) does not mention the economy at all, nor does the still more recent *Palgrave Advances in Renaissance Historiography* (2005), which consists of 13 chapters on recent Renaissance scholarship, none on the economy.

To the extent that the search for a Renaissance economy continues, it has been conducted primarily by Italianists, and in particular those interested in business history and major urban centers. The term remains popular also in studies of conspicuous consumption, now treated not only in its economic context, but as a broader cultural, material, and intellectual phenomenon that serves as a metaphor for the Renaissance itself. On a lower key, the Renaissance label continues to be used in general studies as a loose marker under which to place economic innovations, such as urbanization and advanced accounting techniques.[105]

Notes

1 Giovanni Boccaccio, *The Decameron*, trans. by Mark Musa and Peter Bondanella (New York, 1977): 3–7.
2 Adam Smith, *The Wealth of Nations*, ed. by Edwin Canaan, vol. 2 (London, 1930), p. 125 (bk. iv, ch. vii).
3 Karl Marx, *Capital* in *The Marx-Engels Reader*, ed. by Robert C. Tucker (New York, 1978): 433–4.
4 Werner Sombart, *Der Moderne Kapitalismus*, 3 vols. (Leipzig, 1902); Max Weber, *The Protestant Ethic and the Spirit of Capitalism*, trans. by Talcott Parsons (New York, 1933, original German edn. 1904–5).
5 Frank Nussbaum, "The Economic History of Renaissance Europe: Problems and Solutions during the Past Generation," *Journal of Modern History* 13, 4 (1941): 527; Wallace K. Ferguson, "Recent Trends in the Economic Historiography of the Renaissance," *Studies in the Renaissance* 7 (1960): 55.
6 François Simiand, *La méthode positive en science économique* (Paris, 1912); Camille-Ernest Labrousse, *La Crise de l'économie française à la fin de l'Ancien Régime et au début de la Révolution* (Paris, 1943); Emmanuel Le Roy Ladurie, "Motionless History," *Social Science History* 1, 2 (Winter 1977): 115–36.
7 Peter Musgrave, *The Early Modern European Economy* (New York, 1999).
8 H. Koht, "Le problème des origines de la Renaissance," *Revue de synthèse historique* 37 (1924): 107–16.
9 Alfred von Martin, *Sociology of the Renaissance* (New York, 1963, originally published as *Soziologie der Renaissance* in 1932).
10 H. M. Robertson, *Aspects of the Rise of Economic Individualism* (Cambridge, 1933).
11 Henri Pirenne, *Medieval Cities: Their Origins and the Revival of Trade* (Princeton, 1980, originally published 1925), p. 161.
12 Henri Pirenne, *Early Democracies in the Low Countries: Urban Society and Political Conflict in the Middle Ages and the Renaissance* (New York, 1963, originally published in 1915).

13 Henri Pirenne, *Economic and Social History of Medieval Europe* (London, 2006, originally published in 1933).

14 Edward P. Cheyney, *Dawn of a New Era* (New York, 1936): 1–2.

15 Alfons Dopsch, *Economic and Social Foundations of European Civilization* (New York, 1937). See also K. Pagel, *Die Hanse* (Brunswick, 1952); Philippe Dollinger, *The German Hanse*, trans. by D. Ault and S. Steinberg (Stanford, 1979).

16 Gino Luzzatto, "The Study of Medieval Economic History in Italy: Recent Literature and Tendencies," *Journal of Economic and Business History* 4 (1931–2): 708–27.

17 Armando Sapori, *La crisi delle compagnie mercantili dei Bardi e dei Peruzzi* (Florence, 1926), *Una compagnia di Calimala ai primi del Trecento* (Florence, 1932), *Libri di commercio dei Peruzzi* (Milan, 1934), *Liber tercius Frescobaldorum* (Florence, 1947), and *I libri degli Alberti del Guidice* (Milan, 1952). Sapori's major articles are collected in *Studi di storia economica medievale* (Florence, 1945).

18 Frederic C. Lane, *Venetian Ships and Shipbuilders of the Renaissance* (Baltimore, 1934), "Venetian Bankers, 1496–1533," *Journal of Political Economy* 45 (1937): 187–206, and "The Mediterranean Spice Trade: Its Revival in the Sixteenth Century," *American Historical Review* 45 (1940): 581–90; Eileen Power, *The Wool Trade in English Medieval History* (London, 1941); Sylvia Thrupp, *The Merchant Class of Medieval London, 1300–1500* (Chicago, 1948); Abbott Payton Usher, *The Early History of Deposit Banking in Mediterranean Europe* (Cambridge, 1943); Richard Ehrenberg, *Capital and Finance in the Age of the Renaissance* (New York, 1963); Jakob Strieder, *Jacob Fugger the Rich: Merchant and Banker of Augsburg, 1454–1525* (New York, 1932); Ernst Hering, *Die Fugger* (Leipzig, 1939).

19 Hans Sieveking, "Studio sulle finanze genovesi nel medioevo," trans. by O. Soardi, *Atti della Società Ligure di Storia Patria* 35 (1905): 3–261; Bernardino Barbadoro, *Le finanze della repubblica fiorentina: imposta diretta e debito pubblico fino all'istituzione del Monte* (Florence, 1929); Gino Luzzatto, *I prestiti pubblici della Repubblica di Venezia* (sec. XIII–XV) (Padua, 1929); Frederic C. Lane, "Venture Accounting in Medieval Business Management," *Bulletin of the Business Historical Society*, 19 (1945): 161–72 reprinted in his *Venice and History: The Collected Papers of Frederic C. Lane* (Baltimore, 1966), pp. 99–108.

20 N. S. B. Gras, "Business History," *Economic History Review* 4 (1934): 385–98 and *Business and Capitalism: An Introduction to Business History* (New York, 1939).

21 Florence Edler de Roover, "Early Examples of Maritime Insurance," *Journal of Economic History* 5 (1945) and "Lucchese Silks," *Ciba Review* 80 (1950); Raymond De Roover, *Money, Banking and Credit in Medieval Bruges* (Cambridge, MA, 1948) and *The Rise and Decline of the Medici Bank, 1397–1494* (New York, 1966).

22 William Caferro, "The Silk Business of Tommaso Spinelli, Fifteenth-Century Florentine Merchant and Papal Banker," *Renaissance Studies* 10 (Dec. 1996): 417–39 and "L'Attività bancaria papale e la Firenze del Rinascimento: Il caso di Tommaso Spinelli," *Società e storia* 55 (Summer 1996): 717–53.

23 The vast literature includes David Herlihy, *Medieval and Renaissance Pistoia: The Social History of an Italian Town, 1200–1430* (New Haven, 1966); Frederic Lane and Reinhold Mueller, *Money and Banking in Medieval and Renaissance Venice: Coins and Moneys of Account* (Baltimore and London, 1985); Reinhold C. Mueller, *The Venetian Money Market: Banks, Panics, and the Public Debt, 1200–1500* (Baltimore, 1997); Herman Van der Wee, ed., *The Rise and Decline of Urban Industries in Italy and in the Low Countries: Late Middle Ages–Early Modern Times* (Leuven, 1988): Edwin S. Hunt, *The Medieval Super-Companies: A Study of the Peruzzi Company of Florence* (Cambridge, 1994); Richard A. Goldthwaite, Enzo Settesoldi, and Marco Spallanzani, eds., *Due libri mastri degli Alberti: Una grande compagnia di Calimala, 1348–1358*, 2 vols. (Florence, 1995); Richard Goldthwaite, "Local Banking in Renaissance Florence," *Journal of European Economic History* 14 (Spring 1985): 5–55; Claude Carrère, *Barcelone: Centre économique à l'époque des difficultés, 1380–1462* (Paris, 1967); Angus MacKay, *Money, Prices and Politics in Fifteenth-Century Castile* (London, 1981); Teofilio F. Ruiz, *Crisis and Continuity: Land and Town in Late Medieval Castile* (Philadelphia, 1994); Carla Rahn Phillips and William D. Phillips, *Spain's Golden Fleece: Wool Production and the Wool Trade from the Middle Ages to the Nineteenth Century* (Baltimore, 1997); Kathryn Reyerson, *Business, Banking, and Finance in Medieval Montpellier* (Toronto, 1985); Maureen Mazzaoui, "The Cotton Industry of Northern Italy in the Late Middle Ages, 1150–1450," *Journal of Economic History* 32 (1972): 262–86; Hidetoshi Hoshino, *L'arte della lana in Firenze nel basso medioevo: il commercio della lana e il mercato dei panni fiorentini nei secoli XIII–XV* (Florence, 1980); Thomas Blomquist, "The Early History of European Banking: Merchants, Bankers, and Lombards of XIIIth-Century Lucca in the County of Champagne," *Journal of European Economic History* 14 (Winter 1985): 521–36; Paolo Malanima, "Pisa and the Trade Routes to the Near East in the Late Middle Ages," *Journal of European Economic History* 16 (Fall 1987): 335–56; Franco Franceschi, *Oltre il "Tumulto": I lavoratori fiorentini dell'arte della Lana fra Tre e Quattrocento* (Florence, 1993); Luca Molà, *The Silk Business of Renaissance Venice* (Baltimore, 2000); Sergio Tognetti, *Da Figline a Firenze. Ascesa economica e politica della famiglia Serristori (secoli XIV–XVI)* (Florence, 2003) and *Il banco Cambini: Affari e mercati di una compagnia mercantile-bancaria nella Firenze del XV secolo* (Florence, 1999).

24 Abraham Udovitch, "At the Origins of the Western Commenda: Islam, Israel, Byzantium?" *Speculum* 37 (1962): 198–207.

25 Reinhold C. Mueller, "The Role of Bank Money in Venice, 1300–1500," *Studi Veneziani*, n.s., 3 (1979): 47–96.

26 Frederic C. Lane, "Venture Accounting in Medieval Business Management," *Bulletin of the Business Historical Society* 19 (1945): 161–72; Basil S. Yamey, "Scientific Bookkeeping and the Rise of Capitalism," *Economic History Review* 2 (1948–9): 99–113; Raymond de Roover, "The Development of Accounting prior to Luca Pacioli according to Account Books of Medieval Merchants," in *Business, Banking and Economic Thought in Late Medieval and Early Modern Europe*, ed. by Julius Kirshner (Chicago, 1974), pp. 119–80; J. R. Edwards, *A History of Financial Accounting* (London, 1989).

27 T. A. Lee, Ashton C. Bishop, and R. H. Parker eds., *Accounting History from the Renaissance to the Present: A Remembrance of Luca Pacioli*, (New York, 1996); Christopher Nobles, ed., *The Development of Double Entry: Selected Essays* (New York, 1984); Robert H. Parker and Basil S. Yamey, *Accounting History: Some British Contributions* (Oxford, 1994); John F. Padgett and Paul D. MacLean, "Organizational Invention and Elite Transformation: The Birth of Partnership Systems in Renaissance Florence," *American Journal of Sociology* 111 (March 2006): 1463–568.

28 Jakob Strieder, *Jacob Fugger the Rich* (New York, 1932); Iris Origo, *The Merchant of Prato* (New York, 1957); Robert S. Lopez, *Genova marinara nel Duecento: Benedetto Zaccaria, ammiraglio e mercante* (Messina, 1933); Robert S. Lopez, *The Commercial Revolution of the Middle Ages, 950–1350* (Cambridge, 1976), pp. 139–41.

29 A. B. Kerr, *Jacques Coer, Merchant Prince of the Middle Ages* (New York, 1927); Kathryn Reyerson, *Jacques Coeur: Entrepreneur and King's Bursar* (London, 2005), p. 3.

30 Yves Renouard, *Les hommes d'affaires italiens du Moyen Age* (Paris, 1949).

31 M. M. Postan, *The Medieval Economy and Society* (Berkeley and Los Angeles, 1975), p. 212.

32 Romolo Caggese, "Classi e comuni rurali nel medioevo italiano," vol. 1 (Florence, 1907); Gaetano Salvemini, "Un comune rurale nel secolo XIII," in *Opere di Gaetano Salvemini*, ed. by Ernesto Sestan, vol. 2 (Milan, 1972), pp. 274–97; Enrico Fiumi, "Sui rapporti tra città e contado nell'età comunale," *Archivio Storico Italiano* 114 (1956): 18–68; William Caferro, "City and Countryside in Siena in the Second Half of the Fourteenth Century," *Journal of Economic History* 54 (March 1994): 85–110.

33 De Roover, *Medici Bank*, p. 7.

34 William C. Jordan, *The Great Famine: Northern Europe in the Early Fourteenth Century* (Princeton, 1996).

35 W. Abel, *Agrakrisen und Agrarkonjunktur in Mitteleuropa vom 13 bis zum 19 jahrhundert* (Berlin, 1935); M. M. Postan and J. Z. Titow, "Heriots and Prices on Winchester Manors," *Economic History Review* 11 (1956): 392–411.

36 Robert S. Lopez, "Hard Times and Investment in Culture," in *The Renaissance, Medieval or Modern?* ed. by Karl H. Dannenfeldt (Boston, 1959).

37 Edward Miller, Cynthia Postan, and M. M. Postan, eds., *The Cambridge Economic History of Europe* (Cambridge, 1952). For textbooks see Brian Pullan, *A History of Early Renaissance Italy* (New York, 1973) and Norman J. G. Pounds, *An Economic History of Medieval Europe*, 2nd edn. (London, 1994), pp. 482–5. Douglass North and Robert Paul Thomas (1973) referred to the fourteenth and fifteenth centuries as ones of "contraction." Douglass C. North and Robert Paul Thomas, *The Rise of the Western World* (Cambridge, 1973). In 1976 Duane Osheim noted the triumph of the Lopez thesis. Duane Osheim, "Rural Population and the Tuscan Economy of the Late Middle Ages," *Viator* 7 (1976): 329–46.

38 Alison Brown, *The Renaissance* (London, 1999), pp. 18–19.

39 Pirenne, *Medieval Cities*, p. 167.

40 Pirenne, *Economic and Social History*, p. 191.

41 See, among others E. A. Kosminsky, "Peut-on considerer le XIVe et le XVe siècles comme l'époque de la decadence de l'économie européenne?" in *Studi in onore di A. Sapori*, vol. 1 (Milan, 1957), pp. 551–69; David Herlihy, "Population, Plague and Social Change in Rural Pistoia, 1201–1430," *Economic History Review* 18 (1965): 225–44. The papers of the plenary session at the New England Renaissance Conference in 1989 summarized developments in economic history in terms of the Lopez thesis. Judith C. Brown, "Prosperity or Hard Times in Renaissance Italy?" *Renaissance Quarterly* 42 (1989): 760–80.

42 Carlo M. Cipolla, "Economic Depression of the Renaissance?" *Economic History Review* 16 (1964): 519–24 and *Before the Industrial Revolution* (New York, 1994, originally published in 1976), p. 200. For Lopez's response see R. S. Lopez, "Economic Depression of the Renaissance," *Economic History Review* 16 (1964): 525–7.

43 John Day, *The Medieval Market Economy* (Oxford, 1987), pp. 203–11.

44 Benjamin Z. Kedar, *Merchants in Crisis: Genoese and Venetian Men of Affairs and the Fourteenth-Century Depression* (New Haven, 1976).

45 David Herlihy, *The Black Death and the Transformation of the West* (Cambridge, MA, 1997), pp. 49–50.

46 Robert Duplessis, *Transitions to Capitalism in Early Modern Europe* (Cambridge, 1997), p. 65.

47 Julius Klein, *The Mesta: A Study in Spanish Economic History, 1273–1836* (Cambridge, MA, 1920).

48 Harry A. Miskimin, *The Economy of the Early Renaissance* (Englewood Cliffs, NJ, 1969), pp. 138–63 and *Money and Power in Fifteenth Century France* (New Haven, 1984); John Day, "The Great Bullion Famine of the Fifteenth Century," *Past and Present* 79 (1978): 3–54. See also Nicholas Mayhew, "Population, Money Supply, and the Velocity of Circulation in England, 1300–1700," *Economic History Review*, 2nd ser., 48 (May 1995): 238–57.

49 John H. A. Munro, *Wool, Cloth and Gold: The Struggle for Bullion in the Anglo-Burgundian Trade, 1340–1378* (Toronto, 1972) and *Bullion Flows and Monetary Policy in England and the Low Countries* (Leiden, 1992).

50 Peter Spufford, *Money and its Use in Medieval Europe* (Cambridge, 1988), pp. 339–62.

51 Nathan Sussman, "The Late Medieval Bullion Famine Reconsidered," *Journal of Economic History* 58, 1 (March 1998): 26–54 and "Debasements, Royal Revenues and Inflation in France during the Hundred Years War," *Journal of Economic History* 53 (March 1993): 44–70.

52 Wilhelm Abel, *Agricultural Fluctuations in Europe from the Thirteenth to the Twentieth Centuries*, 3rd edn. (Berlin, 1978), trans. by Olive Ordish (London, 1980), chs. 1–3, especially pp. 35–48; John Hatcher, *Plague, Population, and the English Economy, 1348–1530* (London, 1977), pp. 11–73; Maarten Prak, ed., *Early Modern Capitalism: Economic and Social Change in Europe, 1400–1800* (New York, 2001), p. 37; John H. Munro, "Wage-Stickiness, Monetary Changes, and Real Incomes in Late-Medieval England and the Low Countries, 1300–1470: Did Money Really Matter?" on his web page www.economics.utoronto.ca/ecipa/archive/UT-ECIPA-MUNRO-00-03.html/, accessed Feb. 2010.

53 Herlihy, *Medieval and Renaissance Pistoia* (New Haven, 1967), p. 136; P. J. Jones, "From Manor to Mezzadria. A Tuscan Case-study in the Medieval Origins of Modern Agrarian Society," in *Florentine Studies*, ed. by N. Rubinstein (London, 1968), pp. 193–24; Philip T. Hoffman, "Sharecropping and Investment in Agriculture in Early Modern France," *Journal of Economic History*, 42 (March 1982): 155–60, "The Economic Theory of Sharecropping in Early Modern France," *Journal of Economic History* 44 (June 1984): 309–20, and *Growth in a Traditional Society: The French Countryside, 1450–1815* (Princeton, 1996), pp. 1–34, 193–205. See also Elio Conti, *La formazione della struttura agraria moderna nel contado fiorentino: Le campagne nell'età precomunale*, vol. 1 (Rome, 1965); G. Biagioli, "The Spread of the Mezzadria in Central Italy: A Model of Demographic and Economic Development," in *Evolution agraire et croissance démographique*, ed. by Antoinette Fauve-Chamoux (Liege, 1987): 1–40; Daniel A. Ackerberg and Maristella Botticini, "The Choice of Agrarian Contracts in Early Renaissance Tuscany: Risk Sharing, Moral Hazard, or Capital Market Imperfections?" *Explorations in Economic History* 37, 3 (July 2000): 241–57; R. J. Emigh, "The Spread of Sharecropping in Tuscany: The Political Economy of Transaction Costs," *American Sociological Review* 62 (1997): 423–42.

54 Christopher Dyer, *Standards of Living in the Later Middle Ages* (Cambridge, 1989).

55 Charles M. De La Roncière, *Prix et salaires à Florence au XIVe siecle, 1280–1380* (Rome, 1982).

56 Jacob Burckhardt, *The Civilization of the Renaissance in Italy*, trans. S. G. C. Middlemore (New York, 1982), p. 57.

57 David Herlihy and Christiane Klapisch-Zuber, *Tuscans and their Families* (New Haven, 1985, originally published in French as *Les Toscans et leurs familles*, 1978).

58 Hans Baron, "Franciscan Poverty and Civic Wealth as Factors in the Rise of Humanistic Thought," *Speculum* 13 (1938): 1–37. Hans Baron explicitly stated his opposition to the Lopez thesis in an exchange of letters to the editor of the *American Historical Review* in 1956, reproduced in Karl Dannenfeldt's *Renaissance: Medieval or Modern?* pp. 62–3.

59 Richard A. Goldthwaite *The Building of Renaissance Florence* (Baltimore, 1980), "The Renaissance Economy: The Preconditions for Luxury Consumption," in *Aspetti della vita economica medievale* (Florence, 1985), pp. 659–75, and *Wealth and the Demand for Art in Italy, 1300–1600* (Baltimore, 1993). Sergio Tognetti has attacked the "pessimist" view as the work of "political historians" in *Da Figline a Firenze*, pp. 5–7.

60 Goldthwaite, *Building of Renaissance Florence*, pp. 397, 413, 423, 424.

61 An earlier call to examine the "demand side" is in Cipolla, *Before the Industrial Revolution*, pp. 54–8, 201–4.

62 Goldthwaite, *Wealth and Demand for Art*, pp. 40, 49–51.

63 Goldthwaite dismissed the Lopez thesis as "disembodied." Goldthwaite, *Wealth and Demand for Art*, p. 5; Brown, *Renaissance*, p. 18.

64 Lisa Jardine, *Worldly Goods: A New History of the Renaissance* (New York, 1996), p. 34.

65 Stephen R. Epstein, *Freedom and Growth: The Rise of States and Markets, 1300–1750* (New York, 2000), p. 69; Caferro, "Silk Business of Tommaso Spinelli": 417–39; Sergio Tognetti, "The Development of the Florentine Silk Industry: A Positive Response to the Crisis of the Fourteenth Century," *Journal of Medieval History* 31 (March 2005): 55–69; Franco Franceschi, "I forestieri e l'industria della seta fiorentina fra Medioevo e Rinascimento," in *La seta in Italia* (Venice, 2000), pp. 401–22.

66 For critique of conspicuous consumption see Lauro Martines, "The Renaissance and the Birth of a Consumer Society," *Renaissance Quarterly* 51, 1 (Spring 1998): 193–203.

67 William Caferro, "Warfare and the Economy of Renaissance Italy, 1350–1450," *Journal of Interdisciplinary History* 39, 2 (Autumn 2008): 167–209 and *John Hawkwood, An English Mercenary in Fourteenth-Century Italy* (Baltimore, 2006); Maria Nadia Covini, *L'esercito del duca: Organizzazione militare e istituzioni al tempo degli Sforza, 1450–1480* (Rome, 1998); Fritz Redlich, *The German Military Enterpriser and his Work Force, A Study in European Economic and Social History*, vol. 1 (Wiesbaden, 1964).

68 Anthony Molho, *Florentine Public Finances in the Early Renaissance, 1400–1433* (Cambridge, MA, 1971).

69 William Caferro, *Mercenary Companies and the Decline of Siena* (Baltimore, 1998).

70 John R. Hale, *War and Society in Renaissance Europe, 1450–1620* (Baltimore, 1985).

71 For the debate about the Thirty Years' War, see Theodore K. Rabb, "The Effects of the Thirty Years' War on the German Economy," *Journal of Modern History* 34 (1962): 40–51; Henry Kamen, "The Economic and Social Consequences of the Thirty Years' War," *Past and Present* 39 (1968): 44–61; J. V. Polisensky, *The Thirty Years' War* (London, 1970); S. H. Steinberg, *The Thirty Years' War and the Conflict for European Hegemony* (London, 1971); Christopher R. Friedrichs, *Urban Society in the Age of War: Nordlingen, 1580–1720* (Princeton, 1979). For the Low Countries, see Myron P. Gutmann, *War and Rural Life in the Early Modern Low Countries* (Princeton, 1980).

72 Caferro, "Warfare and Economy": 167–209.

73 Duplessis, *Transitions to Capitalism*.

74 Kenneth Pomeranz, *The Great Divergence: China, Europe, and the Making of the Modern World Economy* (Princeton, 2001); E. L. Jones, *The European Miracle Environments, Economies and Geopolitics in the History of Europe and Asia* (Cambridge, 1987).

75 W. W. Rostow, *The Stages of Economic Growth: A Non-Communist Manifesto* (Cambridge, 1960); Douglass C. North and Robert Paul Thomas, "An Economic Theory of the Growth of the Western World," *Economic History Review* 22 (1970): 1–17.

76 E. J. Hobsbawm, "The General Crisis of the European Economy in the Seventeenth Century," *Past and Present* 5 (1954): 33–53 and "The General Crisis of the Seventeenth Century II" *Past and Present* 6 (1954): 44–65; Jan de

Vries, "Renaissance Cities," *Renaissance Quarterly* 42 (1989): 781–93; Edwin S. Hunt and James Murray, *A History of Business in Medieval Europe* (Cambridge, 1999), p. 227.

77 See lead quote, Smith, *Wealth of Nations*, vol. 2, p. 125.

78 Ralph Davis, *Rise of Atlantic Economies* (London, 1973); James Tracy, ed., *The Rise of Merchant Empires: Long-Distance Trade in the Early Modern World, 1350–1750* (Cambridge, 1990); John J. McCusker and Kenneth Morgan, eds., *The Early Modern Atlantic Economy* (New York, 2000).

79 De Lamar Jensen, *Renaissance Europe: Age of Recovery and Reconciliation* (Lexington, 1981), p. 309.

80 Jonathan I. Israel, *Dutch Primacy in World Trade, 1585–1740* (Oxford, 1957), pp. 5–6.

81 Herman van der Wee, "Structural Changes in European Long-distance Trade, and particularly in the Re-export Trade from South to North, 1350–1750," in Tracy, *Rise of Merchant Empires*, pp. 14–33.

82 E. J. Hamilton, *American Treasure and The Price Revolution in Spain, 1501–1650* (Cambridge, MA, 1934), pp. 283, 305 and *Money, Prices and Wages in Valencia, Aragon and Navarre, 1351–1500* (Cambridge, MA, 1936).

83 North, *Rise of the Western World*, p. 108.

84 Cipolla, *Before the Industrial Revolution*, p. 215.

85 R. N. Salaman, *The History and Influence of the Potato* (London, 1949).

86 J. Thirsk, *Economic Policy and Projects: The Development of a Consumer Society in Early Modern England* (Oxford, 1978).

87 Musgrave, *Early Modern European Economy*, pp. 64–72; Duplessis, *Transitions to Capitalism*, pp. 191–3; John Brewer and Roy Porter, eds., *Consumption and the World of Goods* (London, 1993).

88 Eliyahu Ashtor, "Levantine Sugar Industry in the Late Middle Ages: A Case of Technological Decline," pp. 91–132 and *Levantine Trade in the Later Middle Ages* (Princeton, 1983).

89 R. S. Dunn, *Sugar and Slaves: The Rise of the Planter Class in English West Indies, 1624–1713* (London, 1973); Hugh Thomas, *The Slave Trade: The History of the Atlantic Slave Trade, 1440–1870* (New York, 1997); Sidney Mintz, *Sweetness and Power: The Place of Sugar in Modern History* (New York, 1985).

90 Herbert S Klein, "Economic Aspects of the Eighteenth Century Atlantic Slave Trade," in Tracy, *Rise of Merchant Empires*, pp. 287–93.

91 De Vries, "Renaissance Cities": 781–93; Hunt and Murray, *History of Business*, p. 227.

92 Jan de Vries, *European Urbanization, 1500–1800* (Cambridge, MA, 1984), pp. 8, 253–60.

93 Maurice Dobb, *Studies in the Development of Capitalism* (New York, 1946) p. 17.

94 Rodney Hilton, ed., *The Transition from Feudalism to Capitalism* (London, 1976).

95 Robert Brenner, "Agrarian Class Structure and Economic Development in Pre-Industrial Europe," *Past and Present* 70 (1976).

96 T. H. Aston and C. H. E. Philbin, *The Brenner Debate: Agrarian Class Structure and Economic Development in Pre-Industrial Europe* (Cambridge, 1985).

97 Franklin Mendels, "Proto-Industrialization: The First Phase of the Industrialization Process," *Journal of Economic History* 32 (1972): 241–61; Peter Kriedte, Hans Medick, and Jurgen Schlumbohm, eds., *Industrialization before Industrialization* (1977); Sheilagh Ogilvie and Markus Cerman, eds., *European Proto-Industrialization* (Cambridge, 1996); D. C. Coleman, "Proto Industrialization: A Concept too Many?" *Economic History Review* 36 (1983): 435–48. Criticism of proto-industrialization is in Maxine Berg, Pat Hudson, and Michael Sonenscher, eds., *Manufacture in Town and Country before the Factory* (New York, 1983).

98 Fernand Braudel, *Civilization and Capitalism, 15th–18th Century*, 3 vols. trans. by Siân Reynolds (New York, 1981–4), pp. 396, 400, 621. The first volume was published in 1967 and was trans. in 1973 into English as *Capitalism and Material Life*.

99 Fernand Braudel, *The Mediterranean and the Mediterranean World in the Age of Philip II*, 2 vols. (Berkeley and Los Angeles, 1996).

100 Fernand Braudel, *Afterthoughts on Material Civilization and Capitalism* (Baltimore, 1977), p. 112.

101 De Vries, *European Urbanization*, pp. 8, 253–60, 784.

102 North and Thomas, "Growth of the Western World," pp. 1–17.

103 Immanuel Wallerstein, *The Modern World-System*, 3 vols. (New York, 1974–89). An excellent analysis of Wallerstein's work is in Robert S. Duplessis, "World Systems Analysis and Early Modern European History," *History Teacher* 21, 2 (Feb. 1988): 221–32.

104 Jan de Vries, "An Inquiry into the Behavior of Wages in the Dutch Republic and the Southern Netherlands from 1580 to 1800," in *Dutch Capitalism and World Capitalism*, ed. by Maurice Aymard (Cambridge, 1982), pp. 37–61; Patrick O'Brien, "European Economic Development: The Contribution of the Periphery," *Economic History Review* 35 (1982): 1–18.

105 Karl Appuhn, "Tools for the Development of the European Economy," in *A Companion to the World of the Renaissance*, ed. by Guido Ruggiero (Malden, MA, 2002); John A. Marino, "Economic Encounters and the First Stages of a World Economy," in Ruggiero, *Companion to the Renaissance*, pp. 4, 5.

6

Politics: The Emergence of the Modern State?

It now remains to us to see how a prince should govern his conduct towards his subjects or his friends [...] Since it is my intention to say something that will prove of practical use to the inquirer, I have thought it proper to represent things as they are in real truth not as they are imagined. Many have dreamed of republics and principalities which have never existed. The gulf between how one should live and how one does live is so wide that a man who neglects what is actually done learns the way of self destruction rather than self preservation [...] Therefore if a prince wants to maintain his rule he must learn how not to be virtuous, and to make use of this or not, according to need.

Niccolò Machiavelli[1]

The most characteristic aspect of the discourse on Renaissance politics has been its stress on modernity. The scholarship has followed two general lines: one that traces the development of the modern nation state, and another that traces the rise of republicanism and the democratic tradition. The first has dealt primarily with the monarchies of Northern Europe, in particular France and England. The second has focused on the city-states of Italy, above all Florence.

The terms of discussion follow closely those of the nineteenth century, an era of state-building and nationalism during which there was intense scholarly interest in politics and political forms.[2] The Swiss historian, Jean Charles Léonard (Simonde) de Sismondi (d. 1842) searched for the origins of modern political freedom in Italian city-states.[3] Jacob Burckhardt (d. 1897) placed politics at the center of his great work, emphasizing the role of despots and party quarrels in creating the individualism that brought forth the new modern man. He offered no rigorous examination of institutions; Renaissance states were outgrowths of "unbridled egoism."

The association of politics with modernity has held firm in the literature, the details worked out by an international group of scholars. The "state" remains a focal point of histories of Renaissance Europe, which often begin with the city-states of Italy and proceed to the northern nation states of the sixteenth century, depicting the latter as the culmination of the former.[4] The nation state is represented as the triumph of modernity, a political form that, as a popular textbook asserts, is a "familiar reality" of the contemporary world that takes no act of historical imagination to understand it.[5]

As in other subfields, the term Renaissance is not used in consistent ways. It has been applied to princes and kings, who in Burckhardtian fashion individualistically sought power and patronized Renaissance culture or, in Machiavellian manner, displayed ruthless cunning and opportunism in seeking political advantage.[6] It has been applied also to institutional forms, to the establishment of centralized, rational and "impersonal" bureaucracies, the creation of standing armies and the monopoly by the state of coercive power. The institutional angle reflects the strong influence of the work of the German sociologist Max Weber (d. 1920).[7]

The importance of Niccolò Machiavelli (1469–1527) needs to be stressed. In both implicit and explicit ways he has had a profound effect on scholarly and popular perceptions of Renaissance politics. His career was played out during a key period of political transition, when the northern nation states invaded Italy and his native Florence undertook a new experiment in republican government. Machiavelli's stark and unsentimental (ungodly to some) portrayal of Italian statecraft is viewed as possessing the unmistakable air of modernity. The German scholar Friedrich Meinecke credited Machiavelli with being the founder of modern *raison d'état*.[8] Denys Hay argued for modernity of Renaissance politics in the *New Cambridge Modern History* (1957) on the grounds that a character like Machiavelli was inconceivable earlier.[9]

The scholarly tradition represents, as John Najemy has pointed out, a "top-down elitist" and secular approach to Renaissance politics. It is this tendency that the current scholarship has been revising.[10] The revision has included reappraisal of the meaning of the term "state."[11]

New Monarchy and Nation States

In the early years of the twentieth century, scholars fitted the qualities of the Renaissance nation state under the general rubric of "new monarchy," a term popularized by the English historian Alfred F. Pollard (1907).

New monarchy had both a personal and institutional component. It was characterized in the first instance by an individualistic impulse toward "absolute" authority on the part of rulers, who sought to consolidate their power. They did this by reducing the "multiplicity of competing authorities," i.e., the influence of the aristocracy, church, and representative assemblies (which were not mutually exclusive), replacing them with royal, centralized bureaucracies. Rulers substituted Roman law for local custom and privilege. Roman law had been revived by humanists and affirmed absolute power, with its dictum *Quod principi placuit habet legis vigorem* (Whatever pleases the prince has force of law). Rulers also expanded their tax base, centralized the collection of revenue and created bureaucracies under their direct control.[12]

Advocates of new monarchy stressed its evolutionary nature. It supplanted medieval feudal monarchy and the Italian city-state as "the most complete and effective" political entity, with unprecedented coercive, economic, and military might. The prior forms were compared to "children." The transformation took place primarily in the sixteenth century, contemporaneous with the French invasion of Italy and the Italian Wars (1494–1527) and the Reformation that weakened the Catholic Church. The new monarchies engendered strong "national" feelings, undertook territorial expansion, and created national armies.

The new monarchy remains a starting point for discussion of Renaissance politics in textbooks.[13] It is most typically applied to France, England, and Spain. The states had different trajectories based on geographic, social, and economic considerations, but were similar in that they all experienced an increase in monarchical power and the formation of centralized bureaucracy in the sixteenth century.

France is the most representative example. Centralized monarchical power coalesced in stages, culminating with the absolutist state of Louis XIV in the seventeenth and eighteenth centuries. The historian Roland Mousnier, the staunchest advocate of French new monarchy, examined its genesis. He noted the rise of patriotic national sentiment in the work of the humanists Robert Gaguin (d. 1501) and Guillaume Budé (d. 1540) and the alliance between the crown and the bourgeoisie against the aristocracy. French new monarchy also involved the creation of a centralized royal bureaucracy with the power to dispense justice and levy taxes, a standing army and royal control of the church, initiated by the Pragmatic Sanction of Bourges in 1438. The legal underpinnings of royal power were laid down by jurists who advocated a French style of Roman law known as "mos gallicus," which posited the ruler as a patriarch at the head of the family. This notion was developed by Jean Bodin (d. 1596) in *Les six livres de la république* (Six Books of the Commonwealth, 1576), which argued that the monarch was above the law, his authority limited only by divine and natural law.[14]

The reign of King Louis XI (1463–1483) has been treated as a key formative stage in the development of French new monarchy. Louis was a Renaissance figure, a Machiavellian schemer, with a talent for manipulation that earned him the nickname the "Spider King," for the webs of intrigues he spun.[15] The events of Louis' reign were chronicled by Philippe de Commines (d. 1483), whose *Memoirs* have been compared to Machiavelli in terms of their modern-seeming psychological and political insight into statecraft. Louis consolidated his hold on the state by effectively playing competing sides against each other, allying himself with the rising bourgeoisie, whose material circumstance he improved by supporting business and trade, including establishing a native silk business and trade fairs in the city of Lyons. Louis dressed in bourgeois fashion and wore a felt hat that he believed brought him good luck. He created a coherent royal bureaucracy founded on an efficient tax system, which raised new sources of revenue and increased the king's share, which had previously depended mostly on earnings from his own lands. Under Louis XI public revenue increased by 300 percent in the years from 1470 to 1484. The financial reforms were alone sufficient for the historian Martin Wolfe to label Louis a "Renaissance king" based on his transformation of France's "medieval" fiscal system into a "modern efficient" one.[16] Louis' ability to consolidate power was aided also by military success: the end of the Hundred Years War (1453) and his defeat of Charles the Bold, the powerful duke of Burgundy in 1477.

The Renaissance kingship initiated by Louis "matured" under his successors. One of the most important of these was Francis I (1515–1547). Like Louis, Francis was a Renaissance man, described in a recent biography as "Renaissance warrior and patron."[17] He was, however, more Burckhardtian than Machiavellian – a handsome and dashing figure, who valiantly led armies into battle and patronized a circle of humanist writers and artists. Francis was not an innovator in terms of institutions, but he built upon the bureaucratic machinery left him to increase further royal revenue. Most of all, he created a vibrant Renaissance court that attracted to France such notables as Andrea del Sarto and Leonardo da Vinci (see chapter 4). Francis's collection of manuscripts and artworks formed the bases of the Bibliothèque nationale and the Louvre respectively.

The advent of new monarchy in England is associated with the end of civil strife (the War of the Roses) and the rise of the Tudor Dynasty (King Henry VII) in the fifteenth century. In its oldest formulation, English royal power is seen as having lurched forward under King Henry VII (1485–1509), who strengthened royal institutions. His son Henry VIII (1509–1547) further extended royal power, breaking from the authority of the Roman Church. Henry's daughter Elizabeth I (1558–1603) enhanced royal prestige through skillful manipulation of parliament and public opinion (see chapter 3).[18]

Already in 1955, however, the schema was revised by Walter Cecil Richardson, who de-emphasized Henry VII's role as an institutional innovator and depicted him instead as a monarch, whose skill lay in making existing royal offices more efficient.[19]

The discourse on English new monarchy has focused on institutions and personalities. King Henry VIII (1485–1509), like his French contemporary Francis I, has often been treated as a Renaissance man, who cut a dashing figure (at least in his youth) and served as courtly patron to humanists of the day, including Erasmus and Thomas More (see chapter 4). The historian G. R. Elton, however, looked more closely at Henry's bureaucratic reforms, finding in them the most innovative features of Tudor rule. Elton credited Henry with creating a modern bureaucracy that constituted nothing less than a "Tudor revolution in government." The innovations were the work of Henry's chancellor, Thomas Cromwell, a "remarkable revolutionary," who in the years from 1530 to 1540, during Henry's marital problems and break from the Catholic Church, set in place "a unitary sovereign state." This involved a shift to reliance on highly organized impersonal departments of state, staffed by professional bureaucrats. When Henry's daughter Elizabeth ascended the throne, she inherited a modern state.

The "Tudor revolution in government" has been the subject of its own debate, which, like much of English scholarship, has been conducted largely on its own terms. Scholars have disagreed on the degree to which Cromwell's reforms were revolutionary, the nature of the minister's relationship with the king, as well as the extent to which "medieval" practices persisted. The debate occasioned a special issue of the journal *Past and Present* (1963) as well as a book, 25 years later (1988), summarizing opinions. The "Tudor revolution" thesis remains a point of departure for discussion of English government.[20]

New monarchy in Spain presents a different picture. Its advent is usually dated to the marriage of Ferdinand of Aragon with Isabella of Castile in 1469, which brought together the two largest countries of Spain. Scholars have examined centralizing tendencies, including territorial expansion related to the *reconquista*, which ended with the defeat of the Moors in 1492. They have studied the use of royal officials, *corregidores*, in cities and the creation of a species of national militia though revival of the *hermanidades*, urban protective leagues. But the institutional dimension of Spanish new monarchy was limited. Ferdinand and Isabella had little authority outside of their own domains, which were structurally different (Castile, a largely agrarian state; Aragon, a mercantile one). They had separate laws, coinage, customs, and speech. In the third chapter of his pioneering *Imperial Spain* (1963) John Elliott evaluated Isabella and Ferdinand in terms of the "new monarch" label. He found their example so divergent that he suggested that they either be excluded from the label or that the label itself be changed.[21]

The notion of "Renaissance" politics in Spain is nowadays linked primarily to individual persons. Queen Isabella has been called the "first queen of the Renaissance" in a recent biography.[22] Her grandson Philip II (1545–1551), described by Henry Kamen as a "Renaissance prince," has been subject of a well-known debate regarding his personality. Scholars have questioned whether Philip was, in J. L. Motley's famous view, a Machiavellian "incarnation of evil" or, in Roger Merriman's description, a "most prudent Catholic ruler" whose sincere devotion and attention to administrative detail hampered his rule.[23]

The application of new monarchy to the rest of Europe is still more problematic. The Netherlands emerged in the sixteenth and seventeenth centuries as a major economic power, but it did not have a centralized monarchy. The Holy Roman Empire, the largest political entity in Europe, remained fragmented and Habsburg rulers were elected and had little coercive power. The Polish King Sigismund was a patron of Renaissance artists, but the nobility in his state remained strong, and the peasants were subjugated to them.[24] The Russian Tsar Ivan the Terrible displayed Machiavellian dissimulation and a ruthless will to expand his power, but his reforms proved largely ephemeral. The same was true of Gustavus Vasa of Sweden, who initiated new monarchy style administrative reforms, which did not survive his death. The Hungarian king Matthias I Corvinus patronized artists and architects, created a library (the Corviniana) with 500 illuminated manuscripts, increased royal revenue and even initiated a standing army. But his actions did not endure. Hungary returned to being a weak monarchy after Matthias's death.[25]

The examples bring out the variety of Renaissance political forms, to which we may add also the Ottoman Turks, whose rulers possessed a singularly centralized authority but whose state lacked any semblance of impersonal bureaucratic machinery.[26] It is difficult to apply a single standard to them all.

Indeed, even while accepting the notion of new monarchy, scholars often emphasize the persistence of medieval practices. Marriage alliances, for example, remained an important part of Renaissance royal policy as they had been in the Middle Ages, and wars were fought to secure them. King Louis XI, despite his webs, did not reduce the nobility to subservience. It remained a dominant class, able to escape taxation and retain its privileges. The historian J. Russell Major affirmed the existence of new monarchy in sixteenth-century France, but he argued that its most pronounced characteristic was its feudal dynastic structure.[27] He saw France not as an absolute monarchy, but as a "consultative" one that relied on the consent of provincial councils and on patronage to raise money. The weaknesses of the royal bureaucracy were revealed most clearly during the Wars of Religion (1562–1598), when raising royal revenue became very difficult. It was only in the seventeenth century that French absolutism emerged and kings possessed "the vertical ties necessary to hold society together."[28]

A particularly forceful statement of continuity with the Middle Ages was that by Joseph R. Strayer. Strayer also accepted the new monarchy thesis and argued that the period from 1450 to 1600 was one in which rulers substantially strengthened their hold on governments. But rather than transforming institutions, rulers worked with existing forms. In *On the Medieval Origins of the Modern State*, Strayer argued that the modern European state was already developed in embryo by 1300, particularly in France and England, whose political ideas and institutions were then widely imitated elsewhere.[29] Strayer defined the modern state in much the same way as the adherents of new monarchy had done. He argued that it was characterized by strong central authority, permanent and impersonal political institutions and substitution of loyalty to church and family for loyalty to the state. The real skill of the sixteenth-century new monarchs was their ability to get the privileged classes to cooperate and accept their leadership.

The persistence of feudal forms also lay at the heart of Perry Anderson's comprehensive survey of the development of European absolutism. Anderson took a Marxian approach that stressed the role of class in the process of political centralization and monarchical power. He cast the issue of emerging royal power in terms reminiscent of the "transition debate" outlined in chapter 5. He sought the point at which feudalism gave way to capitalism, associating the latter with the advent of absolute monarchy.[30] Anderson argued that preexisting class structures in different countries (like Robert Brenner, see chapter 5) created different political outcomes. Throughout Europe, even in France and England, the aristocracy was never fully dislodged from political power. Rather than empowering a nascent bourgeoisie, Anderson described absolutism as a "new political carapace," which "redeployed and recharged the apparatus of feudal domination." The nobility lost political power, but gained economic power; the peasants were subject to them. Thus key features of the old system remained. Anderson nevertheless saw these changes, which he dated to the sixteenth century, as unique in themselves and constituting a "decisive rupture" with the past.

The diversity of Renaissance political forms remains a key feature of scholarly studies. It is reflected in the political writing of the era. The sixteenth century saw intense interest in Roman law, which advocated greater power for the ruler. But there existed several concurrent themes in political thought, including advocacy of limits to royal power, mixed monarchy and critiques of the contemporary status quo. Thomas More, Lord Chancellor to Henry VIII, criticized growing central power and inequality among the classes. In *Utopia* (1516), More portrayed an ideal society in which all property was held in common and the authority of a singe ruler was limited. The larger intention of More's work, filled with irony and satire, is the subject of its own debate. But More's close friend, Erasmus gave a similar critique of the political landscape in *Education of a Christian Prince* (published the same year as *Utopia*), condemning overweening princes who transgressed the common good. Erasmus's French contemporary, Claude de Seyssel, advisor to King Louis XII and trained in Roman law, advocated limits to absolute power. In *The Monarchy of France* (1515–19), Seyssel argued for constraints on royal power based on religion, justice, and customary institutions. The best government was the one that governed best, which Seyssel saw as a balance between the king and the nobility. The English writer Thomas Starkey (1538) suggested that the aristocracy serve as overseers of the political order, a sentiment expressed also by the anonymous author of *Discourse of the Common Weal* (1549, published 1581).

Coercion, Standing Armies, and Military Revolutions

It is important to stress the role played by bureaucratic forms in the discussion of Renaissance politics. For many scholars, the core of the Renaissance state, whatever its particulars, was the existence of institutions that transcended individual personalities and could be passed on to the next ruler. The discourse owes greatly to Max Weber (1864–1920), whose authority is not always explicitly acknowledged. Weber devoted several influential works in the early twentieth century to the state. He linked modernity to impersonal bureaucracies staffed by professionals trained for the task. He also saw as an essential feature of the modern state its "monopoly of legitimate coercive power."[31]

The notion of the coercive state power has received a great deal of attention. Scholars have associated it in the first instance with the establishment of standing armies. The French, here as elsewhere, were leaders, instituting the so-called *ordonnance* companies in 1445–6 under King Charles VII, which called for a permanent force of approximately 7, 200 men. The army, modified further by Louis XI, reflects not only the growing power of the state over private interests, but also the frequency of warfare during the period, which made the expedient necessary in the first place. Warfare had powerful political consequences, galvanizing the citizenry behind the ruler, helping to solidify sovereign claims and evoke national sentiment.

The emergence of a standing army in France and the monopolization of coercive power by the state provided the context for Norbert Elias famous "sociogenesis" interpretation of absolutism (1939).[32] Elias argued that the creation by French rulers of armies made up of professional soldiers – hired men, year round – enabled them to depend less on the feudal aristocracy. It enhanced the power of the king, while transforming the nobility from a warrior class into courtiers. The attainment by the king of absolute power thus had a "civilizing effect" on the nobility, who were domesticated at court and became preoccupied with issues of manners and civility, behavioral traits that Elias saw as emblematic of the Renaissance (see chapter 2). The epicenter of change was sixteenth-century France, the "most influential" court society in Europe, from where the practice diffused to the rest of Western Europe.[33]

Elias's thesis emphasized the importance of changes in royal bureaucracy and the structure of armies. But it gave curiously little attention to war itself, and how this may itself have conditioned changes in armies and bureaucracies. The subject was taken up by military historians, who saw elements of modernity in the very practice of Renaissance warfare. Michael Roberts coined the term "military revolution" (1955) to describe the military changes that occurred in the years from 1560 to 1660. The revolution involved basic changes in tactics, training, and strategy. Most of all it involved the introduction of firearms on the battlefield, which increased the role of infantry and led to the growth in size of armies that were direct precursors of twentieth century (i.e., modern) developments. The reforms occurred in the armies of Maurice of Orange and King Gustav Adolphus of Sweden.[34]

Roberts's military revolution thesis gained wide currency among scholars, in part owing to the influence Sir George Clark, who included it in his well-known general studies of European politics.[35] Geoffrey Parker, however, pushed the thesis back temporally to the fifteenth century, to the Italian peninsula and the Italian Wars fought by the Spanish and French. Parker stressed the transformative effects of artillery, in particular the development of a more effective cannon. The new cannon reduced the role of cavalry, which was no match for the weapon in the field, and, as in Roberts's thesis, increased the recourse to infantry, which grew to great proportions, vastly enlarging the size of armies. The cannon also necessitated changes in fortifications, which were now vulnerable to attack. Defenders responded by making thicker, more angled walls, the so-called *trace italienne*, which started in Italy and diffused eventually to the rest of Europe.[36]

Parker's variation represents a reworking of the old gunpowder thesis evident already in the seventeenth-century writings of Francis Bacon. It has, however, sparked its own considerable debate among military historians, which is ongoing. Some have challenged Parker's use of sources and figures. Others have pushed the military revolution forward temporally to the eighteenth century; still others have moved it back into the Middle Ages. Some would deny the military revolution altogether.[37]

A key aspect of Renaissance warfare about which there is, however, little dispute is that it was enormously costly (see chapter 5). Essential to the theses of both Roberts and Parker was that fifteenth and sixteenth century wars became far more expensive than ever before. Larger armies and new fortifications greatly raised costs, which placed substantial fiscal burdens on states. Rulers needed to dredge money from their citizenry, which challenged the extent of their coercive power. The all-out search for revenue also placed great burdens on bureaucratic (fiscal) institutions, which were required to handle enormous sums of money and effect speedy and efficient turnover of them. Regular sources of revenue were insufficient to meet expenses during war. Governments made up the shortfall by imposing extraordinary levies and borrowing money from citizens. Success at this was critical to a state's ability to establish a "modern" bureaucracy.

These political/economic implications of war were raised by military historians, but not systematically explored by them. The details have been studied primarily by economic historians, under the rubric of public finance (see chapter 5).[38] The compartmentalization of research has produced, however, a misshapen discourse, in which the two sides (military and economic historians) have not addressed each other directly. The difficulties have been exacerbated by the highly complex nature of the fiscal practices and tax structures of Renaissance states, which have occasioned specialized monographs that are not easily incorporated into the more generalist approach of military historians (see chapter 5).[39] Marvin Becker's work on fourteenth-century Florence represents an early attempt to bring the sides together. Becker argued that warfare connected private interest with public state interest. This was achieved largely through the establishment by Florentine officials of an effective consolidated debt (known locally as the "*monte*" or mountain) which gained the support of the monied elite by promising regular repayment of loans and allowing speculation and ultimately substantial profit for the wealthy.[40]

Public finance and consolidated debts have also been the subject of studies for Northern Europe. James Tracy spoke of a "financial revolution" in sixteenth-century Holland as a result of the expensive Habsburg-Valois Wars (1515–1559), which necessitated large-scale borrowing from citizens. Government officials issued *renten*, annuities that, like the Florentine *monte*, reduced high rate short-term loans into low rate long-term ones. They allowed speculation in *renten* shares, opening a market for profit. The practices regularized Dutch revenue and created confidence among lenders.[41]

P. J. Dickson and John Brewer outlined a "financial revolution" in the late seventeenth and eighteenth centuries in England, owing largely to the conversion of short- into long-term debt.[42]

The studies of public finance did not, however, affirm notions of Renaissance political modernity. The Netherlands saw the formation of a centralized bureaucracy, but not the emergence of a strong central state or monarchy. Power remained largely in the hands of urban officials. The English financial revolution ultimately enhanced the power of Parliament rather than the monarchy and in any case occurred much later than the Renaissance or Elton's Tudor revolution.

What is nevertheless clear from the studies is that wars were expensive and that the manner in which states dealt with them helped determine their political success and structure. This point was elaborated on by Charles Tilly, who traced the effects of warfare on European states over a thousand-year period. He argued that state structure depended directly on the ruler's ability to "acquire the means of war" and that "wars made states and vice versa," a statement that has gained wide currency. Tilly saw as critical the period from the fifteenth to the seventeenth century, during which the "national" state (the term he preferred to nation state) was established. The successful states were those that were commercialized or "capital intensive," like England and France, which were better able to handle the economic burdens of war. The unsuccessful states were agricultural or "coercion intensive" and could not bear the costs. Tilly excluded Italian city-states on the grounds that they lacked the scale of their northern counterparts, and thus were inherently limited.[43]

Ritual, Religion, and Imagined Communities

The top-down approach of Tilly has been joined by more social and anthropologically based studies that investigate the ways in which states exercised coercive power internally through control of crime and violence, and management of gender and family relations (see chapter 3).[44] Historians have devoted greater attention to law and language, to ritual and ceremony. Following Clifford Geertz, they have shown how ritual practices helped create a "ceremonial constitution" that encouraged an idea of the state that transcended individuals, and how ritual activities themselves, in David Kertzer's words, helped "promote schematic thinking."[45]

European kingship involved performance. Rulers used public ceremonies as a species of theater to extend their authority and manipulate public opinion. This was, as we have seen in chapter 3, an important means by which female monarchs (Elizabeth I) asserted their power. Monarchs employed a variety of devices, including triumphal "entries' into cities, coronation ceremonies and public burials. The entry of French kings into the city of Paris has been described as a "social drama" with both secular and religious overtones.[46] It allowed the king to enforce his authority over that important city, while at the same time allowing Parisian officials and corporate bodies to assert their privileges before the king.

Coronation ceremonies and public burials likewise had religious and secular overtones. Kings, as Ernst Kantorowicz famously argued, possessed two bodies, a mortal one that was defective and a kingly one that was perfect (a dual nature reflected in Christ, who was both man and God). When the mortal body of the king died, the kingly body lived on. The custom in France since 1422 was to place a wax effigy of the king on his coffin after he died, to avoid displaying the decomposing body. His successor remained hidden from sight until after the death rites. He was formally crowned a few weeks later at Rheims.[47]

The projection of royal images enhanced notions of political stability and order, while evoking local pride and national consciousness. The role of national consciousness in the development of the nation state has been explored in a broad and provocative manner by the anthropologist Benedict Anderson. Anderson argued that the sixteenth century was a critical point during which national feeling developed in Europe. This owed to the advent of what Anderson called "print capitalism," which resulted from the invention of printing press and presence in Europe of an incipient capitalist culture. The presses commercialized the book industry and made widely available volumes in vernacular languages. This established the basis of a "massive conversation of ideas" based on a common language, which formed the embryo of national consciousness. Common language created an "imagined community" among people who did not know each other personally, but could nevertheless communicate and relate to each other as members of the same nation. The break with the Middle Ages was sharp. An "imagined community" was impossible earlier, owing to the monolithic nature of the Catholic Church and the dominance of the Latin language in books and official documents, the use of which was restricted to an elite few.[48]

Although Anderson's work contains factual errors, it nevertheless has inspired historians to examine language and imagined solidarity as features of emerging states. Historians have studied relational forces, the role of borderlands and people in helping create national identities (see chapter 2).[49] They are joined by medievalists, who debate the degree to which national sentiment applied also to their era, as well as the distinctions between notions of nationality and ethnicity.[50] Opinion is sharply divided. The anthropologist Ernst Gellner and historian Eric Hobsbawm have argued that the term "nation" is a historically new one, appropriate only to developments of the eighteenth century and later.[51]

The process of revision has in any case substantially weakened the equation of Renaissance politics with modernity. Recent histories take the long view of developments and stress continuities with the Middle Ages as well as with the eighteenth and nineteenth centuries. Renaissance monarchy was, as a recent comparative study has emphasized, its own distinct entity to be understood in its own distinct terms.[52]

Renaissance Italian States

The discourse on politics for Italy has shared many characteristics with that of Northern Europe. Scholars of the peninsula were among the first to explore the role of ritual and representation in politics, the use of public ceremonies to display authority.[53] The historian Federico Chabod investigated the "modernity" of the fifteenth- and sixteenth-century Milanese state, stressing in Weberian terms the centralized impersonal nature of the local bureaucracy, staffed by professional officials.[54] Garrett Mattingly traced the development of "modern style" diplomacy and statecraft to Italy.[55] He argued that permanent resident embassies and balance of power politics began in the fifteenth century in synchrony with great Renaissance achievements in art (e.g. Masaccio's painting of the Brancacci Chapel). The practices radiated out to the rest of Europe and were further developed by northern monarchs in the sixteenth century.

Italy's diplomatic legacy remains a strong and largely uncontested point of connection to Northern Europe. M. S. Anderson's recent survey of the European state system gives pride of place to the Italian tradition as inspiration for the latter.[56] But the Italian political situation differed fundamentally from that of the north. No ruler or state achieved absolute power or gained dominion over the peninsula. The Church, the emblem of the Middle Ages, remained a powerful and physical presence in Italy, where it was its own temporal state, the nature of which is not easy to define by existing categories. Italy in short lacked a national dimension and with it national sentiment. Federico Chabod pointedly excluded nationalism from his study of the Milanese state, seeing it as anachronistic given that Italy would not achieve political unity until the nineteenth century.

The Renaissance Italian political landscape was dominated by independent city-states and civic patriotism. The lack of overarching central power allowed the states substantial freedom and *de facto* practice in self-government.[57] Their close geographic proximity, wealth and power meanwhile occasioned frequent conflict, which was a basic feature of Italian political life. The military situation in Italy has, however, been viewed as different from that of Northern Europe. Where nation states moved toward national armies and military revolutions, Italy remained "backward," relying primarily on mercenary soldiers (*condottieri*), paid men from outside their borders and sometimes (in the fourteenth century) from outside of Italy altogether. The practice was famously condemned by Niccolò Machiavelli, who saw it as a principal cause of Italy's failure to defend itself against the French invasion in 1494 and the subsequent Italian wars.[58] Burckhardt used the figure of the conniving, unfaithful *condottiere* (often of illegitimate birth) as a model of Renaissance individualism and the political culture of Italy.

The portrait of the Italian military situation is, however, overstated, and studies have shown the development of permanent forces in several Italian states – Venice, Milan, and Naples most notably – that mirrored and indeed helped set the pattern for changes up north. Nevertheless the scholarly discourse for Italy remains largely focused on mercenaries: the evolution of their service and their relations to the states that employed them. Thus it is the case that their political meaning, as a function of state coercive power and of centralizing and modernizing institutional tendencies of states, has been ignored. As we shall see, for all the discussion of Florentine political modernity in the fourteenth, fifteenth, and sixteenth centuries little is known of the nature of its army.[59]

The political forms on the Italian peninsula included monarchy, lordships (*signorie*), and republics. The interplay of the diverse entities, and the distinctions in their form, has provided the impetus for much of the scholarly discourse. Monarchy has received the least attention, as has Southern Italy, the region in which it was located.[60] The lordships gained early notice in the work of Jacob Burckhardt and John Addington Symonds. Nineteenth-century Italian nationalist scholars were also interested in the lordships, seeing in them (especially Milan) precursors to modern-day Italian unification and "lordly" rule of King Vittorio Emanuele II (1861–1878). The studies led scholars to emphasize events of the thirteenth century, when the "despots," as Symonds called them, first emerged. More recent scholarship, particularly in the Anglophone academy in the middle and later years of the twentieth century, has focused on the republics. The motivation was similar to that of the earlier literature. It involved search for a distant mirror of current political events, in this instance a Renaissance analog for modern western democracies that triumphed in World War II. The cities of Venice and Florence have been especially popular topics. They were treated as distinct entities, the former presenting the image of republican stability ("the myth of Venice"), the latter of internal faction, party politics, and change.[61]

Scholars have debated the nature of the political forms. Lordships involved rule by despots and tyrants and were ostensibly the opposite of republics, which involved rule by elected officials. But recent studies have shortened the distance between the two forms. Benjamin Kohl rejected the term despot in his examination of the Carrara lordship of Padua on the grounds that it was anachronistic and falsely pejorative when taken out of context.[62] The English historian P. J. Jones provocatively argued that there was virtually no distinction between lordships and republics. Both involved rule by elites and shared the same basic objectives: protecting property rights, acquiring revenue through taxes and controlling lawlessness.[63] On close inspection, the lordships appear more politically inclusive and the republics less so.

It is indeed difficult to find a single workable category into which to fit the various Italian political forms. The papacy is perhaps the most problematic of all. It functioned as a kind of elective monarchy, but with much greater claims to sovereignty and its own laws that theoretically applied to all of Christendom. The monarchies in Southern Italy resembled in some respects the centralizing nation states up north. Alan Ryder has argued that the Aragonese king Alfonso the Magnanimous, who ruled the kingdom of Naples in the middle of the fifteenth century (1442–1458), reformed the state along the lines of the new monarchies, centralizing the bureaucracy and restructuring the army.[64] Scholars have also seen elements of Weberian modern bureaucracy in lordly courts at Ferrara and in the Romagna.[65]

Political centralization in Italy had, however, its own distinctive aspect. The political disputes and wars of the fourteenth and fifteenth century led to the consolidation of power on the peninsula. By the middle of the fifteenth century, the political landscape was reduced from numerous small independent states to five major "Renaissance" states – Venice, Florence, Milan, the papacy, and the Kingdom of Naples. They were territorial states, grown large by incorporating neighboring towns and lands.

The territorial states have been the subject of much recent discussion. Scholars have investigated the nature of their political organization, relations between the "center and periphery," dominant cities and their satellites. As with Northern European states, there was an early tendency to emphasize centralization and modernity. But current research has stressed the persistence of "particularism" over central authority, seeing the states as "aggregations" of diverse centers of power. Giorgio Chittolini argued that even where centralized power developed, Italian states were too distinct to be considered "modern" in any real sense. P. J. Jones denied the existence of the Renaissance "state" altogether, claiming that it was a "fiction to be banned from the books." Whatever their ostensible form, Italian states were confused and contradictory entities, whose common feature was that power was in the hand of a privileged elite.[66]

Territorial states remain an important feature of the current discourse on Italian politics.[67] Archival studies have cast further light on the nature of institutions and internal relations, including from the point of view of subject towns. The portrait is variegated.[68] The research has uncovered the persistence of private interests and the importance of patron and client networks. Even highly centralized Venice, which developed a territorial dominion (in Italy as opposed to colonies outside of the peninsula) later than other Renaissance states, allowed its subject towns much *de facto* autonomy. The city of Vicenza, incorporated into the Venetian state in 1404, retained independence with regard to finance and taxation.[69] The ties that bound together the Florentine state together involved accommodation of peasants in the countryside.[70]

As with the nation state of Northern Europe, research into Italian political developments has been greatly influenced over the past 25 years by social and anthropological studies. Attention has been given to class and gender relations, the internal exercise of coercive power through control of crime and sexual mores as well as management of natural resources.[71] Scholars have paid increasing attention to the role of religious institutions, treating them not as medieval vestiges in opposition to the secular state, but as socio-political entities that were intrinsic to the process of governing (see chapter 7).[72] The studies of ritual by Edward Muir and Richard Trexler have shown how sacred and civic spaces converged and how, as Richard Trexler argued for Florence, sacred processions helped "authenticate" and "display" civic power and authority. States exercised coercive authority through lay religious organizations, notably confraternities, which included a significant portion of the citizenry. Venetian officials borrowed money in times of war from confraternities (known as *scuole*).[73] The Medici extended their political power in the sixteenth century by dominating confraternities and through involvement in pawnbroking banks, the so-called *monte di pietà*, which were used as instruments of political patronage.[74] As Roberto Bizzocchi has demonstrated, the Florentine political elite was closely tied to the church. Government officials often held high church office and benefice, which aided their local political power. The political ascendancy of the visionary monk Girolamo Savonarola (1494–8) is treated not as an aberration, but as part of the broader Florentine political tradition. Savonarola worked with extant political forms, advocated republicanism and undertook reforms that lasted beyond his regime.[75]

Florence and Republicanism

As the proceeding examples show, the city of Florence has been at the center of much of the discussion regarding Renaissance politics.[76] Even Jacob Burckhardt, for all his interest in despots, described Florence as a singular entity, a "workshop of the modern European spirit" and the "first modern state in the world."[77] The twentieth-century scholarship has stressed modernity. Florence is the focal point of two famous discussions regarding the genesis of modern-day republicanism. The first, initiated by Hans Baron, located republicanism in the work of humanists at the beginning of the fifteenth century; the second, by Felix Gilbert, found republicanism and modern political theory in the work of Niccolò Machiavelli and Francesco Guicciardini (1483–1540) at the end of the fifteenth and beginning of the sixteenth century.

The two interpretations are, as we shall see, not unrelated, and both have had an enormous impact that goes far beyond the literature on Renaissance politics. Hans Baron's thesis focused on the struggle between lordships and republics. He examined in particular Florence's war with Milan in the last decades of the fourteenth century. He cast the conflict as one of evil versus good, comparing Milan and its "tyrant" Giangaleazzo Visconti to Nazi Germany and Hitler, and Florence to the allied democracies. In terms of fourteenth-century Italy, the war pitted republican "liberty" (Florence) against hegemonic tyranny (Milan).

Baron laid out his argument in his epochal *Crisis of the Early Italian Renaissance* (1955). He asserted that the war, during which Florence's fate hung in the balance, produced a fundamental change in political outlook in the city among humanists. For the first time, they extolled Florence's republican tradition against the despotic ways of its enemy. The shift was most apparent in the work of the humanist Leonardo Bruni (1369–1444), who drew parallels between Florence and the classical republican tradition of Rome and employed a new political vocabulary centered on the words *civis* (citizen) and *libertas* (liberty). Bruni made his views known in two important treatises, *Dialogues to Pier Paolo Vergerio* and *Panegyric to the City of Florence*, which Baron dated to the end of war in 1402. These ushered in a new era of political thought in which Florence, hitherto seen as the heir of the Roman empire and monarchy (Dante) was now the heir of Republican Rome.[78]

Bruni thus represented a new phase of humanism, which Baron called "civic humanism," a term he first coined in a German review article (*Bürgerhumanismus*) published in 1925. Civic humanism advocated participation in politics, the "vita activa," over the contemplative life, the "vita contemplativa," favored by Petrarch and the earlier generation of humanists. The theme of active political participation became an important part of the Florentine humanist tradition.

It is worth stressing the importance of Baron's thesis.[79] It has, as a recent historian noted, provoked more discussion and research than any scholarly book on the Renaissance in the twentieth century.[80] Baron's broad claims were bold. Florentine republicanism represented a wholly new era in the history of political thought. In this Baron followed Burckhardt in seeing the Renaissance as a turning point in the history of mankind. Baron may also be said to have followed Sismondi in locating political freedom in the Italian republics. But unlike Sismondi, who saw the critical moment as occurring in the twelfth and thirteenth centuries, Baron shifted the key moment to the fifteenth century, when for Sismondi Italian liberty was being squelched by the rise of the Medici.

In any case, Baron's thesis provided a powerful point of reference for further research. William Bouwsma looked for examples of republican liberty in sixteenth and early seventeenth century Venice, in the works of Donato Gianotti (d. 1573), Gasparo Contarini (d. 1542) and, above all, Paolo Sarpi (d. 1623).[81] The political scientist J. G. A. Pocock traced the genealogy of Baron's civic humanism back to antiquity and forward to the American colonies and the founding fathers. In *The Machiavellian Moment: Florentine Political Thought and the Atlantic Republican Tradition*, Pocock credited Bruni and civic humanism with reviving the classical republicanism tradition, which influenced the work of Machiavelli ("Machiavellian moment") who in turn influenced the seventeenth-century English political writer James Harrington. Harrington authored *Oceana* (1656), "a revision of English political theory and history in light of the concepts drawn from civic humanism and Machiavellian republicanism," which exerted a strong influence across the Atlantic.

Pocock's thesis has provoked its own considerable debate, which has engaged scholars and political theorists specialized in the ancient world, Renaissance Italy, modern Europe, and America. For Americanists Pocock offered an alternative reading of the foundations of American democracy that eschewed the traditional emphasis on John Locke, whose role was already being reexamined by scholars such as Bernard Bailyn and Gordon Wood.[82] The debate has, however, been characterized by strong ideological considerations. The participants include conservative theorists, who, inspired by the political philosopher Leo Strauss, have strongly denied any connection between ancient and modern republicanism. They see Machiavelli, the key figure in the transfer of ideas, as an innovator who constituted a distinct break from prior tradition.[83]

The debate among Italianists over civic humanism has likewise been considerable. Historians question the timing and originality of Bruni's call to republicanism and his use of the terms liberty and tyranny.[84] They wonder whether the sentiments expressed by him belong more properly under the heading of humanist rhetoric, aimed at displaying eloquence and rhetorical skill (see chapter 4).[85] They have looked more closely at Bruni's civic sentiments in the context of his career and his other writing, and found them less original.[86] Scholars have also questioned Baron's depiction of Petrarch and the earlier Florentine humanist tradition. They have called attention to the nature of Florentine government, questioning whether it was more oligarchic and hegemonic than Baron allowed and thus not so dissimilar to the "tyranny" of Milan.[87]

The debate has taken on the aspect of a "revolt of the medievalists," although it has not been explicitly presented as such. Several scholars have looked more closely at earlier precedents for civic humanism on the peninsula.[88] D. M. Bueno de Mesquita, for example, pointed to the widespread use of the term "liberty" by northern cities (including Milan) during their struggle with German emperors in the twelfth century.[89] Nicolai Rubinstein and Quentin Skinner have noted the influence of the medieval scholastic tradition and the recovery of the Aristotelian corpus in the thirteenth century.[90] Scholastic writers in Italy espoused republican ideology. Ptolemy of Lucca (d. 1327), a student of Thomas Aquinas, rejected royal rule as despotic and advocated republican government in the model of the Roman republic. His contemporary Marsiglio of Padua (d. 1342) drew upon Aristotle's *Politics* to advocate (with respect to the Church) in *Defender of the Peace* (1324) a species of popular sovereignty, government by consent of the governed, in which officials were elected and the laws were made by a legislator, consisting of the "weightier part" of the citizenry.[91] The jurist Bartolus of Sassoferato (d. 1357) condemned tyranny as the worst form of government and affirmed the importance of the participation of citizenry in the political process.[92]

The broader lineage of republicanism did not at once deny the validity of Baron's thesis.[93] Quentin Skinner spoke of a "cultural *longue durée*" dating back to medieval times in which Bruni and the Florentine civic tradition nevertheless constituted a distinct phase, whose novelty lay in Bruni's equation of political freedom with power.[94] John Najemy, employing a wide array of archival evidence and sources, argued that Florence had participated in republicanism a century and a half before Bruni. This was "guild republicanism," based on "corporate" politics of the city's guild system. Political power in Florence was since 1292 in the hands of craft guilds, which were organized according to profession. They possessed an egalitarian structure in which each member was equal. But guild membership was restricted and only a small percentage of citizens actually belonged to them. Florentine guild government was thus oligarchic, but nevertheless elective.

Najemy argued that the great uprising of the lower classes, the Ciompi rebellion in 1378, which occurred in the wake of the Black Death, constituted a "guild revolution." The uprising led to the expansion of political participation to the lesser guilds and thus lower classes. The prospect of sharing political authority with that group frightened the elites, who had dominated politics. They abandoned corporatism in favor of consensus politics, which they were able control. Consensus politics formed the context of civic humanism.[95]

Najemy's interpretation allowed Florentine government its dual oligarchic and Republican nature. Najemy also added an important class element to Florentine politics that was largely missing from Baron's thesis, which argued from the vantage of political elites. The contradictions of Florentine politics have nevertheless continued to fuel animated scholarly discussion. The start of Medici rule in 1434 appeared to move the city further from republicanism to oligarchy and lordship. The family manipulated the voting process and political institutions from behind the scenes.[96] Anthony Molho posed the question whether Cosimo de' Medici, the head of the family, should be considered "pater patriae," the father of the state, or "padrino," a Mafioso king pin.[97] According to Dale Kent, the Medici regime represented the triumph of private over public interest.[98]

Machiavelli: Republican or Monarchist?

The contradictions of Florentine politics, and of Italian politics more generally, are perhaps most apparent in the career of Niccolò Machiavelli, with whom we began this chapter and with whom it seems fitting to end it. Machiavelli was born in Florence during the Medici regime (1469), served in high office (1498–1512) during their exile and lost his position when the Medici returned to the city. Machiavelli's career coincided with the invasion of Italy by France and Spain – a signal moment in the ascendancy of nation states – and the "reinvention" of Florentine government and the advent of a "tougher" republicanism in the city.[99] During his forced retirement from Florentine politics, Machiavelli wrote his most famous works, including *The Prince* and *Discourses on Livy*, in which he laid out his political ideas.

But Machiavelli presents a deeply ambiguous persona that has flummoxed historians for generations.[100] Already in 1949 the political philosopher Benedetto Croce wondered if "the puzzle" that was Machiavelli would ever be solved.[101]After 60 years, this does not appear to be the case. Machiavelli was steeped in Roman classics and even dressed in classical garb and "conversed" with the ancients in his private moments. His ideas nevertheless possess a distinctly modern ring, a directness that shocked his contemporaries and have resonated through the ages. This was not the least because of his seemingly ambivalent view toward Christianity, which in *The Prince* appears as a tool for political power.

Historians debate how to situate Machiavelli. Was he backward looking or forward looking? Was he part of the humanist tradition or a modernist and herald of an entirely new type of politics? Was he a proponent of republican style government, the subject of the *Discourses*, or of one-man rule, the subject of *The Prince*? If the former, how does he fit with the tradition of

Leonardo Bruni that preceded him in his native Florence?[102] Or was Machiavelli, as Garrett Mattingly famously asked, little more than a satirist whose intention was simply to vex and "shock" his audience?[103]

The questions are difficult ones. The universality of Machiavelli's work has prompted so many scholarly studies that it is difficult to make a final verdict. In terms of Renaissance political tradition, the subject of this chapter, the judgment has been mixed. Hans Baron saw Machiavelli as an advocate of republicanism, and stressed his role as writer of *Discourses*, in which Baron saw continuities with Bruni.[104] J. G. A. Pocock treated Machiavelli as the key figure in the transfer of the classical republican tradition in Renaissance Italy to England and then America. Harvey Mansfield and Paul Rahe, however, have argued that Machiavelli was strikingly original, a teacher of wickedness and thus a secular man distinct from the context in which he lived.[105]

It is nevertheless difficult to separate any historical figure from his context. Felix Gilbert struck an early and influential note of compromise, in a powerful reading of Machiavelli that accounted for his originality as well as his context. He asserted that Machiavelli represented a turning point and "modern stage" in Renaissance political thought, but nevertheless argued that Machiavelli belonged "to the climate of the time" which in sixteenth-century Florence included humanist political discussions in the Rucellai gardens. Machiavelli was influenced by these and included several of the participants as characters in his *Art of War*. Throughout his writings, Machiavelli used conventional forms to make unconventional arguments. The *Prince* is patterned after treatises on ideal rulers, a common medieval form. The *Discourses* was cast in the familiar genre of a commentary on a classical author.[106]

Whatever Machiavelli's true intentions, the sustained interest in his writing, from his own era to the present, makes clear that he represented, regardless of specific influences, a distinctive moment in Renaissance political tradition, a point on which there is general agreement.

Notes

1 Niccolò Machiavelli, *The Prince*, trans. by George Bull (New York, 1977), pp. 90–1 (ch. 15).

2 Nineteenth century scholarship included heightened interest in "national" histories. The statements made by Michelet (d. 1874) on the Renaissance were, for example, in his multi-volume *History of France*. The study of politics was particularly popular in the German academy, in the work of Leopold von Ranke (1795–1886) and later Karl Lamprecht (1852–1915), Friedrich Meinecke

(1862–1954), and Max Weber (1864–1920). Anthony Molho, "The Italian Renaissance, Made in the USA," in *Imagined Histories: American Historians Interpret the Past* (Princeton, 1997), p. 271; Harry Liebersohn, "German Historical Writing from Ranke to Weber: The Primacy of Politics," in *A Companion to Western Historical Thought*, ed. by Lloyd Kramer and Sarah Maza (Malden, MA, 2002), pp. 166–84.

3 J. C. L. Sismondi, *A History of the Italian Republics* (New York, 1907, originally published as *Histoire des républiques italiennes du moyen âge*, Paris, 1809–18). On Sismondi's career, see J. B. Bullen, *The Myth of the Renaissance in Nineteenth Century Writing* (Oxford, 1994), pp. 50–8.

4 Edward Muir has recently affirmed the notion that the Renaissance "invented the idea of the state." Edward Muir, "Governments and Bureaucracies," in *A Companion to the Worlds of the Renaissance*, ed. by Guido Ruggiero (Malden, MA, 2002), p. 107. Quentin Skinner has argued that the term "state" came to be used in its modern sense in sixteenth-century England and France. Quentin Skinner, *The Foundations of Modern Political Thought*, vol. 1 (Cambridge, 1978), p. x.

5 Eugene F. Rice and Anthony Grafton, *The Foundations of Early Modern Europe, 1460–1559* (New York, 1994).

6 Michael Cherniavsky, "Ivan the Terrible as Renaissance Prince," *Slavic Review* 27, 2 (June 1968): 195–217.

7 Max Weber, *Economy and Society: An Outline of Interpretive Sociology*, ed. by Guenther Roth and Claus Wittch (Berkeley, 1978, originally published 1914); Liebersohn, "German Historical Writing," p. 178.

8 Friedrich Meinecke, *Die Idee der Staatsräson in der neueren Geschichte* (Berlin, 1924). This was translated into English by Douglas Scott as *Machiavellism: The Doctrine of Raison d'État and its Place in Modern History* (New Brunswick, 1998, originally published in London, 1947).

9 Denys Hay, "The Renaissance 1493–1520," in *The New Cambridge Modern History*, vol. 1, ed. by G. R. Potter, (Cambridge, 1957), pp. 5–6.

10 John Najemy, "Politics and Political Thought," in *Palgrave Advances in Renaissance Historiography*, ed. by Jonathan Woolfson (New York, 2005), p. 270.

11 James J. Sheehan, "The Problem of Sovereignty in European History," *American Historical Review* 111, (Feb. 2006): 1–15.

12 A. F. Pollard, *Factors in Modern History* (London, 1907), pp. 52–78. See also Gerhardt Ritter, *Die Neugestaltung Europas in 16 Jahrhundert* (Berlin, 1950) and Carl Ingvar Andersson, *History of Sweden*, trans. by Carolyn Hanny (New York, 1956).

13 For recent references to "new monarchy" see Mark Kishlansky, Patrick Geary, and Patricia O'Brien, *Civilization in the West* (New York, 2008), p. 358 and Mortimer Chambers, Barbara Hanawalt, Theodore K. Rabb, Isser Woloch, and Raymond Grew, eds., *The Western Experience* (New York, 2005) p. 478.

14 Roland Mousnier, *Histoire générale des civilisations: Les XVIe et XVIIe siècles* (Paris, 1961). See also Arthur J. Slavin, ed., *The New Monarchies and Representative Assemblies* (Boston, 1964), pp. 11–12.

15 Friedrich Meinecke described Louis as an example of the "unscrupulous and rational art of government." Meinecke, *Machiavellism*, p. 29.
16 Martin Wolfe, *The Fiscal System of Renaissance France* (New Haven, 1972), pp. 1–24.
17 R. J. Knecht, *Renaissance Warrior and Patron: The Reign of Francis I* (Cambridge, 1994) and *French Renaissance Monarchy: Francis I and Henry II* (London, 1996, originally published in 1984).
18 A. D. Innes, *England under the Tudors* (London, 1905); F. York Powell and R. F. Tout, *History of England* (London, 1906).
19 Walter Cecil Richardson, *Tudor Chamber Administration, 1485–1547* (Baton Rouge, 1952).
20 G. L. Harriss and Penry Williams, *A Revolution in Tudor History* (London, 1963); Christopher Coleman and David Starkey, *Revolution Reassessed: Revisions in the History of Tudor Government and Administration* (Oxford, 1988). See also John Guy, *Tudor England* (Oxford, 1988). See also J. J. Scarisbrick, *Henry VIII* (London, 1968); B. W. Beckinsale, *Thomas Cromwell, Tudor Minister* (London, 1978); Steven J. Gunn, *Early Tudor Government 1485–1558* (Houndmills, 1995).
21 J. H. Elliott, *Imperial Spain 1469–1716* (New York, 1963), p. 65.
22 Nancy Rubin, *Isabella of Castile: The First Renaissance Queen* (New York, 1991).
23 Henry Kamen, *Spain, 1469–1714*, 2nd edn. (New York, 1991), pp. 10, 151; Roger Merriman, *The Rise of the Spanish Empire*, 4 vols. (New York, 1918–34).
24 Kenneth F. Lewalski, "Sigismund I of Poland: Renaissance King and Patron," *Studies in the Renaissance* 14 (1967): 49–72; Cherniavsky, "Ivan the Terrible": 195–217.
25 Marianna Birnbaum, *The Orb and the Pen: Janus Pannonius, Matthias Corvinus and the Buda Court* (Budapest, 1996).
26 Carole Fink, *Osman's Dream: The Story of the Ottoman Empire 1300–1923* (London, 2005).
27 J. Russell Major, *Representative Institutions in Renaissance France, 1421–1559* (Madison, 1960), pp. 3–4, 10 and *From Renaissance Monarchy to Absolute Monarchy: French Kings, Nobles, and Estates* (Baltimore, 1994).
28 Major, *Renaissance Monarchy*, pp. xx–xxi.
29 Joseph R. Strayer, *On the Medieval Origins of the Modern State* (Princeton, 1970), p. 12.
30 Perry Anderson, *Lineages of the Absolute State* (London, 1974), pp. 15, 18, 20, 142.
31 Weber, *Economy and Society*.
32 Norbert Elias, *The Civilizing Process: Sociogenetic and Psychogenetic Investigations*, trans. by Edmund Jephcott, rev. edn. ed. by Eric Dunning, Johan Goudsblom, and Stephen Mennell (Oxford, 1994).
33 Elias, *Civilizing Process*, pp. 181, 188, 191.
34 Michael Roberts, "The Military Revolution, 1560–1660," in *The Military Revolution Debate*, ed. by Clifford J. Rogers (Boulder, CO, 1995), pp. 13–35.
35 George Clark, *War and Society in the Seventeenth Century* (Cambridge, 1958), pp. 72–5.

36 Geoffrey Parker, "Military Revolution, 1560–1660: A Myth?" *Journal of Modern History* 48 (1976): 196–214 and *The Military Revolution: Military Innovation and the Rise of the West, 1500–1800* (Cambridge, 1988).

37 Jeremy Black, *A Military Revolution?: Military Change and European Society, 1550–1800* (London, 1991); Clifford Rogers, "The Military Revolutions of the Hundred Years War," *Journal of Military History* 57 (1993): 258–75. See also Brian M. Downing, *The Military Revolution and Political Change: Origins of Democracy and Autocracy in Early Modern Europe* (Princeton, 1992); On Bacon's views see Eugene F. Rice Jr, *Foundations of Early Modern Europe, 1460–1559* (New York, 1970), pp. 14–16.

38 Richard Bonney, ed., *Economic Systems and State Finance* (Oxford, 1995) and *The Rise of the Fiscal State in Europe, c.1200–1815* (Oxford, 1999); Wantje Fritschy, "A 'Financial Revolution' Reconsidered: Public Finance in Holland during the Dutch Revolt, 1568–1648," *Economic History Review* 56, 1 (Feb. 2003): 57–89.

39 The earliest studies were those of major Italian commercial centers (Genoa, Venice, and Florence), which focused on economic issues without explicit reference to politics. Hans Sieveking, "Studio sulle finanze genovesi nel medioevo," trans. by Onorio Soardi, *Atti della Società Ligure di Storia Patria* 35 (1905): 3–261; Bernardino Barbadoro, *Le finanze della repubblica fiorentina: imposta diretta e debito pubblico fino all'istituzione del Monte* (Florence, 1929); Gino Luzzatto, *I prestiti pubblici della Repubblica di Venezia* (sec. XIII–XV) (Padua, 1929).

40 Marvin Becker, "Some Common Features of Italian Urban Experience," *Medievalia et Humanistica*, n.s. 1 (1970): 175–201 and *Florence in Transition*, 2 vols. (Baltimore, 1967–8).

41 James Tracy, *A Financial Revolution in the Habsburg Netherlands* (Berkeley and Los Angeles, 1985).

42 P. J. Dickson, *A Financial Revolution in England. A Study in the Development of Public Credit, 1688–1765* (London, 1967); John Brewer, *The Sinews of Power. War Money and the English State, 1688–1783* (New York, 1989).

43 Charles Tilly, *Coercion, Capital and European States* (Oxford, 1992), pp. 76, 81, 190.

44 J. A. Sharpe, *Crime in Early Modern England 1550–1750* (London, 1984); Steve Hindle, *The State and Social Change in Early Modern England 1550–1640* (New York, 2000); Michael J, Braddick, *State Formation in Early Modern England, 1550–1700* (Cambridge, 2000), p. 1.

45 Clifford Geertz, *Negara, The Theater of State in Nineteenth-Century Bali* (Princeton, 1981); David I. Kertzer, *Ritual, Politics, and Power* (New Haven, 1988); David Potter, *A History of France, 1460–1560: The Emergence of a Nation State* (London, 1995), p. 17. See also Victor Turner, *The Ritual Process: Structure and Anti-Structure* (Chicago, 1969); Edward Muir, *Ritual in Early Modern Europe* (Cambridge, 1997).

46 Lawrence M. Bryant, "The Medieval Entry Ceremony at Paris," in *Coronations: Medieval and Early Modern Monarchic Ritual*, ed. by János M. Bak (Berkeley and

Los Angeles, 1990); Alice Hunt, *The Drama of Coronation: Medieval Ceremony in Early Modern England* (Cambridge, 2008).

47 Ralph E. Giesey, *The Royal Funeral Ceremony in Renaissance France* (Geneva, 1960).

48 Benedict Anderson, *Imagined Communities: Reflections on the Origin and Spread of Nationalism* (London, 2003, originally published in 1983), pp. 6, 18, 37–46.

49 Peter Sahlins, *Boundaries: The Making of France and Spain in the Pyrenees* (Berkeley, 1991).

50 Ernst Gellner, *Nations and Nationalism* (Oxford, 1983) and *Nationalism* (London, 1997); Eric Hobsbawm, *Nations and Nationalism Since 1780* (Cambridge, 1990).

51 Patrick Geary, *The Myth of Nations: The Medieval Origins of Europe* (Princeton, 2002); Robert Bartlett, "Medieval and Modern Concepts of Race and Ethnicity," *Journal of Medieval and Early Modern Studies* 31,1 (2001): 52; R. R. Davies, "The Peoples of Britain and Ireland, 1100–1400, I: Identities," *TRHS*, 6th ser., 4 (1994): 1–20; Simon Forde and Alan V. Murray, eds., *Concepts of National Identity* (Leeds, 1995).

52 Glenn Richardson, *Renaissance Monarchy: The Reigns of Henry VIII, Francis I, and Charles V* (New York, 2002).

53 Edward Muir, *Civic Ritual in Renaissance Venice* (Princeton, 1981); Richard Trexler, *Public Life in Renaissance Florence* (New York, 1980); Loren Partridge and Randolph Starn, *Arts of Power. Three Halls of State in Italy, 1300–1600* (Berkeley and Los Angeles, 1992).

54 Federico Chabod, "Y a-t-il un État de la Renaissance?" in *Actes du colloque sur la Renaissance* (Paris, 1958), pp. 57–74 and an English language translation "Was there a Renaissance State?" in *The Development of the Modern State*, ed. by Heinz Lubasz (New York, 1964), pp. 26–42. For the influence of Weber on Chabod, see Julius Kirshner, "The State is Back In," in *The Origins of the State* (Chicago, 1996), p. 1.

55 Garrett Mattingly, *Renaissance Diplomacy* (New York, 2008, originally published in 1955), pp. 51–2.

56 M. S. Anderson, *The Origins of The Modern European State System, 1494–1618* (New York, 1998).

57 John M. Najemy, "Political Ideas," in Ruggiero, *Companion to the Renaissance*, pp. 384–40.

58 Piero *Pieri*, "Alcune questioni sopra la fanteria nel periodo comunale," *Rivista Storica Italiana* 50 (1933): 561–614 and *Il Rinascimento e la crisi militare italiana* (Turin, 1952). On military developments in Italy, see Michael Mallett, *Mercenaries and Their Masters* (Totowa, 1974); John R. Hale, *War and Society in Renaissance Europe, 1450–1620* (Baltimore, 1985) and with Michael Mallett, *The Military Organization of a Renaissance State: Venice, 1400–1617* (Cambridge, 1984); Bert S. Hall, *Weapons and Warfare in Renaissance Europe* (Baltimore, 1997); Maria Nadia Covini, *L'esercito del duca: Organizzazione militare e istituzioni al tempo degli Sforza, 1450–1480* (Rome, 1998); William Caferro, *Mercenary Companies and the Decline of Siena* (Baltimore, 1998) and *John Hawkwood: An English Mercenary in Fourteenth-Century Italy* (Baltimore, 2006).

59 William Caferro, "Continuity, Long-Term Service, and Permanent Forces: A Reassessment of the Florentine Army in the Fourteenth Century," *Journal of Modern History* 80 (June 2008): 303–22.
60 David Abulafia, "The South," in *Italy in the Age of the Renaissance, 1300–1550*, ed. by John Najemy (Oxford, 2004), pp. 208–25.
61 Burckhardt called Venice a city of "political silence" and Florence a city of "incessant movement." For the myth of Venice, see James S. Grubb, "When Myths Lose Power: Four Decades of Venetian Historiography," *Journal of Modern History* 58, 1 (Mar. 1986): 43–94.
62 Benjamin G. Kohl, *Padua under the Carrara, 1318–1405* (London, 1998); Christine Shaw, *Popular Government and Oligarchy in Renaissance Italy* (Leiden, 2006).
63 Philip J. Jones, "Communes and Despots in Late Medieval Italy," *TRHS*, 5th ser., 15 (1965): 71–96.
64 Alan J. Ryder, *The Kingdom of Naples under Alfonso the Magnanimous. The Making of a Modern State* (Oxford, 1976), pp. 16–17. For parallels in the fourteenth century, see Samantha Kelly, *The New Solomon. Robert of Naples (1309–1343) and Fourteenth-Century Kingship* (Leiden, 2003).
65 Muir, "Governments," in Ruggiero, *Companion to the Renaissance*, p. 109; Paolo Prodi, *Il sovrano pontefice: Un corpo e due anime. La monarchia papale nella prima età moderna* (Bologna, 1982); John Larner, *Lords of the Romagna: Romagnol Society and the Origins of the Signorie* (Ithaca, 1965) and Werner Gundersheimer, *Ferrara: The Style of Renaissance Despotism* (Princeton, 1973).
66 Marino Berengo, "Il Cinquecento," in *La storiografia italiana negli ultimi vent'anni*, 2 vols. (Milan, 1970); Giorgio Chittolini, *La formazione dello stato regionale e istituzioni del contado: Secoli XIV e XV* (Turin, 1979) and "Cities, City-States and Regional States in North-Central Italy," *Theory and Society* 18 (Sept. 1989); Elena Fasano Guarini, *Lo stato mediceo di Cosimo I* (Florence, 1973) and "Center and Periphery," in Kirshner, *Origins of the State*.
67 William J. Connell and Andrea Zorzi, eds., *Florentine Tuscany: Structures and Practices of Power* (Cambridge, 2000).
68 See among others Judith Brown, *In the Shadow of Florence: Provincial Society in Renaissance Pescia* (Oxford, 1982); Edoardo Grendi, *Il Cervo e la Repubblica: Il modello ligure di antico regime* (Turin, 1993); William J. Connell, *La città dei crucci: Fazioni e clientele in uno stato repubblicano del '400* (Florence, 2000).
69 J. S. Grubb, *Firstborn of Venice: Vicenza in the Early Renaissance* (Baltimore, 1991).
70 Samuel K. Cohn Jr, *Creating the Florentine State: Peasants and Rebellion, 1348–1434* (Cambridge, 1999).
71 John K. Brackett, *Criminal Justice and Crime in Late Renaissance Florence, 1537–1609* (Cambridge, 1992); Andrea Zorzi, "La cultura della vendetta nel conflitto politico in etá comunale," in *Le storie e la memoria: In onore di Arnold Esch* (Florence, 2002); Trevor Dean and K. J. P. Lowe, eds., *Crime, Society and the Law in Renaissance Italy*, (Cambridge, 1994); Karl Appuhn, "Inventing Nature: Forests, Forestry and State Power in Renaissance Venice," *Journal of Modern History* 72 (2000): 861–89.

72 David Peterson, "Out of the Margins: Religion and the Church in Renaissance Italy," *Renaissance Quarterly* 53 (2000): 835–79; John Najemy, "The Dialogue of Power in Florentine Politics," in *City States in Classical Antiquity and Medieval Italy*, ed. by Anthony Molho, Kurt Rauflaub, and Julia Emlen (Ann Arbor, 1991); Samuel K. Cohn, *The Laboring Classes in Renaissance Florence* (New York, 1980).

73 Brian Pullan, *Rich and Poor in Renaissance Venice* (Oxford, 1971); David M. D'Andrea. *Civic Christianity in Renaissance Italy: The Hospital of Treviso, 1400–1530* (Rochester, NY, 2007).

74 Carol Bresnahan Menning, *Charity and State in Late Renaissance Italy: The Monte di Pieta of Florence* (Ithaca, 1993).

75 Roberto Bizzochi, *Chiesa e potere nella Toscana del Quattrocento* (Bologna, 1987); Donald Weinstein, *Savonarola and Florence: Prophecy and Patriotism in the Renaissance* (Princeton, 1970); Lorenzo Polizzotto, *The Elect Nation: The Savonarolan Movement in Florence, 1494–1545* (Oxford 1994).

76 Gene A. Brucker, *Florentine Politics and Society, 1343–1378* (Princeton, 1962) and *The Civic World of Early Renaissance Florence* (Princeton, 1977); Lauro Martines, *The Social World of Florentine Humanists* (Princeton, 1963) and *Lawyers and Statecraft in Renaissance Florence* (Princeton, 1968); Alison Brown, *The Medici in Florence: The Exercise and Language of Power* (Florence, 1992); Melissa Bullard, *Filippo Strozzi and the Medici: Favor and Finance in Sixteenth-Century Florence and Rome* (Cambridge, 1980); Humphrey Butters, *Governors and Government in Early Sixteenth-Century Florence, 1502–1519* (Oxford,1985); Paula C. Clarke, *The Soderini and the Medici: Power and Patronage in Fifteenth-Century Florence* (Oxford, 1991).

77 Jacob Burckhardt, *The Civilization of the Renaissance in Italy*, trans. by S. G. C. Middlemore (New York 1982), pp. 55, 63–4.

78 Hans Baron, *The Crisis of the Early Renaissance: Civic Humanism and Republican Liberty in an Age of Classicism and Tyranny* (Princeton, 1955), pp. 3–78, 83–93.

79 On the importance of Baron see John M. Najemy, "Review Essay of Baron's 'Essays on the Transition from Medieval to Modern Thought,'" *Renaissance Quarterly* 45 (1992): 340–2; Riccardo Fubini, "Renaissance Historian: The Career of Hans Baron," *Journal of Modern History* 64 (1992): 541–74; James Hankins, "The 'Baron Thesis' After Forty Years and Some Recent Studies on Leonardo Bruni," *Journal of the History of Ideas* 56 (1995): 309–38.

80 Ronald Witt, "Hans Baron's Renaissance Humanism," *American Historical Review* 101 (Feb. 1996): 111.

81 Bouwsma saw the papal interdict of the republic in 1605–7 as a turning event in political feeling. William Bouwsma, *Venice and the Defense of Republican Liberty*, pp. 53, 95.

82 Bernard Bailyn, *The Ideological Origins of the American Revolution* (1967) and Gordon Wood, *The Creation of the American Republic, 1776–1987* (1969). An excellent summary is in William J. Connell, "The Republican Idea," in

Renaissance Civic Humanism, Reappraisals and Reflections, ed. by James Hankins (Cambridge, 2000), pp. 22–4.

83 Leo Strauss, *Thoughts on Machiavelli* (Glencoe, IL, 1958); Paul A. Rahe, *Republics Ancient and Modern*, 3 vols. (Chapel Hill, 1992); Harvey C. Mansfield, *Machiavelli's Virtue* (Chicago, 1996).

84 For recent evaluation of Baron's dating see James Hankins, *Plato in the Italian Renaissance*, vol. 2 (Leiden, 1990), p. 371.

85 Jerrold E. Seigel, "Civic Humanism or Ciceronian Rhetoric," *Past and Present* 34 (1966): 3–48; Robert Black, "The Political Thought of Florentine Chancellors," *Historical Journal* 29 (1986): 991–1003. For an excellent evaluation of the debates, see Connell, "Republican Idea," pp. 14–29.

86 James Hankins, "Rhetoric, History and Ideology: The Civic Panegyrics of Leonardo Bruni," in *Renaissance Civic Humanism*, p. 143.

87 Peter Herde, "Politische Verhaltensweisen der Florentiner Oligarchie, 1382–1402," in *Geschichte und Verfassunggefuge: Frankfurter Festgabe fur Walter Schlesinger*, ed. by Klaus Zernack (Wiesbaden, 1973).

88 Nicolai Rubinstein, "Political Theories in the Renaissance," in *The Renaissance: Essays in Interpretation*, ed. by A. Chastel (London, 1982).

89 D. M. Bueno de Mesquita, "The Place of Despotism in Italian Politics," in *Europe in the Late Middle Ages*, ed. by John Hale, Roger Highfield, and Beryl Smalley (London, 1965).

90 Rubinstein, "Political Theories"; Quentin Skinner, *The Foundations of Modern Political Thought*, vol. 1 (Cambridge, 1978).

91 David S. Peterson, "Conciliarism, Republicanism and Corporatism: The 1415–1420 Constitution of the Florentine Clergy," *Renaissance Quarterly* 42, 2 (Summer 1989): 183–226.

92 Charles T. Davis, *Ptolemy of Lucca and the Roman Republic in Dante's Italy* (Philadelphia, 1984); James M. Blythe, "Civic Humanism and Medieval Political Thought," in Hankins, *Renaissance Civic Humanism*.

93 Witt, "Hans Baron's Renaissance Humanism": 113–15.

94 Quentin Skinner, "The Vocabulary of Renaissance Republicanism: A Cultural longue durée?" in G. Bock, Q. Skinner, and M. Viroli, eds., *Machiavelli and Republicanism* (Cambridge, 1990).

95 John M. Najemy, *Corporatism and Consensus in Florentine Electoral Politics, 1280–1400* (Chapel Hill, 1982).

96 Nicolai Rubinstein, *The Government of Florence Under the Medici (1434 to 1494)* (Oxford, 1966); Herde, "Politische Verhaltensweisen der Florentiner Oligarchie".

97 Anthony Molho, "Cosimo de' Medici: Pater Patriae or Padrino," *Stanford Italian Review* 1 (1979): 5–33.

98 Dale Kent, *The Rise of the Medici: Faction in Florence 1426–1434* (Oxford, 1978).

99 John M. Najemy, *A History of Florence, 1200–1575* (Malden, MA, 2006), pp. 381 and "Politics Ideas," in Ruggiero, *Companion to the Renaissance*, p. 392.

100 Villari, *Niccolò Machiavelli*; Oreste Tommasini, *La vita e gli scritti di N. M. nella loro relazione col machiavellismo* (Rome, 1883–1911); Friedrich Meinecke, *Die Idee der Staatsräson* and Bendetto Croce, *Elementi di Politica* (Bari, 1925).

101 Benedetto Croce, "Una questione che forse non si chiuderà mai: La questione del Machiavelli," *Quaderni della Critica* 5, 14 (1949): 1–9.

102 Federico Chabod, *Machiavelli and the Renaissance* (London, 1958).

103 Garrett Mattingly, "Machiavelli's Prince: Political Science or Political Satire," *American Scholar* 27 (1958): 482–91.

104 To strengthen the connection, Baron dated the *Prince* much earlier than the *Discourses*. This therefore did not represent Machiavelli's final opinion. Hans Baron, "Machiavelli the Republican Citizen and the Author of the Prince," in *In Search of Civic Humanism: Essays on the Transition from Medieval to Modern Thought*, 2 vols. (Princeton, 1988); John M. Najemy, "Baron's Machiavelli and Renaissance Republicanism," *American Historical Review* 101 (Feb. 1996): 119–26.

105 Strauss, *Thoughts on Machiavelli*, pp. 202–3; Paul A. Rahe, "Situating Machiavelli," in Hankins, *Renaissance Civic Humanism*, p. 307; Mansfield, *Machiavelli's Virtue*.

106 Felix Gilbert, *Machiavelli and Guiccardini: Politics and History in Sixteenth Century Florence* (New York, 1985, originally published 1965), pp. 29, 48, 125, 153, 156 and "Bernardo Rucellai and the Orti Oricellari: A Study in the Origins of Modern Thought," *Journal of the Warburg and Courtauld Institutes* 12 (1949): 101–31.

7

Faith and Science: Religious or Rational?

I was led, as I believe, by a heavenly gift from the Father of lights, from whom comes every excellent gift, to embrace incomprehensible things incomprehensibly in learned ignorance and through a transcending of humanly knowable incorruptible truths. Thanks to him who is Truth I have now expanded this learned ignorance in these books, which [. . .] proceed from one and the same principle.

Nicholas of Cusa[1]

To us, it seems that sixteenth century learning was made up of an unstable mixture of rational knowledge, notions derived from magical practices, and a whole cultural heritage whose power and authority had been vastly increased by the rediscovery of Greek and Roman authors.

Michel Foucault[2]

The opposition of religion and rationality was an important feature of the early historiography of the Renaissance. The Middle Ages represented an "age of faith," during which the Catholic Church played a dominant role. The Renaissance was a progressive and modern era, characterized by the emergence of rational thought and personal freedom. The French philosophe Voltaire stated the notion already in the eighteenth century, in his *Essay on Manners and the Spirit of Nations* (1756). He attributed the revival of the arts in fifteenth- and sixteenth-century Italy to the "triumph of reason and genius" which was intrinsically linked to "irreligious attitudes, moral confusion, and criminal tendencies." Jacob Burckhardt made moral confusion, superstition and corruption preconditions for the great achievements of the

Renaissance, which included scientific discovery and a wholly new appreciation of the natural world.[3]

The image of a secular and rational Renaissance remains part of popular perceptions of the period. Modern scholars have, however, largely abandoned the view. They treat Renaissance society as at once religious and secular and blur the distinctions among its scientific, philosophic, spiritual, and superstitious activities.[4]

A Border Region between the Late Middle Ages and the Reformation

In the old narrative – still evident in textbooks and general studies – Renaissance religion occupies a hazy border region between the "crises" of late medieval Christendom and the Reformation.[5] The former were characterized by institutional difficulties and heresies coinciding with the cycle of famine, plague, and warfare in the fourteenth and fifteenth centuries. The papacy abandoned Rome for Avignon, initiating the Babylonian Captivity of the Church (1309–77). This was followed by the Great Schism (1378–1415), which saw the advent of two and briefly three popes, and the Conciliar Movement that attempted to heal the breach by means of a Church council (see chapter 6). John Wycliff (d. 1384) and the Lollards challenged established church practices in England, as did Jan Hus (d. 1415) and his followers in Bohemia.

The events formed the prelude to the Renaissance papacy that, in Burckhardt's words, "acted in the spirit of secular principalities."[6] Popes displayed the same traits of "individualism" as Renaissance princes. They patronized humanist writers and artists, collected books and manuscripts and, in the case of Nicholas V and Pius II, were humanists themselves (see chapter 4). As with secular rulers, their individualism shaded into debauchery. Pope Innocent VIII (1482–1492) fathered 16 children; Alexander VI (1492–1503) held sex parties at the Vatican; Julius II (1503–1513), the "warrior" pope, led armies into battle. This "march of folly," as one popular writer called it, brought the calls for reform that led directly to the Protestant Reformation.[7] The central role of the papacy in this development is made clear by the elevation to the Holy See of members of the Medici family. It was Giovanni de' Medici, son of Lorenzo the Magnificent, who, as Pope Leo X (1513–1521), issued the call for indulgences (to beautify the Vatican) that provoked Martin Luther's Ninety-Five Theses. It was likewise Leo who initially misjudged Luther's dissent, believing it that of "a drunken German."

The relationship between the Renaissance and Reformation has since been a focal point of scholarly discussion. Modern debate has centered primarily on the role of humanism (see chapter 4). The nineteenth-century art critic John Ruskin equated humanism with paganism and thus saw it as inherently anti-Christian. The twentieth-century Italian historian Delio Cantimori stressed humanism's anticlerical aspect and connection to Italian heretical movements in the sixteenth century.[8]

Few now hold such stark views. The occasional humanist such as Gemistos Pletho (d. 1454) abjured Christianity in favor of paganism. But the vast majority remained Christians, whose interest in classics was not contrary to their faith.[9] This was, as we have seen in chapter 4, particularly true of Jacques Lefèvre d'Étaples and Desiderius Erasmus, whose "Christian" humanism involved study of the bible and church fathers in their original languages. The historian Charles Trinkhaus forcefully argued that humanism remained fundamentally Christian in nature. In his study *In Our Image and Likeness* (1970), Trinkhaus demonstrated that Italian humanists viewed classics as a means of deepening their faith rather that as an alternative to it. The notion of man's "dignity" and perfection was grounded in scripture, in Genesis 1:26, which stated that man was created in God's image, whose likeness he reflected. "There was never in Petrarch's mind or in those of his contemporary humanist friends the slightest doubt about the truth of the Christian revelation, nor could there have been."[10]

The acceptance of a religious component of humanism left open how to situate it in terms of the Reformation. As rhetoricians and grammarians, humanists were usually not interested in religious reform. Conversely, Protestant reformers, though sometimes educated in the humanist tradition, showed little interest in eloquence and rhetoric. Direct access to the language of patristic texts and the bible nevertheless encouraged critique and skepticism. Erasmus famously ridiculed Church abuses, particularly those involving monasteries and the papacy. His stress on inner heartfelt piety and "philosophia Christi" has parallels with Luther's "justification by faith" and Reformation theology. Nevertheless, Erasmus ultimately repudiated Luther and the reformists.[11]

Modern scholarship has centered on two opposing interpretations: one that has seen the Reformation as the inevitable consequence of humanism and the other that has seen the Reformation as a reaction against it. The recent trend has been to seek a middle ground, to stress, in Peter Matheson's felicitous phrase, how humanism and Reformation were "married" but not in a "monogamous" way.[12] The two movements modified and balanced each other. Martin Luther, Philip Melanchthon, and Ulrich Zwingli read humanist works, which had gained wide currency through the printing press and were available in schools. Melancthon advocated the adoption of humanist curricula at universities as a counter to "Catholic" scholasticism. His educational program was similar to that of the great English humanist Thomas

More. Both viewed humanist study as a means of preparing men for public service and the proper worship of God. The radical Swiss reformer Thomas Müntzer (d. 1525) amassed a sizable library of humanist texts.

Renaissance Religion

It is necessary to stress, however, the importance of the revision of the scholarship that occurred in the early 1970s. Charles Trinkhaus's work initiated a spate of studies that have transformed the field over the last 40 years.[13] Scholars have reexamined institutional and intellectual developments. They have emphasized the points of intersection between religious and secular authority (see chapter 6). Drawing on the cultural anthropological approaches of Émile Durkheim and Clifford Geertz, they have explored the meaning of religious rites and rituals; how they, in Durkheim's phrase, created "mental states" that ordered Renaissance society.[14] Scholars have likewise investigated "popular" aspects of religion. They have traced the experiences of women (see chapter 3) and of ordinary citizens below the level of the elite. They have sought to move beyond traditional disciplinary boundaries, treating religious developments as part of the basic social, cultural, and economic fabric of society.

The result is that Renaissance religion has been raised, in the words of Timothy Verdon, to an "equal coefficient" of the Renaissance. The transformation has occurred, however, even if the precise line of demarcation with the Middle Ages is not always clear.[15] The term "late medieval" remains a popular one for events prior to the sixteenth century. It lives on in studies of the institutional crises and heresies of the fourteenth century and in studies, such as Andre Vauchez's influential analysis of the social construction of ("late medieval") sainthood in the thirteenth to sixteenth centuries, that take the long view of events.[16] The Renaissance label is rarely applied to developments in German lands, the epicenter of the Reformation, for which "medieval" seems a more appropriate precursor. Renaissance has been more comfortably applied to Italy and France, though not in a consistent manner.

A distinctive feature of the recent scholarship on Renaissance religion has been its emphasis on lay practices. Scholars have traced the ways in which traditionally secular spaces became increasingly "sacralized" during the era. They observe a Renaissance tendency toward the "laicization of spirituality" and contrast this to the Middle Ages during which sacred spaces – monasteries and nunneries in particular – were physically set apart from the rest of society. The interpretation allows the Renaissance its own distinct religious coloring while at the same time creating a more meaningful bridge to the

Reformation, when the separation between lay and sacred space decreased still further, with the elimination altogether of the cloister by reformers.[17]

Popular and Civic Religion

A form of religious expression that has received a great deal of attention from Renaissance scholars has been confraternities. They were voluntary associations at the intersection of institutional and popular religious practice. Their basic function was to promote piety and solidarity among members and prepare them for the afterlife. They existed in a variety of forms, most typically as *laudesi*, who sang hymns and prayed, and *disciplinati*, who purged and flagellated themselves. Their members represented a broad sector of society, including men and women of varying social status. According to one estimate, a third of all urban households in Italy belonged to confraternities in the late sixteenth century. Clergy sometimes participated, but confraternities were mostly lay associations, whose members pledged an oath and remained in the world.[18]

Given their ubiquity and diversity, confraternities offer important insights into everyday life during the Renaissance. They sponsored feasts and festivals, staged plays and held public processions in honor of patron saints and funerals for members who died. The confraternity of the Archangel Raphael in Florence was composed of young boys, whose joint activities included singing, playing cards, and billiards. As corporations, confraternities patronized the arts, hiring musicians and artists for some of the most renowned commissions of the Renaissance. They distributed charity to the poor and functioned also as hospitals, especially during times of the plague. They helped create networks that allowed members to cross social and economic boundaries and make connections beyond their neighborhoods. In Italy, confraternities played a leading role in public executions, acting as comforters to prepare the condemned for the afterlife.[19]

As noted in chapter 6, confraternities also had important political functions. The Venetian government relied on confraternities, the so-called *scuole*, for loans in times of war and fiscal crises.[20] The consolidation of Medici rule in Florence in the sixteenth century included manipulation of confraternities as part of a larger strategy aimed at extending authority over the church. This was a general trend throughout Europe, where political centralization involved closer control of the religious institutions. David Peterson has traced points of convergence between the republican movement in Florence in the late fourteenth and fifteenth centuries and Conciliar thought. He noted how both argued against one-man rule and in favor of popular participation in government.[21]

The coincidence between politics and religion is particularly apparent in public rituals. The pioneering studies of Edward Muir and Richard Trexler in the 1980s for the cities of Venice and Florence respectively emphasize the ways in which sacred and civic spaces coincided and how governments used rituals to validate and display civic authority. Local officials undertook a variety of activities, including processions honoring local saints, burials of important citizens, celebrations of military victories, diplomatic missions and the ascension to office of local politicians and rulers. In Venice, the election of a doge was an elaborate ceremony, in which the new ruler was transported to the sea in a gold-painted barge. He dropped a gold ring into the water, symbolic of his union with it. As Christ was bridegroom and master of the church, the Venetian doge was bridegroom of the sea. In Florence, the Medici family inserted itself into the festival of the Magi, a popular procession originally sponsored by local confraternities. After assuming *de facto* control of Florence in 1434, Cosimo de Medici joined the Magi processions and commissioned works of art relating to the theme. His participation symbolically enforced his prince-like power.[22]

The examples highlight the civic use of religion in Renaissance society. Rituals projected power, both inside the state and outside of it. There was little distinction between secular and sacred images.

The confluence of secular and religious themes is evident also in the popular preaching of the era.[23] The tradition is viewed prima facie as at odds with the Renaissance, as representative of a distinctly medieval trend and reaction against the elite cultural and intellectual currents of the era. But there was during the Renaissance a strong mystical and prophetic culture that included "living saints" such as Catherine of Siena (1347–1380) and Teresa of Avila (see chapter 3) and itinerant charismatic preachers such as Bernardino of Siena (1380–1440) and the Girolamo Savonarola (1452–1498).[24]

Scholars now treat the culture as a fundamental part of Renaissance society, whose roots lay in the Middle Ages. Bernardino and Savonarola were Franciscan and Dominican monks respectively and represented a mendicant tradition of preaching that dated to the thirteenth century. Medieval Franciscan and Dominican preachers drew large crowds and spoke on issues relating to modesty, penance, peace, and charity. Bernardino and Savonarola undertook the same themes. They railed against personal vanity and worldliness, warning listeners to tend first to their souls. The stirring sermons of Bernardino involved prophetic visions and culminated in bonfires of vanities, as listeners, often women, placed false hair, teeth and other symbols of worldliness into fires. Savonarola's oratory also involved prophetic visions. He created in Florence a cadre of *piagnoni* or criers to keep watch on the moral fiber of the populace.[25]

Savonarola has had a special place in discussions of the Renaissance. In his nineteenth century biography, Pasquale Villari posited Savonarola as an emblem of Renaissance spirit of individuality.[26] More recent scholars treat Savonarola in terms of his milieu, in particular as part of the Florentine political tradition in which he participated. Savonarola's brief rule of the city is seen not as an aberration, but as evidence of important connection between religion and politics, which was not inconsistent with Florentine republican ideology (see chapter 6).[27]

The tradition of Renaissance popular preaching gained its distinct aspect from its connection to the crises of the era. Bernardino of Siena's career took place against a backdrop of plague and warfare, which were important themes in his sermons. The outbreak of the Black Death occasioned the so-called Bianchi movement, made up of a cross section of society that traveled throughout northern and central Italy in the summer of 1399 preaching peace and the need to end feuds and civil strife. Ottavia Niccoli has argued that prophetic popular preaching reached a peak in Italy during wars and political crises stemming from the French invasion of 1494.[28]

The Bianchi sought peace and concord and, as Daniel Bornstein has demonstrated, evoked generally positive responses from civic authorities. Other groups were, however, less pacific. Samuel Cohn has cataloged a wide array of contemporary popular movements that were often violent and had as their goal political and social change.[29] The Black Death gave rise in German lands to the flagellants, whose calls for peace and penance were coupled with the denunciation of Jews, whom they accused of causing the plague. In Spain, the Black Death set off massacres and forced conversions of Jews in 1391. The "marranos," as the converts were pejoratively known, were targets of sporadic violence and persecution throughout the fifteenth century.[30] Charges of ritual murder were levied against the Jewish community in Trent in 1475 and found their way into work of humanists and in popular sermons.[31] Bernardino of Siena virulently condemned Jews in his sermons. The end of the *reconquista* in Spain in 1492 brought the expulsion of Jews, who dispersed throughout Europe and to the Ottoman Empire.[32]

Muslims, Amerindians, and Africans were likewise victims of stereotypes and mistreatment. The culmination of the *reconquista* in 1492 brought the political subjugation of the last Islamic outpost in Spain (Granada) and the expulsion of Muslims along with Jews. The military threat of the Ottoman empire meanwhile stoked fears about Islam. Humanists depicted Muslims as "savages," who threatened the survival of civilization and good letters.[33] New World natives were also depicted as savages and were subjugated and enslaved by their European conquerors (see chapter 2). As with Muslims, humanists applied pejorative language and images to them drawn from classical antiquity. Charges of cannibalism against Amerindian natives led, as we saw in chapter 2, to a debate in Europe about the meaning of humanity.

The discovery of the New World meanwhile stimulated trade in black Africans from the sub-Sahara, who, like the American natives, were seen as slaves by nature. Europeans associated black skin color with evil, which trumped all prior social status and nationality.[34] The Spanish sneezed when black Africans passed by them, to ward off evil. Local stereotypes included depiction of Africans as lazy, shiftless, and sexually promiscuous. The concept of "blackness" was, however, a variable one. Italian financial records suggest differences in price according to skin color: the lighter the skin, the higher the price for a slave. Even among indigenous Europeans there appears to have been distinction according to hue and color of skin.[35]

The Renaissance atmosphere of intolerance also involved repression of heretics and witches. Witchcraft was, as we saw in chapter 3, perceived as an international conspiracy and charges of demonic possession were most typically leveled against women. Fears were heightened by religious fervor arising from Protestant reform and Catholic counter-response. Local authorities undertook extraordinary efforts to control heresy, creating tribunals and inquisitorial commissions to root out disbelief and dissent. Carlo Ginzburg's well-known sixteenth century miller Menocchio was a victim of one such purge. Menocchio's creative comparison of God's creation of the universe to the formation of cheese and worms (the latter representing angels) brought condemnation by the inquisition at Friuli, where he was burned alive at the stake.[36]

Repressive measures were also taken against vagrants, vagabonds, and homosexuals, who were often fitted into the same category. The charge of sodomy, a crime in Renaissance Europe, was leveled at heretics and witches. In his sermons Bernardino of Siena equated Jews with witches, heretics, and sodomites on the grounds that all were in league with the devil. The portrait of intolerance includes a whole lexicon of national typologies. Germans described the Poles as "thieves" and Hungarians as "violent and drunkards, who flapped their arms when inebriated."[37]

The portrait is not, however, without nuance. Black Africans gained praise – albeit as objects – for their physical prowess and "exotic" qualities. They functioned at the court of Catherine of Austria of Portugal as symbols of royal power. Not all Africans were slaves. Some served as ambassadors, others as musicians (drummers and trumpeters) at Renaissance courts; a black confraternity was founded in Lisbon. Amerindians of the New World were seen by contemporaries, such as Michel Montaigne, as noble and virtuous, if in a primitive way. Despite fears of the Ottomans, there was significant cultural and artistic interaction between the Muslim and Christian worlds. The Muslim convert Al-Hassan Al-Wazzan was one of the most popular writers of the early sixteenth century. And despite fierce repression, there remained vibrant Jewish communities in Europe. The historian Ariel Toaff has cataloged the presence of these in fourteenth and fifteenth century Italy. Jews worked as doctors, blacksmiths, and innkeepers and played an important role in Italian economic life.[38] Jews participated in confraternities in Venice. The seventeenth-century Venetian rabbi Leon Modena wrote an autobiography that scholars have seen as reflecting the broad Renaissance spirit of individualism. Even in Spain, after the forced conversions, there remained important Jewish communities, such as at Morvedre, which flourished economically in the fifteenth century. Robert Bonfil has described Jewish life in Italy as neither wholly good nor bad, but as serving as a mirror of Christianity, and providing a means by which Christians defined themselves.[39]

Renaissance and Scientific Revolution

The studies of religious developments make clear the complex and contradictory nature of Renaissance society. The question remains however whether, amid the many social, economic, and political forces, the Renaissance was at all a secular age? This has in many ways been the most difficult question for scholars. It requires evaluating the Renaissance in terms of the Scientific Revolution of the seventeenth century, the "century of genius," which challenged ancient authority, overturned the medieval worldview, and developed – in the work of Galileo (1564–1642) and Newton (1642–1727) – a wholly new understanding of nature and set of physical laws.[40] On the surface, there appears little connection between the two movements. The Renaissance sought to recapture antiquity rather than move beyond it. Writing in 1949, the historian of science Herbert Butterfield saw a stark contrast. The Scientific Revolution constituted "the real origin of the modern world" and the Renaissance and Reformation were "mere episodes, internal displacements, within the system of medieval Christendom."[41] The statement struck at the core of the issue. Both eras lay claim to modernity, but the Scientific Revolution's claim was stronger.

The notion of a "scientific renaissance" therefore presents scholars with notable challenges. They need to evaluate it in terms of humanism, the most representative intellectual movement of the era, which focused on imitation rather than innovation and rhetoric rather than empirical observation. They must also situate scientific developments in terms of Renaissance philosophy. There was strictly speaking no such thing as "science" during the period. Such speculations fell under the heading of natural philosophy, the term used by Isaac Newton in the title of his *Mathematical Principles of Natural Philosophy (Philosophiae Naturalis Principia Mathematica*, 1687), which redrew the laws of the physical world. The Renaissance recovery of the full corpus of Plato and the work of Neoplatonist writers represented a *de facto* boon to science in that it weakened the primacy of Aristotle, whose natural system dominated the medieval worldview. But Platonism, and Renaissance philosophy more generally were ambiguous entities. They possessed strong magical and religious components. Two of the greatest figures of the age, Marsilio Ficino (1433–1499) and Giovanni Pico della Mirandola (1463–1494) sought in the study of Platonism a unifying vision of the world that brought together their faith and understanding of the natural world. Finally, scholars must assess the role of a vernacular and technical tradition of scientific inquiry and whether advances in Renaissance science owed only to elite intellectual trends. This involves consideration of the work of obscure artisans and practical men of the Renaissance, who gained knowledge and expertise by direct experience and whose methods bore resemblance to the empiricism of the seventeenth century.

In keeping with his view of the Renaissance as a period of progress and modernity, Jacob Burckhardt stressed the scientific achievements of the age. He cited in particular increased knowledge of the world and appreciation of nature. His evidence of the former included Dante's depiction of the cosmos in the Divine Comedy and of the latter, the "clever" breeding practices of horses at the Gonzaga court. These were hardly convincing and elicited an early and forceful "revolt" from medievalist scholars.[42] Lynn Thorndike openly ridiculed Burckhardt's assertions, claiming that the Renaissance represented in fact a backward period for science. Thorndike argued that medieval science was both technically and intellectually superior. He noted the sketchbooks of thirteenth century French builder Villard de Honnecourt (d. 1250?), which contained drawings of sophisticated and innovative machines, the treatises of Albertus Magnus (d. 1280), who wrote about animals and plants, and the work of John Buridan (d. 1358), who investigated laws of motion. Thorndike accused humanists of "show rather than substance" and suggested that the lack of Renaissance achievement in science may have owed to a talent drain into painting and the visual arts.[43]

The priority of the Middle Ages was reinforced in studies by Pierre Duhem, Alistair Crombie, George Sarton, and J. H. Randall. Pierre Duhem, a physician as well as historian, gave primary place to the thirteenth century. He stressed the role of Arabic mathematical and scientific texts that entered Europe at the time.[44] J. H. Randall argued for the existence of a direct link between the medieval science and seventeenth century Scientific Revolution through the University of Padua. He noted that many of the most important scientific figures of age, including Andreas Vesalius, Copernicus, and

Galileo, studied there. The university curriculum focused on Aristotle, who was synonymous with the medieval worldview. But the study of Aristotle at Padua was not, as elsewhere, grounded in theology and scholasticism, but in the study of medicine and the natural world. Students also read the works of Galen and the Greek medical tradition as well as Arabic texts and the Muslim tradition, the most advanced of the era. Randall pointed to a tradition of professors of medicine (Jacopo of Forlí, d. 1410; Hugo Benzi, d. 1439; Giacomo Zabarella, d. 1589), who did not so much solve particular problems regarding physics and medicine as establish a method of scientific inquiry that was at times critical of Aristotle and facilitated the later scientific achievements of Copernicus and Galileo.[45]

The medievalist revolt was influential and was incorporated into Renaissance textbooks, many of which take the long view of Renaissance science, starting with developments in the thirteenth century. The revision was less successful, however, among historians of science, who continued to treat the seventeenth century in its own terms as a period of innovation and fundamental change. In his influential study of the Scientific Revolution, Alexandre Koyré placed Galileo in a chapter entitled "Things Never Seen Before and Never Thought."[46]

The singularity of the period received strong additional support in the seminal studies of the historian of science/philosopher Thomas Kuhn. In *The Structure of Scientific Revolutions* (1962), Kuhn denied the progressive nature of scientific inquiry. He argued that science moved forward not by means of a cumulative process, but by "paradigm shifts," breaks from prior knowledge and approaches, initiated by those who sought to explain anomalies in accepted theories. The thesis left little room for Renaissance science as a precursor to the Scientific Revolution.[47]

Humanism and Science

The influence of Kuhn notwithstanding, a more positive view of Renaissance science has emerged over the last 30 years. The revision is linked to a re-evaluation of humanism (see chapter 4). Eric Cochrane, Cesare Vasoli, Anthony Grafton, Ann Blair, and Pamela O. Long have argued that humanism played an important role in the development of science and constituted a meaningful prelude to the career of Galileo.[48] Although concerned with eloquence and rhetoric, humanists did a fundamental service to science by recovering and translating much of the ancient corpus of scientific writings. The translations, whatever the motive for their production, helped create an intellectual and social climate receptive to scientific advancement.[49] In making classical texts more readable, humanists also made them less sterile and more accessible. Meanwhile, humanism's inherent hostility toward tradition rendered more reasonable the proposition that the ancients, for all their skills, were fallible men. The humanists' penchant for self-promotion and the advent of the printing press allowed the new knowledge to be communicated to the widest possible audience. The audience included those not directly interested in science. The Renaissance recovery of Lucretius' *De rerum natura*, for example, inspired Niccolò Machiavelli (1469–1527), who copied an edition by hand in the 1490s and found correspondences between Lucretius' atomistic view and the political actions of men.[50]

The influence of humanism is, however, particularly evident in the field of mathematics. By the middle of the sixteenth century, humanists had translated and produced new editions of the work of the major Greek mathematicians, including Euclid, Apollonius, and Archimedes. Archimedes was especially important. His idea that motion was susceptible to mathematical investigation became a key feature of the new view of the physical world.[51] It inspired the studies by Niccolò Tartaglia (d. 1557) of falling bodies (*Nova scienza*) as well as those (relating to machines) of Del Monte (d. 1607), who was a patron of Galileo. Archimedes also influenced the work of mathematician, physician, and polymath Girolamo Cardano (1501–1576) and the artist Piero della Francesca (1415–1492), who transcribed a Latin edition of Archimedes by hand.

The effect of humanism on mathematics is perhaps most apparent in the career of Regiomontanus (1436–1476), the pen name of Johan Müller. Regiomontanus was both a mathematician and humanist. He authored the earliest systematic work on plane and spherical geometry (*On Triangles of All Kinds*), and produced an abridged edition of the *Almagest* of Ptolemy, a second-century Greek mathematician, who had revised Aristotle's schema of the cosmos. Regiomontanus's *Epitome of the Almagest* helped, as Peter Dear has asserted, "transfer the language of the humanism" to the arena of mathematical science.[52] Regiomontanus's success owed to his very conscious efforts to popularize the work of the ancients. In humanist fashion he collected Greek scientific manuscripts and set up a printing press at Nuremberg, the first scientific press in Europe, to publish the vast corpus. Regiomontanus issued a prospectus of what he planned to print that included virtually all the mathematical works of classical antiquity. He unfortunately died before completing the project. But his collection of texts nevertheless facilitated later study.

It was Regiomontanus's edition of Ptolemy that Nicolaus Copernicus (d. 1543) used to formulate his famous heliocentric view that ultimately revised the prevailing view of the cosmos. Copernicus laid out his intentions in humanist fashion in the preface of his famous *On the Revolution of Celestial Bodies*. Copernicus wrote that he canvassed the work of the ancients for precedent, in the hope of restoring views that had previously been held. Indeed, the Hellenistic Greeks had speculated about a sun-centered cosmos back in the third-century BC. Copernicus's conclusions nevertheless would go on to have revolutionary consequences. Copernicus was himself aware of this and did not publish his treatise until 1543, the year of his death, for fear of censure by the Church, for which he worked as a canon at Frauenburg Cathedral in his native Poland.

The contradictions have raised questions among historians about how precisely to place Copernicus. Was he an innovator or a conservative? The historian of science Marie Boas described Copernicus as the "embodiment of the culture of the Renaissance."[53] Nevertheless, Copernicus had studied Aristotle at Padua and accepted much of Aristotle's cosmology, including the notion that the universe was a finite sphere with fixed stars. Copernicus's primary objective in *On the Revolution of Celestial Bodies* was to simplify the Ptolemaic system, to reduce the number of epicycles, and remove errors. He placed the sun at the center by means of mathematical conjecture, not observational data. But Copernicus's decision to stress the primacy of mathematical logic ultimately pitted him against Aristotelian physics and contemporary Church teachings, which was, as Robert S. Westman has argued, a revolutionary stance.[54]

Humanism also had a considerable influence on Renaissance medicine. The Aldine press in Venice published the complete works of Galen in 1525 and Hippocrates in 1526. The recovery of the entire Galenic corpus stimulated the study of anatomy.[55] Andreas Vesalius (d. 1564), a student at Padua and later professor there, was inspired by Galen to perform dissections and autopsies. In *On the Structure of the Human Body*, published in the same year as Copernicus's treatise, Vesalius corrected some of Galen's errors and provided a detailed description of the body, which included carefully drawn anatomical images that greatly facilitated study. Vesalius believed that it was necessary to know how the body worked in order to properly treat disease. Like Copernicus, Vesalius explicitly drew on humanist principles in the preface of his book, stating his desire to restore the study of anatomy to the level it had reached under the ancients. Vesalius's work proved a turning point in the medical view of the human body and in the status of anatomy as a field of study. The historian Andrew Cunningham has spoken of "anatomical Renaissance" in the sixteenth century. Anatomy became at that time a formal part of the curriculum of medical schools.[56]

The study of anatomy and medicine was accompanied by heightened interest in the natural world. Botany became a part of the medical curriculum in universities in the sixteenth century. Humanists provided new and better translations of the works of Theophrastus, Dioscorides, and Pliny the Elder. This encouraged a whole genre of Renaissance naturalist treatises, which, like their counterparts on anatomy, coupled descriptive language with meticulously drawn visual images. Otto Brunfels's *Living Portraits of Plants* (1530) contained more than 500 illustrations taken from nature and went through numerous editions. Leonard Fuchs's *History of Plants* (1542) was even more lavishly illustrated and offered a kind of Renaissance naturalist ethos, stating that there was "nothing more delightful in life than to wander over woods and plains garlanded and adorned with little flowers and plants of various and elegant sorts."[57]

Interest in the natural world was further stimulated by the Atlantic voyages and discovery of the New World, which brought to light entirely new objects. Contemporaries were fascinated by these and sought to categorize them. Nature became, as Paula Findlen has argued, a "collectable entity." This was reflected in the widespread establishment of natural museums, known as "wonder rooms" and "cabinets of curiosities." Princes and wealthy citizens collected rare and exotic plants, gathered animals in menageries and built special gardens. The act of collecting functioned as a means of establishing identity as well as patronage for friends and clients. The practice connected well to the Renaissance habit of collecting books and amassing libraries. Brian Ogilvie has spoken of the "professionalization" of the study of nature in the sixteenth century, during which time it became its own distinctive field of inquiry.[58]

It should be stressed, however, that the work of humanism did not preclude the importance also of medieval ideas. As Nancy Siraisi has argued, the medical profession benefited from a "series of receptions of the ancient heritage," which began already in the twelfth century. Each reception was distinct. The medieval period drew much from Arabic texts. The Renaissance, which Siraisi dated from the fourteenth to the sixteenth century, was shaped by fuller knowledge of the Greek tradition that helped set the stage for a later critique of it.[59]

The Renaissance was also distinct in terms of the effects on it of exogenous forces, notably the plagues and demographic crisis of the fourteenth and fifteenth centuries. These had a profound impact on the medical profession. They created greater demand for services, which broadened the profession. They heightened the search for cures, and altered the organization of medicine and its social role.[60] The era saw greater use of vernacular medical textbooks and the emergence, particularly in Southern Europe, of a "medical marketplace," in which practitioners competed for patients. It witnessed the widespread establishment of hospitals to care for the sick and dying. In the city of Florentine, as John Henderson has shown, hospitals were set up along monastic lines and involved both spiritual and physical healing. Henderson argued, contra Michel Foucault (*The Birth of the Clinic*), that premodern hospitals were not "hell holes," but carefully planned places with separate wards for patients, living quarters for staff, refectories, chapels, and pharmacies. Some specialized in treating plague victims, others in caring for foundlings, still others in general care. Patients ate and drank well during their stays, though doctors were poorly paid.[61]

Technology, the Artist-Engineer-Genius, and Leonardo da Vinci

The line between intellectual and technical developments is, however, difficult to draw. Medicine was as much a practical art as an intellectual one. The lower end of the profession included men and women with little book learning, who gained expertise primarily through hands-on experience. Mathematics was likewise a practical art. Those who studied the subject often did so for the purposes of applying it to the real world, particularly to warfare. Niccolò Tartaglia studied falling bodies to gain a better understanding of ballistics. Federico Commandino (d. 1575), who translated Archimedes and Euclid, was employed by the duke of Urbino to help improve fortifications and devise machines for war. Leon Battista Alberti – Burckhardt's all-sided Renaissance man – applied his study of linear perspective to fortification and devoted a portion of his famous treatise on architecture (*De re aedificatoria*, 1485) to the issue. The artists Leonardo da Vinci and Michelangelo also worked on military projects. Leonardo speculated on ways to build portable bridges, armored vehicles, and various types of catapults and flamethrowers.[62] His designs included a plan for a navigable canal between Pisa and Florence.

The examples highlight the role of "the artist-engineer-genius" – as Erwin Panofsky called him – in the development of Renaissance science. Some of the most important technical innovations of the era were the work of artists. Panofsky credited the men with playing a unique role in bringing together the manual and intellectual arts, a conjunction that distinguished the Renaissance period from the Middle Ages, during which the two spheres were completely separate. The artists "intellectualized" the mechanical professions, of which they, as artisans in the first instance, were a part (see chapter 2).[63]

Leonardo da Vinci's career has been judged particularly significant in this regard. His famous *Notebooks* contained speculations on a wide array of subjects, ranging from anatomy to the mechanics of motion. Leonardo included in the margins of the work pithy and brilliant insights that have tantalized scholars ever since. His detailed drawings of the human body were sufficient to gain for Leonardo recognition as a pioneer in the field of anatomy or more specifically a pioneer in the artists' empirical tradition of

Table 7.1 *Categorization of Leonardo da Vinci in Renaissance textbooks*

Author	*Artist/Scientist/Engineer*	*Artist*
Henry S. Lucas (1934)	X	
Eugene Rice (1970)	X	
Lewis Spitz (1971)	X	
De Lamar Jensen (1981)	X	
Margaret L. King (2003)		X
Robert Ergang (1967)	X	X
Robin Kirkpatrick (2002)	X	X

Sources: Henry S. Lucas, *The Renaissance and the Reformation* (New York, 1934), p. 361; Eugene Rice, *Foundations of Early Modern Europe, 1460–1559* (New York, 1970), pp. 20–1; Lewis Spitz, *The Renaissance and Reformation Movements* (St Louis, MO, 1971), pp. 187–8; De Lamar Jensen, *Renaissance Europe* (Lexington, MA, 1981), pp. 165–8; Margaret L. King, *The Renaissance in Europe* (London, 2003), p. 129; Robert Ergang, *The Renaissance* (New York, 1967), pp. 168–172, 277–280; Robin Kirkpatrick, *The European Renaissance, 1400–1600* (London, 2002), pp. 145–150.

anatomical study that grew alongside the humanist approach of Vesalius. The historian Ernst Cassirer went so far as to credit Leonardo with being the father of the modern experimental method.[64]

Other scholars have, however, been less sure of Leonardo's credentials as a scientist. They note that he worked in isolation, that his approach was unsystematic and that his contemporary reputation was far less distinguished than his posthumous one has been. Indeed, Leonardo's fame as a scientist owes largely to modern scholarship and popular textbooks, which, for the sake of brevity and effect (in the case of textbooks) have often taken him as the apotheosis of Renaissance science (see table 7.1). Nevertheless it is not easy to connect Leonardo to contemporary trends. He did not attend university, was not a humanist or did not in fact know the Latin language well. But Leonardo was friends with the humanists Paolo Toscanelli and John Argyropoulos and the mathematician Luca Pacioli. Leonardo mentions Archimedes in his *Notebooks*. Even if his contribution to Renaissance science has been "overrated," Leonardo's career suggests how far the culture of science and technology had diffused by the end of the fifteenth century.

The culture of science and technology included the work of artisans and engineers of lesser renown. In his influential three-volume *Geschichte der neusprachlichen wissenschaftlichen Literatur* (1919–27) (History of Scientific Literature in the Modern Languages), Leonardo Olschki pointed to a strong vernacular tradition of scientific writing in the Renaissance. The treatises were written by practical men, who employed the techniques of trial and error, a methodology used also by Galileo and Newton.[65] The work of the artisans raises questions about the importance of humanism and the Renaissance elite intellectual tradition to science. But recent research has minimized the distinctions. Ann Blair has demonstrated that humanism and empiricism were not mutually exclusive. The latter was in fact often the subject of former. Humanists argued that empirical skill could be learned by book study.[66] They expressed appreciation for labor and technical knowledge and rejected the classical and scholastic opinion that the mechanical arts were inherently inferior to intellectual ones. George Bauer's humanist treatise on mining (*De re metallica*, 1556) not only explained the technical aspects of refining metallic ores, but argued against the prevailing view that mining was "sordid toil."[67]

Magic and Philosophy

A key component of Renaissance science was magic. Magic was, as noted above, perceived as an operative force in Renaissance society.[68] It fell into two basic categories: demonic magic (i.e., witchcraft), which was evil, and natural magic, which was positive. Natural magic had substantial appeal among Renaissance intellectuals, who believed that it allowed access to the hidden powers of nature, the "occult" in the literal Latin sense of the word, representing the secret meanings of things. Heinrich Cornelius Agrippa (d. 1535), author of a compendium on the occult, described natural magic as "a faculty of wonderful power" and the "most perfect branch of knowledge."[69] Magic was important to the study of mathematics. Numbers were perceived as having metaphysical properties. Perfect squares, for example, corresponded to the harmonies of the universe and provided insight into them. Numerology was a key component of astrology, which was popular during the Renaissance, as it had been in the Middle Ages. Astrology was a marketable skill, suitable for employment at the courts of kings and princes, who wished to know the course of future events as well as the most propitious time to mobilize armies, arrange weddings and coronations. Johannes Kepler, who formulated the theory of elliptical orbit of planets, worked as an astrologer/mathematician at the court of Emperor Rudolf II in Prague. Medical doctors often doubled as astrologers.[70] According to Nancy Siraisi, the plagues of the fourteenth and fifteenth centuries stimulated interest in astrology, which played a larger role in post-plague medicine than it had before.[71]

A prevalent form of magic was alchemy. Alchemists sought the magical elixir or agent of transmutation that turned base metal into gold and silver. Like astrologers, they received widespread support for their activities from princes, who were interested in alchemy's potential profits and, as Bruce T. Moran has pointed out, its congruence with their broader political aims.[72] One of its most enthusiastic proponents of the practice was the medical doctor Paracelsus (d. 1541), the pseudonym for Theophrastus Philippus Aureolus Bombastus von Hohenheim. Paracelsus's interest in alchemy derived from his study of the human body, which he saw as a reflection of the spiritual and occult sympathies of the universe. His search to understand these sympathies led him beyond inherited convention, to seek alchemical cures for disease. He denied the medieval notion of balance of humors, but saw diseases instead as having specific causes due to agents, which could be counteracted by specific remedies. He favored the use of drugs, including inorganic and poisonous substances such as mercury. The novel approach has gained for Paracelsus recognition from modern scholars as an initiator of the field of experimental chemistry.[73]

Paracelsus was a passionate and colorful character, who has been described as being as much a madman (D. P. Walker) as an innovator. He nevertheless represented a clear break from prior tradition. He publicly burned the books of Galen and expressed contempt for the contemporary medical establishment and university training. His very name, which he gave himself, suggested his defiance of tradition. It means "surpassing the work of Celsus," the great Roman medical writer. But Paracelsus's ideas found broad support, as did alchemy more generally, which influenced also Isaac Newton.[74]

Renaissance magic was closely connected to study of the natural world. The search for the hidden meanings of objects heightened interest in things that were "novel," "wondrous," or even "monstrous."[75] There emerged in the sixteenth century a new genre of books, "the secrets of nature" literature, which contained exotic recipes, the hidden properties of plants and gems and other "tricks of the trade." Alessio Piemontese's *Secrets* (1555) was a prototype. It was a best seller that included alchemical recipes, practical information on quotidian tasks and "unknown" cures for illness. The book, and others of the genre, were lavishly illustrated and their authors became known as "professors of secrets." The books gained wide circulation by means of the printing press and were popular with the urban middle-class. William Eamon has credited them with validating a new view of scientific discovery in which the experimenter undertook the role of the hunter, treating nature like a dense wood in which secrets lay hiding. The tradition influenced the modern experimental methods of Francis Bacon and the English Royal Society.[76]

Along with the professors of secrets, there emerged in the middle of the sixteenth century the work of the so-called "philosophers of nature," who wholly rejected Aristotle's worldview and sought direct empirical study of nature according to its own principles.[77] Bernardino Telesio (1509–1588), one of first of the natural philosophers, asserted in *On the Nature of Things according to Their Own Principles* that the "structure of the world and nature [...] are not to be sought from reason, as the ancients did, they must be perceived from sensations." His example was followed by Girolamo Cardano and Tommaso Campanella (d. 1639), both of whom rejected Aristotle in favor of direct observation of nature. Campanella, a supporter of Galileo and devotee of the occult and astrology, wrote that he learned more from examining "the anatomy of an ant [...] than from all the books written from the beginning of time."[78]

The examples demonstrate the close connection between the Renaissance magical/scientific tradition and Renaissance philosophy.[79] Campanella's rejection of Aristotle owed in part to the influence on him of Platonism, which as we have seen was an important intellectual trend in the Renaissance. The "moving spirit" of Renaissance Platonism was the Florentine medical doctor and philosopher, Marsilio Ficino (1433–1499). Ficino translated the ancient Neoplatonic texts of Porphyry, Proclus, Plotinus, and Hermes Trismegistus and produced a complete Latin edition in 1484 of Plato's dialogues. With the patronage of Cosimo de' Medici, Ficino formed about him a circle of friends, a Platonic academy, at a villa at Careggi in Florentine countryside. From there his ideas projected outward and gained an international audience, which included Paracelsus and Kepler, among many others. Ficino inspired also Giovanni Pico della Mirandola who studied the mysteries of the universe in Jewish Kabbalistic texts.[80]

The recovery of Plato and Neoplatonic works stimulated interest in occult forces and the mysteries of the universe. For Ficino and Pico they allowed access to arcane knowledge that linked to an occult system in which individual parts of the universe reflected the cosmos as a whole. Of particular importance in this regard was Ficino's translation of the corpus Hermeticum. The corpus was believed to be the work of Hermes Trismegistus, the "thrice-great" Hermes, who lived just after the time of Moses and venerated by the Egyptians as the god Thoth. Hermes' writings had the status in the Christian world of *prisca theologia*, an ancient pagan theology that confirmed the truth of Christian scripture. In reality, Hermes' writings dated from the first centuries of Christianity, but these fraudulent origins were not exposed until the seventeenth century.

In a highly influential study published in 1964, the historian Frances Yates stressed the importance of the Corpus Hermeticum to Renaissance science.[81] She argued that it served as a critical impetus to scientific inquiry in that it allowed humans to interpret the great wonders of the universe. It enhanced the notion of man as "magus" or magician, who was capable of apprehending the mysteries of the universe. This created the context for the careers of broadly speculative thinkers such as Giordano Bruno (d. 1600), who advocated a magical/empirical approach to apprehending nature, and eventually Isaac Newton.

The "Yates thesis" stimulated much scholarly discussion and lifted magic to a central role in the study of Renaissance science.[82] The view gained additional support in Michel Foucault's *The Order of Things: An Archaeology of the Human Sciences* (1966). Foucault equated his Renaissance "episteme" (by which he meant a way of thinking or a field of knowledge) with pervasive magic (see opening quote), which stood as a prelude to his classical "episteme," which saw the birth of the modern scientific approach.[83]

The recent scholarship has, however, reassessed the role of Hermes and magic more generally. Historians point out that the term "hermetic" was more a generic one used in a variety of ways by contemporaries. It served as a catch all for a style of thinking rather than an actual philosophy. It had an exotic ring to it, but Renaissance magic was eclectic and derived also from other sources.[84] Moreover, not all contemporaries in fact believed in magic. Bernardino Telesio advocated direct observation of nature, but denounced astrology. The same is true of Giovanni Pico della Mirandola, who wrote a treatise against astrology that remained unfinished at his death.

Scholars have meanwhile examined more closely the distinctions between occult and non-occult forces. Brian Vickers has argued that the two represented distinct traditions, involving different thought processes and mental categories. The occult discourse was largely symbolic. Nature was of interest less for its own sake than as a means of gaining insight into human destiny. The non-occult discourse was more empirical and it was this tradition that formed the prelude to modern science. The Renaissance saw a battle between the two approaches, which constituted a kind of "high-level intellectual pugilism."[85]

In rejecting an all-consuming role for magic, scholars have nevertheless found it difficult to locate in Renaissance science aspects that were entirely new. Brian Copenhaver noted that for all the work of humanists, technicians, and philosophers the period saw no unique set of concepts and theories, no achievements in science that were comparable to those in the fields of arts and letters.[86] There is general agreement that heightened interest and attention to nature and natural phenomena were distinctive features of the era, and that much of Renaissance scientific inquiry took place outside of universities, at courts.[87] There is also agreement that the many trends are not easily reconcilable. While some philosophers rejected Aristotle, others like Pietro Pomponazzi (d. 1525), remained within the Aristotelian tradition and nevertheless speculated on natural phenomena.[88] As with other fields, discomfort persists with the Renaissance label itself. The recent *Cambridge History of Science* groups the years 1490 to 1730, inclusive of Galileo and Newton, under the label "early modern."[89]

Consideration of Renaissance science nevertheless reinforces the importance of religion to Renaissance society, the subject that began this chapter. The search for meaning in nature was, as we have seen, often linked to the search for God. The natural philosophers Tommaso Campanella and Giordano Bruno were Dominican friars, whose spiritual concerns were an intrinsic part of their impulse to study nature. Marsilio Ficino was a theologian and priest, whose study of Plato and the natural world was intended to facilitate his understanding of God. The appeal of Plato for Ficino in the first instance lay in the Greek philosopher's support of the immortality of the human soul, which Aristotle had denied. Similarly, Giovanni Pico della Mirandola's search for knowledge of nature was grounded in his search for religious truth and unity. Knowledge of the mysteries of nature provided spiritual consolation.[90] Pico believed that all philosophical and theological schools contained valid insights. In his famous oration on human dignity, he cited a concurrence of opinion in Latin, Greek, Arabic, Hebrew, and even Persian sources. These speculations brought condemnation of him by the church, a fate endured also by Campanella and Bruno. The latter was burned alive at the stake in the Campo de' Fiori in Rome.

The tensions and contradictions are perhaps most apparent in the career of the German polymath Nicholas of Cusa (1401–1464). More so than any other figure, Cusa fits many of the categories covered in this chapter. He was a churchman (priest and bishop), who was involved in the efforts to heal the Great Schism. He was a physician, mathematician, and philosopher. He studied scholasticism and Platonism, was familiar with humanism and a devotee of magic. In Ernst Cassirer's famous judgment, he was the quintessential Renaissance man, the "first modern thinker" whose speculations in *On Learned Ignorance* (1440), his most important work, were a turning point in Renaissance philosophy and science. In that work, Cusa laid the foundation for the modern cosmology and worldview. Cusa posited what Cassirer called the mathematization of the universe, which led him to see the cosmos as infinite and thus remove the earth from its center. Cusa speculated that the earth existed on its own axis and made a daily rotation. His work was known to Copernicus, Johannes Kepler, and Renee Descartes.[91]

But Cusa came to his conclusions on the cosmos by means of mystical contemplation. He saw the universe as a manifestation of God, which, like the deity, was limitless and unknowable. It could be apprehended only by consideration of mathematical symbolism, which was a deeply mystical enterprise. This key element in Cusa's thought aligns him closely, however, with a contemporaneous German mystical tradition, evident in the work of Meister Eckhart (d. 1328) and taken by most scholars as a distinctly medieval phenomenon. Indeed, the historian of science Alexandre Koyré granted

Cusa his priority as herald of a new worldview and mathematization of the universe, but described him as the "last great philosopher of the Middle Ages."[92]

Notes

1 Nicholas of Cusa, *On Learned Ignorance*, trans. by Jaspar Hoskins (Minneapolis, 1985), p. 151 (author's letter to Lord Cardinal Julian).

2 Michel Foucault, *The Order of Things: An Archaeology of the Human Sciences* (New York, 1970, originally published in 1966), p. 32.

3 Voltaire, *Essai sur les moeurs et l'esprit des nations*, vol. 7 (Geneva, 1773), p. 169; Jacob Burckhardt, *The Civilization of the Renaissance in Italy*, trans. by S. G. C, Middlemore (New York, 1982), pp. 299–387.

4 Excellent surveys of historiography of the Renaissance Church are in Anne Schutte-Jacobsen, "Periodization in Sixteenth Century Religious Italian History: The Post-Cantimori Paradigm Shift," *Journal of Modern History* 61 (1989): 269–84; David S. Peterson, "Out of the Margins: Religion and the Church in Renaissance Italy," *Renaissance Quarterly* 53 (2000): 835–79; John J. Martin, "Religion," in *Palgrave Advances in Renaissance Historiography*, ed. by Jonathan Woolfson, (London, 2005), pp. 193–209; Susan C. Karant-Nunn, "Changing One's Mind: Transformations in Reformation History from a Germanist's Perspective, *Renaissance Quarterly* 58 (Winter 2005): 1101–27; Charles G. Nauert, *Humanism and the Culture of Renaissance Europe*, 2nd edn. (Cambridge, 2006).

5 Peterson, "Out of the Margins," pp. 835–6 and "Religion and the Church," in *Italy in the Age of the Renaissance*, ed. by John M. Najemy (Oxford, 2004), pp. 59–81.

6 Burckhardt, *Civilization*, p. 81.

7 Barbara Tuchman, *The March of Folly: From Troy to Vietnam* (New York, 1985).

8 Delio Cantimori, *Eretici Italiani del cinquecento: Ricerche storiche* (Florence, 1939).

9 Douglas Bush, *The Renaissance and English Humanism* (Toronto, 1939); Giuseppe Toffanin, *Che cosa fu l'umanesimo?Il risorgimento dell'antichità classica nella coscienza degli italiani fra i tempi di Dante e la riforma* (Florence, 1919).

10 Charles Trinkhaus, *In Our Image and Likeness: Humanity and Divinity in Italian Humanist Thought*, vol. 1 (Chicago, 1970), p. 26.

11 P. G. Bietenholz, "Luther und die Stillen in Land," *Bibliotheque d'Humanisme et Renaissance* 47 (1985): 27–46; Nauert, *Humanism and Renaissance Europe*, p. 164.

12 Peter Matheson, "Humanism and Reform Movements," in *The Impact of Humanism in Western Europe*, ed. by Anthony Goodman and Angus MacKay (New York, 1990), pp. 23–42; M. Brecht, *Martin Luther. His Road to the Reformation*, trans. by J. L. Schaaf (Philadelphia, 1985), p. 38.

13 Martin, "Religion," pp. 195–6; Charles Trinkhaus, ed., *The Pursuit of Holiness in Late Medieval and Renaissance Religion* (Leiden, 1974).
14 Émile Durkheim, *Elementary Forms of Religious Life*, trans. by Carol Cosman (Oxford, 2001, originally published in France in 1912).
15 Timothy Verdon and John Henderson, eds., *Christianity and the Renaissance: Image and Religious Imagination in the Quattrocento* (Syracuse, 1990), p. 2. For the persistence of the medieval genre of hagiography in the work of humanists, see Alison Knowles Frazier, *Possible Lives: Authors and Saints in Renaissance Italy* (New York, 2004).
16 Andre Vauchez, *Sainthood in the Late Middle Ages* (New York, 1997).
17 Martin, "Religion," p. 200.
18 Christopher F. Black. "Italian Confraternities," in *Early Modern Confraternities in Europe and the Americas*, ed. by Christopher F. Black and Pamela Gravestock (Aldershot, 2006), p. 2 and *Italian Confraternities in the Sixteenth Century* (Cambridge, 1989); Nicholas Terpstra, *Lay Confraternities and Civic Religion in Renaissance Bologna* (Cambridge, 1995) and *Politics of Ritual Kinship: Confraternities and Social Order in Early Modern Italy* (Cambridge, 2000); Konrad Eisenbichler, ed., *Crossing the Boundaries: Christian Piety and the Arts in Italian Medieval and Renaissance Confraternities* (Kalamazoo, MI, 1991).
19 Konrad Eisenbichler, *The Boys of the Archangel Raphael: A Youth Confraternity in Florence, 1411–1785* (Toronto, 1998); John Henderson, *Piety and Charity in Late Medieval Florence* (Oxford, 1994); David M. D'Andrea, *Civic Christianity in Renaissance Italy: The Hospital of Treviso, 1400–1530* (Rochester, NY, 2007); Ronald Weissman, *Ritual Brotherhood in Renaissance Florence* (New York, 1982); Maureen Flynn, *Sacred Charity: Confraternities and Social Welfare in Spain, 1400–1700* (Ithaca, 1989); Andrew E. Barnes, *The Social Dimension of Piety: Associative Life and Devotional Change in the Penitent Confraternities of Marseille (1499–1792)* (Mahwah, NJ, 1994); Nicholas Terpstra, ed., *The Art of Executing Well: Rituals of Execution in Renaissance Italy* (Kirksville, MO, 2008).
20 Brian Pullan, *Rich and Poor in Renaissance Venice* (Oxford, 1971).
21 Paolo Brezzi, *Le riforme cattoliche dei secoli XIV e XVI* (Rome, 1945); Giovanni Miccoli, "La storia religiosa," in *Storia d'Italia*, vol. 2, pt. 1, ed. by Ruggiero Romano and Corrado Vivanti (Turin, 1974), pp. 431–1071; Roberto Bizzochi, *Chiesa e potere nella Toscana del Quattrocento* (Bologna, 1987); Duane Osheim, *A Tuscan Monastery and its Social World: San Michele of Guamo* (Rome, 1989); Peter Partner, *The Pope's Men: The Papal Civil Service in the Renaissance* (Oxford, 1990); Kate J. P. Lowe, *Church and Politics in Renaissance Italy: The Life and Career of Cardinal Francesco Soderini* (Cambridge, 1993); Simon Ditchfield, *Liturgy, Sanctity and History in Tridentine Italy: Pietro Maria Campi and the Preservation of the Particular* (Cambridge, 1995); David S. Peterson, "Conciliarism, Republicanism and Corporatism: The 1415–1420 Constitution of the Florentine Clergy," *Renaissance Quarterly* 42, 2 (Summer 1989): 183–226.
22 Edward Muir, "Representations of Power," in Najemy, *Italy in the Renaissance*, pp. 228–9 and *Ritual in Early Modern Europe* (Cambridge, 1997), p. 235.

23 Daniel Bornstein, *The Bianchi of 1399: Popular Devotion and Orthodoxy in Late Medieval Italy* (Ithaca, 1993); Daniel R. Lesnick, *Preaching in Medieval Florence: The Social World of Franciscan and Dominican Spirituality* (Athens, Georgia, 1989); Peter Francis Howard, *Beyond the Written Word: Preaching and Theology in the Florence of the Archbishop Antoninus 1427–1459* (Florence, 1995).
24 Martin, "Religion," pp. 194–5.
25 Donald Weinstein, *Savonarola and Florence: Prophecy and Patriotism in the Renaissance* (Princeton, 1970); Franco Mormando, *The Preacher's Demons: Bernardino of Siena and the Social Underworld of Early Renaissance Italy* (Chicago, 1999).
26 Pasquale Villari, *The Life and Times of Girolamo Savonarola*, trans. by Linda Villari (New York, 1888), originally published as *La storia di Girolamo Savonarola e de'suoi tempi*, Florence, 1859–61).
27 Lorenzo Polizzotto, *The Elect Nation: The Savonarolan Movement in Florence, 1494–1545* (Oxford, 1994).
28 Ottavia Nicoli, *Prophecy and People in Renaissance Italy* (Princeton, 1990); Miriam Leathers Kunz, *The Appointment of Dionisio: Prophecy and Politics in Renaissance Italy* (University Park, PA, 2001).
29 Bornstein, *Bianchi of 1399*; Samuel K. Cohn, *Lust for Liberty: The Politics of Social Revolt in Medieval Europe, 1200–1425* (Cambridge, MA, 2006).
30 Mormando, *Preacher's Demons*.
31 R. Po Chia Hsia, *Trent 1475: Stories of a Ritual Murder Trial* (New Haven, 1992).
32 B. Netanyahu, *The Marranos of Spain from the Late Fourteenth to the Sixteenth Century* (Ithaca, 1999); Samuel K. Cohn, "The Black Death and the Burning of the Jews," *Past and Present* 191 (Aug. 2007): 2–36.
33 James Hankins, "Renaissance Crusaders: Humanist Crusade Literature in the Age of Mehmed II," *Dumbarton Oaks Papers* 49 (1995): 111–207; Robert Schwoebel, *The Shadow of the Crescent: The Renaissance Image of the Turk 1453–1517* (Nieuwkoop, 1969); Gerald MacLean, ed., *Re-Orienting the Renaissance: Cultural Exchanges with the East.* (Basingstoke, 2005); Nancy Bisaha. *Creating East and West. Renaissance Humanists and the Ottoman Turks* (Philadelphia, 2004); Gerald MacLean, "When West Looks East: Some Recent Studies in Early Modern Muslim Cultures," *Journal for Early Modern Cultural Studies* 7, 1 (Spring/ Summer 2007): 96–112; L. P. Harvey, *Muslims in Spain, 1500 to 1614* (Chicago, 2005); Margaret Meserve, *Empires of Islam in Renaissance Historical Thought* (Cambridge, MA, 2008).
34 Thomas Foster Earle and K. J. P. Lowe, eds., *Black Africans in Renaissance Europe* (Cambridge, 2005), p. vii; Steven A. Epstein, *Speaking of Slavery: Color, Ethnicity, and Human Bondage in Italy* (Ithaca, 2001).
35 K. J. P. Lowe, "The Stereotyping of Black Africans in Renaissance Europe," in Earle and Lowe, *Black Africans*, pp. 17–47.
36 Daniel Bornstein and Roberto Rusconi, *Women and Religion in Medieval and Renaissance Italy* (Chicago, 1996); Carlo Ginzburg, *The Cheese and the Worms: The Cosmos of a Sixteenth-Century Miller* (Baltimore, 1980).

37 Linda Woodbridge, "Renaissance Bogeymen: The Necessary Monsters of the Age," in *A Companion to the Worlds of the Renaissance*, ed. by Guido Ruggiero (Malden, MA, 2002), p. 2. See also, Mormando, *Preacher's Demons*; Michael Rocke, *Forbidden Friendships. Homosexuality and Male Culture in Renaissance Florence* (New York, 1996) and James M. Saslow, *Ganymede in the Renaissance: Homosexuality in Art and Society* (New Haven, 1986).

38 Ariel Toaff, *The Jews in Medieval Assisi, 1305–1487* (Florence, 1979) and *The Jews in Umbria*, 3 vols. (Leiden, 1993).

39 Elliott Horowitz, "Procession, Piety, and Jewish Confraternities" in *The Jews of Early Modern Venice*, ed. by Robert C. Davis and Benjamin Ravid (Baltimore, 2001); Mark R. Cohen, ed., *The Autobiography of a Seventeenth-Century Venetian Rabbi: Leon Modena's Life of Judah* (Princeton, 1990); Mark D. Meyerson, *A Jewish Renaissance in Fifteenth-Century Spain: Jews, Christians, and Muslims from the Ancient to the Modern World* (Princeton, 2004), pp. xx, 272; Robert Bonfil, *Jewish Life in Renaissance Italy* (Berkeley, 1995).

40 For the broad issue of science and the Renaissance, see Brian P. Copenhaver, "Did Science Have a Renaissance?" *Isis* 83, 3 (1992): 387–407 and Brian W. Ogilvie, "Science," in Woolfson, *Palgrave Advances*, pp. 241–63; Peter Dear, *Revolutionizing the Sciences: European Knowledge and its Ambitions, 1500–1700* (Palgrave, 2001).

41 Herbert Butterfield, *The Origins of Modern Science, 1300–1800* (London, 1949), p. viii. George Sarton compared the Renaissance to a "reshuffling of cards that were old" and the Scientific Revolution to a "reshuffling of cards that were mostly new." George Sarton, *Six Wings: Men of Science and the Renaissance* (Bloomington, 1957).

42 Burckhardt, *Civilization*, p. 198.

43 Charles Homer Haskins, *Studies in the History of Medieval Science* (Cambridge, MA, 1924); Lynn Thorndike, "Renaissance or Prenaissance?" *Journal of the History of Ideas* 4 (1943): 65–74, 83, *A History of Magic and Experimental Science*, vol. 5 (New York, 1923–58), p. 5, and *Science and Thought in the Fifteenth Century* (New York, 1963).

44 Pierre Duhem, *Etudes sur Leonard de Vinci: Ceux qu'il a lus et ceux qui l'ont lu*, 3 vols. (Paris, 1906–13) and *Medieval Cosmology: Theories of Infinity, Place, Time, Void, and the Plurality of Worlds*, ed. and trans. by Roger Ariew (Chicago, 1985); Alistair Crombie, *Medieval and Early Modern Science* (New York, 1959); George Sarton, *The Appreciation of Ancient and Medieval Science during the Renaissance, 1450–1600* (Philadelphia, 1955) and *Six Wings*.

45 J. H. Randall, "The Development of the Scientific Method at the School of Padua," *Journal of the History of Ideas* 1 (1940): 179–83 and *The School of Padua and the Emergence of Modern Science* (Padua, 1961).

46 Alexandre Koyré, *From the Closed World to the Infinite Universe* (Baltimore, 1957), p. 66. See also Edwin A Burtt, *The Metaphysical Foundations of Modern Physical Science* (Atlantic Highlands, NJ, 1952) and Michael Sharratt, *Galileo, Decisive Innovator* (Oxford, 1994).

47 Thomas S. Kuhn, *The Structure of Scientific Revolutions* (Chicago, 1962).

48 Eric Cochrane, "Science and Humanism in the Italian Renaissance," *American Historical Review* 81 (1976): 1037–59; Cesare Vasoli, "The Contributions of Humanism to the Birth of Modern Science," *Renaissance and Reformation* 3 (1979): 1–15; Anthony Grafton, "Humanism, Magi and Science," in Goodman, *Impact of Humanism*, pp. 99–117 and *Defenders of the Text: The Traditions of Scholarship in the Age of Science 1450–1800* (Cambridge, MA, 1991), pp. 1–15; Ann Blair and Anthony Grafton, "Reassessing Humanism and Science," *Journal of the History of Ideas* 53, 4 (1992): 535–40; Pamela O. Long, "Humanism and Science," in *Renaissance Humanism, Foundations, Forms and Legacy*, vol. 3, ed. by Albert Rabil (Philadelphia, 1988), pp. 486–512.

49 Dear, *Revolutionizing the Sciences*, p. 8.

50 Alison Brown, "Lucretius and the Epicureans in the Social and Political Context of Renaissance Florence," *I Tatti Studies: Essays in the Renaissance* 9 (2001): 11–62.

51 Paul Lawrence Rose, *The Italian Renaissance of Mathematics: Studies on Humanists and Mathematicians from Petrarch to Galileo*. (Geneva, 1975); Dear, *Revolutionizing the Sciences*, pp. 45–7.

52 Dear, *Revolutionizing the Sciences*, pp. 33–4.

53 Marie Boas, *The Scientific Renaissance, 1450–1630* (London, 1962), p. 68.

54 Robert S. Westman, "The Astronomers Role in the Sixteenth Century: A Preliminary Survey," *History of Science* 18 (1980): 105–47.

55 Anita Guerrini, "Anatomizing the Renaissance," *Early Science and Medicine* 6, 1 (2001): 35–8; Nancy Siraisi, *The Clock and the Mirror: Girolamo Cardano and Renaissance Medicine* (Princeton, 1997).

56 Andrew Cunningham, *The Anatomical Renaissance: The Resurrection of the Anatomical Projects of the Ancients* (Aldershot, 1997).

57 Quoted in Boas, *Scientific Renaissance*, p. 51.

58 Paula Findlen, *Possessing Nature: Museums, Collecting and Scientific Culture in Early Modern Italy* (Berkeley and Los Angeles, 1994); Anthony Grafton and Nancy Siraisi, eds., *Natural Particulars: Nature and the Disciplines in Renaissance Europe* (Cambridge, MA, 1999); Brian W. Ogilvie, *The Science of Describing: Natural History in Renaissance Europe* (Chicago, 2006), pp. 1, 5, 49 and "Science," pp. 256–9.

59 Nancy G. Siraisi, *Medieval and Early Renaissance Medicine: An Introduction to Knowledge and Practice* (Chicago, 1990), p. 187.

60 William Eamon "The Scientific Renaissance," in Ruggiero, *Companion to the Renaissance*, pp. 403–24.

61 John Henderson, *The Renaissance Hospital: Healing the Body and Healing the Soul* (New Haven, 2006).

62 Eugene Rice, *The Foundations of Early Modern Europe, 1460–1559* (New York, 1970), p. 20; Bert S. Hall, *Weapons and Warfare in Renaissance Europe* (Baltimore, 1997).

63 Erwin Panofsky, "Artist, Scientist, Genius: Notes on the 'Renaissance Dammerung,'" in *The Renaissance: Six Essays*, ed. by Wallace K. Ferguson (New York, 1962), pp. 123–52. See also John W. Shirley and F. David Hoeniger, eds., *Science and the Arts in the Renaissance* (Washington, DC, 1985); Samuel Y.

Edgerton, *The Heritage of Giotto's Geometry: Art and Science on the Eve of the Scientific Revolution* (Ithaca, 1991).

64 Carlo Pedretti, *Leonardo: A Study in Chronology and Style* (Berkeley, 1973); Martin Kemp, *Leonardo* (Oxford, 2004).

65 Leonardo Olschki, *Geschichte der neusprachlichen wissenschaftlichen Literatur*, 3 vols. (Heidelberg, Leipzig, Halle, 1919–27); Dear, *Revolutionizing the Sciences*, p. 52.

66 Ann Blair, *The Theater of Nature: Jean Bodin and Renaissance Science* (Princeton, 1997).

67 Paolo Rossi, *Philosophy, Technology and the Arts in the Early Modern Era*, trans. by Salvatore Attanasio and ed. by Benjamin Nelson (New York, 1970) and *The Birth of Modern Science*, trans. by Cynthia Nardi Ipsen (Oxford, 2001), pp. 31–3; Blair and Grafton, "Reassessing Humanism and Science," p. 537; Pamela O. Long, "Humanism and Science," pp. 492–4.

68 Guido Ruggiero, "Witchcraft and Magic," in *Companion to the Renaissance*, pp. 475–90; Bengt Ankarloo and Stuart Clark, eds., *Witchcraft and Magic in Europe*, vol. 3 (The Middle Ages) (Philadelphia, 2002); Richard Kieckhefer, *Forbidden Rites: A Necromancer's Manual of the Fifteenth Century* (University Park, PA, 1998); and Claire Farago, ed., *Conjuring Spirits: Texts and Traditions of Medieval Ritual Magic* (University Park, PA, 1998).

69 Henry Cornelius Agrippa, *Three Books of Occult Philosophy*, trans. by James Freake and ed. by Donald Tyson (St Paul, MN, 1993); Stuart Clark, "Witchcraft and Magic in Early Modern Culture," in Ankarloo and Clark, *Witchcraft and Magic*, pp. 147–8.

70 Anthony Grafton, *Cardano's Cosmos: The Worlds and Works of a Renaissance Astrologer* (Cambridge, MA, 2000).

71 Siraisi, *Medieval and Renaissance Medicine*, pp. 67–9, 189.

72 Bruce T. Moran, *The Alchemical World of the German Court: Occult Philosophy and Chemical Medicine in the Circle of Moritz of Hessen (1572–1632)* (Stuttgart, 1991); Urszula Szulakowska, *The Alchemy of Light: Geometry and Optics in Late Renaissance Alchemical Illustration* (Leiden, 2000).

73 A. P. Debus, *The Chemical Philosophy: Paracelsian Science and Medicine in the Sixteenth and Seventeenth Centuries*, 2 vols. (New York, 1977) and *Man and Nature in the Renaissance* (Cambridge, 1978); Owen Hannaway, *The Chemists and the Word: The Didactic Origins of Chemistry* (Baltimore, 1975).

74 Betty Jo Teeter Dobbs, *The Janus Faces of Genius: The Role of Alchemy in Newton's Thought* (Cambridge, 1991).

75 Lorraine Daston and Katherine Park, *Wonders and the Order of Nature, 1150–1750* (New York, 1998); Zakiya Hanafi, *The Monster in the Machine: Magic, Medicine, and the Marvelous in the Time of the Scientific Revolution* (Durham, 2000); Peter Pesic, *Labyrinth: A Search for the Hidden Meaning of Science* (Cambridge, MA, 2000).

76 William Eamon, *Science and the Secrets of Nature: Books and Secrets in Medieval and Early Modern Culture* (Princeton, 1994) and "Scientific Renaissance," p. 403.

77 Nauert, *Humanism and Renaissance Europe*, pp. 203–7; Brian P. Copenhaver and Charles B. Schmitt, *Renaissance Philosophy* (Oxford, 1992), pp. 303–28; Eamon, "Scientific Renaissance," pp. 423–4.

78 Copenhaver and Schmitt, *Renaissance Philosophy*, p. 311.

79 Early influential studies of the nexus between Renaissance philosophy and the occult are in Paul Oskar Kristeller, "Ficino and Pomponazzi on the Place of Man in the Universe," *Journal of the History of Ideas* 5 (1944): 220–6; and Eugenio Garin, La cultura filosofica del Rinascimento italiano (Florence, 1961) and *Science and Civic Life in the Italian Renaissance* (Garden City, 1969). See also D. P. Walker, *Spiritual and Demonic Magic: From Ficino to Campanella* (University Park, PA, 2000, originally published in London in 1958).

80 Copenhaver and Schmitt, *Renaissance Philosophy*, pp. 15–16, 127–63; Arthur Field, *The Origins of the Platonic Academy of Florence* (Princeton, 1988); Michael J. B. Allen and Valery Rees, with Martin Davies, eds., *Marsilio Ficino: His Theology, His Philosophy, His Legacy* (Leiden, 2002).

81 Frances Yates, *Giordano Bruno and the Hermetic Tradition* (Chicago, 1964), pp. 17–18, 152–6.

82 R. S. Westman, "Magical Reform and Astronomical Reform: The Yates Thesis Reconsidered," in *Hermeticism and the Scientific Revolution*, ed. by R. S. Westman and J. E. McGuire (Los Angeles, 1977), pp. 1–91; Charles B. Schmitt, "Reappraisals in Renaissance Science," *History of Science* 16 (1978): 200–14: Brian P. Copenhaver, "Natural Magic, Hermeticism and Occultism in Early Modern Science," in *Reappraisals of the Scientific Revolution*, ed. by David C. Lindberg and Robert S. Westman (Cambridge, 1990), pp. 261–301, and "Hermes Trismegistus, Proclus and a Philosophy of Magic," in *Hermeticism and the Renaissance* (Washington, 1988), p. 80.

83 Ian Maclean, "Foucault's Renaissance Episteme Reassessed: An Aristotelian Counterblast," *Journal of the History of Ideas* 59, 1 (Jan. 1998): 149–66.

84 Clark, "Witchcraft and Magic," pp. 156–7, 159.

85 Brian Vickers, ed., *Occult and Scientific Mentalities in the Renaissance* (Cambridge, 1984), pp. 2–3, 6–9, 13.

86 Ogilvie, "Science," p. 259.

87 Mario Biagoli, "The Social Status of Italian Mathematicians, 1450–1600," *History of Science* 27 (1989): 41–95.

88 Copenhaver, "Did Science Have a Renaissance?" pp. 388–9.

89 Katherine Park and Lorraine Daston, eds., *The Cambridge History of Science, Early Modern*, vol. 3 (Cambridge, 2006).

90 Nauert, *Humanism and Renaissance Europe*, p. 63.

91 Ernst Cassirer, *The Individual and the Cosmos in Renaissance Philosophy* (New York, 1964, originally published in 1927).

92 Koyré, *Closed World*, pp. 7–8.

Further Reading

This list does *not* represent a comprehensive bibliography. It is intended only to highlight some secondary sources cited in the text, for the purposes of teaching. With this in mind, the sources are arranged by chapter and include accessible works in English, with citation, where possible, of the most recent editions. Fuller bibliographies can be found in the chapters themselves.

The materials below may be supplemented by additional bibliographic resources. The I Tatti Renaissance library, edited by James Hankins, publishes the works of Renaissance humanists, philosophers, and writers. Similarly, the University of Chicago's The Other Voice in Early Modern Europe series is publishing works by Renaissance women writers, as well as men, concerned with issues of gender. An excellent bibliography of the secondary literature relating to economic history may be found on Professor John Munro's web page (www.economics.utoronto.ca/munro5/WebBib.htm). Comprehensive surveys of works on science are available from Isis Current Bibliographies. These were begun in 1913 by George Sarton and are published yearly in the journal *Isis*. They can also be accessed online through OCLC's HistSciTechMed database (www.ou.edu/cas/hsci/isis/website/index.html) which is available to members of the History of Science Society. For recent bibliographies of other Renaissance topics, readers may consult the six-volume *Encyclopedia of the Renaissance*, edited by Paul F. Grendler, published by Charles Scribners and Sons (2000) and the six-volume *Europe 1450 to 1789, An Encyclopedia of the Early Modern World*, edited by Jonathan Dewald, also published by Scribners (2004). The forthcoming *Oxford Bibliographies Online* will provide still more comprehensive and up-to-date bibliographies of many fields.

General

Brown, Alison. *The Renaissance* (London: Longman, 1999).
Burckhardt, Jacob. *The Civilization of the Renaissance in Italy*, translated by S. G. C. Middlemore and introduced by Peter Gay (New York: Penguin, 1982, originally published in 1860).
Burke, Peter. *The European Renaissance: Centres and Peripheries* (Oxford: Blackwell, 1998).
Burke, Peter. *The Renaissance*, 2nd edn. (London: Macmillan, 1997).
Dannenfeldt, Karl H., ed. *The Renaissance: Medieval or Modern?* (Boston: D. C. Heath and Company, 1959).
Ferguson, Wallace K. *The Renaissance in Historical Thought: Five Centuries of Interpretation* (Cambridge, MA: Houghton Mifflin, 1948).
Fletcher, Stella. *The Longman Companion to Renaissance Europe* (New York: Longman, 2000).
Hale, John R. *The Civilization of Europe in the Renaissance* (New York: Harper, 1993).
Hay, Denys., ed. *The Renaissance Debate* (New York: Holt, Rinehart and Winston, 1965).
Huizinga, Johan. *The Autumn of the Middle Ages*, translated by Rodney J. Payton and Ulrich Mammitzsch (Chicago: University of Chicago Press, 1996, originally published in 1919).
Jensen, De Lamar. *Renaissance Europe: Age of Recovery and Reconciliation* (Lexington, MA: D. C. Heath, 1981).
King, Margaret L. *The Renaissance in Europe* (London: Laurence King, 2003).
Kirkpatrick, Robin. *The European Renaissance, 1400–1600* (London: Longman, 2002).
Martin, John J., ed. *The Renaissance World* (New York: Routledge, 2007).
Najemy, John M., ed., *Italy in the Age of the Renaissance* (Oxford: Oxford University Press, 2004).
Rabb, Theodore K. *The Last Days of the Renaissance and the March to Modernity* (New York: Perseus, 2006).
Rice, Eugene, and Anthony Grafton. *The Foundations of Early Modern Europe, 1460–1559* (New York: W. W. Norton, 1994, originally published in 1970).
Ruggiero, Guido, ed. *A Companion to the Worlds of the Renaissance* (Malden, MA: Blackwell, 2002).
Spitz, Lewis W. *The Renaissance and Reformation Movements*, vol. 1 (St Louis, MO: Concordia, 1987, originally published in 1971).
Symonds, John Addington. *The Renaissance in Italy*, 2 vols. (New York: Modern Library, 1935, originally published 1875–98).
Woolfson, Jonathan, ed. *Palgrave Advances in Renaissance Historiography*, (New York: Palgrave Macmillan, 2005).

Chapter 1

Bloom, Harold, ed. *Selected Writings of Walter Pater* (New York: New American Library, 1974).
Bouwsma, William J. *A Usable Past: Essays in European Cultural History* (Berkeley and Los Angeles: University of California Press, 1990).

Brown, Alison, ed. *Language and Images of Renaissance Italy* (Oxford: Oxford University Press, 1995).

Bullen, J. B. *The Myth of the Renaissance in Nineteenth-Century Writing* (Oxford: Clarendon Press, 1994).

Connell, William J., and Giles Constable. *Sacrilege and Redemption in Renaissance Florence: The Case of Antonio Rinaldeschi* (Toronto: University of Toronto Press, 2005).

Davis, Natalie Zemon. *The Return of Martin Guerre* (Cambridge, MA: Harvard University Press, 1984).

Elias, Norbert. *The Civilizing Process: Sociogenetic and Psychogenetic Investigations*, translated by Edmund Jephcott, revised edition edited by Eric Dunning, Johan Goudsblom, and Stephen Mennell (Oxford: Blackwell, 1994, originally published in 1939).

Foucault, Michel. *The Order of Things: An Archaeology of the Human Sciences* (New York: Pantheon, 1970).

Geertz, Clifford. *The Interpretation of Cultures* (New York: Basic Books, 1973).

Gombrich, E. H. "The Renaissance – Period or Movement," in *Background to the English Renaissance*, edited by A. G. Dickens, J. B. Trapp, et al. (London: Gray-Mills, 1974), pp. 9–30. (Reprinted in Robert Black, ed., *Renaissance Thought: A Reader*. London: Routledge, 2001).

Gossman, Lionel. *Basel in the Age of Burckhardt: A Study in Unseasonable Ideas* (Chicago: University of Chicago Press, 2000).

Grendler, Paul F. *The European Renaissance in American Life* (Westport, CT: Greenwood, 2006).

Haskins, Charles Homer. *The Renaissance of the Twelfth Century* (Cambridge, MA: Harvard University Press, 1927).

Hay, Denys. *The Italian Renaissance in Its Historical Background* (Cambridge: Cambridge University Press, 1976).

Hunt, Lynn, ed., *The New Cultural History* (Berkeley and Los Angeles: University of California Press, 1989).

Iggers, Georg G. *The German Conception of History: The National Tradition of Historical Thought from Herder to the Present* (Middletown, CT: Wesleyan University Press, 1983, originally published 1968).

Law, John E., and Lene Østermark-Johansen, eds. *Victorian and Edwardian Responses to the Italian Renaissance* (Aldershot: Ashgate, 2005).

Lopez, Robert S. *The Three Ages of the Italian Renaissance* (Charlottesville, VA: University Press of Virginia, 1970).

Molho, Anthony. "The Italian Renaissance, Made in the USA," in *Imagined Histories, American Historians Interpret the Past*, ed. by Anthony Molho and Gordon S. Wood (Princeton: Princeton University Press, 1997).

Muir, Edward. "The Italian Renaissance in America." *American Historical Review* 100 (Oct 1995): 1107–8.

Panofsky, Erwin. "Renaissance and Renascenses." *Kenyon Review* 6 (1944): 201–36. (Reprinted in *Renaissance and Renascences in Western Art*, Boulder, CO: Westview, 1972.)

Southern, Richard W. *Medieval Humanism and Other Studies* (New York: John Wiley and Sons, 1984, originally published in 1970).

Starn, Randolph. "A Postmodern Renaissance?" *Renaissance Quarterly* 60 (2007): 1–24.

Thorndike, Lynn. *A History of Magic and Experimental Science*, 8 vols. (New York: Columbia University Press, 1923–58).

Chapter 2

Amelung, James S. *The Flight of Icarus: Artisan Autobiography in Early Modern Europe* (Stanford: Stanford University Press, 1998).

Barolsky, Paul. *Michelangelo's Nose: A Myth and its Maker* (University Park, PA: Penn State Press, 1990).

Barolsky, Paul. *Why Mona Lisa Smiles and Other Tales by Vasari* (University Park, PA: Penn State Press, 1991).

Bartlett, Robert. *The Making of Europe: Conquest, Colonization and Cultural Change, 950–1350* (Princeton: Princeton University Press, 1993).

Bell, Rudolf. *How to Do It: Guides to Good Living for Renaissance Italians* (Chicago: University of Chicago Press, 1999).

Biagioli, Mario. *Galileo, Courtier: The Practice of Science in the Culture of Absolutism* (Chicago: University of Chicago Press, 1993).

Brading, D. A. *The First America: The Spanish Monarchy, Creole Patriots, and the Liberal State 1492–1867* (New York: Cambridge University Press, 1991).

Bynum, Caroline Walker. *Jesus as Mother: Studies in the Spirituality of the High Middle Ages* (Berkeley and Los Angeles: University of California Press, 1982).

Certeau, Michel de. *The Writing of History*, translated by Tom Conley (New York: Columbia University Press, 1988).

Cohn, Samuel K. *Black Death Transformed: Disease and Culture in Early Renaissance Europe* (London: Arnold, 2002).

Cohn, Samuel K. "Burckhardt Revisited from Social History," in *Language and Images of Renaissance Italy*, edited by Alison Brown (Oxford: Oxford University Press, 1995).

Cohn, Samuel K. *The Cult of Remembrance and the Black Death: Six Renaissance Cities in Central Italy* (Baltimore: Johns Hopkins Press, 1997).

Connell, William J., ed. *Society and Self in Renaissance Florence* (Berkeley and Los Angeles: University of California Press, 2002).

Davis, Natalie Zemon. *Trickster Travels: A Sixteenth-Century Muslim between Worlds* (New York: Hill and Wang, 2006).

Edgerton, Samuel Y. *The Renaissance Rediscovery of Linear Perspective* (New York: Harper & Row, 1975).

Fernández-Armesto, Felipe. *Amerigo: The Man Who Gave His Name to America* (New York: Random House, 2007).

Foucault, Michel. *Power/Knowledge: Selected Interviews and Other Writings, 1972–1979*, edited and translated by Colin Gordon (New York: Pantheon, 1980).

Frazier, Alison Knowles. *Possible Lives: Authors and Saints in Renaissance Italy* (New York: Columbia University Press, 2004).

Gardner, Victoria C. "*Homines non nascuntur, sed figuntur*: Benvenuto Cellini's Vita and Self-Presentation of the Renaissance Artist." *Sixteenth Century Journal* 28, 2 (Summer 1997): 447–65.

Grafton, Anthony. *New Worlds, Ancient Texts: The Power of Tradition and the Shock of Discovery* (Cambridge, MA: Harvard University Press, 1995).

Greenblatt, Stephen. *Marvelous Possessions: The Wonder of the New World* (Chicago: University of Chicago Press, 1991).

Greenblatt, Stephen. *Renaissance Self-Fashioning: From More to Shakespeare* (Chicago: University of Chicago Press, 1980).

Gurevitch, Aaron. *The Origins of European Individualism*, translated by Katharine Judelson (Oxford: Blackwell, 1995).

Hay, Denys. *Europe: The Emergence of an Idea* (New York: Harper Torch Books, 1966, originally published in 1957).

Hennessy, John Pope. *The Portrait in the Renaissance* (Princeton: Princeton University Press, 1966).

Jardine, Lisa. *Erasmus, Man of Letters: The Construction of Charisma in Print* (Princeton: Princeton University Press, 1993).

Lacan, Jacques. *The Language of the Self: The Function of Language in Psychoanalysis*, translated by Anthony Wilden (Baltimore: Johns Hopkins Press, 1997, originally published in 1968).

Le Goff, Jacques. *The Birth of Europe*, translated by Janet Lloyd (Oxford: Blackwell Press, 2005).

Meserve, Margaret. *Empires of Islam in Renaissance Historical Thought* (Cambridge, MA: Harvard University Press, 2008).

Morris, Colin. *The Discovery of the Individual, 1050–1200* (Toronto: University of Toronto Press, 1972).

Martin, John Jeffries. *European Encounters in the New World* (New Haven: Yale University Press, 1993).

Martin, John Jeffries. *The Fall of Natural Man: The American Indian and the Origins of Comparative Ethnology* (New York: Cambridge University Press, 1982).

Pagden, Anthony. "Inventing Sincerity, Refashioning Prudence: The Discovery of the Individual in Renaissance Europe." *American Historical Review* 102, 5 (December 1997): 1309–42.

Pagden, Anthony. *Myths of Renaissance Individualism* (New York: Palgrave Macmillan, 2004).

Paoletti, John T., and Gary M. Radke. *Art, Power and Patronage in Renaissance Italy*, 3rd edn. (Upper Saddle River, NJ: Prentice Hall, 2005).

Parry, J. H. *The Age of Reconnaissance* (Cleveland and New York: World, 1963).

Porter, Roy, ed. *Rewriting the Self: Histories from the Renaissance to the Present* (London: Routledge, 1997).

Prescott, William H. *History of the Conquest of Mexico* (New York: Harper and Sons, 1843). Full text available online at the Scholar's Lab, University of Virginia Library, at http://etext.virginia.edu/toc/modeng/public/PreConq.html, accessed Feb. 2010.

Rubenstein, Jay. *Guibert of Nogent: Portrait of a Medieval Mind* (London: Routledge, 2002).
Rubin, Patricia Lee. *Images and Identity in Fifteenth-Century Florence* (New Haven: Yale University Press, 2002).
Said, Edward. *Orientalism* (New York: Vintage, 1978).
Todorov, Tzvetan. *The Conquest of America and the Question of the Other*, translated by Richard Howard (Oklahoma City: University of Oklahoma Press, 1999, originally published in 1984).
Weissman, Ronald F. E. "The Importance of Being Ambiguous: Social Relations, Individualism and Identity in Renaissance Florence," in *Urban Life in the Renaissance*, edited by Susan Zimmerman and Ronald F. E. Weissman (London: Associated University Presses, 1989).
Wittkower, Rudolf. "Individualism in Art and Artists: A Renaissance Problem." *Journal of the History of Ideas* 22, 3 (July–September, 1961): 291–302.
Woods-Marsden, Joanna. *Renaissance Self-Portraiture* (New Haven: Yale University Press, 1998).

Chapter 3

Baskins, Cristelle. *Cassone Painting, Humanism and Gender in Early Modern Italy* (Cambridge: Cambridge University Press, 1998).
Bennett, Judith. "History that Still Stands: Women's Work in the European Past." *Feminist Studies* 14, 2 (Summer 1988): 269–83.
Bennett, Judith. "Medieval Women, Modern Women: Across the Great Divide," in *Feminists Revision of History*, edited by Ann Shapiro (New Brunswick, NJ: Rutgers University Press, 1994).
Bock, Gisela. *Women in European History* (Oxford: Blackwell, 2002).
Brown, Judith, and Robert C. Davis, eds. *Gender and Society in Renaissance Italy* (New York: Longman, 1998).
Brown, Judith, and Jordan Goodman. "Women and Industry in Florence." *Journal of Economic History* 40, 1 (1980): 73–80.
Bynum, Caroline Walker. *Holy Feast and Holy Fast: The Religious Significance of Food to Medieval Women* (Berkeley and Los Angeles, University of California Press, 1987).
Chojnacki, Stanley. *Women and Men in Renaissance Venice* (Baltimore: Johns Hopkins Press, 2000).
Clark, Alice. *Working Life of Women in the Seventeenth Century*, edited and introduction by Amy Louise Eriksson (London: Routledge, 1992, originally published in 1919).
Davis, Natalie Zemon. "Women's History in Transition: The European Case." *Feminist Studies* 3 (1975/6): 83–103.
Davis, Natalie Zemon. *Women on the Margins: Three Seventeenth-Century Lives* (Cambridge, MA: Harvard University Press, 1995).
Diefendorf, Barbara. *From Penitence to Charity: Pious Women and the Catholic Reformation in Paris* (Oxford: Oxford University Press, 2004).

Ferguson, Margaret W., Maureen Quilligan, and Nancy J. Vickers, eds. *Rewriting the Renaissance: The Discourses of Sexual Difference in Early Modern Europe* (Chicago: University of Chicago Press, 1986).

Hanawalt, Barbara A., ed. *Women and Work in Preindustrial Europe* (Bloomington: Indiana University Press, 1986).

Herlihy, David. *Opera Muliebria: Women and Work in Medieval Europe* (Philadelphia: University of Pennsylvania Press, 1990).

Howell, Martha C. *The Marriage Exchange: Property, Social Place and Gender in the Cities of the Low Countries* (Chicago: University of Chicago Press, 1998).

Hufton, Olwen. *The Prospect Before Her: A History of Women in Western Europe, 1500–1800* (London: Harper Collins, 1995).

Hughes, Diane Owen. "From Brideprice to Dowry in Mediterranean Europe." *Journal of Family History* 3 (1978): 262–96.

Hutson, Lorna, ed. *Feminism and Renaissance Studies* (New York: Oxford University Press, 1999).

Jordan, Constance, ed. *Renaissance Feminism: Literary Texts and Political Models* (Ithaca: Cornell University Press, 1990).

Kelly, Joan. "Did Women Have a Renaissance?" in *Becoming Visible: Women in European History*, edited by Renate Bridenthal and Claudia Koonz (Boston: Houghton Mifflin, 1977): 137–64.

Kelly, Joan. "Early Feminist Theory and the Querelle des Femmes," in *Women, History and Theory: The Essays of Joan Kelly* (Chicago: University of Chicago Press, 1984), pp. 65– 109.

King, Margaret. *Women of the Renaissance* (Chicago: University of Chicago Press, 1991).

King, Margaret, and Albert Rabil, Jr. *Teaching Other Voices: Women and Religion in Early Modern Europe* (Chicago: University of Chicago Press, 2007).

Kirshner, Julius, and Suzanne F. Wemple. *Women of the Medieval World: Essays in Honor of John H. Mundy* (Oxford: Oxford University Press, 1985).

Klapisch-Zuber, Christiane. *Women, Family, and Ritual in Renaissance Italy* (Chicago: University of Chicago Press, 1985).

Kuehn, Thomas. *Law, Family, and Women: Toward a Legal Anthropology of Renaissance Italy* (Chicago: University of Chicago Press, 1994).

Labalme, Patricia H., ed. *Beyond Their Sex: Learned Women of the European Past* (New York: New York University Press, 1984).

Laqueur, Thomas. *Making Sex: Body and Gender from the Greeks to Freud* (Cambridge MA: Harvard University Press, 1990).

Larner, Christina. *Enemies of God: The Witch Hunt in Scotland* (London: Chatto and Windus, 1981).

Lerner, Gerda. *The Creation of Feminist Consciousness: From the Middle Ages to Eighteen-Seventy* (New York: Oxford University Press, 1993).

Maclean, Ian. *The Renaissance Notion of Woman* (Cambridge: Cambridge University Press, 1988).

Quilligan, Maureen. *The Allegory of Female Authority: Christine de Pizan's* Cité des Dames (Ithaca: Cornell University Press, 1991).

Rose, Mary Beth, ed. *Women in the Middle Ages and Renaissance: Literary and Historical Perspectives* (Syracuse: University of Syracuse Press, 1986).

Scott, Joan. "Gender: A Useful Category of Historical Analysis." *American Historical Review* 91 (1986): 1053–75.

Strocchia, Sharon. *Women in Medieval Italian Society* (London: Longman, 2001).

Strocchia, Sharon T. "Convent Culture," in *Oxford Bibliographies Online.*

Skinner, Patricia. *Nuns and Nunneries in Renaissance Florence* (Baltimore: Johns Hopkins Press, 2009).

Stuard, Susan Mosher, ed. *Women in Medieval History and Historiography* (Philadelphia: University of Pennsylvania Press, 1987).

Tilly, Louise A., and Joan W. Scott, eds. *Women, Work and Family* (New York: Holt, Rinehart and Winston, 1978).

Whitney, Elspeth. "The Witch 'She'/The Historian 'He': Gender and the Historiography of the Witch Hunts." *Journal of Women's History* 7 (1995): 77–101.

Wiesner, Merry E. *Women and Gender in Early Modern Europe*, 2nd edn. (Cambridge: Cambridge University Press, 2000).

Chapter 4

Black, Robert. *Humanism and Education in Medieval and Renaissance Italy* (Cambridge: Cambridge University Press, 2001).

Celenza, Christopher S. *The Lost Italian Renaissance: Humanists, Historians, and Latin's Legacy* (Baltimore: Johns Hopkins Press, 2004).

Eisenstein, Elizabeth L. *The Printing Press as an Agent of Change*, 2 vols. (Cambridge: Cambridge University Press, 1979).

Eisenstein, Elizabeth L. *The Printing Revolution in Early Modern Europe* (Cambridge: Cambridge University Press, 1983).

Fubini, Riccardo. *Humanism and Secularization, Petrarch to Valla*, translated by Martha King (Durham: Duke University Press, 2002).

Garin, Eugenio. *Italian Humanism: Philosophy and Civic Life*, translated by Peter Munz (New York: Harper & Row, 1965).

Goodman, Anthony, and Angus Mackay, eds. *The Impact of Humanism on Western Europe* (New York: Longman, 1990).

Gouwens, Kenneth. "Perceiving the Past: Renaissance Humanism after the 'Cognitive Turn,'" *American Historical Review* 103, 1 (February 1998): 55–82.

Grafton, Anthony, and Lisa Jardine. *From Humanism to the Humanities* (Cambridge, MA: Harvard University Press, 1986).

Grendler, Paul F. *Schooling in the Renaissance: Literacy and Learning, 1300–1500* (Baltimore: Johns Hopkins Press, 1989).

Hankins, James. *Plato in the Italian Renaissance*, 2 vols. (Leiden: Brill, 1990).

Joachimsen, Paul. *Geschichtsauffassung und Geschichtschreibung in Deutschland unter dem Einfluss des Humanismus* (Aalen: Scientia Verlag, 1968, originally published in 1910).

Joachimsen, Paul. "Humanism and the Development of the German Mind," in *Pre-Reformation Germany*, edited by Gerald Strauss (New York: Harper & Row, 1972).
Jurdjevic, Mark. "Hedgehogs and Foxes: The Present and Future of Italian Renaissance Intellectual History." *Past and Present* 195 (2007): 241–68.
Kelley, Donald R. *Renaissance Humanism* (Boston: Twayne, 1991).
Kohl, Benjamin. *Renaissance Humanism, 1300–1550: A Bibliography of Materials in English* (New York: Garland, 1985).
Kraye, Jill, ed. *The Cambridge Companion to Renaissance Humanism* (Cambridge: Cambridge University Press, 1996).
Kristeller, Paul Oskar. *Renaissance Concepts of Man and other Essays* (New York: Harper & Row, 1972).
Kristeller, Paul Oskar. *Renaissance Thought II: Papers on Humanism and the Arts* (New York: Harper & Row, 1965).
Kristeller, Paul Oskar. *Renaissance Thought and Its Sources* (New York: Columbia University Press, 1979).
Martines, Lauro. *The Social World of Florentine Humanists, 1390–1460* (Princeton: Princeton University Press, 1963).
Mazzocco, Angelo, ed. *Interpretations of Renaissance Humanism* (Leiden: Brill, 2006).
Nauert, Charles G. *Humanism and the Culture of Renaissance Europe* (Cambridge: Cambridge University Press, 2006, originally published in 1995).
Rabil, Albert, Jr, ed. *Renaissance Humanism, Foundations, Forms and Legacy*, 3 vols. (Philadelphia: University of Pennsylvania Press, 1988).
Rummel, Erika. *The Humanist-Scholastic Debate in the Renaissance and Reformation* (Cambridge, MA: Harvard University Press, 1995).
Southern, R. W. *Scholastic Humanism and the Unification of Europe*, vol. 1 (Oxford: Blackwell, 1995).
Ullmann, Walter. *Medieval Foundations of Renaissance Humanism* (Ithaca: Cornell University Press, 1977).
Voigt, Georg. *Die Wiederbelebung des classischen Alterthums oder das erste Jahrhundert des Humanismus*, 2 vols. (Berlin: Reimer, 1859).
Weiss, Roberto. *The Dawn of Humanism in Italy* (London: H. K. Lewis, 1947).
Weiss, Roberto. *The Spread of Italian Humanism* (London: Hutchinson University Library, 1964).
Witt, Ronald G. *"In the Footsteps of the Ancients": The Origins of Humanism from Lovato to Bruni* (Leiden: Brill, 2000).
Witt, Ronald G. "Medieval '*Ars Dictaminis*' and the Beginnings of Humanism: A New Construction of the Problem." *Renaissance Quarterly* 35, 1 (Spring 1982): 1–35.

Chapter 5

Aston, T. H., and C. H. E. Philpin. *The Brenner Debate: Agrarian Class Structure and Economic Development in Pre-Industrial Europe* (Cambridge: Cambridge University Press, 1985).

Ashtor, Eliyahu. *Levantine Trade in the Later Middle Ages* (Princeton: Princeton University Press, 1983).

Braudel, Fernand. *Civilization and Capitalism, 15th–18th Century*, 3 vols. (*The Structures of Everyday Life, The Wheels of Commerce, The Perspective of the World*) translated by Siân Reynolds (New York: Harper & Row, 1981–4, originally published in 1979).

Braudel, Fernand. *The Mediterranean and the Mediterranean World in the Age of Philip II*, 2 vols. (Berkeley and Los Angeles: University of California Press, 1996, originally published in 1949).

Caferro, William. "City and Countryside in Siena in the Second Half of the Fourteenth Century." *Journal of Economic History* 54 (March 1994): 85–110.

Caferro, William. *Mercenary Companies and the Decline of Siena* (Baltimore: Johns Hopkins Press, 1998).

Caferro, William. "Warfare and the Economy of Renaissance Italy, 1350–1450." *Journal of Interdisciplinary History* 39, 2 (Autumn 2008): 167–209.

Cipolla, Carlo M. *Before the Industrial Revolution* (New York: W. W. Norton, 1994 originally published in 1976).

Cipolla. "Economic Depression of the Renaissance?" *Economic History Review* 16 (1964): 519–24.

De Roover, Raymond. *The Rise and Decline of the Medici Bank, 1397–1494* (New York: W. W. Norton, 1966).

De Vries, Jan. *European Urbanization: 1500–1800* (Cambridge, MA: Harvard University Press, 1984).

De Vries, Jan, and Ad van der Woude. *The First Modern Economy: Success, Failure, and Perseverance of the Dutch Economy, 1500–1815* (Cambridge: Cambridge University Press, 1996).

Duplessis, Robert. *Transitions to Capitalism in Early Modern Europe* (Cambridge: Cambridge University Press, 1997).

Dyer, Christopher. *Standards of Living in the Later Middle Ages* (Cambridge: Cambridge University Press, 1989).

Ehrenberg, Richard. *Capital and Finance in the Age of the Renaissance*, translated by H. M. Lucas (New York: Harcourt, Brace and Company, 1963, originally published in 1928).

Epstein, Stephen R. *Markets and States in Europe, 1300–1750* (London: Routledge, 2000).

Epstein, Steven A. *Economic and Social History of Later Medieval Europe, 1000–1500* (Cambridge: Cambridge University Press, 2009).

Goldthwaite, Richard A. *The Economy of Renaissance Florence* (Baltimore: Johns Hopkins Press, 2009).

Goldthwaite, Richard A. *Wealth and the Demand for Art in Italy, 1300–1600* (Baltimore: Johns Hopkins Press, 1993).

Gras, N. S. B. *Business and Capitalism: An Introduction to Business History* (New York: F. S. Crofts and Company, 1939).

Herlihy, David. *The Black Death and the Transformation of the West* (Cambridge, MA: Harvard University Press, 1997).

Herlihy, David, and Christiane Klapisch-Zuber. *Tuscans and their Families* (New Haven: Yale University Press, 1985, originally published as *Les Toscans et leurs familles*, 1978).
Jordan, William C. *The Great Famine: Northern Europe in the Early Fourteenth Century* (Princeton: Princeton University Press, 1996).
Hilton, Rodney, ed. *The Transition from Feudalism to Capitalism* (London: NLB, 1976).
Lane, Frederic C. *Venice and History* (Baltimore: Johns Hopkins Press, 1966).
Le Roy Ladurie, Emmanuel. "Motionless History." *Social Science History* 1, 2 (Winter 1977): 115–36.
Lopez, Robert S. "Hard Times and Investment in Culture," reprinted in *The Renaissance, Medieval or Modern?* edited by Karl H. Dannenfeldt (Boston: D. C. Heath, 1959).
Lopez, Robert S., and I. I. Raymond. *Medieval Trade in the Mediterranean World* (New York: Columbia University Press, 2001, originally published in 1955).
Mendels, Franklin. "Proto-Industrialization: The First Phase of the Industrialization Process." *Journal of Economic History* 32 (1972): 241–61.
Miskimin, Harry A. *The Economy of the Early Renaissance* (New York: Cambridge University Press, 1969).
Miskimin, Harry A. *The Economy of the Later Renaissance* (New York: Cambridge University Press, 1977).
Mueller, Reinhold C. "The Role of Bank Money in Venice, 1300–1500." *Studi Veneziani*, new series, 3 (1979): 47–96.
Mueller, Reinhold C. *The Venetian Money Market: Banks, Panics, and the Public Debt, 1200–1500* (Baltimore: Johns Hopkins Press, 1997).
Munro, John H. A. *Bullion Flows and Monetary Policy in England and the Low Countries* (Leiden: Brill, 1992).
Musgrave, Peter. *The Early Modern European Economy* (New York: St Martin's Press, 1999).
North, Douglass C. *Institutions, Institutional Change and Economic Performance* (Cambridge: Cambridge University Press, 1990).
Pirenne, Henri. *Economic and Social History of Medieval Europe* (London: Routledge, 2006, originally published in 1933).
Pirenne, Henri. *Medieval Cities, their Origins and the Revival of Trade* (Princeton: Princeton University Press, 1980, originally published in 1925).
Pomeranz, Kenneth. *The Great Divergence: China, Europe, and the Making of the Modern World Economy* (Princeton: Princeton University Press, 2001).
Prak, Maarten, ed. *Early Modern Capitalism: Economic and Social Change in Europe, 1400–1800* (New York: Routledge, 2001).
Robertson, H. M. *Aspects of the Rise of Economic Individualism* (Cambridge: Cambridge University Press, 1933).
Thomas, Hugh. *The Slave Trade: The History of the Atlantic Slave Trade, 1440–1870* (New York: Simon and Schuster, 1997).
Tracy, James, ed. *The Rise of Merchant Empires: Long-Distance Trade in the Early Modern World, 1350–1750* (Cambridge: Cambridge University Press, 1990).
Von Martin, Alfred. *Sociology of the Renaissance* (New York: Harper & Row, 1963, originally published in 1932).

Wallerstein, Immanuel. *The Modern World-System*, 3 vols. (New York: Academic Press, 1974–89).
Weber, Max. *The Protestant Ethic and the Spirit of Capitalism*, translated by Talcott Parsons (Mineola, NY: Dover, 2003, originally published in 1904–5).
Yamey, B. S. "Scientific Bookkeeping and the Rise of Capitalism." *Economic History Review* 2 (1948–9): 99–113.

Chapter 6

Anderson, Benedict. *Imagined Communities: Reflections on the Origin and Spread of Nationalism* (London: Verso, 2003, originally published in 1983).
Anderson, M. S. *The Origins of the Modern European State System, 1494–1618* (New York: Longman, 1998).
Anderson, Perry. *Lineages of the Absolute State* (London: NLB, 1974).
Appuhn, Karl. "Inventing Nature: Forests, Forestry and State Power in Renaissance Venice." *Journal of Modern History* 72 (2000): 861–89.
Baron, Hans. *The Crisis of the Early Renaissance: Civic Humanism and Republican Liberty in an Age of Classicism and Tyranny* (Princeton: Princeton University Press, 1955).
Baron, Hans. *In Search of Civic Humanism: Essays on the Transition from Medieval to Modern Thought*, 2 vols. (Princeton: Princeton University Press, 1988).
Birnbaum, Marianna. *The Orb and the Pen: Janus Pannonius, Matthias Corvinus and the Buda Court* (Budapest: Balassi, 1996).
Bock, Gisela, Quentin Skinner, and Maurizio Viroli, eds. *Machiavelli and Republicanism* (Cambridge: Cambridge University Press, 1990).
Bonney, R., ed. *The Rise of the Fiscal State in Europe, c. 1200–1815* (Oxford: Oxford University Press, 1999).
Braddick, Michael J. *State Formation in Early Modern England, 1550–1700* (Cambridge: Cambridge University Press, 2000).
Caferro, William. "Continuity, Long-Term Service, and Permanent Forces: A Reassessment of the Florentine Army in the Fourteenth Century." *Journal of Modern History* 80 (June 2008): 303–22.
Chabod, Federico. "Was There a Renaissance State?" in *The Development of the Modern State*, edited by Heinz Lubasz (New York: Macmillan, 1964): 26–42.
Chittolini, Giorgio. "Cities, City-States and Regional States in North-Central Italy." *Theory and Society* 18 (September 1989): 689–706.
Coleman, Christopher, and David Starkey. *Revolution Reassessed: Revisions in the History of Tudor Government and Administration* (Oxford: Oxford University Press, 1988).
Elliott, John. *Empires of the Atlantic World: Britain and Spain in America 1492–1830* (New Haven: Yale University Press, 2006).
Elliott, John. *Imperial Spain, 1469–1716* (New York: St Martin's Press, 1963).
Fink, Carole. *Osman's Dream: The Story of the Ottoman Empire 1300–1923* (London: John Murray, 2005).

Geary, Patrick. *The Myth of Nations: The Medieval Origins of Europe* (Princeton: Princeton University Press, 2002).

Gilbert, Felix. *Machiavelli and Guiccardini: Politics and History in Sixteenth Century Florence* (New York: W. W. Norton, 1985, originally published in 1965).

Grubb, James S. "When Myths Lose Power: Four Decades of Venetian Historiography." *Journal of Modern History* 58, 1 (March 1986): 43–94.

Hankins, James. "The 'Baron Thesis' After Forty Years and Some Recent Studies on Leonardo Bruni." *Journal of the History of Ideas* 56 (1995): 309–38.

Hankins, James. ed., *Renaissance Civic Humanism, Reappraisals and Reflections* (Cambridge: Cambridge University Press, 2000).

Hindle, Steve. *The State and Social Change in Early Modern England 1550–1640* (New York: Palgrave Macmillan, 2000).

Jones, P. J. "Communes and Despots in Late Medieval Italy." *Transactions of the Royal Historical Society*, 5th series, 15 (1965): 71–96.

Knecht, R. J. *French Renaissance Monarchy: Francis I and Henry II* (London: Longman, 1996, originally published in 1984).

Kohl, Benjamin G., and Ronald G. Witt, eds. *The Earthly Republic Italian Humanists on Government and Society* (Philadelphia: University of Pennsylvania Press, 1978).

Major, J. Russell. *From Renaissance Monarchy to Absolute Monarchy: French Kings, Nobles, and Estates* (Baltimore: Johns Hopkins Press, 1994).

Mallett, Michael. *Mercenaries and their Masters* (Barnsley: Pen and Sword Books, 2009, originally published in 1974).

Mattingly, Garrett. *Renaissance Diplomacy* (New York: Cosimo Classics, 2008, originally published in 1955).

Meinecke, Friedrich. *Machiavellism: The Doctrine of Raison d'État and its Place in Modern History*, translated by Douglas Scott (New Brunswick, NJ: Transaction, 1998, originally published in 1924).

Muir, Edward. *Civic Ritual in Renaissance Venice* (Princeton: Princeton University Press, 1981).

Muir, Edward. *Ritual in Early Modern Europe* (Cambridge: Cambridge University Press, 1997).

Najemy, John M. *Corporatism and Consensus in Florentine Electoral Politics, 1280–1400* (Chapel Hill: University of North Carolina Press, 1982).

Najemy, John M. "Politics and Political Thought," in *Palgrave Advances in Renaissance Historiography*, edited by Jonathan Woolfson (New York: Palgrave Macmillan, 2005).

Parker, Geoffrey. *The Military Revolution: Military Innovation and the Rise of the West, 1500–1800* (Cambridge: Cambridge University Press, 1988).

Partridge, Loren, and Randolph Starn. *Arts of Power. Three Halls of State in Italy, 1300– 1600* (Berkeley and Los Angeles: University of California Press, 1992).

Pocock, P. G. A. *The Machiavellian Moment: Florentine Political Thought and the Atlantic Republican Tradition* (Princeton: Princeton University Press, 1975).

Pollard, A. F. *Factors in Modern History* (London: G. P. Putnam and Sons, 1907).

Potter, David. *A History of France, 1460–1560. The Emergence of a Nation State* (London: Macmillan, 1995).

Pullan. Brian. *Rich and Poor in Renaissance Venice* (Oxford: Oxford University Press, 1971).
Richardson, Glenn. *Renaissance Monarchy: The Reigns of Henry VIII, Francis I, and Charles V* (New York: Arnold, 2002).
Rogers, Clifford J., ed. *The Military Revolution Debate* (Boulder, CO: Westview, 1995).
Rubinstein, Nicolai. *The Government of Florence under the Medici (1434 to 1494)* (Oxford: Oxford University Press, 1966).
Sahlins, Peter. *Boundaries: The Making of France and Spain in the Pyrenees* (Berkeley and Los Angeles: University of California Press, 1991).
Shaw, Christine. *Popular Government and Oligarchy in Renaissance Italy* (Leiden: Brill, 2006).
Sheehan, James J. "The Problem of Sovereignty in European History." *American Historical Review* 111 (February 2006): 1–15.
Sismondi, J.-C.-L. de. *A History of the Italian Republics* (New York: Everyman Library, 1907, originally published in 1809–18).
Skinner, Quentin. *The Foundations of Modern Political Thought*, vol. 1 (Cambridge: Cambridge University Press, 1978).
Slavin. Arthur J., ed. *The New Monarchies and Representative Assemblies* (Boston: D. C. Heath, 1964).
Strayer, Joseph R. *On the Medieval Origins of the Modern State* (Princeton: Princeton University Press, 1970).
Tilly, Charles. *Coercion, Capital and European States 990–1992* (Oxford: Blackwell, 1992).
Tracy, James. *A Financial Revolution in the Habsburg Netherlands* (Berkeley and Los Angeles: University of California Press, 1985).
Trexler, Richard. *Public Life in Renaissance Florence* (New York: Academic Press, 1980).
Weber, Max. *Economy and Society: An Outline of Interpretive Sociology*, edited by Guenther Roth and Claus Wittich (Berkeley and Los Angeles: University of California Press, 1978, originally published 1914).

Chapter 7

Ankarloo, Bengt, and Stuart Clark, eds. *Witchcraft and Magic in Europe*, vol. 3 (Philadelphia: University of Pennsylvania Press, 2002).
Black, Christopher F. *Italian Confraternities in the Sixteenth Century* (Cambridge: Cambridge University Press, 1989).
Black, Christopher F., and Pamela Gravestock, eds. *Early Modern Confraternities in Europe and the Americas* (Aldershot: Ashgate, 2006).
Blair, Ann. *The Theater of Nature: Jean Bodin and Renaissance Science* (Princeton: Princeton University Press, 1997).
Bonfil, Robert. *Jewish Life in Renaissance Italy* (Berkeley and Los Angeles: University of California Press, 1995).

Bornstein, Daniel, and Roberto Rusconi, eds. *Women and Religion in Medieval and Renaissance Italy* (Chicago: University of Chicago Press, 1996).

Cassirer, Ernst. *The Individual and the Cosmos in Renaissance Philosophy* (New York: Harper & Row, 1964, originally published in 1927).

Cochrane, Eric. "Science and Humanism in the Italian Renaissance." *American Historical Review* 81 (1976): 1037–59.

Copenhaver, Brian P. "Did Science Have a Renaissance?" *Isis* 83, 3 (1992): 387–407.

Copenhaver, Brian P., and Charles B. Schmitt. *Renaissance Philosophy* (Oxford: Oxford University Press, 1992).

Daston, Lorraine, and Katherine Park. *Wonders and the Order of Nature, 1150–1750* (New York: Zone Books, 1998).

Davis, Robert C., and Benjamin Ravid, eds. *The Jews of Early Modern Venice* (Baltimore: Johns Hopkins Press, 2001).

Dear, Peter. *Revolutionizing the Sciences: European Knowledge and its Ambitions, 1500–1700* (New York: Palgrave Macmillan, 2001).

Debus, A. P. *Man and Nature in the Renaissance* (Cambridge: Cambridge University Press, 1978).

Eamon, William. *Science and the Secrets of Nature: Books and Secrets in Medieval and Early Modern Culture* (Princeton; Princeton University Press, 1994).

Earle, Thomas Foster, and K. J. P. Lowe, eds. *Black Africans in Renaissance Europe* (Cambridge: Cambridge University Press, 2005).

Eisenbichler, Konrad. *The Boys of the Archangel Raphael: A Youth Confraternity in Florence, 1411–1785* (Toronto: University of Toronto Press, 1998).

Findlen, Paula. *Possessing Nature: Museums, Collecting and Scientific Culture in Early Modern Italy* (Berkeley and Los Angeles: University of California Press, 1994).

Grafton, Anthony, and Nancy Siraisi, eds. *Natural Particulars: Nature and the Disciplines in Renaissance Europe* (Cambridge, MA: Harvard University Press, 1999).

Hall, Bert S. *Weapons and Warfare in Renaissance Europe* (Baltimore: Johns Hopkins Press, 1997).

Henderson, John. *Piety and Charity in Late Medieval Florence* (Oxford: Oxford University Press, 1994).

Henderson, John. *The Renaissance Hospital: Healing the Body and Healing the Soul* (New Haven: Yale University Press, 2006).

Hsia, R. Po-Chia. *Trent 1475: Stories of a Ritual Murder Trial* (New Haven: Yale University Press, 1992).

Karant-Nunn, Susan C. "Changing One's Mind: Transformations in Reformation History from a Germanist's Perspective." *Renaissance Quarterly* 58 (Winter 2005): 1101–27.

Koyré, Alexandre. *From the Closed World to the Infinite Universe* (Baltimore: Johns Hopkins Press, 1957).

Kuhn, Thomas S. *The Structure of Scientific Revolutions* (Chicago: University of Chicago Press, 1962).

Lindberg, David C., and Robert S. Westman, eds. *Reappraisals of the Scientific Revolution* (Cambridge: Cambridge University Press, 1990).

Long, Pamela O. *Openness, Secrecy, Authorship: Technical Arts and the Culture of Knowledge from Antiquity to the Renaissance* (Baltimore: Johns Hopkins University Press, 2001).

Martin, John J. "Religion," in *Palgrave Advances in Renaissance Historiography*, edited by Jonathan Woolfson, (London: Palgrave Macmillan, 2005): 193–209.

Meyerson, Mark D. *A Jewish Renaissance in Fifteenth-Century Spain: Jews, Christians, and Muslims from the Ancient to the Modern World* (Princeton: Princeton University Press, 2004).

Moran, Bruce T. *The Alchemical World of the German Court: Occult Philosophy and Chemical Medicine in the Circle of Moritz of Hessen (1572–1632)* (Stuttgart: F. Steiner, 1991).

Mormando, Franco. *The Preacher's Demons: Bernardino of Siena and the Social Underworld of Early Renaissance Italy* (Chicago: University of Chicago Press, 1999).

Ogilvie, Brian W. *The Science of Describing: Natural History in Renaissance Europe* (Chicago: University of Chicago Press, 2006).

Panofsky, Erwin. "Artist, Scientist, Genius: Notes on the 'Renaissance Dammerung,'" in *The Renaissance: Six Essays*, edited by Wallace K. Ferguson (New York: Harper & Row, 1962).

Park, Katharine. *Secrets of Women: Gender, Generation and the Origins of Human Dissection* (New York: Zone Books, 2006).

Park, Katharine, and Lorraine Daston, eds. *The Cambridge History of Science, Early Modern*, vol. 3 (Cambridge: Cambridge University Press, 2006).

Peterson, David S. "Out of the Margins: Religion and the Church in Renaissance Italy." *Renaissance Quarterly* 53 (2000): 835–79.

Randall, J. H. "The Development of the Scientific Method at the School of Padua." *Journal of the History of Ideas* 1 (1940): 179–83.

Rocke, Michael. *Forbidden Friendships: Homosexuality and Male Culture in Renaissance Florence* (New York: Oxford University Press, 1993).

Ruggiero, Guido. *The Boundaries of Eros: Sex Crime and Sexuality in Renaissance Venice* (Oxford: Oxford University Press, 1985).

Sarton, George. *Six Wings: Men of Science and the Renaissance* (Bloomington: Indiana University Press, 1957).

Schmitt, Charles B. "Reappraisals in Renaissance Science." *History of Science* 16 (1978): 200–14.

Schutte-Jacobsen, Anne. "Periodization in Sixteenth Century Religious Italian History: The Post-Cantimori Paradigm Shift." *Journal of Modern History* 61 (1989): 269–84.

Siraisi, Nancy G. *Medieval and Early Renaissance Medicine: An Introduction to Knowledge and Practice* (Chicago: University of Chicago Press, 1990).

Terpstra, Nicholas. *Lay Confraternities and Civic Religion in Renaissance Bologna* (Cambridge: Cambridge University Press, 1995).

Trinkhaus, Charles. *In Our Image and Likeness: Humanity and Divinity in Italian Humanist Thought*, vol. 1 (Chicago: University of Chicago Press, 1970).

Trinkhaus, Charles. ed. *The Pursuit of Holiness in Late Medieval and Renaissance Religion* (Leiden: Brill, 1974).
Vauchez, Andre. *Sainthood in the Late Middle Ages* (New York: Cambridge University Press, 1997).
Verdon, Timothy, and John Henderson, eds. *Christianity and the Renaissance: Image and Religious Imagination in the Quattrocento* (Syracuse: Syracuse University Press, 1990).
Walker, D. P. *Spiritual and Demonic Magic: From Ficino to Campanella* (University Park, PA: Penn State University Press, 2000, originally published in 1958).
Yates, Frances. *Giordano Bruno and the Hermetic Tradition* (Chicago: University of Chicago Press, 1964).

Index